GAMING THE WORLD

HOW SPORTS ARE RESHAPING
GLOBAL POLITICS AND CULTURE

GAMING THE WORLD

ANDREI S. MARKOVITS & LARS RENSMANN

PRINCETON UNIVERSITY PRESS   PRINCETON AND OXFORD

Published by Princeton University Press, 41 William Street,
Princeton, New Jersey 08540
In the United Kingdom: Princeton University Press, 6 Oxford Street,
Woodstock, Oxfordshire OX20 1TW
press.princeton.edu

Library of Congress Cataloging-in-Publication Data

Markovits, Andrei S.
Gaming the world : how sports are reshaping global politics and culture /
Andrei S. Markovits and Lars Rensmann.
p. cm.
Includes index.
ISBN 978-0-691-13751-3 (hardcover : alk. paper)
1. Sports and globalization—Europe.   2. Sports and globalization—United
States.   3. Nationalism and sports—Europe.   4. Nationalism and sports—
United States.   5. Sports—Political aspects—Europe.   6. Sports—Political
aspects—United States.   I. Rensmann, Lars.   II. Title.
GV706.35.M3525 2010
306.483—dc22
2010006187

British Library Cataloging-in-Publication Data are available

This book has been composed in Janson and Bank Gothic

Printed on acid-free paper. ∞

Printed in the United States of America

10 9 8 7 6 5 4 3 2 1

For
Kiki
Ina
Samira
and
Cleo Rose
◇◇◇◇◇◇◇◇◇

CONTENTS ◇◇◇◇◇◇◇◇◇◇◇◇◇◇◇◇◇◇◇◇◇◇◇◇◇◇◇◇◇◇◇◇◇◇◇◇

PREFACE AND ACKNOWLEDGMENTS ◇◇◇◇◇◇◇

This project started in June 2006 when Andrei Markovits, to his immense delight, assumed the summer position of "*Fußball-Professor*" (soccer professor) at the University of Dortmund when that city featured one of host Germany's most eminent venues of the World Cup soccer tournament. Dortmund also happens to be Lars Rensmann's place of birth and the home of his parents. It was Markovits's honor to meet Gerd Rensmann, Lars's father (now deceased), and one of Germany's most renowned sports journalists, before the two proceeded to the city's famed Westfalenstadion, home to Rensmann's beloved Borussia, to watch Brazil defeat Ghana.

That fall, Rensmann commenced his position, co-sponsored by the German Academic Exchange Service (*Deutscher Akademischer Austauschdienst*—DAAD) at the University of Michigan. We are very grateful to the DAAD and the University of Michigan for giving us the institutional possibility to expand our friendship into a scholarly collaboration that both of us enjoyed immensely. Our being colleagues at the same university led us to coauthor a number of publications, not least a book on sports entitled *Querpass: Sport und Politik in Europa und den USA* (Verlag Die Werkstatt, 2007). This book constitutes at best a distant sketch to our current work and is in no way its German precursor, let alone equivalent. Above all, being colleagues at the wonderful University of Michigan has provided us many hours of priceless visits to the Big House to watch football, Yost Arena to attend hockey games, Crisler Arena to witness a long-overdue resurgence in Michigan basketball; and the professional sports' offerings in the Detroit metropolitan area, including our enjoying the Red Wings at "the Joe," the Pistons at the Palace of Auburn Hills, and the Tigers at Comerica Park. Alas, we have yet to attend a Lions game at Ford Field together. But we are certain that this will happen soon.

Permit us to say a few words about the sports terminology that informs this book. As bicontinental sports fans, we know that our readers in Britain would have preferred our using the word "supporters" instead of "fans." We are fully aware of the common language that divides us, none more gravely than in the world of sports. We know that "pitch" has a different meaning in Britain than it does in America. Since this book was coauthored by an American and a German teaching at an American university, published by an American university's press, and meant mainly for American audiences, we have chosen to follow the language common to the American sports world. Thus, when we speak of football, we mostly mean the game played with an oblong ball on the gridirons of North America; and soccer to us connotes its cousin played with a round ball propelled by legs, head, and body though never hands on a slightly larger field. However, we refused to be dogmatic about the usage of such terms and trust the reader's intelligence and good will in understanding our meaning from the context wherein a particular term appears. We are convinced that our liberal usage of a transatlantic vocabulary will not confuse the reader's understanding but enhance it, perhaps even shed some light on the complexities of meaning that these terms connote to their respective carriers and players.

All books owe their existence to many more people than their authors. This one is no exception. Markovits expresses his most profound gratitude to the Center for Advanced Study in the Behavioral Sciences (CASBS) of Stanford University, whose leadership consisting of Claude Steele, Anne Petersen, Lynn Gale, and Linda Jack in 2008–9 made his stay at this unique place possible. Without the Center's intellectual ambiance and, above all, the luxury of granting its fellows time to think and write, this book would never have happened. Any serious reading of this work will reveal the bevy of knowledge that Marion Fourcade, Kieran Healy, Philip Howard, John Lucy, Gina Neff, Charles Phelps, Woody Powell, Martin Ruef, and Abigail Saguy imparted to Markovits in the course of this enriching experience. Their learned insights and brilliant ideas enhance the book's intellectual value immeasurably. Markovits would also like to thank the University of Michigan for various mini-grants over the years that, when compounded, have proven to be quite maxi. A book on sports is perhaps a better forum than any other in which to express his utmost gratitude to the University of Michigan, which has been exceptionally good to him in every conceivable way. Go Blue!

Apart from the DAAD, which has been supportive of his work in so many ways, Rensmann is grateful to the University of Michigan, its Department of Political Science and, most importantly, the people that shape it. They have provided an invaluable, indeed superb, academic environment. It is a fabulous place to teach, to do research, and to think "outside the box"—to invoke an image so congruent with this book in more ways than one. There are many colleagues and friends to whom Rensmann owes insights and ideas that appear in this book. He is especially grateful to Seyla Benhabib, Lisa Disch, Klaus Drechsel, Joshua Ehrlich, Samir Gandesha, Malachi Haim Hacohen, Donald Herzog, Christoph Kopke, Mika Lavaque-Manty, Cosimo Ligorio, Cas Mudde, Jennet Kirkpatrick, Anne Manuel, Duston Moore, Anthony Pinnell, Dirk and Jörg Rensmann, Arlene Saxonhouse, Elizabeth Wingrove, and Mariah Zeisberg for their comments, criticism, and intellectual presence—and in some cases also for great conversations about sports. Most important, he is greatly indebted to Markovits for his tremendous academic and intellectual support of all of Rensmann's scholarly pursuits over the years—far beyond the scope of this collaboration. Rensmann would also like to thank his mother Ingrid, who has always been there for him, and his father Gerd, who passed away in 2007. Gerd would have enjoyed reading this work.

Both of us would like to express our thanks to our research assistants Ravi Dev, Julian Trobe, and David Watnick who, at various stages of our project, proved wonderfully helpful. David Smith has been an invaluable resource and sounding board for every imaginable topic in politics, culture, economy, society—and sports. His erudition never ceases to amaze us. Clara Platter proved to be a stellar editor in every imaginable manner from the book's conception to its publication. Our manuscript's two anonymous readers offered us comments and insights that most decidedly improved the quality of our final product. We are grateful to them for the diligence and deliberations that they devoted to our work. Lastly, we owe everything to our respective families, who sustain us with their love and humor that transform the travails that accompany the writing of any book into a pleasurable experience. It is to them that we dedicate this work.

Ann Arbor, February 7, 2010—Super Bowl Sunday

GAMING THE WORLD

CHAPTER 1 ◇◇◇◇◇◇◇◇◇◇◇◇◇◇◇◇◇◇◇◇◇◇◇◇◇◇◇◇◇◇◇◇◇

INTRODUCTION: GOING GLOBAL—SPORTS, POLITICS, AND IDENTITIES

Sports matter. They hold a singular position among leisure time activities and have an unparalleled impact on the everyday lives of billions of people.[1] We show how, why, and for whom this has been the case for well over a century on both sides of the Atlantic. Analyzing the continuities and changes that have characterized sports cultures in the United States and Europe, we find complex processes involving global transformations alongside persistent local and national factors.

This book poses the following questions: How has a continuing process that we call "postindustrialization" and "second globalization" transformed sports? More specifically, How have developments since roughly the 1970s—in the advanced industrial capitalist economies of the liberal democracies of the United States and Europe—altered key aspects of contemporary sports cultures? And, to what degree have globalized sports and their participating athletes in turn influenced postindustrial societies and identities? Which role do sports play in globalization, and to what extent are they an engine of cosmopolitan political and cultural change? At the same time, how have sports successfully maintained traditions in the continuing battles for their very identities? And how have sports reconciled

[1] A humoristic and exaggerated example of a sports fan's dedicated life can be found in Joe Queenan, *True Believers: The Tragic Inner Life of Sports Fans* (New York: Henry Holt, 2003). Of course, in Queenan's ironic book the problem of political fanaticism among mass movements resonates, which is the subject of Eric Hoffer's 1951 social science classic; see Eric Hoffer, *The True Believers: Thoughts on the Nature of Mass Movements* (New York: HarperCollins, 2002 [1951]).

the new challenges that have emerged by their becoming globalizing cultural forces with new affiliations and allegiances far beyond local and national venues? To resolve this puzzle, we examine the global, national, and local layers of the dynamics that comprise present-day sports in Europe and America.[2]

Our approach follows the Hegelian notion of *Aufhebung*, a German term that means both "preserving" and "transcending." Many of the distinctive cultural narratives and special patterns that first shaped sports cultures as we know them in the late nineteenth century—in the wake of globalization's first wave—now continue unabated, perhaps even augmented, in a global arena. Yet, we argue that even as the national and the local continue to be resilient forces, the substantial changes befalling sports through the processes of second globalization—and the cosmopolitan changes accompanying it—also transcend national and local affiliations.

Both terms—cosmopolitanism and globalization—are equally disputed. We conceive of cosmopolitanism broadly as the respect for strangers and the universal recognition of individuals independent of their cultural or racial background, citizenship, and heritage. Thus hegemonic sports, as part of popular culture, play a crucial role in shaping more inclusive collective identities and a cosmopolitan outlook open to complex allegiances.[3] While local fans identify with their teams, they also want to watch the very best players perform at the peak of their game. This, in turn, leads these fans to accept, even admire and love, "foreign" players and those belonging to ethnic minorities whom these fans otherwise might have ignored, or possibly disdained and hated. In other words, the sport consumers' wish to watch and follow the best of the best may enhance acceptance of an otherwise possibly disliked "other." Sports, in this cosmopolitan context, fulfill what Robert Putnam has so aptly called "bridging capital," an integrative force among different groups and their cultural boundaries. Yet, in the very

[2] When we speak of "America," we refer to the United States of America. While we are aware that the United States is only part of North America, we use "America" here as a signifier that corresponds to its popular use.

[3] In contrast to multiculturalism, which has received broad criticism for resting upon rather rigid notions of culture and group belonging, we use instead the term "cosmopolitanism" to avoid the pitfalls of essentialism or all-or-nothing understandings of identity. See Bhikhu Parekh, *Rethinking Multiculturalism: Cultural Diversity and Political Theory* (Cambridge, MA: Harvard University Press, 2000); Steven Vertovec and Robin Cohen, "Introduction: Conceiving Cosmopolitanism," in Vertovec and Cohen, eds., *Conceiving Cosmopolitanism: Theory, Context, and Practice* (Oxford: Oxford University Press, 2002), p. 2. On variations of political cosmopolitanism see Seyla Benhabib, *Another Cosmopolitanism* (Oxford: Oxford University Press, 2006) and Daniele Archibugi, *The Global Commonwealth of Citizens: Toward Cosmopolitan Democracy* (Princeton: Princeton University Press, 2008).

process of doing so, sports also conjure up forces that reaffirm emotions and identities akin to Putnam's "bonding capital," a hardening of boundaries among different constituencies and their cultures.[4]

Global Players, the Power of Sports, and Globalization

Sports shape and stabilize social and even political identities around the globe; and, we are certain, that they do so today to an unprecedented extent. They mobilize collective emotions and often channel societal conflicts. Small wonder then that sports are also the subject of a vast array of popular literature on heroes, legends, club histories, championships, and games. Sports subjects appear in popular movies, television series, and various other narratives that captivate millions, even billions, of people around the world. Sports have evolved into an integral part of the global entertainment industry. In recent years, this formidable feature of our cultural landscape has attracted increasing interest and legitimacy as an important subject of intellectual inquiry.

Sporting events are far and away *the* most watched television programs in the world. The last World Cup Tournament—held in Germany in the summer of 2006—attracted approximately thirty billion viewers, with more than two billion of the world's population watching the final match alone.[5] And one need only consider the record number that tuned in to watch at least some events of the most recent summer Olympics in Beijing. Billions watched the sensational feats of Michael Phelps in the pool and Usain Bolt on the track. While the global audience for the Beijing Olympics was enhanced by the Internet for the first time, thus boosting the global viewership well beyond its traditional television boundaries, this event, like all televised Olympics since the Rome Games in 1960, created a

---

[4] It is interesting, that Robert Putnam uses a sport metaphor for the title of his book, which arguably has been among the most important statements in the social sciences of the past two decades. And sure enough, his seminal book's main concern is central to all sports: that of creating a community in the context of competition, of fostering solidarity in the framework of contestation. See his *Bowling Alone: The Collapse and Revival of American Community* (New York: Simon and Schuster, 2001).

[5] The 2006 World Cup in Germany drew a cumulative viewership of 26.29 billion across 214 countries. The final between Italy and France attracted 715.1 million television viewers; see http://www.fifa.com/aboutfifa/marketingtv/news/newsid=111247.html. Retrieved July 10, 2007. According to FIFA data of 2006, 265 million people (male and female) are actively playing soccer, an increase of 10 percent compared to 2000; see FIFA Communications Division, Information Services, May 31, 2007.

global village around sports like few other events ever have.[6] Thus, for example, the National Football League's (NFL) annual Super Bowl reaches an estimated 160 million people across the globe, while the European Champions League final bests that number by almost fifty million. Add to that the hundreds of millions that watch the Rugby World Cup, the Cricket World Cup, and the NBA Finals on a regular basis, and it is clear that these sports have become global spectacles.

Sports' major protagonists have mutated into global icons. Soccer heroes such as David Beckham, Zinedine Zidane, Ronaldinho, Lionel Messi, and Thierry Henry are recognized and admired the world over.[7] So are their basketball equivalents: Michael Jordan, Kobe Bryant, Yao Ming, Dirk Nowitzki, and LeBron James. And Tiger Woods is in a class all by himself. Many teams also exhibit this kind of global charisma: Real Madrid CF, FC Barcelona, Manchester United FC, Chelsea FC, Liverpool FC, Arsenal FC, FC Bayern München, Juventus Turin, AC Milan, and FC Internazionale Milano (Inter) in soccer; the Los Angeles Lakers, the Chicago Bulls, the Boston Celtics in basketball; the New York Yankees in baseball; the Dallas Cowboys in American football; and an array of teams from the National Hockey League (NHL) have attracted attention well beyond the immediate confines of their actual purview. Likewise for some team owners, sports embody symbolic, social and "cultural capital"[8] at least as much as they fulfill monetary interests. In many cases, such teams are not even profitable and represent a financial burden. However, they invariably serve as sources of pride and social status for their owners.

[6] The 2008 Bejing Olympics beat all kinds of records. They reached a cumulative global audience of 4.7 billion viewers; see http://blog.nielsen.com/nielsenwire/media_entertainment/beijing-olympics-draw-largest-ever-global-tv-audience. Retrieved October 30, 2008. With 211 million American viewers in total, this was the most-watched U.S. television event of all time; China had 842 million viewers. One of this tournament's highlights was the first round China vs. U.S. men's basketball game, which was watched by more than a billion people, making it the most-watched basketball game of all time. See Mark Heisler, "US Men's Basketball routs China, 101–70, in Olympic opener," *Los Angeles Times*, August 11, 2008, http://articles.latimes.com/2008/aug/11/sports/sp-olymenhoop11 (retrieved December 12, 2008).

[7] See Peer Hull Kristensen and Jonathan Zeitlin, *Local Players in Global Games: The Strategic Constitution of a Multinational Corporation* (Oxford: Oxford University Press, 2004); Fredr Soderbaum and Luk van Langenhove, eds., *The EU as a Global Player: The Politics of Interregionalism* (New York: Routledge, 2007). In political science, of course, influential rational choice and game theories also employ the "players" metaphor as a conceptual tool; see among many works, George Tsebelis, *Veto Players: How Political Institutions Work* (Princeton: Princeton University Press, 2002).

[8] As "symbolic capital" and "cultural capital" we understand the symbolic (respectively cultural), nonmaterial value of goods and their nonmaterial benefits for individuals and collectives. They entail social recognition, public attention, and collective practices and identities.

There is sound evidence that sports teams are rarely profitable on either side of the Atlantic and yet they are hotly desired treasures. Abu Dhabi's ruling family purchased Manchester City from the former Thai prime minister and multibillionaire Thaksin Shinawatra in good part to outdo their rivals, the rulers of Dubai, who have succeeded in making their Persian Gulf spot among the premier sports venues of the world. It is indeed mainly for ornamental reasons that investors are so keen on owning prestigious sport teams. More than half of the English Premier League's twenty clubs are owned by foreign businessmen and virtually none of them purchased these clubs for profit.[9] To be sure, the acquisition of professional sports teams is much easier in the franchise system dominating the North American sports scene as well as the increasingly corporate structure of top-level English football than the club-based system still common on the European continent where even the most prominent teams in such eminent leagues as Spain's *Primera Division* and Germany's *Bundesliga* are owned by the clubs' members. The German-speaking world's "Verein" which all of Austria's and Germany's soccer clubs are, constitutes a sort of pre- or extra-capitalist structure and culture where "regular" market-based exchange and property relations in terms of club ownership do not pertain. Yet despite the proliferation of foreign owners in the English Premier League, and the increasingly global appeal and multicultural value of these eminent sports entities, virtually all team owners are citizens of the countries in which these clubs are located. Thus, for example, in the big four American sports, all principal team owners continue to remain North American with the exception of Hiroshi Yamauchi, third president of the Japanese video game giant Nintendo, who, since 1992, has been the majority owner of Major League Baseball's (MLB) Seattle Mariners. At the time of this writing (fall of 2009), there is movement afoot to have Mikhail D. Prokhorov, widely considered the richest man in Russia, become the second non–North American principal owner of a major sports franchise, in this case the NBA's New Jersey (perhaps soon-to-be Brooklyn) Nets.[10] So the local and national have far from disappeared from the ownership even of the most globalized entities in modern sports, let alone their local representatives.[11]

[9] Rob Hughes and Landon Thomas, Jr. "English Soccer Club Sale Reveals Emirates' Rivalry," *New York Times*, September 3, 2008.

[10] Charles V. Bagli, "Richest Russian's Newest Toy: An N.B.A. Team," *New York Times*, September 24, 2009. In May 2008, Chinese investors purchased 15 percent of the NBA's Cleveland Cavaliers.

[11] This persistence of the national pertains to the top management structure of virtually all major so-called "multinational" companies. Yes, there are the Carlos Ghosns (Nissan and

Sports bestow much social capital and ornamental prestige not only on such flamboyant men as Mark Cuban, owner of the NBA's Dallas Mavericks; Jerry Jones, owner of the NFL's Dallas Cowboys; Silvio Berlusconi, owner of Italian soccer's AC Milan; and George Steinbrenner in his early days as owner of the New York Yankees; but also on quiet, indeed quasi-stealthy, media-shy ones like the legendary, almost mythical Philip F. Anschutz. He still operates four Major League Soccer (MLS) franchises in the United States, and is arguably the sole reason that this fledgling league has existed and survived. It is thus not surprising that MLS's ultimate championship trophy be named the Philip F. Anschutz Cup, and that this man's efforts on soccer's behalf in the United States were rewarded by his subsequent induction into the United States Soccer Hall of Fame in Oneonta, New York. Tellingly, *SoccerAmerica*, the country's leading soccer publication, graced the cover of its thirty-fifth anniversary issue with a photograph of Anschutz and listed him as top choice among the thirty-five people (players, officials, journalists, coaches, managers, owners) deemed by the magazine as having had the greatest impact on American soccer.[12] Anschutz not only maintains the largest investment by anybody in American soccer, through his Anschutz Entertainment Group (AEG), but also owns the Los Angeles Kings of the NHL and the city's fabled Staples Center, the Berlin hockey team Eisbären and their O2 Arena, as well as the eponymous entertainment venue in London. Moreover, AEG—among its myriad sports and entertainment projects around the globe—is in the process of teaming up with the NBA to build many state-of-the art basketball arenas in China. Even though it is unlikely that anybody can rival Anschutz as a major player in international sports, he refuses any and all interviews, eschews all publicity, and continues his pioneering work away from the glare that such sports can—and do—bestow on those that seek it.

And somewhere between the flamboyance of the Berlusconis, the Joneses, and the Cubans on the one hand, and the secretiveness of the Glazers (owners of the English Premier League's glamour club Manchester United and the NFL's Tampa Bay Buccaneers) and Anschutz's on the other, is

---

Renault), the Howard Stringers (Sony) and the Josef Ackermanns (Deutsche Bank) of this world, but on the whole Germany-based multinational companies are run by German CEOs, CFOs and top managers with very few, if any, foreigners having decisive agenda-setting and policy-making positions; and the same pertains to their Japanese, French, British, Russian, and American counterparts. So while today's multinational corporations act globally in terms of their market reach and the presence of their products, their management remains firmly in the realm of the local and national.

[12] *SoccerAmerica* (November 2006), cover; and pp. 16 and 17.

Lamar Hunt, legendary Texas oilman and member of the Professional Football Hall of Fame (inducted in 1972), the Soccer Hall of Fame (inducted in 1982), and the International Tennis Hall of Fame in Newport, Rhode Island (inducted in 1993). Hunt commenced his remarkable sports-team and -league-owning career as a cofounder of the old American Football League, which then mutated into the American Football Conference (AFC) of the NFL in 1970. Hunt's name continues to grace the trophy of the AFC's champion and his heirs (he died in 2006) still own the NFL's Kansas City Chiefs. Hunt was one of the true pioneers of major league professional soccer in the United States. He was a cofounder of the glamorous but short-lived North American Soccer League (NASL) and subsequently a major force behind the establishment of Major League Soccer in 1996. He owned (and his heirs continue to own) the Columbus Crew and FC Dallas. Indeed, the United States Open Cup in soccer, established in 1914 and the oldest annual team tournament in all of American sports, now bears Hunt's name in honor of his pioneering role in that sport.

Clearly, men like Hunt and Anschutz, as well as their counterparts in Europe and now increasingly Asia, represent "global players" first and foremost in the world of business, but also in the world of sports. Indeed, it is mainly by dint of the latter that they are known to a large public and garner much-deserved (and often also much-desired) cultural and social capital.

Yet, "global players" are not just public figures of politics or business and of multinational corporations competing on the world market, or powerful nations in international politics, or global institutions like the United Nations and supranational organizations like the European Union. While we regard the role and meaning of professional sports clubs, including their managers and owners, as multinational enterprises, and while we view supranational sports organizations like the *Fédération Internationale de Football Association* (FIFA), the Union of European Football Associations (UEFA), the International Olympic Committee (IOC) and *Fédération Internationale de Basketball* (FIBA) as influential principals and global players in society, this book features global players in a more literal sense: the actors on the sports fields in the global age, the symbolic and cultural capital they generate, the many millions they attract and mobilize, and the changing public spaces in which they operate.

We focus on sports primarily in relation to its cultural and political impact, that is, its symbolic capital, which clearly exceeds the often claimed and much-lamented commercial importance. As Andrew Zimbalist points out, the entire revenue of the Big Four team sports of football, baseball, basketball, and hockey in a leading sports country like the United States does not exceed $15 billion in an economy that surpasses $11 trillion in size.[13] In purely economic terms, these dominant sports are akin to small-ish industries and even their marquee teams resemble run-of-the-mill, mid-sized firms in terms of their market capitalization.

Global "Cultural Capital" and the Politics of Sports

As sports have gone global they have become more embedded in politics, constituting an important display of political authority and even figuring into the most quotidian political matters. Throughout the twentieth century, dictatorships of various kinds utilized the charismatic power of sports for their own, often nefarious, causes. Examples abound, from Adolf Hitler's harnessing the Berlin Olympics in 1936 for his regime's propaganda purposes, to China's rulers doing the same seventy-two years later[14]; from Benito Mussolini's basking in his country's winning the second World Cup in soccer with Fascist Italy playing host, to the Argentinian military junta's gaining much-needed legitimacy by the national team's triumph in 1978.[15]

[13] Zimbalist adds that, contrary to common expectations, independent economic research shows that sports teams and sports facilities do not have any positive economic impact on an area. A new stadium and arena does not increase the level of per-capita income or that of employment. Zimbalist, an eminent sports economist, adds that the special value of professional sports can be found in its identity-generating role for the community. Having a sports team in your community "galvanizes everyone to actually experience themselves as a community. It gives them an identity." See Andrew Zimbalist, "Sports & Economics," *Sports in America* (Washington, D.C.: U.S. Department of State, 2007), pp. 51–55, here p. 52; also Andrew Zimbalist, *May the Best Team Win: Baseball Economics and Public Policy* (Washington, D.C.: Brookings Institution, 2003). The wealthiest European soccer clubs, Manchester United and Real Madrid, are worth US$1.453 billion and US$1.036 billion respectively. These are values not even close to any significant multinational corporation in the economic world; see http://www.infoniac.com/offbeat-news/forbes-list-of-25-most-valuable-soccer-teams.html. Retrieved July 10, 2008.

[14] Minky Worden, ed., *China's Great Leap: The Beijing Olympic Games and Human Rights Challenges* (New York: Seven Stories Press, 2008).

[15] Argentina's famous national coach, Luis César Menotti, openly distanced himself from the regime and refused the rulers' invitation. He could afford to do so precisely because Argentina's national team won the World Cup at home and he was a national hero whose success shone over the regime and its state terror. See Simon Kuper, *Football Against the Enemy* (London: Orion Books, 1994), pp. 205–36; Alberto Ciria, "From Soccer to War in Argentina: Preliminary Notes on Sports-as-Politics under a Military Regime (1976–1982)," in Arch R. M. Ritter, ed., *Latin America and the Caribbean: Geopolitics, Development and Culture* (Ottawa: Canadian Association for Latin American and Caribbean Studies, 1984), pp. 80–95; Eduardo Archetti, "Argentina 1978: Military Nationalism, Football Essentialism, and Moral Ambivalence," in Alan Tomlinson and Christopher Young, eds., *National Identity and Global Sports*

However, even for politicians in the liberal democracies of the advanced industrial world, it has become commonplace—a well-nigh necessity—at least to feign a deep interest in sports; though, we believe that for the most part such interest is actually genuine. Thus, it was completely natural for Tony Blair, then the British prime minister, to have stopped a crucial cabinet meeting upon receiving the news that David Beckham had broken his right foot and was thus unable to play for England in crucial games. Equally credible was Gerhard Schröder, his German counterpart, scheduling all his cabinet meetings so that they not coincide with the German team's games during the World Cup tournament held in Japan.[16]

It is, of course, de rigueur for every head of state and head of government in Europe (including Schröder's female successor, Angela Merkel) to attend all the important matches that her or his country's national soccer team contests even beyond the World Cup. Ms. Merkel's repeated visits in June 2008 to Austria and Switzerland to attend the German team's games during the European Championship has in the meantime become routine behavior for pretty much any head of state or government. The King of Spain, for example, joined her in watching their respective countries' teams contest the final game of the tournament. Silvio Berlusconi, Italian prime minister on multiple occasions, used his success as president and principal owner of AC Milan to convince the Italian public that he could govern the country with similar results, bringing to Italy the same fame and pride that his club "Milan" attained. Berlusconi's "soccer power" was crucial on his road to attaining the pinnacle of Italy's political power. In addition, Berlusconi's party *Forza Italia* was named after the national soccer slogan "Go Italy." With this slogan Berlusconi successfully used the appeal of Italian national soccer to gain political support for his populist one-man-party in a time of highly divisive and collapsing party politics.[17]

Events: Culture, Politics, and the Spectacle in the Olympics and the Football World Cup (Albany, NY: SUNY Press, 2006), pp. 133–48; B. L. Smith, "The Argentinian Junta and the Press in the Run-Up to the 1978 World Cup," *Soccer and Society* 3 (1), 2002, pp. 69–78.

[16] In recent years a German chancellor is also expected to be a member of a professional soccer club and thus demonstrate passion for soccer as well as one's local ties: Helmut Kohl became an honorary member of his regional club 1.FC Kaiserslautern in 1996; Gerhard Schröder became honorary member of his favorite club Borussia Dortmund in 2001; and Angela Merkel accepted honorary membership in the East German soccer club Energie Cottbus in 2008.

[17] See Michael E. Shin and John A. Agnew, *Berlusconi's Italy: Mapping Contemporary Italian Politics* (Philadelphia: Temple University Press, 2008); Giuseppe Fiori, *Il venditore: Storia di Silvio Berlusconi e della Fininvest* (Milano: Garzanti, 1996); Alexander Stille, *The Sack of Rome* (London: Penguin, 2007); Mauro Grassi and Lars Rensmann 2005, "Die Forza Italia: Erfolgsmodell einer populistischen Regierungspartei oder temporäres Phänomen des ital-

At the time of this writing, serving a third term as prime minister after the 2008 election, Berlusconi continues to use his AC Milan capital directly as cultural capital in international politics: For instance, he trotted out "his" Brazilian stars Dida, Kaka, Ronaldinho, Emerson, and Pato for visiting Brazilian president Luiz Inácio Lula da Silva, who was deeply impressed by this surprise.[18]

Political campaigning, governing, and symbolic politics often entail references to sports. Using sports as "cultural capital" has become commonplace in many societies and is not limited to populist politicians like Berlusconi. Sport as an ornamental tool has turned into a globalized phenomenon, which is part of our ubiquitous and inescapable zeitgeist.[19]

In the United States, presidents have long been deeply involved with sports—their key events and champions. It was a shocked Theodore Roosevelt who, upon seeing the mangled bodies of players from a University of Pennsylvania vs. Swarthmore College football game, called for reforms that eventually led to the establishment of the National Collegiate Athletic Association (NCAA), one of the mainstays of the American sports world. The sitting president has thrown the ceremonial first pitch of the MLB season since William Howard Taft started the tradition in 1910. One of the apocryphal stories used to explain the origins of the seventh inning stretch, an integral part of contemporary baseball culture, is that the same President Taft once got up to stretch his ailing back in the middle of the seventh inning of a game and the rest of the attendants felt obliged to do so as well. The public parading in the White House of every champion in American sport—from the winner of the Super Bowl, to that of the World Series and the NBA championship, as well as all NCAA champions in college sports—is a staple of American political life.

The central role that sports play in the lives of most American male politicians is significant: Richard Nixon regularly drew up plays for his beloved Washington Redskins and communicated them to the team's head coach George Allen; Bill Clinton rushed to watch the Super Bowl with Bill Richardson in the hope of winning the latter's endorsement of Hillary Clinton's candidacy for president; George H.W. Bush captained the Yale baseball team and played first base; George W. Bush was deeply involved

ienischen Parteiensystems?" in Susanne Frölich-Steffen and Lars Rensmann, eds., *Populisten an der Macht: Populistische Regierungsparteien in Ost- und Westeuropa* (Wien: Braumüller, 2005), pp. 121–46.

[18]"Berlusconi praises Brazil exports," *International Herald Tribune*, November 11, 2008.

[19]On the populist "Zeitgeist" in politics, see Cas Mudde, "The Populist *Zeitgeist*," *Government & Opposition* 39 (3), 2004, pp. 541–63.

with the game as part owner of the Texas Rangers, and was present at the 2008 Olympics in Beijing as a supporter of United States national teams; Gerald Ford's public career commenced as a star lineman for his much-loved University of Michigan's Wolverines football team, to which he remained loyal throughout his life; Barack Obama proudly displays his love of basketball, which he played regularly on many campaign stops. He also announced his picks for the 2009 NCAA Men's final tournament (ubiquitously known as the "Big Dance" or "March Madness") on national television, completing his brackets in front of millions. Obama correctly predicted on this program that the North Carolina Tar Heels would emerge as national champions. He scrimmaged with the team the morning of that state's crucial primary win which propelled him to defeat Hillary Clinton for his party's nomination and carried him to the White House nary a year later. And let us not forget Obama's visiting with the players of the American and National Leagues in their teams' respective club houses at MLB's All-Star Game in St. Louis in July 2009, where he threw out the ceremonial first pitch wearing tennis shoes, blue jeans, and the warm-up jacket of his beloved Chicago White Sox. A few innings later, many million Americans saw the president once again, this time perched in the broadcast booth between veteran announcers Tim McCarver and Joe Buck, just three regular guys sitting around "talking baseball." Barely ten days later, the nation once again was privy to Obama's enthusiasm for and knowledge of sports when he gave Mark Buehrle a congratulatory phone call; Buehrle had just completed a perfect game for a White Sox victory, an almost superhuman feat accomplished only 18 times in baseball's 134-year history and with more than 170,000 major league baseball games played between 1903 and 2009. President Obama exhorted Buehrle to buy his teammate DeWayne Wise a "large steak dinner" for the latter's monumental catch in the ninth inning that saved the perfect game, and has in the meantime emerged as one of the greatest catches ever in the history of baseball.

It is no secret that the NBA has harnessed Obama's love for the game of basketball to further its own global appeal. There is also little doubt that the NBA's global presence with stars such as Michael Jordan, Magic Johnson, LeBron James, and Kobe Bryant has helped solidify the legitimacy, attractiveness, and acceptance of African Americans—Barack Obama included—as public figures in the white-dominated societies and cultures of Europe and America. Alas, not even President Obama's immense global popularity, but also his legitimacy as a bona fide sports fan and connoisseur, were sufficient to bring the 2016 Olympic Games to his hometown Chicago. Even the president's last-minute lobbying trip to Copenhagen to amplify his wife's and Oprah Winfrey's advocacy for Chicago's candidacy proved no match for the determination of the International Olympic Committee's delegates to award the games to Rio de Janeiro which, of course, had the Brazilian president Lula in attendance as the city's most prominent advocate. Prime Minister Tony Blair's all-out effort greatly aided London's bid for the 2012 summer games just as Russian President Vladimir Putin's trip to Guatemala in support of Sochi's candidacy for the 2014 winter Olympics helped that venue's cause. Obama's global appeal will surely help the United States' chances of landing another World Cup soccer tournament for 2018 or 2022. In short, sports have steadily increased their presence and importance in political life in the contemporary world.[20] No political leader can "exit" from the culturally and symbolically powerful world of sports, even if he or she would like to do so.[21]

In this book we also look at how sports have reshaped global politics in a much broader sense. We do not refer to the role of sports only in political campaigns, or to the world of diplomacy and international relations in the strict sense. Rather, we explore how sports and sports culture affect political and cultural inclusion, how they both deconstruct and construct national identity, and how, in what manner, and to which extent they facilitate a kind of "global citizenship" and global community.[22] Thus, we conceive

[20] The language and symbolism of the competitive world of sports—from the "slam dunk" to the "home run"—has long made its inroads into everyday usage and the language of politics, particularly in the vernacular of American English and the iconography of American culture. In recent decades, Europe has caught up a bit in this regard. Sports and sports language have long become effective vehicles for political mobilization and support both internationally and domestically.

[21] That also applies to political organizations, and often to even local terrorist groups. Think of Iraq, a country divided by religious, ethnic, and sectarian conflicts and suffering from war and terrorism. It is also a country in which soccer is a powerful unifying force that few would challenge. Soccer "is so beloved here that even Al Qaeda in Mesopotamia, which claims ties to Osama bin Laden's group, has not dared to emulate Mr. bin Laden's theologically based contempt for the game. Matches in Iraq are one of the few types of public gatherings that have never become a target for suicide bombers," who have bombed mosques, schools, funerals, hospitals, shops, bazaars. See Rod Nordland and Sa'ad Al-Izzi, "Soccer in Iraq: Another Field for Argument in a Divided Society," *New York Times*, November 25, 2009, p. A16.

[22] We understand political globalization not only in terms of the increasing relevance of "post-Westphalian" international authorities and institutions, and changes in international law. Political globalization is also characterized and shaped by diverse new transnational publics, associations and communications—including those that are initially not "political" in the strict sense of the word. These publics help generate forms of "global civil society" (Mary Kaldor) or "global political culture" (David Jacobsen) and thus have significant political and cultural ramifications. See Mary Kaldor, *Global Civil Society* (Cambridge: Polity, 2003); David Jacobsen, "The Global Political Culture," in Mathias Albert, David Jacobsen, and Yosef

of sports as an independent variable: as a powerful force of political and cultural change around the globe.

Sports and Cultural Change

Only a very limited number of sports attain the heights of genuine popular culture and reach well beyond the niche of their immediate producers and consumers. Such sports comprise what we have come to call "hegemonic sports culture,"[23] defined by watching, following, worrying, debating, living, and speaking a sport rather than merely playing it. Of course the "following" and the "doing" are related, but only to an extent. This nexus does not necessarily apply to those rare hegemonic sports that comprise a country's sports culture. One need never have kicked a soccer ball or played on any team in order to follow the *Squadra Azzurra* if one is Italian, the *Seleção* if one is Brazilian, or Barcelona if one is Catalan. A New Englander need not know much about baseball to be consumed by the Red Sox and be a rabid member of what has been so aptly called "Red Sox Nation." The same pertains to football, basketball, and hockey. New Englanders follow the Patriots, the Celtics, and the Bruins regardless of when, where, how, and even *if* they ever participated in these sports. The very crux of all hegemonic sports cultures occurs off the playing field or court and centers on ancillary matters between the games or matches proper. The attention surrounding the annual drafts of the NFL and NBA comprise the core of hegemonic sports culture at its best.[24] The same pertains to sports talk

Lapid, eds., *Identities, Borders, Orders: Rethinking International Relations Theory* (Minneapolis: University of Minnesota Press, 2001), pp. 161–79.

[23] On hegemonic sports cultures, see Andrei S. Markovits and Steven Hellerman, *Offside: Soccer and American Exceptionalism* (Princeton: Princeton University Press, 2001), pp. 19–33; see also below.

[24] On the weekend of April 25 and 26, 2009, ESPN celebrated the silver anniversary of its telecast of the NFL draft in which all thirty-two teams of the NFL select college players for their rosters. Whereas the original telecast in 1984 drew a 0.6 rating, its 2009 successor attained a higher than 4.0 rating. According to Nielsen Media Research, first-round coverage of the draft combined an average viewership of 6.3 million on ESPN and the NFL Network. The first telecast lasted ten hours with the latter version having ballooned to sixteen hours of prime time for sport events during the weekend. ESPN deems this event sufficiently worthy to have Chris Berman, arguably its best known and most highly regarded superstar, anchor all sixteen hours over two days. The network's draft guru, Mel Kiper Jr., has become such a legend among American sports fans that he is known to millions of them merely by his first name (akin to Brazilian soccer stars). Additionally, this event is held at New York City's Radio City Music Hall, as iconic in American culture as any building, which is packed by fans who purchased their tickets years in advance. Furthermore, thousands, if not millions, of fans

radio, where, as a rule, one "talks" passionately in minute detail 24/7 about what has already happened and/or what is about to happen in a game, to players, to teams, and to the culture of the sport above and beyond the game on the actual playing field.

Distinct hegemonic sports cultures participate in shaping local, re-gional, national, and transnational collective identities. Affections for a sport, and for a club or team, mark social differences and particular bonds, just as they establish shared languages in public spheres across borders.[25]

---

gather in sports bars across the country, and near their team's facilities to experience this event together, hoping that seven new players will radically alter their team's fortunes for the better. Thus, for example, Markovits experienced the 2009 NFL draft with hundreds, perhaps thousands, of San Francisco 49ers fans in a large venue near the team's facility and home in Santa Clara, California.

And lest we forget, not much actually happens during these sixteen hours over two days: in regular intervals of seven minutes in the first two rounds and five minutes in rounds three to seven, the NFL commissioner (replaced by one of the League's other major officials for the later rounds) emerges to announce into a microphone at a podium that team X just drafted player Y with draft pick Z in each of the seven rounds. The player comes up to the podium, dons the team's cap, holds its jersey aloft, shakes the official's hand, poses for the cameras, and disappears behind the stage. That is it! No games, no runs, no passes, no tackles, no kicks, no scores—no activity at all. But, of course, all of this is accompanied by incessant analyses weeks before the event, obviously during it, and massively following it—all of which dissect in the most detailed minutiae whether the players picked and the teams picking made the correct choices leading to a good match for both. Few things underline the salience of following (as in viewing, discussing, living though not playing) to the maintenance of hegemonic sports culture and the relative marginality of participating in it than the annual NFL draft and—to a somewhat lesser, but also very prominent, extent—its NBA counterpart at the end of June every year.

To put the power of this aspect of sports following into proper perspective, the aforemen-tioned 6.3 million viewers watching the first two rounds of the NFL draft that April weekend surpassed the average viewership for the Sunday night Yankees vs. Red Sox game on ESPN, the Saturday afternoon Yankees vs. Red Sox game on Fox and every NBA and NHL playoff game over the weekend. In all, a record 39 million viewers watched the draft. Draft viewer-ship has increased 66 percent since 2003. For an event that does not highlight any games or contests and consists merely of talk to outdraw the television audience of Yankees vs. Red Sox, without a shadow of a doubt America's foremost rivalry in baseball, arguably all of profes-sional sports, twice on a weekend in prime time is nothing short of sensational and bespeaks football's unique prominence among America's Big Four.

The attention bestowed on these drafts also gives the NFL much cultural prominence and public attention when its season is actually dormant and its sport not performed. The draft thus maintains the NFL's and professional football's salience at a time when its actual absence on the playing fields might open up the sports space for potential rivals to emerge. The NBA draft in late June performs an identical function for professional basketball, though on a much more modest level due to the league's lesser prominence among America's Big Four and the draft's temporal proximity to the end of the NBA season, which often ends in the latter half of June.

[25] A wonderful example is provided by Kwame Anthony Appiah when he discusses the cultural relevance of soccer and European soccer competition in Ghana; see Kwame Anthony Appiah, *Cosmopolitanism: Ethics in a World of Strangers* (New York: W.W. Norton). As K. H.

In particular, professional team sports—in addition to high school and college sports in the United States, as we discuss in chapter 6—featuring some kind of ball-like contraption, have captured the imagination and passion of mainly the male half of the population in postindustrial societies and beyond. However, as we make clear in chapter 4, women have also participated in the course of the past three to four decades, precisely coinciding with the forces that we have come to call "second globalization."

These few games that constitute hegemonic sports culture have by now evolved into independent social forces of hitherto unimagined importance, influencing the cultural consumption and daily habits of millions well beyond the actual producers of these games (that is, the players) or national borders. Asked about the significance of Association Football—better known as soccer—Bill Shankly, the long-time manager of Liverpool explained: "Some people think football is a matter of life or death. I don't like that attitude. I can assure them it is much more important than that."[26] Substitute baseball, football, and basketball for soccer in the context of the United States, hockey in Canada, Rugby Union in New Zealand, Rugby League in the state of New South Wales in Australia with Australian Rules Football assuming a comparable role in nearby Victoria, cricket's cultural hegemony in India, Pakistan, Sri Lanka, the West Indies, South Africa and Australia, and Shankly's statement has its parallels in any of the hegemonic sports cultures the world over. The games in question vary from country to country and continent to continent, but the larger cultural phenomenon that each has come to embody in its respective countries or continents, does not.

Take the world of Association Football, known as "football" in much of the world, but—curiously and tellingly—by its Victorian English slang term of "soccer" in North America. Today this game may very well represent one of the very few "languages" that is understood on a global scale. There can be no question, and opinion surveys confirm this, that Ronaldinho in his heyday was the best-known and most popular Brazilian on the globe, Zidane the best-known and most popular Frenchman, and Franz "Kaiser" Beckenbauer the only German whose name recognition has come

Chen puts it: "The shaping of local people's cultural subjectivity can no longer go back and look for origin, purity, authenticity; it must be connected to the here and now of everyday life." See K. H. Chen, "Voices from the Outside: Toward a New Internationalist Localism," *Cultural Studies* 6 (3), 1992, pp. 347–69. On the democratic and cultural impact of transnational publics, see James Bohman, *Democracy across Borders* (Cambridge, MA: MIT Press, 2007); for an earlier account see Jeremy Waldron, "Minority Cultures and the Cosmopolitan Alternatives," *University of Michigan Journal of Law Reform* 25, 1992.

[26]This famous quote by Shankly, stated in a television interview in 1981, was first published posthumously in the *Sunday Times*, October 4, 1981.

to equal Hitler's (surpassing Heidi Klum and Claudia Schiffer, as well as Johann Wolfgang von Goethe). David Beckham, now also among the prominent athletes in America, ranks among the top of all British celebrities and is a global superstar well beyond the game that he has come to master. All four of these men are now or were once soccer players, sharing in this international language of sports and becoming globalized cultural role models, symbols of an evolving sports culture and market that speaks increasingly to every distant corner of the world.

Their North American counterparts—superstars like Tiger Woods, Michael Jordan, Kobe Bryant, Alex Rodriguez (A-Rod), and Wayne Gretzky— have entered the global lexicon like few other Americans or Canadians, including most movie stars and politicians, as well as businessmen, academics, or scientists. None, quite tellingly, hail from the world of soccer but from those sports that comprise America's hegemonic sports culture. Nevertheless, while Ronaldinho and A-Rod are exquisite masters of different arenas of play, the overall character of their cultural production beyond the immediate playing field is almost identical.[27] These eminent sports figures are the best of the best at their game, which renders them truly global players or—to substitute the less pretentious vernacular of the American inner city for the Latin-based "global"—All World.[28]

Local Identities and Cultural Resilience

This book looks at the interrelations between ongoing transformations in the sports world and the processes of the second or postindustrial globalization, which began more or less three decades ago. Our study illuminates the cosmopolitan role of sports within shifting cultures, identities, and politics, by example of Europe and America. This second globalization, however, can only be understood against the background of the first. The

[27] And all are male. Until very recently, this world has been virtually the exclusive domain of men as consumers and as producers. Moreover, the main carriers of this male world reflected the less propertied and less privileged social strata, operating largely in the confines of a particular nation-state.

[28] "All World" (sometimes even "All Planet") denotes a level of exceptional excellence and rare exclusivity beyond the official assignation in American sports of being an "All American," which, of course, is a rarity and high distinction in and of itself. Indeed, the Philadelphia 76ers shooting guard Lloyd B. Free was considered to be such a sensational shooter, such an amazing dunker, and such a flamboyant player that he was given the sobriquet "World" by his admiring peers on the playgrounds of Brooklyn, where he became a basketball legend. In 1980, Free proceeded to have his first name "Lloyd" changed legally to "World" thus officially becoming World B. Free.

first wave of capitalist globalization that engulfed the world from the second half of the nineteenth century to the beginning of World War I emanated from Britain, home of modern capitalism, and coursed through its empire. During the same period Britain also became the home of modern sports. Indeed, no other country comes close to Britain in its contributions to the contemporary world of sports. Britain's singular feat consisted of transforming its diverse and highly varied local games into modern sports through organization, rationalization, and institutionalization. The origins of the global emanate almost exclusively from the national and local, and the latter two levels continue to persist as crucial characteristics of sports culture.

In addition to giving these entities mutually intelligible rules that henceforth defined their very essences as sports, Britain's modern capitalism—with its accompanying bourgeois institutional order—codified the former local dialects of games into portable sports languages, also confirming the mold for the rigid separation of work and leisure.[29] This separation established the temporal and spatial dimensions of social and cultural life in which modern sport assumed its place. As a major player in the global game of imperialism, Britain exported this model around the globe. And in the process of this first globalization, all of these newly codified sports with their particular rules and regulations became universally intelligible sports languages. Maarten Van Bottenburg, in expanding Norbert Elias's original term "sportization," has best characterized the process as providing the singularly most important aspect of making sports uniform, thus precisely understood by all participants (both players and followers) regardless of time and space—that is, rendering sports profoundly modern.[30] The proliferation and acceptance of English soccer by textile engineers, electrical work-

[29] It is perfectly clear to us that to many linguists our usage of the term "languages" to denote different sports is nothing short of blasphemous and, from their professional vantage point, completely erroneous. We could, of course, opt to call sports "semiotic systems" or "systems of communication," both of which would be more appropriate in a technical sense. Still, we think that for our purposes, using the term "language" as a metaphor conveys what we are trying to say: namely that sports are communicative forms with clearly delineated rules and regulations that have a bevy of meaning, nuances, and levels that are used by those that know them to articulate their emotions and knowledge to others conversant with these forms. To us, each sport has a distinctive symbolic and normative framework comprised of formal rules and informal codes, which in turn generate a penumbra of meaningful practices, symbols, and evaluations. We see these analogous to languages or idioms. In no way do we mean to imply that each sport is a language. Rather, we see each sport as having a distinctive (normative, symbolic, conceptual, and terminological) language associated with it, which constitutes part of that sport's singular culture.

[30] Norbert Elias, "The Genesis of Sport as a Sociological Problem" in Eric Dunning, ed., *The Sociology of Sport: A Selection of Readings* (London: Frank Cass, 1971), pp. 88–115; and

ers, accountants, merchants, and businessmen around the world, but particularly in Latin America and the European continent, characterized the might of Britain's economic model more than its political power. Much less prominently than Britain—and behooving its (self-proclaimed) posture of "splendid isolation"—the North American continent, too, developed crucial sports languages parallel to Britain's in the latter part of the nineteenth century, namely the Big Four of baseball, football, basketball, and hockey.[31]

All of these languages, soccer included, are related and share many common characteristics. Thus, for example, they are all centered on a ball-like contraption of varying shape and size (if we are permitted the indulgence of calling a hockey puck a ball); they are all team sports; they are all modern variants of ancient sports. So, in a sense, they all share an Ur-language as it were, a Latin.

Yet, to some extent they have become and still are mutually incomprehensible, just as today's French is from Portuguese and Romanian. One can make out meanings in the other language, see related patterns in it, sense some parallels with it, but one cannot quite speak or understand it without a long process of acculturation and learning. Just like with languages, the early socialization process is hereby decisive; the earlier one learns to speak baseball, soccer, or basketball, the more proficient one is in all their respective complexities and nuances. Later learning is possible, but since it will in some ways always be accented, it remains an empirical question whether the native speakers will fully accept the newcomer as "authentic."

Though by no means tied to nation-states, these individual sports languages have proven to be immensely resilient over an entire century, from the mid to late nineteenth century until today. America developed its own languages that—in many cases—were related to their British counterparts but emerged in due course as entities all their own. We will devote much attention later to the celebrated presence of college sports as an integral part of American culture way beyond sports, a phenomenon unique to that country.

There are many other examples of this "linguistic" difference between the United States and the rest of the sports world, but at this juncture we

---

Maarten Van Bottenburg, *Global Games* (Champaign: University of Illinois Press, 2001). This will be discussed in greater detail throughout the book.

[31] With the exception of American football, all of the North American sports spread to other countries and cultures in the process of this first globalization. But their success in establishing a lasting cultural prominence in these countries proved to be much more muted and geographically confined than soccer's.

will restrict ourselves to merely four: first, the prevalence of multisport performers at the very top level of American team sports, such as Dave DeBusschere and Danny Ainge in baseball and basketball, Deion Sanders and Bo Jackson in baseball and football, and others such as Charlie Ward who won the Heisman Trophy as the country's very best collegiate football player and seamlessly proceeded to pursue a respectable career as a starting point guard in the NBA.[32] Such two- or even three-sport stars are much more prominent at the college level than among the professional ranks, and are quite common in high schools where many top athletes participate at the varsity level in all three of the American sports languages.[33] This does not exist elsewhere precisely because no other country has the same proliferation of different sports languages that dominate general culture. Despite "His Airness's" inability to hit a curveball, Michael Jordan's failed attempt to become a major league baseball player attests to the uniquely American phenomenon of athletic skill linked with cultural capital that informs the three-pronged (potentially four) nature of America's hegemonic sports culture. The very fact that Jordan played Triple-A ball for two years still bespeaks an inordinate proficiency in two sports. To our knowledge, no comparable European or Latin American soccer star ever attempted to apply his athletic skills or cultural knowledge to another sport. For example, David Beckham never took a leave of absence from Manchester United to try his hand at playing passable professional cricket or rugby, nor did Thierry Henry spend any of his springs or summers on a bicycle participating in that sport's elite events such as the Giro d'Italia,

[32] By all accounts, the Hall-of-Fame baseball players Tony Gwynn and Dave Winfield could have played basketball in the NBA had they chosen to do so (Gwynn as a point guard, Winfield as a power forward); and let us not forget the Cy Young Award and 300-games winning pitcher Tom Glavine who was drafted by the National Hockey League's Los Angeles Kings in 1984 in the fourth round, two rounds ahead of 2009 Hockey Hall of Fame inductees Brett Hull and Luc Robitaille, but chose to join MLB's Atlanta Braves who also drafted him in 1984. The most prominent non-American two-sport star on the top professional level was arguably Denis Compton, the face of Brylcreem, who played cricket for Middlesex and performed in seventy-eight test matches for England while playing football for Arsenal.

[33] Just think of athletes like Drew Henson, who played quarterback for the University of Michigan and was then drafted to play third base for the New York Yankees. Or Jeff Samardzija, a star pitcher for the Notre Dame baseball team, who became one of the very best receivers for its football team and of Football Bowl Subdivision (FBS)—formerly Division I-A—college football as a whole, and was a first-round draft pick for the National Football League, but then chose to become a relief pitcher for the Chicago Cubs (and became a star). And we would be remiss not to mention Stanford University's Toby Gerhart who shattered all the Cardinal's rushing records in his stellar four-year college career, was a serious candidate for the Heisman Trophy in 2009, but also starred on Stanford's baseball team and was poised to commence a fine career either in the NFL or MLB.

the Tour de France, or any of the "classiques"; and we know of no top-level German, Swiss, Austrian, Dutch, or Scandinavian soccer player who also became a well-respected star in any of these countries' diverse winter sports that comprise their respective hegemonic sports cultures.[34] Moreover, in no other country are educational institutions, starting well before high school and culminating in college, so intricately involved in creating expert users, indeed well-nigh masters, of these sports languages. America's hegemonic sports culture has been multilingual as it were, with most countries' cultural equivalence being at most bilingual, with soccer a predominant first among equals.[35]

[34]Václav Nedomanský, the great Czechoslovak hockey star for the national team and for his club Slovan Bratislava, was the closest European whom we could locate as a two-sport star. He performed at the highest levels in hockey and was also an excellent soccer player, and played one match for Slovan Bratislava's soccer club in the Czechoslovak first division. Tellingly, just like in the American cases, soccer and hockey are the two hegemonic languages of Czechoslovak sports culture, thus played by boys and men from an early age. Other European cases do not really constitute a change of sports language: An interesting and in many ways exceptional case is the German soccer star Manfred Burgsmüller, who played for Borussia Dortmund. The fourth all-time leading scorer in the Bundesliga (with an amazing 213 goals) retired from professional soccer in 1990. But he turned to professional football in 1996, starting a second career as the kicker for Rhein Fire, Düsseldorf's American football team. When he ended his career in 2002, Burgsmüller had turned into the most successful kicker in NFL Europe. He won two "World Bowls." Playing at age fifty-two, he was the oldest professional football player of all time. Similarly, Toni Fritsch ("Wembley Toni"), an Austrian soccer player—a regular for SK Rapid Wien, who made it to six caps in the Austrian national team and scored two legendary goals in 1965 in Austria's only win against England at Wembley (without achieving much further fame in that sport thereafter)—emigrated to the United States and became a successful place kicker for the Dallas Cowboys. Both Fritsch's and Burgsmüller's transitions from one football to another were much less dramatic than playing sports as diverse as football, baseball, and basketball on the world's highest levels of each sport.

[35]Australia presents the closest approximation to the Big Four languages of the American sports space. Here, too, one can detect four important sports cultures but the prominence of Australia's main team sports are geographically segmented, in notable contrast to the situation in the United States where only hockey remains regional. Thus, while Rugby League is immensely popular in New South Wales, Queensland, and the Australian Capital Territory, it is hardly followed in Victoria, South Australia, Western Australia, Tasmania, and the Northern Territory, where Australian Rules Football comprises the core of hegemonic sports culture. Cricket has a truly national following and ditto with Rugby Union though the latter's popularity is much stronger in the Rugby League states than in those beholden to Australian Rules Football—with the exception of Western Australia, which has strong Union grass roots due to large numbers of South African and British immigrants. Soccer's Australian profile is not dissimilar to the sport's American counterpart: a rather weak domestic presence but an increasing interest in the national team's international successes. The "Socceroos," rather than the sport of soccer per se, have received major support and interest in Australia since the late 1990s confirming yet again the power of nationalism in creating attraction to an aspiring entrant into a country's sports space and hegemonic sports culture. While the Australian domestic league, the Hyundai A-League, which commenced playing in the 2005–6 season, has

Second, even in the ubiquitous and profoundly modern motor sports, America is different from the rest of the world, speaking a slightly different language as it were. Whereas Formula One has become a global phenomenon, literally contested in races on every continent, there is the marked absence of the United States of America, the world's largest producer and consumer of cars throughout the twentieth century.[36] Of course, Americans did participate in Formula One, and sure enough Phil Hill and Mario Andretti won Formula One's coveted world championship, Dan Gurney emerged as one of its bona fide stars, and races were held at places like Watkins Glen and in the streets of Detroit and Las Vegas. However, Americans have never come close to speaking and truly enjoying the language of Formula One the way they have their own two indigenously produced vernaculars: The National Association for Stock Car Auto Racing (NASCAR), whose product has been catapulted to the second spot—behind only the NFL—as the most watched sport on American television; and open-wheel car (Indy Car) racing, featuring such American classics as the Indianapolis 500 held on Memorial Day every year. But here, too, we observe an increased American engagement with the world of global sports, in that at the time of this writing the first U.S.-based Formula One team since the late 1960s first U.S.-based Formula One team since the late 1960s had just been established with José Maria López of Argentina as its first driver.[37]

Third, there are those unique North American temples and shrines to sports called "Halls of Fame," which celebrate the respective sport's best players, most important coaches and managers, and its most meritorious officials, owners, and broadcasters—in short, that embody the sport's most coveted history and honor the particular language's most original practitioners, its most prolific masters, and its most accomplished users. It is not at all by chance that the French term for the Hockey Hall of Fame has an explicitly religious nomenclature in *Temple de la Renomée du Hockey*. Expressions such as somebody being a "first-ballot-Hall-of-Famer," which denotes singular excellence in the person's métier, are purely part of the American vernacular and unknown to other sports cultures and languag-

---

certainly gained in prominence precisely on the coattails of the Socceroos' success, many of the country's soccer fans tend to quench their quotidian thirst for the game by following their favorite teams of the English Premier League.

[36] This is all the more surprising since 90 percent of Formula One's technology hails from the U.S. aerospace industry and trickles down to the Formula One teams based in Britain and Italy.

[37] "U.S. Formula One Team Names Driver," *New York Times*, January 26, 2010, p. B14.

es.[38] The fact that sports assume, at least to some degree, the cultures and language patterns of local customs that might otherwise not be part of their mainstream presence, is best demonstrated by the fact that soccer in the United States does indeed feature the National Soccer Hall of Fame and Museum, which was opened in 1979 in Oneonta, New York; it is just a few miles up the road from the National Baseball Hall of Fame and Museum in Cooperstown. There is nothing remotely similar in the global culture for soccer. And while legends such as Franz Beckenbauer and Pelé would surely be celebrated members of an edifice and shrine that encompassed world football, or even of their respective countries, Germany and Brazil, they are actually soccer Hall-of-Famers by dint of their induction in Oneonta—an honor that they attained by having played a leading role in American soccer arguably at the tail end of their respective stellar careers and not German and Brazilian football that propelled them to global stardom. We should mention in this context the International Cricket Council's (ICC) Hall of Fame, which was established on January 2, 2009 as part of the ICC's centenary celebrations. This Hall honors the greatest players of cricket from all over the world.

And fourth, the origins of American sports teams as businesses, leading to the system of franchises, is in stark contrast to their European counterparts hailing from the world of clubs. The former lead a mobile existence, moving from place to place following changing conditions in demography and markets. Yet, once in a league, they do not drop to its lower rungs by dint of having had a poor season, nor do they advance to its top tier as reward for good results. By contrast, European clubs remain geographically immutable, but they do get relegated to lower divisions for poor results and promoted for good ones.

Our metaphoric sports languages also exhibit major effects on real languages and their users. Take the term "football," for example. It denotes different sports in the United States, Canada, Australia, and England. Each

---

[38] There are, of course, many halls of fame in the United States. Indeed, virtually every state has a hall of fame to which it inducts its most meritorious athletes and sports figures. But clearly, the most important are the halls of fame of the Big Four American team sports. Not by chance, the oldest and most distinguished of these is The National Baseball Hall of Fame and Museum, opened on June 12, 1939 in Cooperstown, New York—celebrating the centenary of baseball's alleged beginnings then and there. It was followed by The Hockey Hall of Fame (the above-mentioned Temple de la Renomée du Hockey), established in 1943 in Kingston, Ontario and subsequently moved to Toronto in 1958. The Professional Football Hall of Fame followed on September 7, 1963 in Canton, Ohio. Lastly, The Naismith Memorial Basketball Hall of Fame emerged on February 17, 1968 in Springfield, Massachusetts.

of these in turn creates its own nomenclatures and special terms. What the English call "nil," "pitch," "match" (also "fixture"), "supporter," "(goal) keeper," "manager," "penalty," "level" (also "draw"), "batsman," and "bowler," the Americans refer to as "zero" (or "nothing"), "field," "game," "fan," goalie," "coach" (though "manager" in baseball), "PK" (short for penalty kick), "tie(d)," "batter," and "pitcher." Making matters more confusing still is that the exact same terms mean completely different things to their respective speakers. "Pitch" means nothing to an American in terms of referring to a "field" but quite a lot as an integral part of baseball. Any insider perceives any erring in the proper usage of the language as a tell-tale sign of an outsider's ignorance or worse. Indeed, we had to make choices as to what nomenclatures we were to use in this volume, cognizant of the fact that few things divide us more from our British and other English-speaking friends than our common language, particularly that of sports. Woe onto the person who transgresses linguistically by referring to an item by its "improper" name. Nothing carries a greater stigma and fiercer contempt for a "true" English football supporter than to have his game sullied by the usage of improper (i.e., alien and disdained) American terminology.[39] In turn, most American soccer aficionados have to assert their bona fide soccer identity by using the game's English rather than American terminology, which, too, has its problems.[40]

Sports languages shift and move; but they also prove immensely sticky

[39] Indeed, one of us experienced a rare look of unmitigated contempt and hatred on the part of an English fan toward an American patron in an Ann Arbor sports bar when the latter jumped up in the opening minutes of the telecast of the 2006 Champions League Final between Arsenal and Barcelona and screamed at the top of his lungs "This is a PK," when the Arsenal goalkeeper brought down a Barcelona attacker. "It's a f—— penalty for you," hissed the Englishman full of venom and anger.

[40] One of America's foremost soccer journalists and grey eminences of the game, the English-born Paul Gardner, constantly inveighs against what he calls the "Eurosnobs," who appear compelled to enhance their (and perhaps soccer's) legitimacy in America by always using the game's English rather than its American terminologies. Here is Gardner on the origins of the word "soccer" and some of the game's American fans' determination to use the English term "football," which they perceive to be the "correct" nomenclature for the game: "A point about the word soccer: There seems to be a widespread impression that the word is an American invention, It is not. It is pure English, almost as old as the sport itself. Maybe the World Football Challenge people [the organizers of this tournament who insisted on using the word 'football' instead of 'soccer,' which will be discussed in chapter 3], having understood that the word has sturdy Brit Eurosnob origins, will now be able to use it?" Paul Gardner, "Superclubs Tour USA: Pros and Cons," *SoccerAmerica*, July 27, 2009. Even on this level, language in and about sports matters immensely because it bespeaks a deeper identity. Nothing is more upsetting to insiders than outsiders misusing the sport's proper terminology, violating the language's proper grammar as it were. Any and all transgressions in this area disqualify the user

and resilient. Still, the questions remain: How do these languages transform in the global context; How culturally inclusive and cosmopolitan are modern sports; and, What role do sports play in cultural and political change—especially in a world where "globalizations" clash with exclusive identity claims and counter-cosmopolitanism?

Sports are going global for the second time. We will examine the resilience and transformations of the cultural and sports spaces[41] that formed in the first globalization and have remained relevant during our contemporary era, featuring what we call the second globalization. This entails an age of global capitalism and trade, new transnational migration, global communications networks, and cosmopolitan norms and institutions never previously imagined, let alone experienced. These massive shifts create a global culture wherein sports assume pride of place. New transnational identities, markets, events, agents, and communications have emerged. Yet,

---

as an imposter, an unwanted intruder or—in the best case—as a newcomer who needs a lot of seasoning in the particular sports language's nuances.

[41] We use the term "sports space" analogous to what political scientists have come to call party space, meaning both actual physical space and its congruent cultural presence. According to Lipset and Rokkan's ground-breaking theory, the beginning of the modern industrial age until the end of World War I witnessed some "critical junctures" that shaped political spaces and their future paths. Emerging dominant societal cleavages—the most significant between owners and workers—were by and large established by 1920. The party space emerging at that post–World War I juncture, became "frozen," according to Lispet and Rokkan, and remained so until the late 1960s, making it difficult for newcomers to enter this space. The two spaces, party and sports, are actually related because they both hail from the world of industrialization. This process created a spatial and temporal separation between work and leisure; and it is in the latter that in the second half of the nineteenth century spaces arose in which modern sports became located. Thus sports space entails courts, fields, clubhouses—actual edifices and grounds—as well as human beings associated with these institutions, first as a matter of leisurely pursuit but subsequently as their vocations. It is by dint of the last development that very few ball-centered team sports came to attain an importance way beyond their immediate milieus and thus became hegemonic culture in a society's sports space. Analogous to the topography of party systems, this space, created more or less between 1860 and 1920, has become occupied by hegemonic sports, rendering the barrier of entry for newcomers quite difficult. On the concept of party space and its occupation, see Seymour Martin Lipset and Stein Rokkan, "Cleavage Structures, Party Systems and Voter Alignments: An Introduction," in Seymour Martin Lipset and Stein Rokkan, eds., *Party Systems and Voter Alignments* (New York: Free Press, 1967), pp. 1–64; see Ira Katznelson, "Structure and Configuration in Comparative Politics," in Mark Irving Lichbach and Alan S. Zuckerman, eds., *Comparative Politics: Rationality, Culture, and Structure* (Cambridge: Cambridge University Press, 1997), pp. 81–112. For some of the many revisions, defenses, and critiques of the contemporary relevance of this argument see also Peter Mair, *Party System Change: Approaches and Interpretations* (Oxford: Clarendon, 1997); Paul Pennings and Jan-Erik Lane, eds., *Comparing Party System Change* (New York: Routledge, 1998). For the analogy in sports see Markovits and Hellerman, *Offside*, pp.19–30.

these appear to transform, rather than replace, local spaces and ties within the global topography of sports. This second globalization creates new inroads for various global players and professional games, as it further expands the cultural territory of one sport into the hitherto guarded domain of another. Witness the penetration of basketball into Europe's sports space and the reciprocal presence of soccer in America's. Globalizing sports and interests—illustrated, for example, by the fact that for millions in China, Tanzania, or Australia the results of Manchester United's weekend games have become a major concern—overlay new areas of culture onto established sports spaces that do not leave the local unaffected. However, players, teams, and games that have become global do not simply discard their local importance and national salience; rather, to a considerable extent, their newly acquired global stature often reinforces those dimensions.

This happens in two opposed directions. On the one hand, those who adhere to the identity of a local or national sports culture may cling to it all the more trenchantly in the face of absorption into the global. On the other hand, the local or national dimensions of a sports community may constitute one of the points of appeal that these sports have on the global level. "You never walk alone," the famous chant reverently intoned by Liverpool fans, bespeaks most powerfully the essence of being scouse, a native of Liverpool and a member of its local sports culture. Indeed, Liverpool supporters often invoke their scouse identity in explicit opposition to identifying themselves as English, let alone British or belonging to any other national or ethnic category. However, as a trapping of Liverpool's global presence, along with the color red, the legend of Anfield—the team's home stadium with its iconic "This is Anfield" sign that graces the tunnel leading to the pitch, and which every Liverpool player touches with reverence—and "scouse-ness" now may include fans in China, Africa, or anywhere in the world. As teams like Liverpool become global, which community does a motto like, "You never walk alone" embody? Identities that until recently remained strictly local have attained, by virtue of global teams, a reach far beyond their immediate boundaries. In fact, these teams have developed multiple cosmopolitan attachments, from their multiethnic international lineup to dedicated fan communities across the globe. Nevertheless, the local has been far from replaced and it may well continue to resist the global, while it also cannot help but be radically transformed into something new when a sport culture is marketed and communicated around the globe.

The Second Globalization and its Cosmopolitan Turns

We argue that the hegemonic sports cultures that were established between 1860 and 1914 in the United States, Europe, and by extension much of the world, continue to flourish unabated, yet far from unchanged and unchallenged. In postindustrial societies today, professional team sports are not just a crucial part of (global) popular culture but also significant agents of cultural change and global communication. "Globalization" has become an overused catch-word in the social sciences and beyond. However, we think that it points to some striking developments in the postindustrial age. Moreover, we argue that the concept we call the second or postindustrial globalization, starting roughly in the 1970s, embodies causal factors for the aforementioned cosmopolitan changes and the reshaping of sports cultures.

Although the new, post-industrial globalization might be primarily economically induced, it cannot be reduced to the expansion of markets and the increase of social inequalities.[42] This process is instead multicausal and multilayered, entailing a transformation of global communications, the decline of the "television age" and a concomitant prominence of the Internet, globalized publics and cosmopolitan expectations, new transnational identities and migration, as well as the rise of supranational entities and organizations. Cultural interactions are also affected. Even distant local events or deliberate "localisms" are today enmeshed in global relations. Here we adopt the diagnostic definition offered by David Held and his collaborators: globalization is a complex and multidimensional process that "embodies a transformation in the spatial organization of social relations and transactions—exerted in terms of their extensity, intensity, velocity and impact—generating transcontinental or interregional flows and networks of activity, interaction, and the exercise of power."[43] However, we conceptualize this process more specifically as a second, postindustrial globalization. Just like the first, "industrial" globalization, so does

---

[42] On globalization and global inequality see Kate Vyborny and Nancy Birdsall, "Does Free Trade Promote Economic Equality?," in Peter M. Haas, John A. Hird, and Beth McBratney, eds., *Controversies in Globalization: Contending Approaches to International Relations* (Washington, DC: CQ Press, 2010) pp. 55–67.

[43] David Held, Anthony McGrew, David Goldblatt, and Jonathan Perraton, "Rethinking Globalization," in David Held and Athony McGrew, eds., *The Global Transformations Reader* (Cambridge: Polity, 2000), p. 55. Globalization, hence, primarily denotes "the expanding scale, growing magnitude, speeding up and deepening impact of transcontinental flows and patterns of interaction." David Held and Anthony McGrew, *Globalization/Antiglobalization* (Cambridge: Polity Press, 2002), p. 1.

its second, postindustrial variant exert in its own unique way multiple pressures on existing political orders, collective identities, cultural bonds, and societal structures.[44]

First, the postindustrial transformation of technology and emergence of global media have facilitated unprecedented communication between individuals and groups in far-away places. Thus, sports connoisseurs around the world can be part of the most distant sports events. Second, this coincides with new global migration and mobility that has inevitably altered the cultural composition, increasing the diversity of postindustrial societies and, in particular, of sports consumers and producers. Third, funda-

[44] Our claim that this second globalization is multilayered and multicausal is backed by major advances in contemporary scholarship on the subject. We view the second globalization as a set of *processes* that have begun to generate new, complex webs of interdependencies, sprawling networks, and global publics operating far beyond the economic realm. Globalization does not refer to a single (economic) dynamic but a "set of processes that operate simultaneously and unevenly on several levels and in various dimensions." See Steger, *Globalization* (Oxford: Oxford University Press, 2009), p. 36. Moreover, globalization is hardly a unified phenomenon but rather, as James Mittelman claims, a syndrome of changes of social relations that also produces deep tensions. Although globalization entails intensified global exchanges and events (including global sports events) that induce an increased human awareness of interdependence and receding boundaries, the emerging global networks are disparate and fragmented. While globalization refers to the multiplication, expansion and acceleration of activities across political and territorial boundaries, much of contemporary scholarship also insists that globalization is never just a one-way street. It is equally misguided to view globalization only in terms of "cultural imperialism"—as new Western superhighways that pave over local roads and villages. For all the pressures that globalization forces exert on individual cultures, diversity typically increases within society, as Tyler Cohen points out. While globalization relativizes particularisms, political or cultural differences do not simply disappear; they are also recreated. As we will show in chapter 2, this mutual penetration of the universal and the particular, the global and the local is arguably best captured by Roland Robertson's concept of "glocalization." In this process of hybridization of differences neither the global nor the local stay the same. Transnational, national, and local groups are agents in this context: For instance, local cultures and groups may absorb, transform, and reject certain dimensions of globalization. In turn, local politics and cultures (and sports cultures for that matter) may have global impact. Thus, conceptions that view globalization simply as cultural homogenization ("McWorld") fail to grasp the proliferating complexity of global relationships among individuals, institutions, cultures, and organizations. Globalization unfolds a "nonlinear dialectical process in which the universal and the particular, the similar and the dissimilar, the global and the local are to be conceived, not as cultural polarities, but as interconnected and reciprocally interpenetrating principles." Ulrich Beck, *The Cosmopolitan Vision* (Cambridge: Polity Press, 2006), pp. 72–73. See also Arjun Appadurai, *Modernity at Large: Cultural Dimensions of Globalization* (Minneapolis: University of Minnesota Press, 1996); Tyler Cohen, *Creative Destruction: How Globalization Is Changing the World's Cultures* (Princeton: Princeton University Press, 2004); James H. Mittelman, *The Globalization Syndrome: Transformation and Resistance* (Princeton: Princeton University Press, 2000); Roland Robertson, *Globalization: Social Theory and Global Culture* (London: Sage, 1992); James N. Rosenau, *Distant Proximities: Dynamics Beyond Globalization* (Princeton: Princeton University Press, 2003).

mental postindustrial changes in the workplace—the decline of the traditional industrial working class—have also profoundly influenced the audience for sports events. Fourth, we are faced with the globalization of political arrangements, that is, the expansion and increasing relevance of global institutions in the world of sports as well. And, fifth, the globalization of the economy has led to an intensified global outreach on the part of clubs and corporations that invest in sports. Challenging societies to change their ways, this second globalization has thus facilitated the "cosmopolitanization" of global players and arenas, reshaping the sports cultures that we examine.

In particular, we explore the fascinating similarities and differences that inform the sports spaces in America and Europe and analyze the factors and variables that influence continuity and change in them: We observe the resilience ("stickiness") of old habits on both continents that comprise the backbone of all hegemonic sports cultures: the much-maligned (or praised) "couch potato" forms the core of sports consumption. But *his* (sic) world, too, has experienced mighty changes in the course of the second globalization. We witness what one could label the "Europeanization" of America's sports culture and, conversely, the "Americanization" of Europe's. While it is commonplace to talk about the latter and to view globalization more or less as synonymous with Americanization, we demonstrate that Europe, far from being a victim of America's might, very much plays a leading (perhaps *the* leading) role in what arguably has evolved into *the* hegemonic sports culture par excellence on a global level—the world of soccer. Indeed, Europe's massive domination of two of international sport's leading federations, FIFA and the IOC, are well known and beyond dispute. Simply put, while baseball, football, basketball, and hockey—the old mainstays of North America's sports culture for well over one century—continue to comprise the world's undisputed core in these respective sports, it is Western Europe's soccer, with its four leading professional leagues (the English Premier League, *Serie A* in Italy, the *Primera Division*, commonly known as *La Liga* in Spain, and Germany's *Bundesliga*) that furnishes this sport's uncontested core. But Europe's added prominence hails from the fact that the game over which it lords embodies a much wider global product than any of its North American competitors; their global reach, though growing massively since the advent of the second globalization, still remains way behind soccer's, which seems to have built its insurmountable lead during the time of its nineteenth-century predecessor.

How Sports Are Reshaping Global Politics and Culture

Our argument for this study is three-fold.

(1) We submit that hegemonic sports cultures, like political cultures and political party systems, represent "frozen" spaces that resist change and offer newcomers few opportunities for entry. Tradition, collective identity, and socialization matter immensely and continue to define *frozen sports spaces* rooted at the local, regional, and national level. Not surprisingly, these sports spaces have generally created even stronger emotional attachments and more powerful collective identifications than have political parties and ideologies. As such, we argue that these localized sports cultures continue to harbor a strong—and frequently quite successful—resistance to the pressures exerted by contemporary globalization. The relevance of these sports cultures, their languages, affective ties, and narratives of collective identity—even their putative resistance—should not be underestimated. The mostly locally anchored love for these sports and their institutions (such as teams, rules, players, colors, smells, legends, myths, narratives, and pubs or bars) often last a lifetime, at least for men. Sports, in this important sense, will remain, just like politics, perennially local.

(2) At the same time we also suggest that postindustrial globalization puts these frozen spaces under new, unprecedented pressures. It is challenging well-established cultural spaces and national, regional, and local identities on multiple levels. Traditional collective patterns and allegiances, constituting the established cleavages in the frozen landscape of sports and politics, begin to melt around the edges. They face a partial defrosting. There are several indicators that hegemonic sports cultures are becoming increasingly prolific across the Atlantic, well at pace with the development of the whole range of global interdependencies, media, and pop cultures that propagate global spaces.

More importantly, as a crucial part of popular culture globally, sports offer a key medium for cosmopolitan cultural change.[45] In several respects, hegemonic sports—especially but not exclusively contemporary soccer—are *the* vanguard of sociocultural globalization and cosmopolitan turns.

---

[45] Like other new global media and public arenas, sports are often a vehicle for communicating cosmopolitanism and facilitating diversity rather than simply producing cultural homogeneity; on the cosmopolitan impact of global media, see Pippa Norris and Ronald Inglehart, *Cosmopolitan Communications: Cultural Diversity in a Globalized World* (Cambridge: Cambridge University Press, 2009).

Global players on the field, who draw admiration from locals but also from across the world, are both representatives and facilitators of more inclusive cultural self-understandings in today's diverse societies. Sports are often the first cultural space in which migrants gain social recognition. Sports' universalistic focus on individual merit rather than exclusive cultural difference corresponds with, and helps generate, the rise of those egalitarian and inclusive sets of beliefs in postindustrial societies that Ronald Inglehart and Christian Welzel conceptualize as "self-expression values." Such values emphasize individuality, human choice, freedom of expression, liberty, autonomy, and diversity. According to Inglehart and Welzel, they emerge with long-term value change in civil society. Although they are "shaped by economic resources, they have a significant independent impact on democracy."[46]

Accounts that paint a thoroughly grim picture of global sports as mere propaganda for dictatorships, mimicking warfare or as hotbeds of nationalism, are at the very least one-sided.[47] They do not grasp that in a nation like China, which is ruled by an authoritarian regime, a new frenzy for the NBA, international soccer, and global players evade the control of the Communist elite. NBA star Kobe Bryant is arguably more popular in China than any other person in the world. He is now "the hometown favorite."[48] We argue that especially sports—and maybe only sports—render possible a new, totally unprecedented but "actually existing cosmopolitanism."[49] Sports cut across all national and cultural boundaries and transform identities. Sports also have a critical political impact. The increasing popular demands connected to soccer and basketball may in the long run topple the Chinese regime "from below," as Guoqi Xu, an expert on Chinese sport and society, persuasively argues.[50] Thus, far from viewing sports as the opiate of the masses, we regard their contemporary global presence as antinomian forces that challenge encrusted sources of domination.

An emerging cosmopolitan consciousness is in part caused by the sec-

[46] See Ronald Inglehart and Christian Welzel, *Modernization, Cultural Change, and Democracy: The Human Development Sequence* (Cambridge: Cambridge University Press, 2005), p. 182; see also Christian Haerpfer, Patrick Bernhagen, Ronald Inglehart, and Christian Welzel, eds., *Democratization* (New York: Oxford University Press, 2009).

[47] See Jonathan Kay, "War in Lycra," *National Post*, August 12, 2008, p. A14.

[48] David Barboza, "China's Promise Excites the Sports Stars," *New York Times*, August 27, 2008, p. C8.

[49] See Bruce Robbins, *Feeling Global: Internationalism in Distress* (New York: New York University Press, 1999).

[50] See Xu Guoqi, *Olympic Dreams: China and Sports, 1895–2008* (Cambridge, MA: Harvard University Press, 2008).

ond globalization of sports, in particular by the evolution of global sports arenas and broadcasts and the new global migration of players and spectators. Even if one's attachments remain local and specific to a hegemonic sport, one still develops an identity as a participant in an increasingly globalizing sports world that is by necessity culturally inclusive, antiessentialist, and universalistic—racist hooligans in European soccer stadiums and other forms of counter-cosmopolitan exclusions notwithstanding. People love good players, especially ones on "their" team, no matter their origins, the color of their skin, or their religion. And such players are international migrants who woo global audiences with their skillful performances, gaining interest and affection wherever they play.[51] Indeed, if professional teams lack international diversity, they risk being less competitive; this rule applies to other areas of society as well.[52]

Today's sports induce a broad cultural cosmopolitanism to a degree that we do not find anywhere else in a "global society" still divided along social cleavages, national borders, and other conflicts. Nationalism, dictatorship, exclusive identities, power, and money continue to remain important in sports and society. Yet this does not erase the new inclusive attachments, multiple allegiances, and the increasing relevance of new forms of cosmopolitan identity that sports cultures clearly provide. The cosmopolitanism of sports not only facilitates the universal admiration of the very best—thus generating an everyday sense of global commonality[53] and community of sports connoisseurs—but it also *transforms* persistently relevant collective identities. For instance, Germans—who have, until recently, adhered to an exclusive and ethnicity-based interpretation of citizenship, perhaps longer than other advanced capitalist countries[54]—now cheer for

[51] See Daniel A. Nathan, "Travelling: Notes on Basketball and Globalization; or, Why the San Antonio Spurs are the Future," *International Journal for the History of Sport* 25 (6), 2008, pp. 737–50, for a critical account of basketball's global impact in the context of global capitalism. In light of the Michael Jordan phenomenon other authors argue that "when products, images, and services are exported to other societies from some simulated American homeland, to some extent they become indigenized according to the cultural specificities of the local culture in which consumption takes place." See David L. Andrews, Ben Carrington, Steven J. Jackson, and Zbigniew Mazur, "Jordanscapes: A Preliminary Analysis of the Global Popular," *Sociology of Sport Journal* 13, 1996, pp. 428–57, here p. 453.

[52] For a pathbreaking work on the benefits of diversity in multiple areas of society, see Scott Page, *The Difference: How the Power of Diversity Creates Better Groups, Firms, Schools and Societies* (Princeton: Princeton University Press, 2007).

[53] See Ulrich Beck, "The Cosmopolitan Society and its Enemies," *Theory, Culture, and Society* 18 (6), 2001, pp. 17–44.

[54] See Ruud Koopmans and Hanspeter Kriesi, *Citizenship, National Identity and the Mobilisation of the Extreme Right: A Comparison of France, Germany, the Netherlands and Switzerland* (Berlin: Wissenschaftszentrum Berlin für Sozialforschung, 1997).

Olympians who were issued their German passports only a few weeks before the competition. NBA star Chris Kaman, does not even speak the
language of his "home" country. In the German working-class city of
Dortmund, a large proportion of the citizens are passionate about the
black Brazilian soccer player Júlio César, a member of the most successful
squad in the local team's (Borussia) history and among the all-time fan favorites. He has arguably done more to undermine—and delegitimize—
widely spread racial stereotypes and racist hatred in the stands and in town
than most educational campaigns.

The cultural cosmopolitanism of global players and market-induced
cosmopolitanism "from above" thereby meets an inclusive cosmopolitanism "from below." In the long run, this might provide an important bul-
wark against racism and cultural exclusion, and offer a major challenge to
inward-looking identity politics. In Europe, soccer is on its way to becoming a powerful medium for postnational political identity. As we will show,
few other cultural factors are as successful in generating Europeanization
and European identity as soccer, a long-shared grassroots phenomenon
whose common language and passion has become further Europeanized
through club competitions like the Champions League.[55]

Furthermore, following many failures, the global culture of soccer has
also reached the shores of America—often wrongly identified as the sole
source and agent of globalization. The arrival of David Beckham at the
L.A. Galaxy is only one example of this larger phenomenon. American
professional basketball, in turn, has had a major impact in Europe, changing cultural perceptions since the appearance of Larry Bird, Earvin "Magic"
Johnson, and most important of all Michael Jordan, as well as this trio's
participation in the legendary "Dream Team" at the Barcelona Olympic
Games of 1992. European superstars such as Dirk Nowitzki and Tony
Parker, who earn their living in America's arenas but have become global
icons, are direct descendants of these earlier global players who originated
in America's sports culture. All major professional clubs/actors in the contemporary world of sports, many with a global presence since the 1980s,
are represented by international stars with whom fans identify way beyond
the boundaries of these players' actual performance in their respective
sport. That this second sporting globalization had its roots in earlier developments is best attested to by the fact that it was the American professional
soccer club New York Cosmos in the 1970s and early 1980s, that represented the first truly globalized sports club of the modern age, with the

[55] See Anthony King, *The European Ritual: Football in the New Europe* (Aldershot: Ashgate,
2005), pp. 136–66. See also chapters 2 and 3 of this book.

soccer legends Pelé and Beckenbauer at its core. Not coincidentally, this was precisely the period that we regard as the beginning of the second globalization process.

(3) Finally, we realize that the global developments in which these hegemonic sports cultures play such a key role do not go unquestioned and unchallenged. In general, we find strong antimodern reactions that reflect generalized cultural opposition to globalization and cosmopolitanism, especially in traditionally ethnically exclusive societies. Adopting Kwame Anthony Appiah's notion of "counter-cosmopolitanism," which he attributes to religious neofundamentalists whom he portrays as intolerant "universalists," we identify all fundamental opponents to cosmopolitanism and all agents of exclusion on religious, ethnic, or cultural grounds as counter-cosmopolitans.[56] This, of course, also applies to the world of sports. Such reactions often correspond to anticosmopolitan sentiments elsewhere in contemporary postindustrial democracies. Even the *potential* transformation of hegemonic sports culture evokes fears and defensive reactions on both sides of the Atlantic. On the one hand, we perceive resentment against the incursion of "un-American" soccer in the United States, while on the other hand we observe derision in Europe against the allegedly "un-European" "Americanization," "feminization," and "commercialization" of soccer.[57] At its most extreme—though, alas, far from uncom-

[56] Appiah, *Cosmopolitanism*, pp. 137–53. Appiah primarily refers to a new kind of cosmopolitanism's noisiest foes: global Islamists and jihadists. They are by no means "localists" and reject traditional authorities, including religious ones. They also resist the "narrow nationalisms of the countries where they were born." And their outreach is in fact global: They "enlist in a campaign *against* any nation" that gets in the way of what they define as "universal justice." However, they vehemently oppose toleration of diversity and cosmopolitan inclusion regardless of belief or origin.

[57] The purchase of Manchester United by the Glazer family in May and June of 2005 represents a fascinating case in point. The objections by many of United's supporters and much of the British media against this acquisition focused not only on the huge debt that this purchase heaped on the club, but also on the Glazers' being double outsiders to the world of football by dint of their being American: first, thus not being privy to the game's culture, not being fluent in its language and thus not being able to value the true cultural worth of their acquisition; and second, by being American the Glazers were ipso facto steamrolling and globalizing Manchester United. It was fascinating to observe how in the eyes of angry United supporters, this mighty entity—arguably *the* most globalized sports team in the world well before the Glazers' takeover—appeared as this small, local, innocent village club that was a helpless victim against the onslaught of this Yankee monster. To local fans of any club, the identity of their team remains anchored in the local forever, untouched by the club's standing in the rest of the world. That American purchases of European and English football clubs have been particularly anathema to their European fans can best be gauged by the fact that similar deals by others have invoked less ire. The buyers were perceived by the fans as being conversant with the language of football, thus not such blatant outsiders as Americans. Thus, for example, when the Russian billionaire Roman Abramovich acquired the pedigreed Lon-

mon—this backlash manifests itself in the violent, sometimes deadly, racist and ultranationalist fan cultures that inhabit European soccer stadiums. These are perhaps the last uncontested bastions in our advanced liberal democracies where men are "given" the legitimate space to behave badly, that is, to exhibit an unbridled maleness which in turn has to be interpreted as a defense mechanism in light of massive cultural changes and social shifts that have at least questioned, if not substantially challenged, the continued legitimacy of heterosexual male dominance in liberal democracies. And since hegemonic sports cultures have always been, and continue to remain, male domains, many aspects of maleness (including some less flattering ones) come to the fore in these venues.

Nevertheless, amidst the wave of the second globalization, the powerful forces of global communications, international stardom, and economic interests render the cosmopolitan current in sports irreversible. Supported by globalization from above, new culturally inclusive identities emerge from below, with global sports furnishing a major factor in this process. A widening of consciousness and altered cultural repertoires[58] find their most prominent expressions in the global players and cosmopolitan teams with which people identify on the local or national level. Such a new cosmopolitanism, which merges with local ties without replacing them, resonates across the globe.

The Remaining Structure of the Book

Chapter 2 offers an analysis of the history of the globalization of sports cultures—soccer in particular, but also basketball, football, baseball and hockey—and their impact in local, national, and global contexts to the present. Exploring how these games mutated into global languages and cultural systems in the course of the past one hundred and fifty years, we discuss how global arenas have been established and shaped by critical junctures of the first globalization at the end of the nineteenth century and were drastically expanded in the postindustrial, second globalization of the current age.

Showing the cultural relevance and power of sports, we then examine their potential as agents for cosmopolitanism, diversity, and inclusion on the one hand, and resilient politicocultural exclusionism and traditional-

---

don club Chelsea in 2003, there was no animosity comparable to the Glazers' purchase of Manchester United two years later.

[58] See Vertovec and Cohen, "Introduction: Conceiving Cosmopolitanism," p. 4.

ism on the other. As examples for the latter case, soccer has served as a tool for dictators and a vehicle for chauvinism. Indeed, we find hypernationalism still extant, especially in World Cup and European Championship competitions when national soccer teams clash.

In formerly ethnically homogenous Europe, professional soccer has worked as a unique force for diversity, facilitating the democratic inclusion of immigrants since the 1980s. Similarly, Hank Greenberg's remarkable career as MLB's first Jewish superstar symbolized the struggle for the recognition and respect of America's Jews in the 1930s. When Jackie Robinson broke the color barrier in baseball, the effect was even more powerful in terms of opening the door to the overdue and still ongoing process of the formal integration of African Americans into the mainstream of American life. In no other contemporary social arena in Europe have immigrants become more socially accepted and more influential as role models than in the arena of sports and, in particular, soccer. Hence, there can be no question that sports have enhanced the social acceptance of diversity, while at the same time remaining a battleground of primordial identities, exclusive nationalism, and localism.

These inherent tensions are manifested in the inclusiveness of multiethnic and cosmopolitan professional soccer clubs on the one hand, and the exclusivity and particularism of national teams on the other. These dual—and rivaling—organizational principles have defined soccer's existence since the latter part of the nineteenth century. Above all, however, as a globalizing language, sports are among the major engines of actual cosmopolitanism. Especially, but not exclusively, on the top professional level ("from above") and with its global institutions and transnational competitions, sports generate a global arena of cultural and political interaction that resonates with sports cosmopolitanism "from below." With the help of new media such as the Internet, global sports arenas have evolved and set new viewership records. They are part of a global culture that goes beyond established territorial sports spaces. This global sports culture is more diversified and cosmopolitan than any other sphere of society—performance is what matters, not one's ethnic, national, or social background. We see instances of admiration for the world's "best of the best," which clearly transcend nationalism in an unprecedented way. Indeed, even localism tends to become more cosmopolitan today. Supporters increasingly love *their* teams' best players; take note, the emphasis being on "their" with those on the opponents' representing a much more complicated proposition in that any "otherness" in an opponent usually provides a welcome occasion to express hostility and derision. But bespeaking the cosmopolitan dimensions of skill and its proper appreciation by those conversant with the language in which it is being displayed, even opponents come to value—if not worship—a player regardless of her or his background merely by dint of her or his achievements on the field. The merit- and achievement-based dimension of sports has profoundly enlightening and inclusive qualities. Performance, output, and results are ultimately the only things that matter to all involved, sports producers and consumers. Note how Hines Ward, the Pittsburgh Steelers' fine receiver, addresses precisely this issue in describing his difficulties growing up in Georgia as the son of an African American father and a Korean mother: "It was hard for me to find my identity. The black kids didn't want to hang out with me because I had a Korean mom. The white kids didn't want to hang out with me because I was black. The Korean kids didn't want to hang out with me because I was black. It was hard to find friends growing up. And then once I got involved in sports, color didn't matter."[59]

Chapter 3 examines how the globalization of sports affects transnational political cultures and identities across the Atlantic. With the help of an array of pertinent data, we examine whether and to what degree sports cultures have changed in the wake of the second globalization and how each continent's traditional sports space has been penetrated by the others' sports cultures. This chapter is influenced by the conceptually innovative work of Jeannette Colyvas and Stefan Jonsson, who differentiate between what they call "diffusion" and "institutionalization" of cultures and social phenomena across various structures ranging from countries to academic disciplines. We demonstrate how both of these factors have occurred in the course of the second globalization on both sides of the Atlantic, but how diffusion is so much easier—thus perhaps also more fleeting—than institutionalization.[60] Whereas we see diffusion confined to the realm of mimicry and imitation, we regard institutionalization as an anchoring of actual organizations in a new environment. Thus wearing a Yankees cap (diffusion) may have nothing to do with the much more involved institution of knowing baseball and its culture. Clearly these two have vastly different meanings in terms of identity. Still, we find such diffusions indicative of the growing significance of cultural transfers across continents. We mention, for that reason, such oddities as tattoos adorning athletes' bodies,

[59] John Branch, "The Journey toward Acceptance," *New York Times*, November 9, 2009.

[60] Jeannette A. Colyvas and Stefan Jonsson, "Ubiquity and Legitimacy: Disentangling Diffusion and Institutionalization" (Working paper, Northwestern University, 2009; under review for publication in *Social Theory* at the time of our writing). We are grateful to Walter Powell.

melodies shared by fans, and similar "marginalities" that are prima facie ancillary, though far from marginal, to the sports themselves.

Also in this context, we analyze an array of "effects" that tell us much about the nature of these cultural penetrations on the part of various sports and their new locales. Thus, we discuss what we have termed the "Beckham effect," which denotes the arrival of a foreign, bona fide, crossover, global superstar to help a struggling sport in a country where it has languished at the cultural margins. Then, we highlight what we have called the "Nowitzki effect," which features almost the exact opposite of the "Beckham effect": a local boy excels far away from home in a sport that is hugely popular in the country where he now resides but has been secondary in his native land. The sport, however, then grows in popularity in the "sending country," almost solely by dint of the local boy's brilliance and star-status in the sports culture of the "receiving" country and, of course, by virtue of the ever-powerful nature of localism and nationalism. We could just as easily have called this phenomenon the "Parker effect" or the "Petrovic effect" or the "Divac effect" or the "Yao effect," all of whom established the analogous relations to their respective countries of France, Croatia, Serbia, and China. However, our calling this the "Nowitzki effect" goes beyond the fact that one of us is German and the other a professor of German politics. We view the effect as a superb case in point about the qualitatively different dimensions exacted by the second globalization and its shifts in the tectonics of sports cultures on both sides of the Atlantic. After all, Dirk Nowitzki was not the first German NBA star. That distinction will forever belong to Detlef Schrempf, who had a brilliant career playing for three teams. He was an NBA All-Star repeatedly and remains the only German other than Nowitzki to have played in an NBA All-Star game and the NBA finals. And yet, having entered the league in 1985—thus prior to its having become a major force in gobalized sports cultures—and by being a superb player though not quite a superstar, Schrempf remained largely unknown to the German public beyond the country's small basketball acolytes. In other words, the growth in basketball's popularity in Germany and Nowitzki's having become a recognizable personality every bit the equivalent of the country's most prominent soccer stars could not have happened a decade earlier. The "Nowitzki effect's" American analog would be an American soccer player's star status abroad, which in turn helped the growth of the game at home. While there have been quite a few American players in Europe's top leagues, and while some have attained solid respectability, such as goalkeepers Kasey Keller, Brad Friedel, and Tim Howard, we do not discern a "Keller," "Friedel," or "Howard" effect back home in America. This is the case mainly on account of these superb players being goalkeepers, and thus engaged in the less glamorous job of their sport's defense rather than its offense, which, in soccer, like in all four major American sports, invariably accords greater attention beyond the sport's immediate core followers appealing to a larger and less knowledgeable public. The old adage about defense winning championships and accolades by those in the know, and offense wowing the casual fans and leading to a higher payday, pertains to soccer like it does to the North American Big Four. Enter David Beckham with his "effect" precisely to counter this lacuna and lend soccer an institutional anchor beyond the diffusion of its immediate sheen. Whether the Beckham "experiment" has thus far attained its intended "effect"—or whether it ever will—remains well beyond the temporal purview of this book, though we will present our informed conjectures on this matter.[61]

We analyze how "events" in these sports have grown on both sides of the Atlantic, welcoming lasting fans and admirers without, however, necessarily making them permanent fans of the sports as such—most certainly not on the local level, where the quality of teams and leagues is invariably far below what spectators have come to appreciate and admire in the top tier of these sports performed precisely in the context of these events that attracted these newcomers to the sport in the first place. We call this phenomenon "Olympianization," in that, just like with the Olympics, millions of people follow such sports but only as performed in their prime showcase tournaments—all special and major events—that occur every four years or in similar intervals. At the same time, local and quotidian leagues and games barely draw significant attention and remain well behind the established languages of the respective sports cultures in terms of passion and interest. After all, who but those involved in specialized niches follow most of the sports performed at the Olympics any other time! We offer an extended analysis of the "Olympianized" nature of soccer's progress in American sports culture, where the quadrennial World Cup tournaments have developed into significant sporting events with large followings in the United States over the past two decades almost to the point of having entered American sports culture, meaning that the World Cup has become water cooler talk since the early 1990s, which it had not been before. Soccer itself, however, still languishes in its cultural marginality. But in America, too, soccer's position has changed because American society and cul-

---

[61] There can be no better account of the Beckham "experiment" than Grant Wahl's superb reportage in his *The Beckham Experiment: How the World's Most Famous Athlete Tried to Conquer America* (New York: Crown Books, 2009).

ture have changed in the course of the past two decades. In this framework, we shed light on America's premier soccer league, MLS, which has bestowed itself the gravitas of being the sole representative of top-level professional soccer in the United States by never using the definitive article "the" preceding its name (analogous to Major League Baseball's MLB). We will look at the growing influence of the Latino community in America's soccer world as well.

The impact of globalization in the context of the continued relevance of tradition and history is most strikingly displayed by the different trajectories of women's soccer in the United States and Europe. This difference serves as the subject of a comparative case study in chapter 4. It is more than a coincidence that the rise of women's soccer in America was accompanied by a massive change in gender politics and identity across the liberal democracies of the advanced industrial world. Women's soccer, at times with its own professional leagues, has been an overall American success story. Few things better exemplify its cultural significance than the popularity of the American player Mia Hamm, who was a major force in putting women's team sports on the cultural map. Indeed, Hamm has come to spawn some transatlantic counterparts such as the German player Birgit Prinz. However, the feminization of American soccer produces some ambivalent results, not least of which is the sport's denigration by male fans who, despite important shifts and changes, continue to constitute the most important clientele of these cultures. While soccer has a strong feminine presence in North America, the very opposite is true in Europe, where males try to defend their hegemony in soccer as the last resort of male supremacy and exclusiveness. In Europe, the globalized language of soccer coincides with its entrenched and local hegemonic sports culture, leaving women predominantly on the margins, even though women's interest in sports in general, including soccer, is rising on both continents, thus possibly becoming another vehicle of cosmopolitan inclusion.

Chapter 5 looks at nationalist, localist, and racist backlashes against globalization, which we conceptualize as forms of "counter-cosmopolitanism" that oppose cultural inclusion, universalism, and diversity. Here we analyze the ugliest manifestations of sports—a sort of "bonding capital" gone wild, literally[62]; an exclusion of all things foreign, a rejection of equality, a disdain for the weak, a trust only in the self, home, and hearth. We explore racism and violence in sports and political cultures in a comparative perspective, taking into account the ways through which America has battled

---

[62] Of course we use this term from Robert Putnam's work.

overt racism and violence in sports with much success. With racist violence and slander rather marginalized in contemporary American professional sports, our major focus will be the counter-cosmopolitan backlash against globalized—and Europeanized—sports, which has emerged with a vengeance across Europe. In contrast to the virtual absence of violence and marginalization of racism in American sports arenas, anti-Semitism and racism find expression in the mobilization of extreme right-wing movements, hooliganism, and cults of violence in many of Europe's sports arenas. Even superstars like the Cameroon forward Samuel Eto'o have been regularly exposed to racist slander in Spanish stadiums; and extreme right fans in Italy force their club leadership to abstain from signing contracts with foreign players. One of the few American star soccer players, the fine defender Oguchi Onyewu, of Nigerian descent, felt compelled to resort to legal action in his defense against the racist insults inflicted on him during his playing days in Belgium just prior to his transfer to AC Milan, one of the aforementioned pedigreed Italian clubs.

We elaborate in this chapter on the general and specific factors that foster this counter-cosmopolitanism that, to varying degrees, anchors itself in an exclusive hypernationalist identity and uses soccer as its vehicle of public expression. Highlighting examples from Italy, Germany, Spain, England, Austria, Hungary, and Poland, we argue that in Europe soccer arenas function as political battlefields over identities and cosmopolitan change in the age of postindustrial globalization, which is embodied in global players as highly visible minorities on the field. Moreover, anti-Semitic images of a "globalized Jew" have reappeared among fans in European soccer over the last twenty to thirty years, in which the vilest insults and hostilities against Israeli soccer players and professional soccer clubs like Tottenham Hotspurs, Ajax Amsterdam, MTK Hungária Budapest, FK Austria Wien, and Bayern Munich—Europe's so-called "Jew" clubs—have become commonplace. These invectives, often also used against any opponent not even vaguely connected to anything Jewish, demonstrate yet again that anti-Semitism has far from disappeared from Europe's public discourse. Still, we conclude this chapter on an optimistic note by demonstrating how institutional interventions can constrain such expressions of hatred, and how they have successfully done so in a number of places.

We illuminate the persistence of different European and American identities in their respective sports cultures in chapter 6, where we analyze the resilience and relevance of the uniquely American symbiosis of athletics and academics in the form of that "behemoth" called college sports. In order to understand the impact of this phenomenon, we reconstruct the

th of college sports in the context of American history. In this
merican college sports are compared with other university-asso-
rts in Canada and Britain, only to conclude that they have no
match anywhere and are truly unique and sui generis. They thus form the
quintessential American "exception." So do, of course, high school sports.
Just think of the cultural power of high school football in Texas spawning
such iconic nationally watched movies and television series as *Friday Night
Lights*, or of high school basketball's central identity to life in Indiana and
Kentucky, indeed even the public passion surrounding high school wrestling in Iowa for that matter, as we know so well from Mark Kreidler's fine
book, *Four Days to Glory: Wrestling With the Soul of the American Heartland*.
Alas, our not including high school sports in this book is solely due to the
many limitations constraining our work and in no way suggests our lack of
respect for this essential ingredient to the culture of sports in America and
thus American culture as a whole. Just like its collegiate counterpart, high
school sports as currently constituted in America have no counterparts
anywhere in Europe, perhaps elsewhere in the world as well.

College sports also embody a serious counterargument against the globalization thesis. The uniquely American institutions of college sports play
an especially important role in the variations at the local level that may stir
curiosity on both sides of the Atlantic but remain largely untouched by
many of the globalizing developments described above. Despite all the
globalization that has occurred, the persistence of identity formations
within the sports space of college football and basketball has, if anything,
increased over recent decades. Put differently, while the NFL and the
NBA have attained a global presence in the course of the second globalization, nothing remotely similar pertains to the world of college football and
basketball. Whereas their importance in America's sports space has increased markedly over the past thirty years, they remain parochial to the
United States. March Madness (the NCAA division 1 college basketball
championship)—though a ubiquitous and vastly growing phenomenon in
American culture—remains largely unknown and not followed any place
else in the world. We also discuss the enormous, identity-generating significance of college sports and their meaning for American society way
beyond student life and the campus. This remains a sports world still completely alien to Europeans and non-Americans. Conversely, neither the
system nor the logic of the wide array of local clubs and leagues that structure European amateur sports are really accessible to Americans, signifying
the limits of globalization in the realm of sports and beyond. Yet, even in
the local world of American college sports, we encounter increasingly

global and cosmopolitan features that barely existed twenty years ago, namely the continued growth of foreign athletes at America's universities who decide to hone their athletic skills by representing their college in the sport of their choice and specialty, as well as receive an education.

A brief conclusion recaps our argument and offers a coda to the book.

CHAPTER 2 ◇◇◇◇◇◇◇◇◇◇◇◇◇◇◇◇◇◇◇◇◇◇◇◇◇◇◇◇◇◇◇◇

THE EMERGENCE OF GLOBAL ARENAS

MAPPING THE GLOBALIZATION OF SPORTS CULTURES BETWEEN COSMOPOLITANISM, NATIONALISM, AND LOCALISM

In this chapter we will examine the evolution and transitions of hegemonic sports cultures from the nineteenth to the end of the twentieth century. Our story will feature the key cultural characteristics that this process engendered at two stages of global dissemination: the first coincides roughly with the industrial era of the latter two decades of the nineteenth century; the second we place approximately one hundred years later and identify with what has commonly been called the "postindustrial" epoch. While soccer, arguably *the* single most prominent and ubiquitous sports language in the world, is our special focus, we compare its history of globalization with that of other hegemonic team sports, namely basketball, baseball, football, and hockey which—among related phenomena in rugby and cricket—have emerged in an ever-expanding and ever-inclusive "global sports arena."[1]

To a considerable extent, sports cultures march in step with global modernization processes. However, just like these, the globalization of sports cultures lacks a simple plot. While there appears to be an inexorable path toward homogenized global standards, tastes, and mores, the resilience of traditions and the local have not disappeared. If anything, we argue, the very factors that render the globalizing forces so powerful also bolster pur-

---

[1] The notion of a global sports arena originates from the volume, *The Global Sports Arena*, John Bale and Joseph Maguire, eds. (New York: Routledge, 1994).

portedly weak local cultures, giving them renewed vigor, value, and legitimacy. They do so precisely because they create and reinforce collective identities that, at least prima facie, appear to be antidotes to the new cosmopolitan identities fostered by the globalization process. Sports cultures continue to indulge in both. They are in the vanguard of creating global publics on the one hand, and foster local socializations and emotional attachments that are fundamentally exclusive and suspicious of anything new on the other hand, often to the point of being xenophobic and downright hateful towards any change. In addition to reinforcing old local cultures, sports have also created new ones. Both versions of this localism have contributed to forces of fragmentation that scholars have identified as a major factor in the process of globalization.[2]

None have done so more eloquently and prolifically than Roland Robertson over the past two decades. In a series of studies (solo, and with colleagues), Robertson successfully challenged simplistic views of globalization that saw this force as either the ubiquitous bane of all contemporary existence and the destroyer of local life and worthy traditions, or glorified it as a singularly fortuitous development in creating a unified and uniform world. Instead, Robertson offered a much more nuanced analysis in which he demonstrated that global and local actually merge into a new entity that he coined "glocal." This new symbiosis inevitably features the universalization of particularism just as it does its obverse, the particularization of universalism. Robertson observed an intensification of consciousness of the world as a whole.[3] But he also argued that global cultural flows can reinvigorate local particularisms. Thus, "glocalization" refers to complex interactions between the global and the local in which one "borrows" elements from the other. Whereas Robertson commenced his research apart from sports, it is rather telling of sports' absolutely central role that he and his colleagues eventually applied these theories to sports, soccer in particular.[4]

---

[2] Employing the term "fragmentation," James Rosenau, a leading scholar of globalization, points out that globalization does not only entail cultural homogenization and global integration, but also fosters decentralization, fragmentation, and a new localism; see James Rosenau, "Governance in a Global Order," in David Held and Anthony McGrew, eds., *Governing Globalization: Power, Authority, and Global Governance* (Cambridge: Polity, 2002), p. 70.

[3] See Robertson, *Globalization.*

[4] Roland Robertson, "Glocalization: Time-Space and Homogeneity–Heterogeneity" in Mike Featherstone, Scott Lash and Roland Robertson, eds., *Global Modernities* (London: Sage, 1995), pp. 25–44; Richard Giulianotti and Roland Robertson, "The Globalization of Football: A Study in the Glocalization of the 'Serious Life,'" *British Journal of Sociology*, 55 (4), 2004, pp. 545–68; and Richard Giulianotti and Roland Robertson, eds., *Globalization and Sport* (Oxford: Blackwell, 2008).

Beyond National Cultures: The Inherent Cosmopolitanism of Sports as a Global Language

Few things are as widely disseminated, understood, and followed on a mass level as modern sports, with virtually no dissent, opposition, or challenge. Ever-expanding and ever more inclusive in their scope, they are unique in that they are understood and followed unanimously by those conversant with them. We view these sports and their world akin to languages—with their own codes, grammar, dissemination, intelligibility, mastery, elegance, idiosyncrasies, practitioners, and recipients.

This complex construct includes not just the many people actively involved in sports, that is the "doers," but above all the many more millions who regularly follow sports as fans. Fanatical and devoted followers are but one constituent of this category. Also included are sometime followers who, though having a limited mastery of the relevant languages, participate occasionally in this construct, especially during major global sports events. After all, these sports, like languages, have uniquely recognizable characteristics that are ubiquitously and globally accepted. Indeed, the rules, sanctions, number of players, size of the playing field, the counting of success and failure, the tabulation of individual and collective achievements, winners and losers, rituals and symbols of each sport are the same in every country and differentiate one sport from another. The universal intelligibility of each sport gives each its very identity. Thus, from Stockholm to Sidney, tennis players and their followers know everything about volleys, smashes, and double faults, and each game is counted from love to fifteen, thirty, and forty with the oddity of deuce thrown in. From Berkeley to Berlin, basketball players make personal fouls and fight for rebounds. From Delhi to Barbados, white-clad cricket players have lunch or tea in clearly understood and delineated periods within a match. And to use examples from soccer, the most global sport language of all, everybody, from Patagonia to the North Pole, from Japan in the East to Hawaii in the West, knows what a goal is, how a hand play is sanctioned, what a great pass looks like, and why a corner kick is awarded. Just as the rules of language are largely random, the rules of sport follow little rhyme or reason. Thus, there is nothing inherently good or bad about them. And precisely because of their arbitrariness (which renders them value-neutral) they are readily accepted and understood across cultures, nations, communities, and classes—human collectives that often do not want to understand each other otherwise.

In principle, what makes sports so potently global is the perfect intelligibility *and* virtually flawless acceptance of institutionalized rules and informal codes, which are in fact elaborations of the rules in the actual practice of play. Herein included are, of course, the widely understood and exercised circumventions of such rules, which are tacitly approved as part of the metalanguage accompanying every sport. The limits of such rule violations are particular to every sport and completely understood by its practitioners and followers. They comprise the "games being played" in each and every sport.

The very existence of a particular language and set of rules is essential to a particular sport's identity and boundary vis-à-vis all others. The rules, in essence, define the very existence of each sport, as well as its potentially universal legitimacy and attraction. After all, what differentiates soccer from rugby, or cricket from baseball—to use a relatively related dyad of sport languages—is merely the existence of different rules. And these rules, of course, are completely arbitrary. Thus, there is no particular reason why hands are not allowed to propel the ball in soccer, just like there is no particular reason as to why the moon is feminine in French while the sun is masculine. And in German, the exact opposite is true. Yet, a myriad of such odd rules define the essence of what we have come to recognize as French and German. Similarly, not using one's hands to propel a ball in association football (soccer) has come to be a defining characteristic of the game, whereas the involvement of hands is central to its North American and Australian variants and to both rugby codes, Union and League. Analogous to one well-versed in French or German who has acquired the facility not only to gauge what is proper French or German but what is also beautiful in either or both, a fluent sports fan appreciates the beauty of the game he or she witnesses beyond the result-oriented basics of winning or losing. Just as mastery of a language leads to its enjoyment and experience as an aesthetic pleasure, the very same pertains to one who has mastered a sports language and follows it at its highest level. Each passionate practitioner of a language fully believes that it is only *their* language that is aesthetically the prettiest, analytically the most accurate, logically the most sound—simply the best in all respects. Other languages might be accorded tolerance, even respect, but only one language receives unrestricted love; ditto with sports. And in both instances, the devoted fans rhapsodize over the actual construct, expressing much that is beyond the intended original meaning. Sports devotees often ascribe qualities and attributes to their beloved sports that range from life to death, from war to peace, from the seasons to virtually every collective identity imaginable.[5]

And yet there is one crucial dimension in which sports differ markedly in their structure and texture from language, the arts, theater, music, and many other creative categories that so enrich human life: its unscriptedness. Indeed, this is absolutely essential to all modern sports, so much so that were the outcome of any predetermined, they would immediately lose the signifier of "sports" and become theater, spectacle, or something else instead. The World Wrestling Entertainment (WWE) contestants engage in a physically exacting endeavor, probably much more so than their counterparts in Greco-Roman wrestling. And yet, nobody regards the former as a sport precisely because its narrative is scripted, its outcome predetermined. All players for the Harlem Globetrotters were very fine basketball players—just remember Wilt Chamberlain's membership on this team—but because the outcome is scripted the games that they play against the Washington Generals and similar opponents are not categorized as sport but entertainment, regardless of the athleticism involved.[6] The uncertainty of results is arguably *the* greatest difference between sports and related human activities that are very similar to sports, notably entertainment. The inviolability of sports' unscriptedness provides one of the most essential common denominators for all modern sports languages. Any "scriptedness" is tantamount to cheating and the negation of any sport's integrity. The most important ingredient of sport's unscripted nature lies in the totally unexpected outcomes, best known as upsets. No matter how much one contestant—team or individual—is superior to the other, winning the contest is never a foregone conclusion: "That's why they play the game," as veteran ESPN analyst Chris Berman, one of America's most respected sports gurus, never fails to inform us.

All sports—foremost that of the "simple game" of soccer—have evolved into globally recognized cosmopolitan languages. The universal acceptance of sports languages has become so commonplace in the course of the twentieth century (and now the twenty-first) that few seem to be aware of the social and cultural enormity of their dissemination. And yet, the devel-

[5] There exists no more wonderful rhapsodization about any sport anywhere in the world than the late George Carlin's famous "Baseball vs. Football" monologue, known to virtually every American sports fan far and wide (this brilliant comedian contrasts baseball's essential being to football's; and sure enough, the seasons play a role).

[6] However, when the Trotters played the Rens and the Original Celtics, among other leading basketball teams in the 1930s and beyond, they most assuredly engaged in the pursuit of sports and not entertainment.

opment from local variation to international standardization has fundamentally transformed sport. Indeed, it is this aspect alone (what Elias and
Van Bottenburg have called "sportiziation") that distinguishes modern
sport from traditional games. *The* single most decisive dimension differen-
tiating the two constructs is the almost universal intelligibility of the former and the complete lack thereof in the latter. International expansion
and standardization in the course of the first globalization rendered sports
modern and inherently cosmopolitan. Seven other factors accompanied
this process: secularization, egalitarianism, bureaucratization, specialization, rationalization, quantification, and the desire to win as well as to
break records in the process—that is, to compete at the top level and succeed there. And the top includes virtually invariably "the world," as in
world record and world champion even if what comprises the entity
"world" continues to vary by sport. But the very legitimacy of excellence
and supremacy is defined by claiming a global stage. This profound development of the latter half of the nineteenth century embodies a genuine
social and cultural watershed. It represents the first substantial transformation of sports from ritual to record and to professional competition with
mass audiences. Sports mutated from the world of localized (and disorganized) activities to that of globalized following.[7] As such, sports also furnish an organized, informal, *deterritorialized* principle in which different
cultural claims and ways of life may be temporarily mediated, or at least
met on an egalitarian basis.[8]

There are certainly other globally understood and agreed-upon universal languages, such as the laws of the natural sciences. As Lawrence Kitchin
put it as early as 1966, soccer may be the only genuinely accepted and
widely legitimate "global idiom" apart from such sciences.[9] Yet even in
these languages—often understood by elites but not the masses, in significant contrast to sports[10]—local, national, and other kinds of interpreta-

[7] See Allen Guttmann, *From Ritual to Record: The Nature of Modern Sports* (New York: Columbia University Press, 2004).

[8] For the concept of "deterritorialization" in sports, see Raffaele Poli, "The Denationalization of Sport: De-ethnicization of the Nation and Identity Deterritorialization" in *Sport in
Society*, 10 (4), July 2007, pp. 646–61. We will include Poli's arguments in our discussion
below.

[9] Lawrence Kitchin, "The Contenders," *The Listener*, October 27, 1966, quoted in Patrick
Murphy, John Williams, and Eric Dunning, *Football on Trial: Spectator Violence and Development
in the Football World* (London: Routledge, 1990), p. 1.

[10] It is for this reason, among others, that athletes rather than Nobel laureates in physics,
chemistry, or the medical sciences routinely become such sources of collective pride. Hank
Greenberg and Sandy Koufax instilled a much greater joy and appreciation among American
Jews—particularly Jewish men—than many a Jewish Nobel prize winner: everyday citizens

tions render what was thought to be universal quite tenuous. Many presumed universalisms are culture- or country-dependent. At least they often appear that way in different settings.[11] This also applies to political systems. While the terms "republic," "democracy," and "human rights" have become more or less universally accepted catchwords to which most democracies and authoritarian dictators alike subscribe, their meanings and realities differ vastly. What one country sees as the ideal electoral system to sustain democracy, its neighbor views as completely inadequate. Even against the background of new human rights regimes and humanitarian interventions[12]—as well as international institutions like the United Nations and new supra-national polities like the European Union—political entities do not come close to the inherent cosmopolitanism of sports. Not only does the world of politics not approach the ubiquity of sports, it succeeds in using its own narrow national interests to undermine sports' universality. On the one hand it is our cognitive and intellectual side that fosters the universalistic, crosscultural, and cosmopolitan aspects of sport. On the other hand, our emotional attachments, extolling traditions, in short our partisanship, seem much more congruent with sports' less attractive tribal, particularistic, and counter-cosmopolitan dimensions.

Ritualized rivalries and the construction of "enemies," have always constituted part of sports cultures and their development. Very often, collective identifications are instruments that determine distinction, especially between close neighbors that comprise the great traditional rivalries in sports: Boston Red Sox fans despise the New York Yankees (and vice versa) in baseball; Ohio State fans exhibit nothing but contempt and hatred for their Michigan counterparts (and vice versa) in college football; there is nothing but ill will between the supporters of Boca Juniors and River Plate in Buenos Aires; Liverpool and Manchester United fans loath each other and their respective teams with passion; and there is no love lost—put euphemistically—between German fans and their Dutch neighbors in soccer.

Of course, many further examples from other cultures and sports also

---

understood and appreciated the formers' métier whilst they did not the latters'. It is precisely the level of general intelligibility that renders Nobel laureates in literature and peace much more popular than their colleagues in the sciences, thus placing award-winning writers and activists closer to star athletes on the continuum of popular recognition and appreciation.

[11] This observation about different cultural interpretations of universalisms does not justify any cultural relativism or any generalized cultural attributions that homogenize the contradictions within a "culture." See Homi K. Bhabha, *The Location of Culture* (New York: Routledge, 2004).

[12] For a critical analysis see Benhabib, *Another Cosmopolitanism*.

make this point. Localism, parochial "stickiness," regionalism, and nationalist particularisms have characterized various sports cultures from their beginning. Yet everyone who regularly partakes either as a player or a follower, loves these universally recognized games and bitter rivalries. Despite their occasional ugliness, it is these rivalries that form the essence of all sports whose raison d'etre, after all, is unscripted competition. Rivalries may create hatred for opponents but, if anything, they enhance appreciation for the sport—which comprises such a convenient and mutually shared medium for such hatreds—thereby reinforcing the universal character of sports languages. Few means of communication are as classless as sports languages. As Bonnie H. Erickson demonstrates in a case study of the private contract security industry in Toronto, sports knowledge provides *the* single most important bonding capital among men regardless of their educational and social background.[13] Thus, the knowledge of and passion for soccer (substitute any other hegemonic sport) renders the London taxi driver "equal to" his multimillionaire passenger in their joint recognition of a Brazilian player's skills, even if they happen to love different clubs. All soccer speakers—regardless of their particular passion for a player or a team—will understand, know, and appreciate soccer excellence on a global level regardless of who its particular purveyors might be. As such, this language is not only profoundly egalitarian but also deeply universal, that is, for men.[14] Surprising as it may seem to Ohio State and Michigan fans, their mutually shared passion for football (of which their mutual hatred is an integral ingredient), actually creates a common bond between the two rivals that neither would readily admit.

The Incomplete Conquest of the Modern World: From Soccer's First to Its Second Globalization

It is not a coincidence that today's major globalized and "sporticized" sports cultures hail from the English-speaking world. As Walter Russell Mead has cogently argued, the British have emerged on the victorious side in every major conflict in which they have fought since 1688—with the single, but notable, exception of the American Revolution. In other words, the two English speaking powers—Britain and the United States—have either separately or together won every major war since the seventeenth

---

[13] See Bonnie H. Erikson, "Culture, Class and Connections," *American Journal of Sociology* 102 (1), 1996, pp. 217–51, here pp. 244–47.

[14] Ibid., p. 245.

century, and the global system resting on their military and commercial prowess has remained the foundation of the international political and economic order most certainly from the post–Napoleonic era until today.[15]

The Origins of a Global Cultural Phenomenon

Games of all sorts, as well as quasi- or pre-sportlike activities, have existed in every society. Yet between 1875 and 1895, during the rise of industrial modernity, more than seventy new sports associations were founded in Britain, all of which became the structures, loci, and agents of these new languages called sports. "It is the English who have been far and away the world's most inventive when it comes to sports. Soccer, lawn tennis, cricket, hockey, modern boxing and athletics, badminton, bowls . . . all are English products. . . . The English merely stepped in and got them organized, drew up rules and regulations and laid down specifications as to sizes and types of playing area and equipment. If they hadn't, tennis today might still mean bashing a ball against the walls of a mockup of the courtyard of a French chateau."[16]

Variations of football can be traced back to the fourteenth century, most likely much before. Predecessors can be found in locally distinct, largely unregulated, and ritualistic folk games of the common people.[17] Against the background of modernization, sports such as horse racing, golf, boxing, rowing, fencing, and cricket—the sole team sport among these—experienced their first stage of rules standardization already in the late eighteenth century. The development of clubs and federations, written rules, the keeping of detailed records, and regulated competition also occurred in the eighteenth century.[18] All this happened in Britain and there alone.

We agree with Norbert Elias and Eric Dunning's pathbreaking work that sees Britain as the inventor of the entity "sports" (and the mindset and culture that fostered such a creation) for good reason. Britain was also the inventor of modern parliamentary democracy, which meant that losing did not lead to death or exile or shame or some kind of ignominious ending

---

[15] Walter Russell Mead, "Jews and Wasps," *New York Sun*, November 16, 2007.

[16] Wallace Reyburn, *The Men In White: The Story of English Rugby* (London: Pelham Books, 1975), p. 12.

[17] See Norbert Elias and Eric Dunning, "Folk Football in Medieval and Early Modern Britain," in Elias and Dunning, *Quest for Excitement: Sport and Leisure in the Civilizing Process* (Oxford: Basil Blackwell, 1986), pp. 175–90.

[18] Richard Holt, *Sport and the British: A Modern History* (Oxford: Oxford University Press, 1989), pp. 13–43.

but merely was an opportunity to replay the match as it were.[19] This interpretation links well to Elias's earlier work in *The Civilizing Process* (published in 1939), in which he argues that being civilized meant having control over one's body and emotions. Sports in their British development became an excellent venue in which one was permitted—even encouraged—to express one's emotions but to do so in an environment strictly controlled by rules and regulations both outside and inside the lines; in other words, to experience and articulate emotions in a "civilized" manner. This structure and prerequisite continues to characterize all modern sports to this day.

In America of the early to mid-nineteenth century, in essence still a British extension culturally, baseball evolved in East Coast urban centers only to have its New York version codified and institutionalized—thereby joining cricket in the 1840s as the second modern team sport in the world. By 1846, students at Cambridge University were busy establishing a master game of modern football that rationalized all the many variations of the game played throughout the colleges of that university (and to a lesser extent its rival, Oxford). The resulting game emanated from the differing styles played by graduates of Rugby School, who preferred the use of hands and running with the ball, as opposed to graduates of Harrow, Eton, and Winchester, who favored using their feet and dribbling the ball.[20] Unfortunately, we do not have the original rules that these students devised but we do have the ten "laws," as they were grandly called (published in 1862 by the Cambridge man J. C. Thring) for what he so presciently called, "The Simplest Game."[21] These laws provided the basis for the formation of the official rules of the Football Association (FA) in 1863, expanding them to fourteen. With the schism over the use of hands and hacking splitting the minority that favored such action from the majority that did not (laws 9 through 12), the "dribbling" game became hegemonic in the Football Association. Hence, the new game called itself "Association Football" because it was the game sanctioned by the official Football Association (as opposed to what by 1871 would become the ruling body of the "handling" game, Rugby Football, with its own association, the Rugby Football Association [RFA]).[22] The basic rules of soccer have remained remarkably stable over

[19] See Elias and Dunning, *Quest for Excitement.*

[20] See David Goldblatt, *The Ball Is Round: A Global History of Soccer* (London: Riverhead Trade, 2008), p. 30. The process was consolidated by adult members of the upper and middle classes in the 1850s and 1860s.

[21] Paul Gardner, *The Simplest Game: The Intelligent Fan's Guide to the World of Soccer* (New York: Macmillan, 1994).

[22] The term "soccer," mainly used in the United States for the Association game, is a British

time; they are virtually unchanged since 1863, when the game as we know it came to be institutionalized. In the following years, key developments rapidly established and regularized this game and its structure to a degree unimaginable barely a decade before.[23] By 1888, all the ingredients that constitute the structure of soccer in every corner of the earth to this day had emerged.[24] The first globalization of soccer was well on its way.

Much of the world proceeded to call this game simply "football," while some (North Americans and Australians, among others) have used the name "soccer," since football came to denote a different code of the game that had become hegemonic in these societies. Today, the term "football" signifies *the* culturally and socially most accepted version that has evolved since the split between the "handling" code of the game and its "dribbling" variant in 1863. Thus, Americans mean their version of football when they use the term "football", just like to Canadians the term conjures up their version of the game. For Australians in Victoria, South Australia, Western Australia, and Tasmania the term connotes their dominant Australian Rules Football while for their compatriots in New South Wales and Queensland, football (or "footy") means Rugby League, occasionally also Rugby Union if the speakers hail from the milieu of private schools. In South Africa, "football" to whites occasionally still denotes Rugby Union, whereas to blacks it always signified the Association code, that is, soccer. The word "soccer," used in North America and a few other parts of the globe for the less popular "dribbling" code, represents an English slang abbreviation of the term "association." It is thus as English as can be and not another American abomination as Englishmen and Europeans continue to believe. If anything, the term "soccer" should sound archaic to English ears, rather than American. Whatever version of the game emerged as the majoritarian language in any society, its speakers monopolized the term "football" (and its equivalent in the local language á la Fussball, futbol, etc.) for this hegemonic language, thereby relegating all rival variants

---

slang term for "association." And the words "Association Football" live on until today in their French version in the name of the most powerful international sports body on earth: FIFA, which stands for Fédération Internationale de Football Association.

[23] See Murphy, Williams, and Dunning, *Football on Trial*, pp. 5, 6. This was in many ways both a "civilizing" and modernizing development because it involved the increasing abandonment of mass games according to customary rules played by an unrestricted number of people. Strict self-control and control of force replaced more archaic encounters.

[24] See Bill Murray, *The World's Game: A History of Soccer* (Champaign: University of Illinois Press, 1998); for the most detailed and comprehensive account of the world history of soccer, see Goldblatt, *The Ball Is Round*; for a general overview on the history and politics of soccer, see also Eduardo Galeano, *Soccer in Sun and Shadow* (New York: Verso, 2003).

of the game to be saddled with signifiers other than "football," with "soccer" being the most commonly known and used.

Modernization and Internationalization

Below are just a few key historical stepping-stones of soccer's standardization, modernization, and expansion. In 1871, The Football Association purchased a cup for twenty pounds and inscribed it with the words, "The Football Association Challenge Cup." Immediately, traditionalists denounced this innovation as something that might lead to the importance of winning, competition, and—perish the thought—professionalism. In 1872, the first international game was played between England and Scotland, the idea being that each country should be represented by its eleven best native-born players.[25] The Football Association selected the team representing England. It chose players from ten different clubs; only Oxford University was represented by more than one player among the eleven members of the team. The method of selecting a national team—effectively an all-star squad assembled only for international games in which the country's representation mutates into a club—has in principle remained identical all over the world to this very day. The players selected obviously had to obtain permission from their clubs to play, but because of the great honor involved in this "international" (i.e., intra-British, Anglo-Scot) contest, the clubs released the players. This precedence pertains to this very day, even though, objectively speaking, releasing players for national duty is clearly to the clubs' potential detriment.

More formal mechanisms of control—penalties, referees, and linesmen—were also introduced in the process of the game's diffusion from the upper middle to the middle and working classes. Referees emerged in 1874, and from 1877 onwards they were even entitled to enter the field and eject players from the game who committed brutal fouls in this relatively non-violent team sport.[26] Control problems, however, were exacerbated as soccer at the highest level began to attract large crowds in the wake of its professionalization. By the early 1880s the game had already spread from southern English upper-class strongholds into working-class neighborhoods north of the Wash, embodied, for instance, in the primarily work-

---

[25] In 1882, Ireland played England. By then, the game was already no longer only a British matter.

[26] See Andreas Schiendorfer, "Die englische Krankheit erreicht die Schweiz," *emagazine. credit-suisse.com*, September 1, 2003. Some of the few later modernizations in the twentieth century especially affect the goalkeeper, who has been entitled to use his hands only in the penalty area since 1903; yellow and red cards were introduced as late as 1970.

ing-class team Blackburn Rovers. The Celtic nations also welcomed the game at this time.[27] In 1882, the Football Associations of the four British football nations formed an international board that became the first *supranational authority* lording over the game's every aspect. This board was, in effect, FIFA's predecessor. In 1888, William McGregor, chairman of the Aston Villa club in Birmingham and an early advocate of professionalizing the game, finally succeeded in having the English clubs and the Football Association adopt the structure of baseball's National League (founded in 1876, the National League of Professional Base Ball Clubs featured professional teams playing each other on a regular basis). The Football League thus divided into two divisions (eighteen teams in each). Within each division, each team played the others twice (on a home-and-home basis), receiving two points for a win, one for a draw, and zero for a loss. At the end of each season, the bottom two teams of Division One were relegated to Division Two and the top two from Division Two advanced to Division One. With minor variations, this construct spread over many, though certainly not all, parts of the globe in less than twenty years. The widespread dissemination of Association football thus completed what has arguably remained one of the most successful and thorough global transfers of any structure ever devised.

Cultural Resistance, Sources of Identity

By the late nineteenth and onwards into the twentieth century, professional soccer clubs increasingly competed in the league (which was long dominated by teams from Northern England). Football mania became favorite organized leisure-time activities for all classes, but particularly the working class.[28] Workers also constituted a large share of the ever increasing numbers of spectators, which facilitated soccer professionalism and cultural expansion. By the 1870s, the game had its first professional in Scotsman James Lang.[29] The 1888 Football Association Cup final attracted a crowd of 17,000. In 1913, when the game was moved to the Crystal Palace in London, 120,081 witnessed Aston Villa beat Sunderland.[30] This amazing rise in popularity over such a short time cannot be explained simply by the fun and excitement of the game itself. As David

---

[27] See Goldblatt, *The Ball Is Round*, p. 37.

[28] See Tony Mason, *Association Football and English Society* (Brighton: Harvester Press, 1980).

[29] See Graham Curry, "Playing for Money: James J. Lang and Emergent Soccer Professionalism in Sheffield," *Soccer and Society* 5 (3), 2004, pp. 336–55.

[30] Goldblatt, *The Ball Is Round*, p. 60.

Goldblatt points out, civic pride and local identity constituted key factors in the game's very success. Indeed, the identity-generating, class-affirming localism remained ingrained in soccer's universal, standardized, and class-transcending language from its early cultural rise in the late nineteenth century to the present. Soccer, alone among the many forms of urban working-class cultures, "provided an opportunity for a gathering of people whose origins, identity, and purpose cut across local neighborhoods, industrial occupations, employers, trade union membership—and united them around a bigger but comprehensible geographical location and identity. It also served to insert these nascent forms of working-class localism into a national framework and institutions."[31] At the same time, of course, race, class, regional and national conflicts, and hostilities became increasingly mirrored on the field, though they had—at least prima facie—no relation to the actual sport whatsoever, especially with soccer's being far and away the gentlest of the many football games that emerged at this time. Thus, the old adage of football (i.e., soccer) as a gentle game played by ruffians and rugby as a rough game played by gentlemen aptly depicts the different social milieus informing these two initially related but increasingly diverging sports.

Whereas the origins of soccer's globalization are found in nineteenth-century England, the game quickly moved to the European continent and Latin America as the century drew to a close. The first continental football associations emerged in 1889 in Denmark and the Netherlands. It was in these countries and their Scandinavian and Benelux neighbors that leagues arose soon thereafter, which is not surprising since these areas constituted part of Britain's informal empire and exhibited a considerable penchant for Anglophilia.[32] By the turn of the nineteenth to the twentieth century, football had also taken hold in Northern Italy's industrial centers of Genoa, Turin, and Milan and subsequently found followers in the southern cities of Naples and Rome. Here, like in other European countries such as Germany and Austria, the game diffused from the urban upper middle classes to the lower social order, primarily the working class, within two- to three decades of soccer's introduction to the respective countries.[33]

Soccer's rapid expansion to the European continent initially met considerable resistance and outright hostility. When soccer arrived in Germany at the end of the nineteenth century, it certainly did not receive enthusiastic approval. Many intellectuals reveled in a nationalistic bombast

[31] Ibid., p. 59.
[32] Ibid., p. 120.
[33] Ibid., pp. 152–53.

extolling "good" German physical exercise as opposed to "evil" English sports in their emphatic rejection of soccer. "English sports" were proclaimed to be anathema to the German body and gauged as a dangerous alternative to the "gymnastics" that had swamped German public spaces by the late nineteenth century. "Turnen," that is, gymnastics, hailed from the post-Napoleonic inspirations of the anti-Semite and German nationalist Friedrich Ludwig Jahn. Jahn was a Prussian educator who instituted gymnastics on a vast national scale to harden the German nation in its quest for national glory after the ignominy of having been defeated by France's Napoleonic armies. Thus dubbed "Turnvater Jahn" (Jahn, father of gymnastics), this man also became the spiritual founder of Germany's dueling student fraternities (*Burschenschaften*), which like gymnastics became potent mainstays of Germany's hypernationalism and right-wing politics until the fall of the Third Reich in 1945.

In addition to this nationalist dimension, Germans came to view gymnastics as a holistic construct designed to enhance body and spirit.[34] The hostility to soccer is best exemplified by an infamous pamphlet penned by high school teacher Karl Planck, entitled *Fußlümmelei: Über Stauchballspiel und englische Krankheit* (1898)—best translated as *Soccer Loutishness: On the Crushing Ball Game and English Disease*[35]—which mobilized fears and explicitly identified soccer with the "English disease" of infant spine inflammation. National youth organizers, who were deeply worried about soccer's arrival and its rising cultural popularity, employed the war cry, "do away with soccer loutishness (*Fußlümmelei*)." Of course, as Roman Horak points out, the ideological emphasis on a different exercise culture also contained a political message, "concealed in the contrasting natures of modern, achievement and record-oriented sports, and the philosophy and model of 'natural' gymnastics upheld by the Germans."[36] The odd alternative reflected the conflict between the imperial aspirations of Wilhelmine Germany and the colonial British Empire. But cultural resistance against soccer also expressed a conflict between traditionalism and modernization.

The opposition to soccer by German cultural elites had a significant impact, retarding soccer's success in this major central European country.

---

[34] For a fine analysis of this culture clash between "English sports" and the German middle class, see Christiane Eisenberg's definitive study, *"English Sports" und deutsche Bürger. Eine Gesellschaftsgeschichte 1800–1939* (Paderborn: Ferdinand Schöningh, 1999).

[35] Karl Planck, *Fußlümmelei: Über Stauchballspiel und englische Krankheit* (Münster: LIT Verlag, 1982 [1898]).

[36] Roman Horak, "Germany versus Austria: Football, Urbanism, and National Identity," in Alan Tomlinson and Christopher Young, eds., *German Football: History, Culture, Society* (London: Routledge, 2006), p. 24.

Until the first decade of the twentieth century, soccer did not achieve a substantial breakthrough in Germany. The cultural elite's opposition to this English import only started to lessen in the context of other, large-scale modernization pressures shortly before, during, and in the wake of World War I—when Wilhelminian Germany's outdated social and political organizations eroded considerably.[37]

Despite this massive resistance by cultural elites and gymnastics enthusiasts, soccer's attraction became irresistible first to the German middle classes and subsequently to its working class. Early German organizers of the game even added their own elaborate specifications and regulations to it. By 1896, a German rule proclaimed that "the soccer field needs to be free from trees and bushes."[38] The game underwent a massive "Germanization" in its terminology, when the German national soccer federation (*Deutscher Fußball-Bund*, DFB), founded in 1900, made certain that "everything foreign was to be eradicated" by exacting that German expressions should replace the hated "Engländerei" (usage of English words).[39] The game gained in societal relevance decade after decade despite the Nazis' disdain for soccer and their initial attempt to decrease its popularity because of its "un-German" English roots.[40] But with the Nazis—and other German nationalist elites—unable to oppose soccer's growing popularity among the German (male) public, the game mutated into one of the most powerful vehicles of German nationalism and *völkisch* ideology, which remained alive and well in both Germanies after the war with remnants still present to this day.[41]

Whereas Germany provides one of the most dramatic examples of an

---

[37] See Dietrich Orlow, *A History of Modern Germany*, 7th ed. (New York: Prentice Hall, 2007), pp. 42–44.

[38] See Schiendorfer, "Die englische Krankheit erreicht die Schweiz."

[39] Arthur Heinrich, *Der Deutsche Fußball-Bund. Eine politische Geschichte* (Cologne: Papy-Rossa Verlag, 2000), pp. 33–36.

[40] Only with the advent of World War II did the Nazi regime consider soccer to be an important factor to keep up the morale of the population. In fact, by then the regime, and especially the SS, invested resources and effort to maintain league play because soccer was viewed as critical for the war morale. Along with many armed forces teams joining the leagues, the Nazis' favorite team was the traditionally working-class club Schalke 04, which won six German championships in the Nazi era. Most clubs Nazified enthusiastically, in spite of the Nazis' disrespect for the "English disease." In the last championship final of the Nazi era, Dresdner SC beat Luftwaffen SV Hamburg in Berlin's Olympic Stadium 4-0 in 1944; see Gerhard Fischer and Ulrich Lindner, *Stürmen für Hitler: Vom Zusammenspiel zwischen Fußball und Nationalsozialismus* (Göttingen: Verlag Die Werkstatt, 2002); also www.abseits-soccer .com/essay/nazi. Retrieved January 3, 2009.

[41] Rudolf Oswald, *Fußball-Volksgemeinschaft. Ideologie, Politik und Fanatismus im deutschen Fußball 1919–1964* (Frankfurt: Campus Verlag, 2008).

initial enmity toward soccer, political and cultural opposition to this English import was in no way limited to that country. During soccer's first international expansion and Europeanization, the sport encountered negative reactions elsewhere in Europe, for the most varied of reasons though with less explicitly ethnonationalist or *völkisch* justifications than was the case in Germany. Like any new culture—or language—that seemed irresistible to the masses, so, too, did soccer's arrival upset many establishments, from imperial courts to local clubs, from churches to political parties.

In fact, most socialist parties in Europe initially opposed soccer because they feared that the game would create a culture that they could not control. This resistance is exemplified by the most militant calls on the part of Italian socialist intellectuals in the early twentieth century to sabotage organized sports altogether; they presumably presented illusions about the class character of society and helped obfuscate the evils of capitalism. Needless to say, such policies did not resonate with much success among blue-collar workers in Italy. The British Labour Party was as suspicious of the power of this sport as were the party's continental cousins like the German SPD (the Social Democratic Party of Germany), and the Austrian SPÖ (the Austrian Social Democrats). These parties sensed that soccer was truly attractive for their respective working classes and that it might offer a medium that could easily rival the party and its ancillary organizations as a major agent of mobilization of male, industrial workers.[42] Even though all

[42] To many European socialists of the time, soccer was part of a mass culture that they despised as a capitalist manipulation. They viewed soccer tantamount to religion—that is, as another "opiate of the masses." It is interesting to note that all of Europe's main left establishments either despised soccer outright or remained very skeptical toward it, perhaps all the way until the post–World War II period when the Soviet Union commenced to harness sports, soccer included, for the purposes of national prestige. Although there existed something called the Red Sport International (SPORTINTERN) which worked together with the Communist International (COMINTERN) to advance revolutionary ideas and practices among members of communist and socialist sports clubs, the Bolshevik leadership, just like its social democratic counterparts, viewed sports, and particularly most team sports, as a bourgeois pastime that served no purpose other than to idle the workers, seduce them with bread and circuses, and thus sap them of all revolutionary fervor. The Soviet Union withdrew from the modern Olympic movement following the Russian Revolution and did not participate in any Olympic Games until the summer games in Helsinki in 1952. But in the Soviet Union, too, there occurred a long-lasting tension bordering on incompatibility between socialist ideology and the people's affection concerning soccer. In a fine book, Robert Edelman demonstrates how Spartak Moscow's immense popularity as the people's team often clashed with the ideology and ethos of the workers' state. See Robert Edelman, *Spartak Moscow: A History of the People's Team in the Workers' State* (Ithaca: Cornell University Press, 2009). See also Christiane Eisenberg, "Fußball in Deutschland 1890–1914. Ein Gesellschaftsspiel für bürgerliche Mittelschichten," *Geschichte und Gesellschaft* 20, 1994, pp. 181–210; and Eisenberg, "Zum Span-

socialisms purported to be internationalists to their core, they feared soccer, which they perceived—correctly, as it turns out—as a formidable
global competitor for the hearts and minds of socialism's primary clientele,
the male industrial working class. For socialists in Germany, Austria, and
Italy soccer contained something uncontrollable and seductive that these
parties associated with the alleged evils of other elements of mass culture
such as cinema, jazz, and later rock music. Socialists perceived all of these
as commodified pursuits whose sole purpose was the amassing of profits
for already wealthy capitalists. But let us also not forget that these "evils"
hailed from "the West," represented elements of a globalized world, and
were profoundly rootless. As in many other instances, essential elements of
the left and of the right merged in Europe in their counter-cosmopolitan
antipathy for "Hollywood" and other instances of Anglo-American im-
ports—of which soccer surely was a central one. It is bizarre that team
sports in particular which, after all, depend on the harmonious interaction
of a collective for any kind of success, remained so suspect to most European leftists until World War II, possibly beyond. The left's leaders not
only feared the cultural power of soccer; they also held the game in contempt and viewed it essentially as inauthentic, a disdain similar to the European right's. Despite their alleged internationalism, these socialist cultures were actually profoundly local (and deeply bourgeois for that matter).
In the end, the recurring public attacks against the game were as futile as
the widespread organized opposition to soccer by socialist and worker parties across Europe.

Infact, soccer started to spur a "key moment of modern urban culture."[43]
Along with the rapid sociocultural modernization, industrialization, ur-
banization, and migration of the late nineteenth century, soccer expanded
and moved from a leisure-time activity of the upper middle classes to the

---

nungsverhältnis von kommerzieller Massenkultur und Arbeiterkultur. England aus deutscher
Perspektive," in Hartmut Kaelble and Martin Kirsch, eds., *Selbstverständnis und Gesellschaft der
Europäer. Aspekte der sozialen und kulturellen Europäisierung im späten 19. und 20. Jahrhundert*
(Frankfurt am Main: Lang, 2007), pp. 299–318.

[43] Horak, "Germany versus Austria: Football, Urbanism, and National Identity," p. 27.
Perhaps due to the Habsburg Monarchy's multiethnic nature and Vienna's enjoying a much
greater cultural diversity than virtually any city in the German Reich, Austrian soccer was
never subjected to a forced Germanization of the game's original English terms as happened
in Germany. Thus, well into the 1950s and 1960s, Austrians, especially the Viennese, spoke in
the accent of the local patois, among others, of "referee" instead of "Schiedsrichter," of
"keeper" instead of "Torwart," of "penalty" instead of "Elfmeter," of "corner" instead of "Eck-
ball," and of "hands" instead of "Handspiel." Ironically, this abated and disappeared almost
completely with the advent of television as the major purveyor of the game in which broadcasts dominated by the German networks assumed center stage.

working classes. It was increasingly present in Britain's geographical vicinity, and then speedily spread around the globe. Although, in many cases, this export was related to practices and ideologies of a colonial power (and therefore entrenched in "cultural imperialism"),[44] it constituted a much more complex construct from the very beginning. "Imperial subjects" of the African colonies, such as black Africa's first soccer club Cape Coast Excelsior, already beat European teams at the beginning of the twentieth century. Some local elites, like those in Egypt, for example, fully embraced and excelled at soccer rather than resisted the emergence of the game. In the early stages of soccer's global evolution "this strange compelling European game" was already "providing a platform for the assertion of identity and a quiet declaration of independence."[45] Soccer, thus, can in no way be reduced to a simple colonialist project.[46] Nor can any other of these sports languages, as C.L.R. James so brilliantly demonstrated in the case of cricket.[47] In Austria, for example, soccer by the 1920s at the very latest had become a significant part of popular culture. For instance, Josef Uridil, a player for the "people's team" SK Rapid in Vienna, affectionately called "the tank" by dint of his bulky physique and power-driven game, turned into the country's first true sports star. "Uridil will play today" (*Heute spielt der Uridil*) became *the* most popular song in the Vienna of the 1920s and 1930s, and possibly one of the most popular songs of all time in Vienna's history.[48] Because of his appearance, popularity, and star status way beyond

[44] See Allen Guttmann, *Games and Empires: Modern Sports and Cultural Imperialism* (New York: Columbia University Press, 1994).

[45] Goldblatt, *The Ball Is Round*. pp. 484–86.

[46] See J. A. Mangan, *The Games Ethic and Imperialism: Aspects of the Diffusion of an Ideal* (London: Frank Cass, 1986). Mangan deconstructs ideologies of moralistic athleticism as imperatives in the context of imperial hegemony and cultural assimilation.

[47] In arguably the finest sports book ever written, C.L.R. James—the Afro-Trinidadian Marxist intellectual and life-long critic of British imperialism—demonstrates how cricket, perhaps the most stylized expression of British upper-class demeanor, mutated into the West Indies' hegemonic sports culture and assumed as the sport of the people at least as many moments of resistance against the colonial rulers as it did of complicity and subordination. See C.L.R. James, *Beyond a Boundary* (Durham: Duke University Press, 1993).

[48] Even though Rapid was Vienna's "people's team" and even though workers loved the team and loved the game of soccer, the Social Democrats inveighed against this sport in every possible way available to them. Thus, for example, one of Austrian Social Democracy's leading intellectuals, Jacques Hannak, wrote in the July 1926 issue of *Der Kampf*, one of social democracy's leading publications, how soccer was with "shimmy," and the movies and various forms of gamblimg nothing more than a further expression of the decadence of bourgeois society that was undermining the workers' class consciousness by blinding them to their plight with cheap diversions very much akin to the Roman Empire's bread and circuses. See Roman Horak and Wolfgang Maderthaner, *Mehr als ein Spiel. Fußball und populare Kulturen im Wien der Moderne* (Vienna: Löcker Verlag, 1997), p. 105.

the playing field, Uridil could well be viewed as Austria's and Central Europe's "Babe Ruth"—who resembled Uridil in lifestyle, portliness, and stature and attained a similar sheen via baseball across the Atlantic in New York and beyond.

The Other Football(s): Related Local and Global Sports Languages

By 1953, Geoffrey Green could triumphantly write a book entitled *Soccer: The World Game*.[49] Since that era, the term "world game" has become synonymous with soccer. However, this is not only an incorrect belief and an arrogant claim on the part of soccer's advocates, but also understandably somewhat irritating to those where other hegemonic sports cultures have prevailed. Indeed, our book makes the case that soccer's truly global presence was not attained until the advent of our second globalization. It has in the meantime reached the sports cultures in places such as the United States, Canada, China, Japan, Australia, and India, but its hegemonic presence and future in these areas remains far from certain.[50]

The reason that soccer was perceived to have become *the* global game even during the first globalization of the late nineteenth and early twentieth centuries was simply due to its having been successful in many European and Latin American countries, whereas soccer's major rivals remained confined to a few (though large and sometimes populous) parts of the British Empire. In some of these countries the other (minoritarian) versions of football featuring the two rugby codes, Union and League, developed as *linguae francae*. Others still, like India, Pakistan, Sri Lanka, and the West Indies did not take to any of these footballs and made cricket into the hegemon of their respective sports cultures.[51] Soccer thus embodied a convincing testimony to Britain's economic power, its informal empire as it were, since the game attained popularity in countries not ruled by Britain;

---

[49] Geoffrey Green, *Soccer: The World Game: A Popular History* (London: Phoenix House, 1953).

[50] Thus, for example, Kieran Healy challenged the concept of America's soccer exceptionalism and argued that America, far from being exceptional, was actually part of a larger global norm. If one pooled the populations of India, China, Pakistan, the United States, Canada, Australia, New Zealand, and other "nonsoccer" countries, Healy thought that perhaps it might be more sensible to speak of a soccer exceptionalism rather than an American one since the number of people on the globe who did not have soccer as their primary sports culture exceeded those who did. This occurred in the discussion of Markovits's lecture on comparative sports cultures at the Center for Advanced Study in the Behavioral Sciences (CASBS) of Stanford University on September 24, 2008.

[51] C.L.R. James, *Beyond a Boundary*.

whereas cricket and both rugby codes became the legacy of Britain's political power by occupying the sports spaces of countries that were directly governed by Britain as its colonies.

The aforementioned paper by Colyvas and Jonsson, which disentangled the difference between diffusion and institutionalization, will clarify the varying weights that hegemonic sports assume in a country's sports space. In Europe and Latin America, soccer's institutional presence and cultural diffusion have been "widespread, conventional and appropriate" to use Colyvas and Jonsson's terminology, whereas in the United States, Canada, Australia, New Zealand, India, and other "non-soccer" countries, the game's institutional existence was "accepted" (Colyvas and Jonsson) long ago though its cultural diffusion has remained tenuous and marginal to this day. Reverse this pattern to understand the situation in Europe where the North American Big Four have had an institutional presence for quite some time, though their cultural diffusion remains subordinate to that of soccer.

Suffice it to say that the globalization of Association and rugby football did not mean the total destruction of football's numerous local versions. Many are still played to this day. At the very same time that the World Cup tournament enters its key stages in late June every four years, the Piazza Santa Croce in the city of Florence witnesses three matches of its annual "Calcio Fiorentino," a descendent of the Roman game of *harpastum* that became a mainstay of Florentine public life since the sixteenth century. There are twenty-seven men to a team, both hands and feet are used throughout the game, and the winner is the team with the most points—called "cacce," hence "calcio."[52] In Florence itself, this traditional competition might in fact draw a bigger crowd than a World Cup game featuring any team other than Italy's national team, the beloved *Squadra Azzurra*.

It is this Florentine game's name that the Italians bestowed upon Association football that reached the peninsula in the last few years of the nineteenth century and has since become what it is today: an unparalleled national passion covered by three daily newspapers, among them the publication with the highest circulation of all papers in Italy, the *Gazzetta dello Sport*. Indeed, in an attempt to counter the global dimension of Association football and to de-emphasize its English roots, the Italian nationalists exhumed the term "calcio" from the old Florentine game and placed it on the new international game of "football," thereby "Italianizing" this originally

---

[52] For an extensive historical account see Horst Bredekamp, *Florentiner Fußball: Die Renaissance der Spiele* (Frankfurt am Main: Wagenbach, 1993).

English but soon-to-be global sport.[53] Yet no matter whether Calcio Fiorentino is a resilient or a revived, even invented tradition, the local version of traditional calcio persists and remains popular against all pressures of modernity.[54]

Other, even better examples of the survival of local, traditional football games in a contemporary environment are found on British territory. Cnapan (also spelled Knapan or Knappan), an archaic version of football, is still played in the western counties of Wales, especially Cardiganshire and Pembrokeshire. So too is the Eton Field Game and the Eton Wall Game—two independent versions of football still played at the elite secondary school of Eton in England. It took a long time for this game and, of course, the Eton student body, to transcend gender barriers; the first all-female Wall Game was played on July 15, 2005. Both genders have continued to play this game with verve.

Eton's closest rival, Harrow, also plays its own brand of football on a regular basis. It is Harrow's version of the game that was the most influential in creating the Cambridge Rules of 1848, and it can thus be viewed as the forerunner to today's global game of soccer. The third of the major elite secondary schools, Winchester, naturally has *its* own game. Lovingly called "Winkies" or "WinCoFo" (short for Winchester College Football), it is, like the games at Eton and Harrow, a local football game that continues to enjoy popularity, shows no signs of abating, and remains proudly content in its confinement to this particular public school.

Other popular local versions of football that continue to exist to this day are: Haxie Hood and Hurling the Silver Ball in England; Kemari in Japan; La Soule in Brittany, Normandy, and Picardy; and Marn Grook which,

---

[53] The name *calcio*, given to the Association game in Italy, constitutes a piece of nationalist, invented history. It was only adopted after nationalist representatives of the gymnastics movement acquired a majority on the Italian Football Federation's governing council in 1908. They insisted on dropping all English terms for the game and had them replaced with more "authentic" and "indigenous" Italian ones. The new leadership initially also banned foreign players from that year's national competition; recall our mentioning above the identical measures taken by the German authorities at the same time. See Goldblatt, *The Ball Is Round*, pp. 16 and 154. Tellingly, the Italian Fascists also resisted the game's international impetus by renaming one of the two Milanese clubs from its original "Internazionale" to "Ambrosiana."

[54] For the counter argument, namely that with the rise of soccer as we know it the traditional football games were already anachronisms, see Goldblatt, *The Ball Is Round*, pp. 23, 24. Goldblatt claims that by the end of the nineteenth century games of traditional football had been tamed and then largely extinguished along with the depopulation of nineteenth-century rural England, surviving only "in the most extreme peripheries and backwaters of the kingdom, . . . and extinction loomed." However, Goldblatt does not really keep track of the twentieth-century history of these local sports and their surprising resilience.

contrary to popular opinion, is not a forerunner of Australian Rules Football (that itself is actually an Australian re-organization and expansion of the British import of pre-organized football of the 1850s, thus preceding the founding of the Football Association in London in 1863[55]) but very much a game all its own in Victoria, Australia.

No specific event of these local and pre-globalized versions of football is better known than the Royal Shrovetide Football Match of Ashbourne in Derbyshire in England, which has been contested every year on Mardi Gras and Ash Wednesday since at least the twelfth century. The game is played on both days from 2 PM until 10 PM. The two goal posts are three miles apart and each team—the Up'Ards (featuring Ashbourne's denizens living north of the river) and the Down'Ards (those living south of the river)—has hundreds, perhaps even thousands, of players. The term "derby" is far and away the most important bequest that this annual "premodern" football game has bestowed on the global language of the very modern Association game. In many languages across the globe it denotes the most contested local rivalries: as in the Merseyside Derby of Everton FC vs. Liverpool; the North London Derby of Arsenal vs. Tottenham Hotspurs; the Milanese Derby of Inter vs. AC Milan; and—perhaps the fiercest derby of them all—the Glaswegian "Old Firm" showdown between Celtic FC and Rangers FC. Such derbies exist in American sports as well, apart of course from the Kentucky Derby, arguably America's most pedigreed horse race, where the very word appears. Substitute "rivalry" for "derby" and one need only mention such classics (among many others) of American sports culture as Ohio State vs. Michigan in college football, Duke vs. North Carolina in college basketball, Red Sox vs. Yankees in baseball, and Green Bay Packers vs. Chicago Bears in professional football.[56] The essential character of all such derbies remains identical across

[55] Indeed, the oldest, still extant and flourishing football clubs do not reside in England but in Australia, where the Melbourne Football Club founded in 1858 and the Geelong club founded one year later are testimony to the game's arrival and acceptance in Australia's state of Victoria well before the split between the Association's kicking game and the various running versions of rugby and its descendants. In a fascinating way, Australian Rules Football represents a sort of "Ur-football" predating the decisive split of 1863. But in contrast to the various localized folk games that we mentioned that remained largely noncommercial and basically amateur, Australian Rules Football has mutated into a huge enterprise, boasting some of the largest stadiums in the world, featuring teams, leagues, championships, and, of course, professional players. By any measure, this game has earned the sobriquet of being "big time."

[56] Nowhere in American sports is the structure of derby better institutionalized than in college football, in which traditionally and until recently the very last game of the season occurred between the two most established rivals of the particular league: Cal vs. Stanford; Harvard vs. Yale; Florida vs. Florida State; Alabama vs. Auburn; USC vs. UCLA; Michigan vs.

all cultures and sports: regardless of that particular season's standings, regardless whether one is up or down that year, one *always* wants to defeat one's bitter rival. Needless to say, one *always* wishes them ill, and the concept of *Schadenfreude* has arguably never experienced a more manifest, indeed proud, existence than in this construct.

The most interesting, long-lasting, and expressly political resistance to both football games—Association and rugby—hailed from Ireland where these British games were identified with the enemy and thus shunned, if not forbidden, by those committed to the Republican cause. In their stead, there emerged the Gaelic games of hurling and football that, arguably, became together with the Catholic Church perhaps *the* most important hegemonic institutions of Irish identity over many decades. Dublin's Croke Park, Europe's fourth largest stadium, has since 1884 been the hallowed headquarters of the Gaelic Athletic Association (GAA), Ireland's biggest sporting organization and a bastion of Irish nationalism and identity. Croke Park has hosted the so-called Gaelic games, most notably the annual finals of the All-Ireland Senior Football Championship and the Senior Hurling Championship. Soccer and rugby were relegated in Dublin to the much smaller Landsdowne Road venue, owned by the Irish Rugby Football Union (IRFU), a distant second in importance to the GAA. Perhaps the clearest sign that the long-lasting internecine conflict between Irish Catholics and Protestants was in the fortuitous process of its final demise occurred when Croke Park permitted the playing of rugby and soccer games on its grounds during the refurbishing of the Landsdowne Road venue, which commenced in 2006 and is to be completed by 2010.

Explaining Soccer's Early and (Almost) Global Success

In comparison to rugby in all its variants, surely soccer's closest "relatives," soccer proved to be the more widely disseminated team sport. In the process of its first globalization, soccer quickly diffused to many corners of the globe. Meanwhile, rugby—with a few notable exceptions like France, Argentina and in more recent times Italy, Romania, Russia, and Japan—has remained restricted to countries of the former British Empire.[57] But why did the Association game become almost global in this first globalization from the nineteenth to the early twentieth century? Why did soccer succeed over its many rivals, particularly other modernized team sports hail-

---

Ohio State. Indeed, ESPN has popularized the term "rivalry week" to denote the buildup to these grudge matches or "rivalry games".

[57] Murphy, Williams, and Dunning, *Football on Trial*, p. 6.

ing from Britain but also the United States? Three key elements need to be mentioned in this context:

First and foremost, J. C. Thring was indeed correct. The Association game was the "simplest game" by far. Its fourteen laws were minimal compared to those of its other rival sports languages of the time. Soccer became the most cross-culturally intelligible and transferable team sport by dint of its simplicity. With the possible exception of the offside rule, no others are complicated. It was this simplicity that helped soccer's dissemination to countries and cultures as diverse as Brazil and Germany; Uruguay and Romania; Mexico and Switzerland.[58] Whereas the respective aims of baseball and cricket are not prima facie evident for an ignorant outsider, soccer's aims are crystal clear to all but the simplest minds. It is the defense in both baseball and cricket that holds and controls the ball via its pitchers and bowlers, while the offense tries to get rid of it via its batters and batsmen—who comprise all players on a team but never have them present at the same time on the field. Even in comparison with the much less complex but still muddled football codes of the rugby games and American football—where clarity is not always evident to the untrained eye—the Association game is burdened by none of these complexities. To this day, soccer never developed the numerical intricacies and statistical measures that became essential to a proper understanding of cricket and baseball, and to a lesser extent football and the rugby games. There are no box scores in soccer. Virtually any person in any culture can quickly understand the game's aims and thus its purpose and process.

Second, soccer is a profoundly democratic sport in that it never favored players with particular physical attributes. There have been many legend-

---

[58] As mentioned before, the interpretation of each of these rules is never simple and never clear-cut. Recall the (in)famous Geoff Hurst goal (or non-goal) at Wembley in 1966 for which we have yet to meet a German, regardless of her or his political beliefs, age, profession, gender, class, or status to whom this was a goal (other than, allegedly, the Federal Republic of Germany's second president Heinrich Lübke), and for which we have yet to meet an English person for whom this was not a goal. Interpretations and adjudications of all rules in all sports are always controversial and contingent and never automatic, which is one of the many reasons that render modern sports, that, by virtue of their modernity, are so routinized and rote, so interesting and exciting—and unpredictable in terms of the contest's final result. Remember how it is precisely this unpredictability of outcome and unscripted nature that differentiates sports from other forms of entertainment. But the aim, the essence, of the Association game is extremely simple and is prima facie evident to anybody with a modicum of intelligence and interest. As Simon Kuper points out, American football has 83 penalties in its rule book, compared with soccer's 17 fouls. Against this backdrop it is "easy to see why football—like cricket—is tough to export." Quoted in Eliott C. McLaughlin, "Super Bowl is king at home but struggles on world stage," http://www.cnn.com/2010/US/02/05/super.bowl.vie wers.profit/index.html?hpt=CI; retrieved February 7, 2010.

ary contributors to the game's history who were not particularly tall, strong, fast, or even athletic but who nevertheless mastered the game superbly. Also democratic is the fact that it can be played virtually on any surface, under any weather conditions, and with little equipment—not even a real ball is necessary. To name one player of many, the famous Ferenc "Öcsi" Puskás, of the Hungarian national squad that dominated world soccer in the early 1950s, taught himself the game using a bundle of rags instead of a ball. Moreover, Puskás's stout physique, short legs, and undeniable paunch, surely did not furnish the ideal bodily prerequisites to becoming one of the greatest masters in the game's pedigreed history. Soccer is also democratic by its being inexpensive. Essentially, the game can be played anywhere by anyone with pretty much anything. The barriers to its entry are exceedingly low concerning all important criteria.

Third, the game's global proliferation is a testimony to Britain's economic might of the late nineteenth century, not its political power. Britain's commercial dominance spread the game all across the globe. Textile engineers, railway workers, electricians, language teachers, and, most important of all, natives of many lands who went to England—or came in touch with English experts in their own country—to study modern business practices and become proficient in commercial professions, participated in the global sharing of Association football. It is in this context that they got to know and fell in love with this game.

While inherently cosmopolitan and international by dint of its globalized existence, soccer featured two structures from its outset that prima facie followed two contradictory logics: the inclusiveness of the professional club, and the exclusion of the national team. Let us elaborate.

Two Emerging Logics of Soccer: Transnationalism and Nationalism

The aim of club soccer was to win a country's (or a division's) championship in league play as well as to win the national cup tournament in a country-wide knock-out competition among all clubs regardless of their divisional or league-specific belonging. Winning was the mindset and mentality that emerged in this process, which could be best attained by attracting talent regardless of geographic origins or other particularistic attributes. The logic of winning at all costs emphasized achievement, which gradually, but nonetheless in an inevitable manner, fostered a talent search that might find players of the "wrong" ethnic origin, a distant geographic location, or any other dimension that was construed as an undesirable "other." Of course, the method of professionalism—that is, paying participants a living wage to play what was essentially a children's game—emerged at different junctures in different countries. Still, even in the world of committed amateurism a specialization of skills and desirability of talent developed that grew way beyond the local and extended to the national, sometimes even beyond. There were, for instance, more mining-related players hailing from the mining town of Gelsenkirchen in Germany's Ruhr region who represented Schalke 04, and steel-related men playing for nearby Borussia and anchored in the steel town of Dortmund, than were present at Bayern Munich or other south German clubs hundreds of miles from any colliery or steel plant. Of course, clubs recruited players from their immediate environs. This is still the case today, even in such a geographically and socially mobile society like the United States, where a disproportionate number of both Ohio State and University of Texas players hail from their respective states. Our point is merely that the logic of professionalism and winning mitigated particularistic ties, including localism. Concretely, what we are saying is that many of the Schalke 04 and Borussia Dortmund players belonged to neither the mining nor the steel-working milieus and hailed from different geographic locations in Germany.

Ever since the world's very first professional team in any team sport assembled in 1869, baseball's Cincinnati Red Stockings, the logic of excellence, of winning, of acquiring league points mitigated against the romantic notion of an idealized localism and an alleged loyalty to home and hearth. Incidentally, only first baseman Charlie Gould was a native on this unbeaten Cincinnati Red Stockings team (57 wins, 0 losses). All other players hailed from the East Coast. Vince Lombardi's well-known motto of winning being not only everything, but the only thing, comprises the meritocratic core of all modern sports, not only American football. What matters is output, results, and winning. This logic certainly pertains to the club world of soccer as well. It was not by coincidence that the Nazis, at least officially, did not just vehemently oppose soccer as the "English game" but also its professionalization, denouncing it as "Jewish" thereby underlining their counter-cosmopolitan mindset that hatefully equated "Englishness"—let alone "Jewishness"—with commercialism and the cold pursuit of profits.[59] In principle, the logic of modern club sports knows no local or national limits. Recruitment is only constrained, for example, by nationalist regulations on the part of the governing bodies in professional European soccer leagues. Issued by national soccer federations, these regulations restrict the amount of non-European players allowed to play for a

[59] See Fischer and Lindner, *Stürmen für Hitler.*

club. However, Article 39 of the European Treaty and the European Court of Justice's so-called "Bosman ruling" (the Belgian player Jean-Marc Bosman successfully brought a lawsuit against UEFA and the Belgian soccer association for being denied labor mobility in the EU that is accorded every one of its citizens) banned any restrictions on the freedom of movement and employment of European citizens within the European Union. Now all European players can transfer freely to the club of their liking.

In general the club logic operates below and above the national level; it encompasses competition among teams within a country but also features transnational contests such as the European Champions League or the Copa Libertadores in South America. Although local attachments to teams are of crucial importance, the logic of clubs and the cultural diversity of the global migrant-players representing them since the early days of soccer's professionalization, points to the inherent transnationalism and cosmopolitanism of this track.[60] Thus, soccer's club mode contained from the 1880s onward the logic of what Raffaele Poli has aptly called "denationalization" and "deterritorialization," which he locates temporally as coinciding with the era of our second globalization and not its nineteenth-century precursor, which, for Poli, is largely characterized by what he calls "the nationalization of sport."[61]

We could not agree more that such nationalization did indeed exist at the time and shaped most sports, soccer included. But we see such nationalization not in the logic of the clubs but in that of the national teams. From the very first international match in 1872 between England and Scotland, featuring the best English and Scottish players, the game's nation-based enterprise was a much different one from that of the club world. With no regularity, league, or organized competition following a clearly delineated structure, teams emerged based on nothing else but country.

[60] See King, *The European Ritual*, pp. 9–12. King argues that this transnationalism has only become truly manifest with the Europeanization of soccer. For him, 1999 marks a significant turning point because it had become legitimate in England to support Bayern Munich (in this case the "underdog") in the European Champions League Final against the English powerhouse Manchester United. This perceived shift away from what King calls the "nationalist interpretation," however, underestimates that according to the logic of club soccer various top dog vs. underdog notions always played a role—as do local rivalries. For example, many German fans always want to see Bayern lose because they are the country's top dog. Hardly any true 1860 Munich fan wanted to see Bayern win and was surely delighted to see Manchester United defeat their much-despised crosstown rivals. Of course, the very same holds true in the parallel universe of Manchester, where the antipathy borne by Manchester City supporters toward hated United remains boundless. Thus, it is quite reasonable to assume that City fans were rooting for Bayern in its match against United.

[61] Poli, "The Denationalization of Sport."

From the very beginning, the "we" in this particular soccer track was solely based on nationalism, both for the players as well as the fans; in many European countries, this "soccer nationalism" was for the longest time ethnically exclusive even where "regular" nationalism had been defined by politically inclusive, civic terms. Thus, it is not surprising that simply by wanting one's team to win, one ipso facto mutated into a nationalist, perhaps even a chauvinist. It surely is no coincidence that in most countries where soccer assumes the role of hegemonic sports culture, the national team and its "owner" —the national federation—has disproportionately been on the political right of that country's spectrum. This is the case precisely because the federation's main legitimacy is anchored in the raison d'etre of an intense partisanship based solely on nationalism. Unlike with clubs, where there are many reasons to be partisan, this is not the case with the national team. The playing of the national anthems before every contest, the raising of the flags, and many other symbolic gestures anchored solely in nationalism further facilitate its construction as the sole emotive reason to support a particular team. The structured competition among national teams was a latecomer compared to the club world, since it was not until the World Cup in 1930 that such competition became regularized.[62]

Of course, soccer was played by national teams at the Olympic Games before then, but it remained one among many other sports that lacked the prominence that the club game had already come to enjoy in most of what came to be known as the "world of soccer."[63] More than just a marginal

[62] Still, into the 1960s the World Cup remained *relatively* unimportant as a global sports event. For example, as late as 1962, Austria refused to participate in the World Cup in Chile because "the necessary preparations for a national team would take too much time, as a consequence of which the national club competition would suffer severely." In addition, the national federation argued that the trip would "cost too much money." Edi Finger, "Österreichs 'Njet' zur Fußball-WM: Der Österreichische Fußballbund hat es abgelehnt, an der Fußball-weltmeisterschaft 1962 in Chile teilzunehmen," *Sport und Toto*, February 1, 1959, facsimile in Wolfgang Maderthaner, Alfred Pfoser, and Roman Horak, eds., *Die Eleganz des runden Leders* (Göttingen: Verlag Die Werkstatt, 2008), p. 219. Such a decision on the part of the Austrian, or any other national soccer federation in the world would, of course, be absolutely unthinkable today.

[63] Of course, there developed "classic" national rivalries such as Scotland and England—the two countries competed in the first official game of international football, a 0–0 on November 30, 1872—as the oldest and first contest with "nations" as teams (the two played each other 111 times until 2000, and contested in an annual fixture until 1989 but have not played each other since the 2000 qualification playoff) followed by Argentina vs. Uruguay, who have played each other a record 196 times since they first met on May 16, 1901 (since the 1990s, this South American contest has been replaced by Argentina vs. Brazil, who met 91 times until 2008, as the biggest regional rivalry); and then by Hungary vs. Austria, who first played each other on October 12, 1902 and met each other 136 times until 2006. Tellingly, the oldest

national spectacle, it can be argued that the national soccer team and its success had a crucial importance in nation-state formations or the consolidation of national identities in a number of cases.[64] Eric Hobsbawm's apt analogy applies in full: "The imagined community of millions seems more real in the form of 11 named people."[65]

For example, the much-celebrated 3–2 victory of Austria's squad over Germany at the 1978 World Cup—in a symbolic match with no competitive importance for the Austrians who, even with a victory, could not advance in the tournament—is the greatest moment in the shared collective memory of Austria's soccer history. Furthermore, it is also a key instance in which Austria's still fragile postwar national identity was forged and finalized. With the help of that epochal experience, Austrians solidified their identity apart from Germans to a point that rendered any sentiment of them joining in any meaningful political union, beyond the one binding them together in the European Union, the property of the marginalized extreme right, if that. Austria's soccer victory over Germany in far-away Argentina mutated Austria into another German-speaking country whose population had come to enjoy, even extol, its political sovereignty as a democratic republic shedding any of its hitherto unresolved identity issues of its own "Germanness" and its relations with Germany.[66] In a sense, this victory in Cordoba had finally resolved Austria's "German question," which had informed key aspects of the country's politics and identity since 1806 at the very latest. Even the vaguest notions of an "Anschluss" in any shape or form were rendered politically meaningless. Cordoba became one of many instances in Europe's postwar history in which the "German question" —that had caused so much instability and pain in Europe's nine-

---

international soccer contests between countries outside the British Isles were the games between the United States and Canada in 1885 and 1886, showing that soccer existed on the North American continent from its very beginning. But indicative, too, of soccer's marginal cultural presence in the sports cultures of both of these North American countries, is how unimportant and virtually unknown these games were since they led to no important follow-ups. Indeed, these games' actual occurrence remains disputed.

[64] For a general discussion of sports' impact on civic and ethnic national identity formation, see Alan Bairner's brilliant study *Sport, Nationalism, and Globalization: European and North American Perspectives* (Albany: State University of New York Press, 2001).

[65] Eric Hobsbawm, *Nations and Nationalism since 1780: Programme, Myth, Reality* (Cambridge: Cambridge University Press, 1990).

[66] For the most erudite analysis and detailed presentation of Austria's "Germany complex" in football and beyond, see Gerhard Urbanek, *Österreichs Deutschland-Komplex. Paradoxien in der österreichisch-deutschen Fußballmythologie* (Vienna: University of Vienna, doctoral dissertation, 2007; self-published book, 2009).

teenth- and twentieth-century history—became defanged and was ultimately rendered harmless.[67]

West Germany's 1954 World Cup victory, to take a related example, was
a crucial stepping-stone in the formation of the Federal Republic's postwar
identity and self-discovery.[68] It, too, could—and should—be seen as a
building bloc toward the "normalization," "Westernization," and "Europeanization" of Germany, and a solid ingredient in a lengthy process that
ended Germany's destructive impulses of the twentieth century's first half.

[67] There is probably no Austrian alive today who does not know the screams of "I wer narrisch, I wer narrisch" ("I am going nuts, I am going nuts" in Austrian patois) of the hyperven-
tilating broadcaster Edi Finger celebrating Austria's victory over Germany. By the time of the
"follow-up game" between Austria and (West) Germany, which occurred in Gijón four years
later during the World Cup in Spain in 1982, Austria's cultural and national independence
was much more settled. Emotions will always be high, especially for the Austrians, when the
two countries meet on the soccer field in a competitive match. A case in point is the political
and media frenzy before the EURO 2008 group stage match in Vienna, which many Austrian
publications viewed as the "match of the century," while for the Germans it was more or less
just a group stage game. In 1982, however, the "German question" was basically settled, and
emotions boiled over for a different reason: Austria and Germany faced off in the final group
match, and both group leader Austria and third-ranked Germany settled for a German 1–0
victory. After the German goal by Horst Hrubesch in the eleventh minute, the Austrian and
German players remained almost idle and did not even try to get near the opponent's goal for
the remaining seventy-nine minutes instead kicking the ball leisurely from side to side, almost from team to team. This result secured both teams a place in the so-called "final round,"
while Algeria, who had previously beaten Germany 2–1 in one of the biggest upsets in soccer
history, was eliminated. Austria and Germany had ignominiously conspired with one another,
leaving an indelible stain on the tournament and the sport of soccer in general. The "shame
of Gijon" changed the World Cup forever. It prompted FIFA to alter the rules in subsequent
tournaments. Since Gijon, all final games of the group stage have to be played simultaneously
lest such manipulations occur. In both Germany, who eventually proceeded to the World Cup
final, and Austria, this game—arguably the worst and openly most scandalous soccer game in
history often referred to as the Anschluss game—received as much public outrage as in the
rest of the world; see Ulrich Hesse-Lichtenberger, *Tor! The Story of German Football* (London:
WSC Books Ltd., 2003); see cbcsports.ca/sports/soccer/story/2008/06/16, (accessed June 16,
2008).

[68] See Arthur Heinrich, "The 1954 Soccer World Cup and the Federal Republic of Germany's Self-Discovery," *American Behavioral Scientist* 46 (11), 2003, pp. 1491–505. From the
beginning of the twentieth century, soccer has provided in Argentina a strong nucleus for
representing nationality. A series of international successes, and a list of football "heroes,"
commenced an epic narrative, in which football contributed, in an important way, to the "invention of a nation." Starting from the populist experience of early Peronism in the 1940s,
the relationship between football (sport) and nationality intensified, with a visible climax in
the 1980s and the 1990s, through the "Maradonian saga." See Pablo Alabarces and Maria
Graciela Rodriguez, "Football and Fatherland: The Crisis of National Representation in Argentinean Football," in Gerry P. T. Finn and Richard Giulianotti, eds., *Football Culture: Local
Conflicts, Global Visions* (London: Frank Cass, 2000). Similar phenomena exist in Brazil, Italy,
and many nations in which soccer constitutes hegemonic sports culture.

Toward the Second Globalization of Soccer

Although soccer continued to expand its cultural, political, and social significance and popularity over the twentieth century—especially with the beginning of the television age in the 1950s—the structure and territorial scope of soccer culture was basically established by the 1920s. The first globalization had created a global soccer language cutting across cultures and classes, and had prepared the ground for the emergence of global competitions like the World Cup, transnational migrations and encounters, and the emergence of global arenas. Yet only with the beginning of the second, postindustrial globalization in the 1980s and the rise of new global technologies, was the near-global language of soccer able to find major new inroads in terms of cultural impact and territorial outreach. Soccer's new presence enabled spectators around the world to follow various national and transnational competitions beyond the World Cup. Soccer is still in the process of truly "arriving" in North America, Oceania, and Asia, including China, India, and Japan.

In China, for instance, professional soccer is not really professional in its methods, organization, and performance orientation. Yet China also offers the most dramatic example of the cultural power of globalization and the impact of global sports on the transformation of national cultures. In today's China, soccer and basketball are very popular. Sweeping away cultural traditions, they have displaced table tennis and other former hegemonic sports within a decade in terms of what millions follow rather than play. As an expression of globalization, the European Champions League receives enormous attention. While Kobe Bryant, the NBA superstar, is arguably the most popular athlete in China and among the most popular individuals in the country, soccer is on level terms with basketball as China's favorite sport. Although China's men's soccer team has lacked success in any international forum, the Chinese women's team belongs among the top six nations of the world. Chinese soccer connoisseurs, enthusiasts, and the sports-interested public adore global players such as Ronaldinho, Lionel Messi, and David Beckham, who give Kobe a run for his money as China's most popular sports star.[69]

Notwithstanding the simultaneity of multiple local, national, and supra-

---

[69] Edward Wong, "China Loves Its Soccer. But Its Team? Don't Ask," *New York Times*, August 15, 2008, p. A10. Although there is no necessary trade-off, table tennis, the old English parlor game particularly popularized by Mao Zedong, is losing some of its cultural significance. While table tennis is still very popular among the elderly, most young athletes in China no longer indulge in table tennis but bounce different balls—on soccer fields and bas-

national competitions of many leagues around the world, much of global attention focuses on the professional leagues in Europe and the supranational European Champions League. With very few exceptions, it is in these Europe-centered forums in which almost all of the world's best players compete. Apart from the quadrennial World Cup tournament, Europe undoubtedly comprises soccer's global core. In terms of worldwide attention accorded the game, the Big Four of England, Italy, Spain, and Germany without any doubt comprise soccer's inner sanctum, with countries in the rest of the world fluctuating between the game's semiperiphery and periphery. Of course, this does not obviate the fact that soccer fans in the latter two worlds continue to follow their local teams and players with passion.

Before reflecting further on the second globalization's intersections and dynamics of sports cultures, we briefly take a look at the history of political and cultural disseminations of four other major professional team sports around the world. Our subjects here are baseball, basketball, hockey, and football—sports that either originated or matured in North America, and later achieved varying degrees of global expansion.

The Globalizations of Baseball, Hockey, Basketball, and Football: Different Trajectories

Because of particular class-related characteristics of British colonial rule, it was the languages of cricket and rugby football, instead of the Association game, that became the linguae francae of the respective contemporary hegemonic sports cultures of India, Pakistan, Australia, New Zealand, South Africa, and the West Indies. The United States and Canada also fall into this category of (former) British colonies that did not adopt soccer as their primary hegemonic representative; the game languished on the peripheries. But in contrast to other British colonies (with the possible exception of Australia, by dint of its Australian Rules Football), the United States and Canada *transformed* extant British games into North American sports that then blossomed into their own sports culture: rounders into baseball; rugby football into American (and Canadian) football; field hockey into ice hockey; and netball into basketball (though this is a debatable issue, with

---

ketball courts. See John Branch, "In China, Table Tennis Is for Gramps," *New York Times*, August 17, 2008, Sunday Styles Section, p. 1.

the completely legitimate claim that basketball is a pristinely North American invention by the Canadian educator Dr. James Naismith in Springfield, Massachusetts in 1891).

The American Pastime: The Limited Globalization of Baseball

Contrary to still maintained myths, Abner Doubleday did not invent baseball in Elihu Phinney's cow pasture in Cooperstown, New York in 1839. Rather, like most modern sports, baseball evolved out of preexisting sports with rules changing gradually from one community to the next until the game, as we know it today, became solidified. The first known reference to baseball in America is found in a 1791 bylaw from Pittsfield, Massachusetts, which banned "baseball" playing within eighty yards of a building. Notably, the statute also mentions "wicket," "cricket," "batball," "football," and "cats and five" distinctly from baseball.[70] Beyond that, evidence from the early nineteenth century shows a game known as "base," "townball," or "baseball" growing popular on the American East Coast. Most historians agree that this game was the descendant of an English ball-and-stick game known as "rounders." In 1845 Alexander Cartwright produced a formal list of baseball rules, and in 1846 the first recorded baseball game occurred on the Elysian Fields of Hoboken, New Jersey, as the New York Baseball Club beat Cartwright's Knickerbockers. The game of baseball continued to grow in popularity, and in 1857 a convention for amateur teams was organized to discuss the game's rules. Twenty-five teams sent delegations. The first organized baseball league surfaced already in 1858 with the National Association of Base Ball Players—slightly ahead but roughly parallel to the evolution of soccer at England's Cambridge University. By 1868 the convention of the National Association of Base Ball Players attracted delegates from over one hundred teams.

In 1869 Harry and George Wright made the Cincinnati Red Stockings the first totally professional baseball team, which meant the very first in any sport in the world. Perhaps the fact that professional sports teams in America emerged as businesses from their very beginning—and remain so until today—hails all the way back to the Wright brothers' founding of the Cincinnati Red Stockings. The brothers later moved to Boston, thus establishing the peripatetic nature of American sports "franchises," which re-

[70] Frank Ceresi and Carol McMains, "National Treasures: The Origins of Baseball," *Baseball Almanac* (2004). www.baseball-almanac.com. Retrieved August 12, 2008.

mains anathema to Europe's club system. Despite the changes wrought by modern communication and the massive onslaught of commercialization in all its facets throughout the twentieth century, this system has remained largely intact to this very day. In terms of key features such as their geographic immutability and their existence apart from their attractiveness as profit-generating entities, the European clubs and their system bear a greater similarity to America's college sports than they do to that of their professional establishment.

With the formation of the National Association in 1871, baseball had its first professional league.[71] The National Association of Professional Base Ball Players became the National League of Professional Base Ball Clubs in 1876, and then the American League of Professional Baseball Clubs emerged in 1901 as the ultimate survivor among other competing leagues that rose and fell in the last two decades of the nineteenth century.[72] The first World Series, in 1903, drew over 100,000 spectators in eight games. By 1912, the eight-game attendance surpassed 250,000.[73] Baseball provided the lower classes a venue in which they could excel as players and found entertainment and pleasure as spectators. Few structures in American life offered such a meritocratic—indeed welcoming—space for immigrants to make their mark as Americans.[74]

Baseball's eventual role in integrating all ethnic groups into the American mainstream was delayed by overt racism from the 1880s until after World War II. The game was racially segregated most certainly after Adrian Constantine "Cap" Anson, baseball's most esteemed player and manager at the time, stated his unequivocal refusal to play on the same field with any team that included blacks on its roster. Anson's polemic thereby introduced and solidified Jim Crow laws that dominated America's pastime for more than half a century.[75] In 1920, the National Negro League, the first organized "negro league," was formed. A variety of "negro leagues" would come and go until the breaking of the color barrier in 1947, which integrated

[71] See Sean Lahman, "A Brief History of Baseball: Part I: Origins of the Game," in *The Baseball Archive* (December 1996). www.baseball1.com. Retrieved August 12, 2008.

[72] See "The History of Baseball," www.rpi.edu/~fiscap/history_files/history2.htm. Retrieved August 13, 2008.

[73] See "World Series Gate Receipts" (2007), in *Baseball Almanac*, www.baseball-almanac .com. Retrieved August 15, 2008.

[74] See Robert Elias, *Baseball and the American Dream* (Armonk, NY: M. E. Sharpe Press, 2001). p. 158.

[75] The vile racism by some of the game's all-time greats, such as Ty Cobb for example, needs no further elaboration here.

baseball and led to the demise of the Negro League one decade later.[76] Women's teams began appearing throughout the country at the end of the nineteenth century, and were common until the Midwest's notable All-American Girls Baseball League ended in 1954.[77] After that point, women were mostly left to play softball, a sport in which they had participated since its development in 1904.[78]

Baseball became not only America's pastime but also its "people's game," very much the structural and cultural equivalent to soccer in Europe and Latin America. It developed into an essential part of American identity and became the country's most important sport until the late 1950s. Indeed, many baseball expressions entered the American vernacular to a degree unparalleled by any other sport in any other language. Thus, baseball became an integral linguistic ingredient of American English, demonstrating prima facie the game's profound importance for American culture and the actual affinity between a hegemonic sport's identity as a language and its "real" language.[79]

Yet, the game's international reach remained rather limited. In a recent study on the globalization of baseball, Alan Klein argues that baseball "entered the global arena in an institutional and business sense later than the National Basketball Association and the National Football League." However, Brooklyn Dodgers General Manager Branch Rickey commenced baseball's internationalization seventy years ago. Rickey not only lifted the barriers that had kept African Americans out of organized baseball. His unconventional approach and innovative methods also led him to recruit players from around the world as early as the 1940s.[80]

Yet, baseball's limited first international reach began long before that. In

[76] See Todd Bolton, "History of the Negro Major Leagues," *Negro League Baseball Players Association*. Retrieved August 13, 2008, from www.nlbpa.com.

[77] See Ellen Klages, "The Girls of Summer," Exploratorium.edu. Retrieved August 13, 2008.

[78] See "Historical Facts About Softball," www.athleticscholarships.net. Retrieved August 13, 2008.

[79] No team sport anywhere in the world has spawned nearly the amount of literature as has baseball. Jacques Barzun, the great French-born student of American culture and legendary professor at Columbia University, knew whereof he was speaking when he stated: "Whoever wants to know the heart and mind of America had better learn baseball, the rules and realities of the game—and do it by watching first some high school or small-town teams." Markovits assembled fifty-six baseball expressions that have become integral parts of the American vernacular. We are certain that there are many more. See Markovits and Hellerman, *Offside*, pp. 65 and 66.

[80] Alan M. Klein, *Growing the Game: The Globalization of Major League Baseball* (New Haven: Yale University Press, 2006), pp. 5, 6. This initial integration can be viewed as a local strategy with global repercussions. Dodgers owner Walter O'Malley's following efforts in

the 1870s, Albert Spalding, whose sporting goods empire was to cover the world market already before World War I, toured the world—Europe included—in order to export baseball to other countries and cultures. This failed abysmally for reasons beyond our purview, though the apparent complexity of the game and the fleeting presence of the teams engaged in these exhibitions certainly did not help endear this game to these populations.. But baseball most assuredly became a popular sports language in parts of the Caribbean and a bit later in Japan. In places like the Dominican Republic, Cuba, Venezuela, Puerto Rico, Panama, Mexico, Japan, South Korea, and Taiwan (referred to as Chinese Taipei in baseball), baseball attained great local and national significance. These countries' top players have regularly entered Major League Baseball, the game's pinnacle, since the 1950s; however, coinciding with the time frame of second globalization, their presence has rendered what was previously largely an American endeavor into one of the most international cultural entities on North American soil.

Still, the ongoing internationalization of MLB needs to be placed into its proper historical context. Dominicans and Cubans were the first to make the game their own in the late nineteenth century, around the time that soccer started to spread to the European continent from England. In the Dominican Republic, for example, the formal inauguration of the game is claimed to have occurred in 1891, when the two clubs El Cauto and Cervecería were founded (though the game was actually played earlier in a pre-club, less organized fashion). After a period of steady growth under the aegis of amateurism, Dominican baseball became increasingly professionalized in the 1920s. Parallel to baseball's development in Mexico, the game took root in the Dominican Republic's urban centers and the upper classes, from where it spread to general society.[81]

In the early twentieth century, baseball experienced major growth in much of the Caribbean. The professionalization of Dominican baseball "coincided with an increased presence of the best clubs of Cuba, Puerto Rico, and Venezuela, as well as Americans affiliated with the military. First they came on casual visits, then as part of the U.S. Marines' occupation of the country from 1916 to 1924."[82] Dominican players went abroad, and the professional league hired foreign players in turn. By the 1937 season, Do-

---

protoglobalization, by building ties with Japan and the Caribbean, opened subsequent global possibilities.

[81] See Alan M. Klein, *Baseball on the Border: A Tale of Two Laredos* (Princeton: Princeton University Press, 1997).

[82] Klein, *Growing the Game*, p. 93.

minican professional baseball excited the masses with an unprecedented
level of play and competition and arguably some of the world's best teams.
The defending champions San Pedro de Macorís' roster was mainly
Cuban, showing yet again the potentially cosmopolitan nature of professional sports.

After Ciudad Trujillo's championship victory, which was celebrated by
crowds dancing in the capital, professional baseball fell into a deep crisis in
the Dominican Republic and collapsed shortly thereafter—a development
that is paralleled in other Caribbean states. Steady growth and professionalization were no guarantees for economic success and the spawning of
elaborate organizational structures in the form of lasting leagues. Nonetheless, the game's long tradition and cultural rootedness enabled baseball's later Dominican revival. By 1955, the Dominican game had become
serious again, and its international relationship with powerful Major
League Baseball was formalized in many ways, of which the talent acade-
mies were merely one.[83] Klein argues that only in the age of the second
globalization have the "changes that have been wrought in and through
baseball in the Dominican Republic . . . been so far-reaching as to force all
of us to rethink the trajectory of the sport there."[84] Nationalism and cultural resilience—expressed, for example, in preferences for local over foreign caps—against perceived American baseball colonialism has given way
to a new professionalization,[85] through which Dominican managers have
become counterweights to MLB's hegemony. Meanwhile Dominican superstars in the American major leagues—like Pedro Martinez, Alex Rodriguez, Manny Ramirez, Miguel Tejada, Sammy Sosa, and David "Big Papi"
Ortiz, to mention but a few among the dozens of players from the Dominican Republic who comprise the largest contingent of foreign players
in MLB—are not only national heroes but also serve as multinational role
models to a cosmopolitan and transnational generation of fans well beyond
the Dominican Republic (the country of their origin) and the United
States (the country of their performance). These exceptional figures have
indeed become global players in every sense of how we construe this term
in our study.

Rounding out this very quick Caribbean tour, the Cuban prowess in
baseball needs no elaboration. The island has been a constant feeder of

[83] Ibid., p. 95.

[84] Ibid., p. 124.

[85] See Tim Wendel, *The New Face of Baseball: The One-Hundred-Year Rise and Triumph of Latinos in America's Favorite Sport* (New York: Rayo, 2003); Alan M. Klein, *Sugarball: The American Game, the Dominican Dream* (New Haven: Yale University Press, 1991).

superb talent to the stateside majors. It has produced players like Minnie Minoso ("The Cuban Comet") who, by signing with the Cleveland Indians in 1948, was among the first Latin players to join the "Bigs"; and legendary pitchers like Luis Tiant ("El Tiante") and the Hernandez brothers Orlando ("El Duque") and Livan. During the Castro regime, Cuba came to dominate international baseball, especially the Olympics.[86] Lastly, we would be remiss not to mention Venezuela, the land of legendary shortstops—from Chico Carrasquel through Luis Aparicio, Dave Concepcion, Ozzie Guillen to Omar Vizquel—whose smooth elegance and excellence have graced the majors for more than six decades; Curaçao, which has produced first-rate major league players like Andruw Jones; and, of course, Panama, homeland of Mariano Rivera, without any question the greatest relief pitcher of all time.

But baseball went beyond America's most proximate geographic purview during the early consolidation of sports cultures. In Japan, the emergence of baseball as a hegemonic sport and national pastime was intimately linked to modernization. It is no coincidence that the rise of baseball correlated with the growth of nationalism in the Meiji Restoration (1868–1912), a movement that facilitated Japan's formation as a modern state and expedited the country's rapid introduction to Western culture. Under the Meiji Emperor Mutsushito's government, administrative and educational institutions followed European and American models; and baseball received pride of place as part of the new Japanese physical educational system introduced by the American missionary teacher Horace Wilson.[87] Identified with the United States and its perceived cutting-edge philosophy of education, the game quickly took root and gained importance in Japan in the late nineteenth century. The Japanese reconfigured baseball to become "Japanese" by fusing it with traditional elements and by disseminating it from the elite level to the masses. In fact baseball became "one area in which tensions between emerging modernism and hallowed traditions were defused."[88] At the same time, the imported sport of baseball immediately served as a Japanese cultural tool for anti-Western nationalism when it was turned into an expression of an independent Japanese culture. And nothing created a greater thrill and more emphatic nationalist

[86] We would like to draw the reader's attention to Roberto González Echevarria's *The Pride of Havanna: A History of Cuban Baseball* (New York: Oxford University Press, 1999) as a superb account of that country's hegemonic sports culture.

[87] See Allen Guttmann and Lee Thompson, *Japanese Sports: A History* (Honolulu: University of Hawaii Press, 2001); Klein, *Growing the Game*, pp. 147, 148.

[88] Klein, *Growing the Game*, p. 147.

celebrations than a victory over an American team even before the start of the twentieth century.

Baseball's special path in Japan as part of an imported, transnational sports culture, on the one hand, and tradition-bound assertions of a specifically molded modern nationalism on the other, find their reflection in the game's development until the era of our contemporary globalization. Only now have company-owned teams operating under the aegis of Japanese nationalism and protectionism, come under increasingly "postindustrial" pressure. The all-star series between MLB and Nippon Professional Baseball dates back to 1908, when the Reach All–Americans went to Japan for a nineteen-game tour.[89] American all-star teams have toured Japan regularly in the past and a number of former big leaguers and MLB managers joined Japanese clubs.

In the contemporary era of the second globalization process, we have begun to see an increasingly transnational flow of the game to and from Japan, with Japanese star players like Hideki Matsui, Ichiro Suzuki, and Daisuke Matsuzaka, among others, becoming stars stateside. Also, a contract is in place that pays MLB $275 million for the rights to have its games televised and broadcast in Japan.[90] MLB treats its extensive contacts with Japan as its most important global asset.[91] Japan's singularly important position in MLB's international endeavors has also emerged by way of commencing the 2008 MLB season in Japan. The Boston Red Sox and the Oakland Athletics played the first two games of their 162-game season in Japan, not as exhibitions, but as meaningful contests that counted in the pennant race.

Only in recent years did baseball make significant headway in countries like Italy, Holland (with many of its players and fans hailing from Curaçao and other islands of the Netherlands Antilles), Russia, China, South Korea, South Africa, and Australia. The sport can now claim to have a legitimate presence in these country's sports cultures. Indeed, baseball celebrated its second World Baseball Classic in March of 2009. Very much following

[89] Ibid., p. 241.

[90] Increasingly, Japanese spectators want to see the best of the best. Of course, this transnational success of the world's best baseball league is also due to a nationalist element, namely the increasing presence of Japanese players in MLB. The Japanese star players in MLB have a coterie of Japanese reporters following their every move and reporting to the Japanese baseball-obsessed public on every detail of their lives in the Big Leagues. Games in which these stars play draw huge television audiences in Japan despite the fact that most of these games occur at inconvenient viewing times, most typically very early in the morning on weekdays.

[91] Klein, *Growing the Game*, p. 242.

soccer's World Cup model, MLB has organized a quadrennial tournament in March before the beginning of the regular season, in which national all-star teams representing the top sixteen baseball-playing countries compete for a world championship. The World Baseball Classic tournament enjoys increasing popularity among players, organizers, and, most important of all, fans.[92] As a consequence of this recent internationalization of the game, many more foreign players have entered the purview of American top-level baseball teams. The Minnesota Twins, for instance, had sixteen Australians under contract in 2005. Even in countries such as Germany and England, baseball is in the process of gaining a tentative footing in scattered pockets. We would be remiss not to mention the Little League World Series, which has been held annually in Williamsport, Pennsylvania

[92] A particularly sad setback for baseball has been its being banned from the Olympics as of the London Games in 2012. Together with its close cousin, women's softball, baseball became the first sport to be dropped from the Olympic program since polo in 1936. Baseball became a demonstration sport in 1984 and had been a medal sport since 1992. Cuba won three of the five gold medals since then, with the United States claiming gold in 2000 with a team of minor leaguers representing the country. The South Korean team prevailed at the 2008 Olympics in Beijing, where the Americans won the bronze medal. In a surprising follow-up to the vote to drop baseball and softball, the IOC first decided not to add any sports to take their place. However, at its meeting of August 13, 2009, the IOC reversed itself by making golf and rugby sevens—not even the game's union or league codes—Olympic sports as of 2016, once again maintaining its exclusion of baseball and softball. In the banning of baseball and softball, we are witnessing a willful, though constantly denied, anti-Americanism by the Europe-dominated IOC, which has repeatedly voiced its irritation with things American. The IOC has disliked softball on account of vast American dominance, which has led the American women to destroy their opposition in every single Olympic contest they played on their way to three Olympic gold medals in 1996, 2000, and 2004. Ironically, after the IOC had banned softball from the London Olympics in 2012, Team USA lost the gold medal game to Japan in the Beijing Olympics, thereby becoming the victim of one of the largest upsets in the history of team sports (most assuredly the least expected outcome of the entire Beijing Games). Oddly, the U.S. team's loss to Japan should have been prima facie evidence that the alleged domination of the Americans was at least being contested by other teams, if not yet permanently challenged. If the IOC banned women's softball on account of the American dominance at the Olympic games, it proceeded to do the same with men's baseball in good part because its officials felt irritated by MLB's categorical rejection of the IOC's wishes to have the season interrupted in the middle of August—just as the pennant races begin to capture the attention of the American sports public—to have the game's stars represent their respective home countries at the Olympics. With the National Hockey League obliging the IOC by suspending its season in the middle of February in having its stars play for their countries at the winter Olympics, the IOC expected no less from MLB. MLB's refusal to comply with the IOC's wishes irked the latter, since it was clear that the Olympic baseball tournament did not attract the top players in the game, with the possible exception of the Cubans. In fairness to the IOC, MLB's steroid problems did not help its cause with a crowd that was a priori ill-disposed toward the game. Baseball—too weak; softball—too strong; both cases fed the IOC's anti-American sentiments to take punitive measures against two sports which have been important to American sports culture.

since 1947, with international teams prominently participating from the tournament's inception. Consistently gaining in popularity and attention in the United States and all the participating countries where it is avidly followed on television, it is important to note that of the 63 champions thus far, 32 hailed from the United States but 31 from the international sides—with Taiwan (Chinese Taipei) furnishing 17 champions, followed by Japan with 6, Mexico with 3, South Korea and Venezuela with 2 each, and Curaçao with 1.

Even though MLB operates on the world stage now and has launched renewed globalization efforts—after the game's limited successes in the first globalization—and even if there are increasingly international rosters on its professional teams stateside, baseball is by no means yet a major global game and language. Thus, for example, even though 239 international players appeared on the rosters of MLB teams at the beginning of the 2008 season (comprising 28 percent of all major leaguers) the vast majority of these hailed from countries such as the Dominican Republic (which was the leader), Venezuela, Puerto Rico, and other Central American and Caribbean states with players from Japan, South Korea, and Australia still few and far between. For the game to become truly global, baseball will have to find a way to increase the breadth of its geographic reach but, more important perhaps, the depth in the quality of its play and players in the sports spaces of Europe, Africa, parts of Latin America beyond the Caribbean, and in Asia beyond Japan, South Korea, and Chinese Taipei.

Hockey's Internationalization in the Wake of the Second Globalization

A decidedly non-American but instead North American export, the Canadian game of hockey had more success across the Atlantic than baseball; among other things, it shaped the hegemonic sports culture in countries such as Sweden, Finland, the Czech Republic, Slovakia, and most important, of course, the Soviet Union/Russia. The game has also enjoyed considerable success in Germany, Austria, Switzerland, France, and northern Italy. Despite hockey's substantial cultural presence in these countries, the game's impact remained regionalized, just like it did within the United States. Here it became an undisputed part of hegemonic sports culture in the Northeast and the upper Midwest, but has remained well below the cultural significance of baseball, basketball, and football in the rest of the country. Hockey, though popular in key countries of the world, never evolved into a truly universal sport language—played, followed, understood, and appreciated across the globe—quite possibly, of course, by dint of its still being primarily a winter sport and almost exclusively confined to this planet's northern hemisphere. Still, few leagues have witnessed such a speedy transformation from the strictly local to the global as has the NHL. In nary the course of a decade, the league mutated from a Canadian fraternity with a sprinkling of Americans in the mid- to late 1980s, to a highly international construct with players from Finland, Russia, the Czech Republic, Slovakia, Sweden, Germany, Austria, and Belarus displaying their skill and prowess alongside their Canadian and American colleagues by the 1990s. For the 2007–8 season, 213 of the 744 NHL players—28.6 percent—hailed from places outside North America.

Moreover, just like MLB, the NHL also commenced its regular season with games played abroad, first in London in the fall of 2007, followed by immensely successful outings in Prague and Stockholm in 2008, and equally successful season-opening games in Stockholm and Helsinki in 2009.[93] The establishment of the Russian Super League (RSL) in 1999—from the remnants of the old Soviet hockey leagues and divisions—bespeaks of the game's growing internationalization and Russia's increasing financial might in the wake of the second globalization process. The RSL's mutation into the well-financed and highly marketed Kontinental Hockey League (KHL) in the 2007–8 season represents a potential challenge to the NHL's supremacy as the globe's undisputed premier professional hockey entity. Indeed, the KHL has successfully wooed away superstars such as the Czech legend Jaromir Jagr and the Russian forward Alexei Yashin from the NHL. A sufficient number of foreign players earned their keep in the KHL's debut season to have its first All-Star game feature a contest between an all-Russian team led by Yashin and an all-foreigner side captained by Jagr. However, as long as Russia's very best players—superstars like Alexander Ovechkin, Evgeni Malkin, and Pavel Datsyuk—happily and lucratively ply their trade in the NHL, and no top Canadian or American players show any inclination to join the KHL, the NHL will continue to maintain its global hegemony in the sport.

Basketball's Enduring Rise as the Second Most Popular Global Sport

In contrast to hockey, basketball, exported mainly through American missionaries and the Young Men's Christian Associations (YMCA), developed

---

[93] In 2009, the two opening games in Stockholm featured the Detroit Red Wings who—by dint of having eight Swedish players on their roster, some of them superstars—enjoyed home ice for all intents and purposes against the St. Louis Blues. Despite this de facto advantage, the Wings lost both games.

into a global success already at the beginning of the twentieth century and emerged by that century's end as the world's undisputed second most popular sports language following soccer.

Basketball's invention by Dr. James A. Naismith, a Canadian educator at the YMCA Training School in Springfield, Massachusetts, is too well-known to be repeated here in detail. In 1891, hoping to create an indoor sport for his students to play during the winter, Naismith devised the game of basketball as an explicit counterpoint to what he perceived as the brutality of football and the boredom of gymnastics. He authored a list of thirteen rules (which still remain valid in the contemporary game) and, with a soccer ball and two peach baskets, basketball was born in the YMCA gym.[94] Naismith's students would soon export the game to Canada and Japan in its first globalizing move, but it was mostly via American YMCAs—where some of the first competitive games were held—that organized basketball became established. Women played the game almost immediately, when in 1894 Smith College freshmen and sophomores decided to hold a game of their own.

By 1896 a team from Trenton, New Jersey became basketball's first professional outfit on the men's side, and the turn of the century ushered in the era of barnstorming basketball teams mostly from America's East Coast. Eastern schools, some of which now belong to the Ivy League, initiated the first serious college basketball games around the same time. The first lasting professional league, the National Basketball League (NBL), was founded in 1937; it would merge with the Basketball Association of America (BAA) established in 1946, and the two leagues rechristened their merger as the National Basketball Association (NBA) in 1949. When the NBA first emerged as America's premier basketball league, attendance was rather modest. For the 1946–47 season, the Boston Celtics averaged about 3,600 fans per game. Just ten years later, however, that number had jumped to over 10,500.[95] Still, the NBA remained a distant orphan to baseball, then the nation's uncontested sports pastime.

[94] See History of Basketball, "Dr. James Naismith, Inventor of Basketball," *Kansas History Web Sites*. www.kansashistory.us (March 16, 2006). Retrieved August 12, 2008. Some argue that basketball is a distant cousin of the English game netball, which was probably known to Dr. Naismith. Suffice it to say that among all the ball games discussed in this book, basketball is the most likely to be labeled an "in vitro" candidate, meaning that it emerged as a particular person's invention at a particular time and location that we can pinpoint with certainty. In contrast to all the football games (that had predecessors in ancient Rome and China, among other parts of the world), as well as baseball (that belongs to the bat and ball sports that have roots and traces all over the world well into antiquity), basketball has no such early and distant precursors at all.

[95] Boston Celtics Attendance (2007). www.databasebasketball.com. Retrieved August 15, 2008.

The country's first major college tournament, the National Invitational Tournament (NIT), was inaugurated in New York City in 1938, where it continues to feature that tournament's final games to this day. In direct response to the NIT's initiative, the NCAA began sponsoring its own tournament the following year. It pulled even with the NIT in terms of importance and prestige by the late 1940s, surpassed it by the late 1950s, and became the juggernaut of March Madness by the late 1970s which continues to grow in prominence from year to year.[96] (We discuss this in greater detail in chapter 6, which features college sports.)

While East Coast universities introduced basketball to the American elite, community centers like the YMCA brought the game to city dwellers everywhere, even abroad. Though segregation haunted the game early, black teams competed against white ones in the first ballroom and barnstorming leagues.[97] In the 1942–43 season, the NBL broke new ground in America's race relations by allowing black players; the college game would take longer to integrate African Americans.[98] In 1966, the late Don Haskins' all-black starting lineup at regional Texas Western University beat Adolph Rupp's all-white powerhouse University of Kentucky in the national championship to end once and for all segregated basketball in America.[99] There can be no question that this event marked a milestone in America's race relations and its sports culture that nearly equaled Jackie Robinson's playing for the Brooklyn Dodgers in the 1947 season.

Almost as soon as basketball emerged as a viable game, it was ready for export. In addition to Japan and Canada, China, via YMCA missionaries, would also witness the game before the turn of the century.[100] Competitive basketball reached the Philippines in 1912, and professional play began in Italy in 1920[101] and Greece in 1928.[102] By 1936, twenty-two nations competed in the first Olympic basketball contest.[103] Israeli professional play

[96] History of Basketball (2004). www.sportsknowhow.com. Retrieved August 12, 2008.

[97] John Bloom, and Michael Nevin Willard, *Sports Matters: Race, Recreation, and Culture* (New York: New York University Press, 2002), p. 41.

[98] Douglas Stark, "Paving the Way," *Basketball Digest*, February 2001. Retrieved August 12, 2008, from www.findarticles.com.

[99] Hall Of Fame Feature (1997), *Basketball Hall Of Fame*. Retrieved August 12, 2008 from www.hoophall.com.

[100] Grant Farred, *Phantom Calls: Race and the Globalization of the NBA* (Chicago: Prickly Paradigm Press, 2006), p. 3.

[101] Nathan, "Travelling: Notes on Basketball and Globalization," p. 739.

[102] Introduction to Greek Basketball (2008), *Eurobasket*. Retrieved August 15, 2008, from www.eurobasket.com.

[103] Nathan, "Travelling: Notes on Basketball and Globalization," p. 738.

emerged in 1954[104], and in 1958 intercontinental play began in the Euroleague.[105]

Far and away *the* most important agents in the successful globalization of basketball are the Harlem Globetrotters. The "Trotters," founded in 1926 by a London-born Chicago Jew named Abe Saperstein, played legendary games throughout the late 1930s and early1940s against another all-black team called the New York Renaissance Five, better known as the Rens.[106] Indeed, it was the Rens that beat the Trotters in the first tournament labeled a World Championship played in Chicago in 1939, with the Trotters returning the favor one year later. After World War II, the Trotters commenced their continued globe-trotting, which they have yet to stop. They have played well over 20,000 exhibition games in more than 120 countries. Trotters' warm ups to the tune of "Sweet Georgia Brown", their various antics, humor, and fabulous ball skills have delighted hundreds of millions over the years and continue to frustrate their opponents such as the Washington Generals, the Trotters' best-known and most abused hapless foil. The Trotters have performed in front of more live audiences throughout the world than any other sports team of any kind in history.[107] But recall our earlier mention of the Trotters: Since virtually all their games after World War II were scripted, this legendary team has engaged in entertainment rather than in bona fide sports over the past six decades, which in no way is meant to diminish the success and social importance of its endeavors. Rather, it just goes to show how blurry the boundaries between sports and entertainment really are.

While basketball filtered into the world virtually immediately upon its

[104] Maccabi Tel Aviv – History Review. *Maccabi Electra Tel Aviv Basketball Club.* Retrieved August 15, 2008, from www.maccabi.co.il.

[105] "February 22, 1958: The Day It All Started" (2008), *Euroleague Basketball.* Retrieved August 15, 2008, from www.euroleague.net.

[106] For an overview see William Gleason, "Harlem Globetrotters," in Cary D. Wintz and Paul Finkelman, eds., *Encyclopedia of the Harlem Renaissance* (New York: Routledge, 2004); for earlier popular accounts, see Dave Zinkoff with Edgar Williams, *Around the World with the Harlem Globetrotters* (Philadelphia: McRae Smith, 1953); Chuck Melville, *The Harlem Globetrotters* (New York: David McKay, 1978).

[107] The Harlem Globetrotters' game on August 21, 1951 in Berlin's Olympic Stadium attracted more than 75,000 spectators, set the world's record for live attendance at a basketball game. Further enhancing this special event—that occurred on the Trotters' global tour celebrating the twenty-fifth anniversary of their founding—was the fact that just before the game, a helicopter landed in the middle of the stadium with Jesse Owens emerging from the chopper. This record stood until December 13, 2003, when the Kentucky Wildcats defeated the Michigan State Spartans in front of 78,129 spectators at Detroit's Ford Field. But on February 14, 2010, the NBA's 59th All Star Game, held at Cowboys Stadium in Arlington, Texas, attracted an incredible 108,713 spectators.

invention in America, it has been mainly in the past two- to three decades that the game experienced unprecedented growth in many countries. Today, FIBA (basketball's international governing body) has more than 210 national federation members; more than 450 million people play the sport worldwide,[108] among them an estimated 300 million Chinese. While the United States thoroughly dominated international competition from its onset, recent years have seen a much more even playing field. In 2004, Argentina took Olympic gold, and Spain earned the title at the 2006 World Championships.[109]

Certainly the present state of the NBA furnishes a solid example of the recent internationalization of basketball. The NBA boasted 81 foreign players from 35 countries, amounting to 17.8 percent of the league's players in 2008,[110] with 3 of the previous 6 number one draft picks having been foreign.[111] The growing presence of foreign draftees in the league has been remarkable. Thus, only 4 foreign players were drafted by NBA teams in 1994, while this figure nearly quintupled to 18 in 2005.[112] There is absolutely no doubt that the appearance of the legendary "Dream Team"— anchored by Earvin "Magic" Johnson, Larry Bird, and Michael Jordan at the Barcelona Olympics in 1992—massively contributed to basketball's and the NBA's meteoric proliferation in the world. It is well-known that many NBA stars hailing from abroad, such as Dirk Nowitzki, for example, fell in love with the game via the unique ambassadorship of the 1992 "Dreamers."

The global popularity of the former NBA superstar Michael Jordan represents another stepping-stone and global breakthrough. It marks the beginning of basketball's second globalization in the 1980s and 1990s.[113]

---

[108] Nathan, "Travelling: Notes on Basketball and Globalization," p. 738.

[109] Ibid.

[110] Farred, *Phantom Calls*, p. 11.

[111] Nathan, "Travelling: Notes on Basketball and Globalization," p. 738.

[112] Farred, *Phantom Calls*, pp. 11–2.

[113] See Andrews, Carrington, Jackson, Mazur, "Jordanscapes." Andrews et al. argue too economistically, however, because they largely focus on Jordan as "everybody's All-American commodity sign," reducing Jordan's immense global popularity and ubiquity to "Nike et al.'s desire to exploit largely untapped external markets," a "hugely successful transnational stratagem [that] resulted in Jordan's thereby Nike's and latterly the NBA's, conclusive entry into the inventory of the 'global popular.'" (pp. 431, 432). The authors do recognize, though, "the emancipatory potential offered via the strategic localized appropriation of global icons such as Michael Jordan" (p. 453). Likewise, Walter LaFeber strongly accentuates the economic aspect of the "globalization of Michael Jordan" and the role of transnational corporations; see Walter LaFeber, *Michael Jordan and the New Global Capitalism* (New York: W. W. Norton, 1996). In opposition to that, we claim that while economic incentives and global outreach represent significant factors in the globalization of sports, complex cultural dynamics are

Today, the more ambitious and increasingly powerful professional European basketball leagues in Spain, Italy, Greece, and Israel are beginning to lure potential, and even current, NBA players to Europe. The Charlotte Bobcats' Earl Boykins transferred to Virtus Bologna, Josh Childress left the Atlanta Hawks for Olympiakos Piraeus, and Carlos Arroyo moved from the Orlando Magic to Maccabi Tel Aviv. Meanwhile CSKA Moscow and Olympiakos have been rumored to woo LeBron James.[114] Even though such courtships will never succeed no matter how much either team is prepared to lavish on James—in good part because a player of such rare talent will always want to earn his living among the best of the best—the very fact that such rumors exist and that such teams even contemplate such an unprecedented step bespeaks of the increasingly successful globalization of this erstwhile American game.

Well before the NHL and MLB began to showcase their respective products outside the United States, an NBA team had already played a top European one in 1987. The Milwaukee Bucks defeated Tracer Milan in the opening game of the first McDonald's Open in Milwaukee. The Bucks then defeated the Soviet National Team in the championship game of the tournament, which was sanctioned by the NBA and FIBA. One year later, the Boston Celtics defeated Real Madrid at the Palacio de Deportes in Madrid, the first time that the McDonald's Championship, sometimes called the McDonald's Open was played in Europe. These tournaments continued on a yearly basis, featuring such NBA teams as, among others, the Atlanta Hawks, the San Antonio Spurs, and the Los Angeles Lakers, and such top European sides as Joventut Badalona, Jugoplastika Split, as well as other fine teams from Spain, Italy, Croatia, and later from Greece and Israel. It was not until 1993 that the first pre-season game between two NBA teams was played in Europe, with the Atlanta Hawks battling the Orlando Magic in two games at London's Wembley Arena. By the beginning of the twenty-first century, the appearance of NBA teams in Europe had attained such regularity and was crowned with so much success that the notion of the NBA's expansion to such cities as Paris, London, Madrid, and Berlin was not out of the question. But nowhere were the NBA's touring teams and games crowned with greater success than in China.

---

much more important to understand the success or failure of global sports and their playing icons like Jordan. Their global popularity and local appropriations cannot simply be viewed as the direct outcome of capitalist advertising strategies. Neither can globalization in general be reduced to economic dimensions.

[114]"Europa gegen die NBA: Kampf um jeden Spieler," http://www.spiegel.de/sport/sonst/0,1518,578790,00.html. Retrieved September 18, 2008.

China, more than any other country, provides the most dramatic example of basketball's second globalization, and displays the most impressive impact made by global players. Only since China's economic boom, temporally coinciding with the second globalization, has the popularity of basketball exploded in that huge country. Basketball, which started in China more than a century ago but was frowned upon during the anti-Western Cultural Revolution,[115] is thereby following, and to some extent even exceeding, soccer's recent successes there. Today both sports compete for the top position in China's sports culture. Starting with the Michael Jordan boom, basketball had already exploded in China in the 1990s; its major breakthrough into cultural hegemony, however, was not complete until Yao Ming entered the scene and became an NBA star and global player. Ming was the Houston Rockets' first pick in the 2002 NBA draft, which elevated basketball's and the NBA's presence in China to another level. A rather unimportant early season game in November of 2007—between the Houston Rockets, featuring Yao Ming, and the Milwaukee Bucks, with Yi Jianlian in the lineup, the sixth pick in the 2007 NBA draft—attracted more than 200 million television viewers and was broadcast by nineteen television networks in China. The Rockets and Yao Ming, now an all-star center, have become daily front-page news in China. A country of 1.3 billion citizens, China, as already mentioned, has more than 300 million active basketball players, with basketball courts everywhere. In recent surveys, 83 percent of Chinese males aged 15 to 24 said they were NBA fans, and more than 40 percent stated that basketball was their favorite sport to play and that four of their top five most favored athletes were NBA players.[116]

The cosmopolitan dynamics and their impact in China extend far beyond the import of a sports culture and the social changes that accompany it. It also exceeds the nationalist enthusiasm for Yao Ming confirming the presence of the "glocal" in these intricate cultural currents and countercurrents. Without the national and local that Yao embodied for millions of Chinese, their interest in the NBA would have remained much more meager. Yet again we have evidence that global attraction gains real traction only if it is somehow linked to the local.

Once such an anchor is secured, then the admiration for the world's best league and the most qualified players transcends national boundaries and local identities. Case in point: Kobe Bryant jerseys outsell Yao Ming's in

[115] See Alexander Wolff, *Big Game, Small World* (New York: Warner Books, 2002).
[116] See http://www.chinatownconnection.com/china-basketball.htm. Retrieved June 1, 2008.

China, and Bryant is arguably China's biggest national celebrity.[117] But he might soon be displaced by LeBron James or Shaquille O'Neal, both of whom have made it their business (quite literally!) to visit China regularly during the NBA's off-season. And both have met with immense popularity and attention by the Chinese media and the public. There are few other, if any, cultural phenomena that similarly signify the cosmopolitan impact of globalized sports in China, or for that matter anywhere in the world.

And in many ways, China's involvement with basketball and the NBA is merely a beginning. Today the NBA has an estimated 450 million Chinese fans. And the NBA supports the country's goal of building 800,000 basketball courts.[118] The NBA and Anschutz Entertainment Group (AEG) announced plans on October 11th, 2008 to design and operate at least a dozen arenas in China, extending the league's presence in its largest foreign market. The arenas could form the infrastructure of an NBA-branded league in China.

The NBA's business interests in China have been growing for nearly thirty years. The league has one hundred employees in four cities, and fifteen marketing partners. A third of the online traffic to NBA.com comes from the Mandarin Chinese part of the site, and league merchandise is sold at 30,000 retailers in China, among them two official NBA stores. In addition, NBA games are available on fifty-one networks in China, where 1.6 billion viewers watched programming in the 2007–8 season. One of China's NBA stars, the aforementioned Yi Jianlian—having departed from the Milwaukee Bucks to play for the New Jersey Nets—has been actively marketed and promoted as linking the New Jersey (future Brooklyn or New York?) Nets and the New York metropolitan region's large Chinese-American community.[119] Indeed, the second Yi–Yao confrontation, with the first meeting between the Houston Rockets and the New Jersey Nets in the 2008 NBA season, was not only a major attraction for Chinese basketball fans in New York City's tri-state region, but it also equalled these two Chinese NBA stars' first encounter in the 2007 season by drawing 200 million viewers back home in China.

Obviously, such speedy, sudden, and gargantuan developments have caused plenty of friction and resistance on the local level. Thus, the NBA's extensive presence in China and the Chinese public's access to the global

---

[117] Pete Thamel, "The N.B.A. and China Are Fans of Each Other: League Has Big Hopes for Basketball-Crazed Country," *New York Times*, August 10, 2008, SportsSunday section, p. 7.
[118] Ibid.
[119] Richard Sandomir, "N.B.A. and Partner to Help Build 12 Arenas in China," *New York Times*, October 12, 2008.

best via the myriad means of communication have also harmed basketball's local existence. "The Chinese Basketball Association has hardly enjoyed a smooth ascendance alongside this country's basketball boom. American agents describe broken contracts, unpaid wages, suspicions of game-fixing and rising resentment toward foreign players," reports Dan Levin in the *New York Times*.[120] While Chinese fans and players might very well adore global stars such as Kobe Bryant and LeBron James, they resent the presence of unknown foreigners, whom they see as making too much money and dominating the game, thereby impeding the careers of local Chinese players. A dosage of counter-cosmopolitan xenophobia and resentment seems hardly surprising as an almost automatic antidote to such a rapidly changing situation in culture and identity. Despite these inevitable tensions, there can be no doubt that by any measure basketball's overall success in China and the world has been nothing short of stellar in the wake of the second globalization.

The (Largely) Failed Globalization of American Football

Like a number of the rugby variants of football that developed in a "Protestant" or "Orthodox" manner (meaning that they became autonomous entities in the countries and regions in which they were established—as in American football, Canadian football, Gaelic football, Australian [Rules] Football—thus differing markedly from the "Catholic" organizing principle of the Association game that, certainly from 1904 onward, established a global hierarchy headed by the pope-like FIFA that never tolerated any country-specific variations whatsoever in the game over which it lorded), American football remained confined to U.S. territory. This is already conveyed prima facie by its name, which often carries the specifying adjective "American" in it when the game is discussed in any context beyond the confines of the United States. The game has gained occasional attention abroad—especially in Europe—since the 1980s.[121] Games draw big crowds

---

[120] Dan Levin, "In Basketball Boom in China, Hard Times for Its Pro League," *New York Times*, July 23, 2009.

[121] Football entered the European cultural space after 1980. Up to 3.7 million British viewers, mostly younger male professionals, and male members of the lower middle-class, watched Channel 4's broadcast of American football in 1987–88 on a regular basis. Before the mid 1980s, football had scant audiences outside the United States. However, 61,000 saw the final for the "World Bowl" in Wembley in 1991. Yet, interest dwindled throughout the 1990s. The final of the competition for the National Bowl in England drew only 2,500 spectators. In Europe, the cultural impact of the game remained at best marginal and had its ups and downs since the 1980s on the local and supranational level. The World Bowl did not survive; neither did the NFL's satellite project NFL Europe and the Euro Bowl. Football's highest popularity

and are appreciated as spectacles in Europe and increasingly beyond. Yet the NFL's main attempt at globalization by forming a real league abroad by way of NFL Europe, collapsed after a few years because it could not gain any lasting cultural traction among large segments of the sports-enthused public across the continent beyond the fleeting interest accorded to spectacles and events. The game did not spread nearly as far or deep as one might have expected, at least at the beginning of the "second globalization" and after the initial positive response it received in the 1980s.[122] This failure thus refuted crude globalization theories that foresaw a cultural homogeneity under an American aegis and that feared the Americanization of Europe's sports culture by, among others, American football's inroads in Europe's sports space at the expense of soccer. Put bluntly, while the Super Bowl has indeed become a global media phenomenon, and NFL jerseys are much-worn and coveted by young Europeans, particularly of the hip-hop generation, the game itself has never come close to becoming part of European sports culture in any meaningful sense—that is, what Europeans "breathe, read, discuss, analyze, compare, and historicize" on a daily basis.[123]

While sports spaces are subject to constant change in that they shrink and expand, such cultural shifts rarely happen overnight and most certainly not on their own. Rather, such changes are linked to agency, altered balances of power between and within nations, and critical junctures at key cultural openings.[124] In a historically informed crossnational comparative study of American football's fate in Europe, Maarten Van Bottenburg explains the game's failure as a spectator sport by pointing to a lack of a basic foundation for the sport at the grass-roots level. In sharp contrast to basketball (as well as volleyball, and forms of hockey on lawn or ice), which

---

is still in Germany (the majority of the NFL Europe's professional teams came from Germany) and, to a smaller extent, in the United Kingdom and the Netherlands, without ever making it anywhere near the realm of hegemonic sports cultures.

[122] This initial response led to overly optimistic (or some would say pessimistic) scholarly predictions about an increasingly expanding spread of football in Europe; these prognoses were clearly premature. See Joe Maguire, "More than a Sporting Touchdown: The Making of American Football in England 1982–1990," *Sociology of Sport Journal* 7(3), 1990, pp. 213–37; Allen Guttmann, *Games and Empires*, p. 112. Guttmann classifies late twentieth-century football as another expression of cultural imperialism, claiming that "gridiron football seems especially appropriate as an example of ludic diffusion impelled by American power."

[123] See Markovits and Hellerman, *Offside*, p. 9. Even the Super Bowl, which has become a de facto holiday in the United States, attracts mostly American viewers. See McLaughlin, "Super Bowl is king at home."

[124] See Markovits and Hellerman, *Offside*. See also Maarten Van Bottenburg, "Thrown for a Loss? (American) Football and the European Sport Space," *American Behavioral Scientist* 46 (11), 2003, pp. 1550–62, here p. 1556.

had flourished on Europe's grass-roots participatory levels by the beginning of the 1920s at the very latest, American football did not follow this trajectory. There are no instances of American football in Europe at this critical juncture: no playing of the game in gym classes across the Continent or on playgrounds. In Britain, Rugby Union and Rugby League, American football's close local cousins, crowded out any possibility of the game's gaining any foothold in that country's overcrowded sports space. Lastly, let us not forget that until the legendary New York Giants–Baltimore Colts NFL championship game of December 28, 1958—the much-touted greatest game ever played—football in the United States remained primarily in the cultural domain of the country's colleges with the National Football League a distant second. And as we will argue in chapter 6, college sports even to this day comprise a virtually unknown enigma to much of the world outside of America's borders, which was a fortiori the case in the 1920s, a crucial era for the proliferation of modern sports cultures and languages in Europe and elsewhere.[125]

The long-term presence of American servicemen in Europe following World War II, and the growing popularity of professional football in the United States in the course of the 1950s, created another opening for the game's proliferation in Europe. Thus, a game in 1952 between two United States Air Force teams representing servicemen stationed in Germany and Britain respectively, filled up mighty Wembley Stadium, hallowed home ground of the England national soccer team. Exactly twenty years later, a football tournament on the western coast of Italy featured four NATO-based American teams and drew respectable crowds. Such relatively rare events could never make any inroads into Europe's sports culture that, in fact, they were not designed to do. Instead, they helped re-create a bit of "home" to American servicemen stationed thousands of miles and for long periods away from the United States. At best, these sporadic football games became one piece in the growing mosaic of "a broader European orientation toward American culture."[126]

Until the 1980s, American football's European presence remained largely confined to inner-American affairs featuring servicemen. In the course of that decade, Europeans commenced to pick up the game and form their local teams and leagues. These usually featured the lone American doctoral student, businessman, or missionary who starred in this amateurish affair played much more for fun than any other motive. This was

[125] Van Bottenburg, "Thrown for a Loss? (American) Football and the European Sport Space," pp. 1556–57.
[126] Ibid., p. 1557.

also an era in which many aspects of American culture were exposed to, if not necessarily liked by, Europeans—with the Super Bowl's annual live telecast in the middle of a late Sunday night or early Monday morning in January becoming a regular staple.

However, American football did not only confront the culturally embedded and organizationally structured dominance of soccer and that of other hegemonic sports such as cycling, Alpine or Nordic skiing, tennis, cricket, or rugby in their respective countries, but it also ran into the issue of Europeans' comparing this football *directly* to "their" football (that is, soccer), which they clearly continued to prefer. The nomenclature of "football" as identified with two competing sports made the acceptance of the American game by Europeans immensely difficult and highly contested. After all, the very fact that each competing party represented two very different games in which each claimed to have the sole legitimacy in calling its product "football," helped the ensconced party's case over the newcomer immensely. Thus, in marked contrast to basketball and hockey, American football's acceptance by Europeans involved an identity issue in that it was viewed as a "non-European sport and a counterpoint to soccer," an "anomaly in the world sporting system," and a particularly keen expression of the "intrinsically headstrong character of American culture."[127] Hence, contrary to basketball, which had built up a reservoir of historical resonance and was never perceived as a direct threat to soccer or as an unwanted cultural "other," American football's existence appeared as a direct challenge to the "real" football.

As the rise of commercial television and the Internet offered new opportunities for American football, with new television stations needing a bevy of sports to fill their available programming, the game gained some ground, especially among a small segment of the population that had traveled frequently to the United States, loved America, wanted to re-create some of its experiences back home in Europe, and clearly viewed itself in opposition to the soccer mainstream and the juggernaut of its cultural hegemony.[128] Despite massive financial and media efforts however, American football never attained any significant cultural presence among the masses and Europe's male sports fans, who continued their allegiance to *their* football with its teams, rivalries, histories, and fan cultures.[129]

---

[127] Ibid., p. 1558.

[128] Ibid., p. 1559.

[129] While Van Bottenburg is right to assume that the size of the audience is often dependent on the scale of sport participation, we think he overstates this link between active and passive sports or the "strong correlation between sport participation and other forms of sport

It should perhaps not come as a surprise that the NFL attempted to conquer the European market for American football "from above" by forming its own league there. The NFL was immensely successful as America's most powerful sports juggernaut, surpassing baseball as the definitive number one in American sports culture in the course of the two decades following the late 1950s, partly based on its superior marketing prowess in the then new medium of television in the United States, without a doubt the most challenging sports and marketing terrain of any in the world. Beginning in 1991, an NFL-owned World League of American Football (WLAF) commenced as a spring league with teams on both sides of the Atlantic. When the league was revamped in 1995 after a two-year hiatus, it was renamed the World League with only European teams aboard after having shed its North American franchises. In 1997 the league rechristened itself as NFL Europe League or NFL Europe. In 2006, the league's name changed yet again, this time to NFL Europa, perhaps changing the English "Europe" to the German "Europa" on account of five of the league's six teams being based in Germany by this time, with the lone other calling Amsterdam its home. On June 29, 2007, NFL Europa ceased operations.

The NFL's fifteen-year European adventure ended in abysmal failure. In many ways, the frequent name changes reflected the daunting task confronting the NFL. By trying to impose an entire sports culture and language from above, without any foundation on which to build, it never succeeded in giving its product a real core. The players were virtually all Americans, though none of them of first-rate quality, which gave the product two strikes right off the bat. Their being Americans allowed no links at all to the local fans, which would not have mattered had they been top players. By making the league(s) a priori second-rate and little more than an experimental recruiting ground for the "real deal" back home in the United States with its genuine NFL, the NFL's European experiment signaled even to the interested European consumer that this endeavor was not "the best of the best" and was unlikely to ever become that. With the lack of a necessary foundation and any pre-existing culture favoring the sport, it was not surprising that a migratory pattern of teams coming and going from place to place emerged that also did not help in creating the desired allegiances and necessary fan backing.

Lastly, the NFL's European escapade also failed on account of its own

---

involvement" (ibid., p. 1559). While many follow a sport without ever actively pursuing it, there are also strong participation sports that have not yet become major spectator sports—as is the case with soccer in the United States.

spectacular success in the United States, which—via all the communication means perfected in the second globalization process—became readily available to the still small but growing number of European aficionados of American football. Given the choice of watching the very best players on television or via the Internet, as opposed to their second and third-tier colleagues live in spaces in which they and their game were imposters—since they performed in stadiums built for and identified with that other football, namely soccer—enough Europeans chose the former option to thus render the NFL's European endeavor impossible.[130] The NFL's failure to have American football become part of Europe's sports culture serves as prima facie evidence of the stickiness and resilience of these cultures, which cannot be simply transplanted wholesale from one context to another, even in the era of the second globalization and even by such brilliant marketers as the NFL's. Watching an NFL game played in the United States from one's European living room does not ipso facto suggest that one is professing undying loyalty to either of the teams, their game, its history, its traditions, its meanings, or its metameanings.

Interestingly, American sports—unlike other items of popular culture such as music, film, and dance that became globalized in the wake of World War I—remained largely (though by no means exclusively) domestic and local until the development that we have termed the second globalization. Indeed, underlining this point, one genre of American film has regularly failed in Europe and elsewhere: those centered on American sports. These films remain successful only back home in the United States, and for obvious reasons. Not one of the 98 motion pictures (films and television shows) on baseball produced in America between 1925 and 2007, the 128 featuring football, the 64 having basketball as their theme, or the 19 centered on hockey have been remotely successful in any market outside North America.[131] These shows' failure abroad demonstrates yet again that entrenched

---

[130] Thierry Henry, star of Arsenal, Barcelona and the French national team, might furnish an excellent case in point. Growing up in a rough neighborhood in Paris in the 1980s, Henry developed a love for American sports by watching them on television. It is via this medium that he became a huge fan of the New York Giants, especially their fierce linebacker Lawrence Taylor—better known to all aficionados as LT—whose game young Thierry came to respect and appreciate.

[131] These numbers hail from a study that Markovits is currently conducting as to how established sports cultures are depicted in various media. The first part of the study centers only on the United States. Interestingly, and tellingly, far and away the most successful among all these movies are the ones featuring baseball, rather than the other three sports, thus confirming that "we [Americans] want to believe in baseball with a deep-rooted faith that we don't bring to other sports. It's why baseball movies work and those about other sports don't so much." Tom Verducci, "Latest News Makes This a Dark, Dirty Day for the Red Sox," http://

sports languages are not automatically or easily transferable, and that their understanding and appreciation takes much time and commitment on the part of producers and consumers. Perhaps, they will never travel with ease to different cultures. Appreciating a guitar riff in a rock 'n' roll song constitutes a much easier proposition of cultural transfer and the likelihood of instant understanding than does a well-delivered fastball, a 14-yard run off left tackle, or an 18-foot jump shot.[132]

Yet, the NFL's European foray does not seem to have been totally for naught, because the league commenced in the 2007 season to play one of its regular-season games in London's newly built Wembley Stadium. The first three of these were impressive successes on all counts, with the games selling out this immense and hallowed stadium in less than thirty minutes precisely because there now exists a small but significant number of European fans of American football who know the game, appreciate its players, and will go to major length to attend a game that matters played by the best of the best. And the NFL fully intends to continue with its regular autumnal forays into Wembley even though views opposing these cross-Atlantic excursions have come from many American NFL fans and sports experts who, among other things, bemoan the fact that the "home" team in Wembley loses one of its only eight home games at its real home in the United States and thereby foregoes home field advantage, one of the most vaunted supports in all of sports. Playing at Wembley may be better than nothing, and it shows some resilient enthusiasm for the sport. But these

---

sportsillustrated.cnn.com/2009/wroters/tom_verducci/07/30/manny.ortiz/index.html. Retrieved on July 30, 2009.

[132] In several cases the creation and proliferation of all of these modern sports cultures and languages exacted costs, mainly at the expense of the local games whose importance diminished but whose existence never quite disappeared. Take the fate of the so-called blood sports. Bear, bull, and badger baiting were common in eighteenth- and nineteenth-century England and America and attracted large crowds in public places. They have disappeared. Cock fighting was ubiquitous but has gone underground in much of the advanced industrial world, though certainly not in places like the Dominican Republic where Juan Marichal, a Hall of Fame pitcher and his friend Pedro Martinez, a Hall of Famer to be, were proudly pictured holding their respective fighting birds just before being launched into their deadly battle. When Martinez was criticized in the United States for his behavior, he responded emphatically that cock fighting constituted an essential part of culture in the Dominican Republic. Bull fighting, which some still regard as essential to the Spanish soul, has lost much of its luster in Spain and might well be exiting that country's mainstream culture in the wake of Spain's integration into the European Union, a key player in the second globalization. And the reaction to football star Michael Vick's involvement in dog fighting—a public outcry, Vick's criminal prosecution, his serving serious jail time, his two-year forced absence from the NFL and his foregoing millions of dollars in lost revenue from cancelled sponsorships—also bespeak a shift in the public perception of blood sports in the advanced industrial world.

few games are a far cry from earlier ambitions to enter the European sports space as a serious player and potent cultural force. To wit: By sheer coincidence, the kickoff between the New England Patriots and the Tampa Bay Buccaneers at Wembley Stadium on Sunday, October 25, 2009 happened one hour after the conclusion of the soccer match between archrivals Manchester United and Liverpool at the latter's home ground of Anfield. Virtually all television sets at the Wembley Stadium media center—let alone those in the rest of England and Britain—featured the contest between these two North-English soccer powers, thus making the NFL game a veritable imposter, an almost inconsequential sideshow. Perhaps nothing underlined the NFL's continued cultural marginality to European publics more than the fact that Tom Brady, the New England Patriot's glamorous quarterback and one of the most recognized celebrities in the United States, was mistaken for being a member of a boy band and repeatedly identified as Brazilian supermodel Gisele Bündchen's husband, bringing to mind baseball's similar cultural insularity when an iconic American sports star of Joe DiMaggio's stature was only known as Marilyn Monroe's husband in Europe and many other places outside the United States.[133] Confirming yet again the NBA's and basketball's most far-reaching and successful presence in global sports culture among the North American Big Four is our educated estimation that their contemporary superstars of the Tom Brady and Derek Jeter variety—say Kobe Bryant and LeBron James—are much better known and more readily recognized in Europe and the world, which, in turn, is almost solely the result of basketball's much deeper, longer, and wider presence in these areas' local sports cultures.

Moreover, the fact that the New England Patriots vs. Tampa Bay Buccaneers game sold out Wembley Stadium in less than thirty minutes but that this game's protagonists remained largely unknown to the larger British sports public, supports our thesis that in the global age only the "best of the best" gain meaningful attention in an established sports culture. In case of football, the transatlantic chasm has remained particularly stark: While the Super Bowl represents America's greatest sporting spectacle, and as such has become a global event as well, the game of American football remains peripheral and regional among the world's sports languages. Liking the Super Bowl has little, if any, bearing on one's affection for football itself.

---

[133] Pete Thamel, "Patriots Too Much For Bucs, Anywhere," *New York Times*, October 26, 2009.

This difference, incidentally, also pertains to a sizable proportion of the 100 million Americans who regularly watch the Super Bowl every year. Many care much more about the half-time show—featuring an absolute A-list of the world's superstars, such as the late Michael Jackson, The Rolling Stones, Paul McCartney, Bruce Springsteen, Prince, Tom Petty and the Heartbreakers, The Who (not to forget Justin Timberlake and Janet Jackson of the famed wardrobe malfunction)—and the commercials than the actual game and its eventual outcome. Thus, any new ambitious European plans by the NFL should be viewed with skepticism. "If you want to grow something, you've got to share it," argues Mark Waller, the NFL's senior vice president of sales and marketing. "Once this takes root here, and it will, people are going to expect to see the best, in the same way that you know the World Cup is the ultimate for soccer and the Olympics is the ultimate for track and other sports. If (the Super Bowl) travels, it makes you part of what the world is today, which is truly a global community."[134] NFL Commissioner Roger Goodell told reporters that "there's a great deal of interest in holding a Super Bowl in London. . . . So we'll be looking into that."[135] Yet even the most enthusiastic supporters of sports globalization, who assume that the NFL is "doing well in non-American markets" because of a full Wembley stadium (or 100,000 plus spectators in Mexico City's Azteca stadium in 2005, for that matter), are critical of a new wave of overoptimistic expansionism: "Apparently the people of Europe want football, and like most they aren't willing to settle for half-hearted attempts (NFL Europe), but I still don't believe that any of the 'Expansionists' are thinking this all the way through."[136]

Perhaps Canada offers a more realistic option for the NFL, as it has for the other three of the Big Four. Starting in the fall of 2009, the Buffalo Bills played one of their eight regular-season home games across Lake On-

[134] Quoted in "Super Bowl in London . . . Revisited," *Sports Business Digest*, October 27, 2007, http://sportsbusinessdigest.com/?p=118. Retrieved December 20, 2008.

[135] Ibid.

[136] See ibid; and "6 Reasons Why the Super Bowl Should Not Be Played in London," *Sports Business Digest*, October 16, 2007, http://sportsbusinessdigest.com/?p=109. Retrieved December 20, 2008. Of course, *Sports Business Digest* is one of the most optimistic promoters of future sports globalization: "Sports is going global. No longer will the World Series just be based on teams from America. The Super Bowl will be worldly. The NBA Finals will hold a global finality. The universal globalization of sports is coming . . . and it will be here sooner than you think. . . . The globalization of sports is coming, but we can't rush into it . . . , nor can we provide anything less than a premium product (NFL Europe, I'm talking to you). But know that it's coming." See "Sports Are Going Global," *Sports Business Digest*, November 19, 2007, http://sportsbusinessdigest.com/?p=146. Retrieved December 20, 2008.

tario in nearby Toronto's SkyDome. This is the home field of the Toronto Argonauts of the Canadian Football League (CFL). Predictably, the game disturbed some local CFL fans who saw this as yet another American encroachment on Canadian culture and autonomy. But it also delighted Canadian sports enthusiasts interested in the NFL's more glamorous and global product.

Of the Big Four American team sports, there can be no doubt that football is the least international and global in terms of the game's essence—as opposed to its ancillaries such as jerseys and other products which include these forays into Wembley Stadium. This is also borne out by the fact that barely 1 percent of the NFL's players in 2008 hailed from places outside the United States, as compared to nearly 30 percent in the NHL and MLB, and almost 18 percent in the NBA.

Global Players, Cosmopolitan Change: The Cultural and Political Power of Sports in the Global Age

Although local cultures remain a powerful and resilient force confronting globalization's "good" (i.e., cosmopolitan) as well as "bad" (i.e., uniform) effects, they are also subject to significant changes precisely by dint of the challenges imposed on them by globalization. Globalization in sports contributes more than "merely another layer that exists in addition to—not instead of—the teams' local roots and parochial milieus."[137] It renders sports' new face into what Robertson has termed "glocal."

The relevance of these glocal spaces can best be illustrated by the two movie versions of *Fever Pitch*. Based on the best-selling English football novel by Nick Hornby, published in 1992, *Fever Pitch* tells the story of a die-hard supporter of the North London club Arsenal who has trouble choosing between the love of his life and the club he has loved since his childhood. The moment when both of his dreams are finally realized occurs in 1989, when Arsenal at long last wins its first title after eighteen futile seasons. The English novel became a successful movie in Britain in 1997. For an American audience, however, the movie had to be *translated* in order to appeal to the mainstream and not merely to the sliver of soccer fans to whom Arsenal and its travails were well-known. Thus, the American movie version, which appeared in 2005, transposed the story from London to Boston and transformed the protagonist's love for the Arsenal

---

[137] Markovits and Hellerman, *Offside*, p. 31.

soccer team into the life-long, passionate love for the Boston Red Sox. The term "pitch," of course, had two different meanings in the two different sports spaces: referring to the actual soccer field in its English context, and to the pitcher throwing the ball in a baseball game in its American counterpart.

The American movie starred Jimmy Fallon and Drew Barrymore, while Nick Hornby himself was executive producer. It was filmed during the 2004 Red Sox season, with many scenes shot in hallowed Fenway Park, as iconic a place in America's hegemonic sports culture as can be. It was entirely coincidental, though, that the happy ending matched the English version: In 2004, of all years, the Red Sox won the World Series for the first time in eighty-six years, so the celebrations depicted in the movie were real. Perhaps they were even more meaningful and heartfelt than in Arsenal's case in North London, since the Red Sox's eighty-six-year championship drought far exceeded Arsenal's mere eighteen and the Bosox's glory being realized by the team's singularly successful vanquishing of its most hated foe, the mighty Yankees of New York.

Even though the respective sports languages of soccer and baseball are incompatible, and the specific histories of each are unique, the very essence of the two protagonists' unconditional love for and knowledge about their respective sports, teams, and players are identical to the point of being completely interchangeable. Two phenomena accompanying the American film further corroborated our argument that globally-induced changes in the local (the thus ensuing "glocal") do not transport as easily in sports as they do in pop music and other media: First, the bitterly snide reactions against the movie by many British film reviewers as well as Arsenal supporters who, beyond the obligatory dismissals that masquerade under the ubiquitously pejorative code word "Hollywood," perceived the very idea (let alone the actual making) of such a motion picture as a blasphemous desecration of a saintly English icon (Arsenal) by ignorant Americans, despite Nick Hornby's full support of and affection for the Boston version of his story; and second, that the film, despite its bankable stars, faired poorly at the box offices everywhere but in North America, demonstrating yet again that sports movies do not travel well from culture to culture.[138] Incidentally, the film version of the British original also failed in the international arena, regardless of the greater global presence there for soccer and Arsenal than for baseball and the Red Sox.

Thus, no matter how thorough an impact the second globalization of

---

[138] We include *Fever Pitch* in the ninety-eight films on baseball mentioned above.

sports cultures might create, it will remain confined—indeed localized— by key limits imposed by the "first" globalization, which will always remain part and parcel of any sport's core identity. The Red Sox and Arsenal will always remain apart and stay deeply anchored in their original milieus regardless of the many commonalities that globalization has accorded them.

The links between the local, national, and global remain multiple. Today one discerns a multitude of networks and knowledge. Sometimes globalization may just add another dimension to established sports cultures; there is no inevitable trade-off between hegemonic sports and newcomers. A college football and basketball fan may still know, love, or show interest in learning the traditionally "alien" language of soccer. As American culture has amply demonstrated for well over a century, it is perfectly possible to follow more than one sport on a regular basis and thus be totally conversant in three or more sports languages. But there is still a huge difference between being conversant with sports comprising one's traditional sports culture and being fluent in sports from outside this comfort zone. Only few people can confidently walk between the worlds of the new and old, and speak the languages of different sports cultures fluently.[139] Furthermore, local attachments and interests need not be replaced by global ones. A local club enthusiast can still support her/his national team and also enjoy watching and following a third-party "neutral" team —usually of the global kind, be it Manchester United on the club level or the Brazilian *Seleção* on the national level. An increasing number of people wants to follow the very best players in their respective sports and turn to the arenas where they perform.

This trend encourages cosmopolitan attachments rather than traditionally local and national ones. It has also generated ever-expanding diaspora communities in different hegemonic cultural spaces. The major finals in each respective sport—World Cup Final, the cricket or rugby World Cup finals, the European Champions League final, the NBA finals, the World Series, and the Super Bowl—have turned into global games that attract diverse viewers around the world. Of course, different viewers display vastly different levels of interest, love, and language proficiency. The New York Yankees, the Los Angeles Lakers, Manchester United, Real Madrid, and AC Milan, for instance, have emerged as both local and global teams today. Hence at the peak of their competitions, the best in each of the

---

[139] Although sports represent a cultural sphere that reaches beyond class distinctions, the likelihood of this "sports cosmopolitanism" increases on the elite level; see Craig Calhoun, "The Class Consciousness of Frequent Travelers: Toward a Critique of Actually Existing Cosmopolitanism," *South Atlantic Quarterly* 101 (4), 2002, pp. 869–97.

sports mobilizes populations around the world, reaching beyond conventional identities and cultural spaces and facilitating new cosmopolitan ties across national boundaries and borders.

The city of Milan could claim to be the most international soccer town on earth. Milan's bitter rivals, Inter and AC, furnished twenty-one players representing ten countries during the 1998 World Cup in France. Only six of those players performed for the Italian team.[140]

Think about how the second globalization of soccer has changed the main protagonists of the infamous "Old Firm," the twice-a-year symbolic religious altercations between Catholic Celtic and Protestant Rangers in Glasgow. With Argentinean, Italian, Czech, Brazilian, and Swedish players on both teams, these contests have become just that: extremely competitive soccer contests, not re-enactments of religious wars from the seventeenth century.[141]

Though this certainly pertains to the situation on the field and for the players, alas it is still not the case for all the fans. Many still resort to a narrow parochialism and revel in counter-cosmopolitan attitudes (and behavior) in the stands. Embodying such an identity receives much encouragement by their like-minded friends and appears to be as indispensable an ingredient to what it means to be a real Celtic or Rangers supporter as wearing the teams' colors and chanting their songs with their frequently vile lyrics. Yet even such entrenched fan cultures have begun to change in the course of the last two decades. Nothing illustrates the silent transformation toward a modernized, more inclusive, postreligious and postethnic collective identity more strikingly than this brief conversation between a Glaswegian man and a Muslim immigrant woman: "What are you?" asks the man, whereupon the woman answers, "I am a Muslim," to which the man responds, "I know that you are a Muslim, but are you a Celtic-Muslim or a Rangers-Muslim?"[142]

There are massive shifts in how we have come to perceive identities in the United States, Canada, Australia, New Zealand, and Western Europe. They are also linked to the rise of the so-called second wave of feminism,

---

[140] Andrei S. Markovits, "Reflections on the World Cup '98," *French Politics and Society* 16 (3), Summer 1998, pp. 7, 8.

[141] Although Northern Ireland, with its dysfunctional sports space, in many ways presents the complementary argument, there are signs that the Belfast Giants ice hockey franchise has played a positive role in the recent improvement of community relations in a place otherwise torn apart by ethnosectarian conflict; see Alan Bairner, "On Thin Ice? The Odyssey, the Giants, and the Sporting Transformation of Belfast," *American Behavioral Scientist* 46 (11), 2003, pp. 1519–32.

[142] BBC International Television, "The War against Terror Within," April 10, 2007.

itself an integral part of the phase of the second globalization, and a major force in altering the topography of sports. Even gender-based exclusion such as the shaping of masculine collective identities and spaces of fraternal bonding—among the most distinctive features of hegemonic sports cultures[143]—has come under increasing pressure over the past two to three decades.

We will now take a closer look at the specific transitions that have occurred in Europe and America in the age of the second globalization. American and European sport spaces furnish the main venues and arenas that attract global attention. Yet they are also perfect places to study multiple forms of cultural resilience when the global meets the national and the local.

---

[143] See J. A. Mangan, ed., *Making European Masculinities: Sport, Gender, Europe* (London, Frank Cass, 2000).

Chapter 3 ◇◇◇◇◇◇◇◇◇◇◇◇◇◇◇◇◇◇◇◇◇◇◇◇◇◇◇◇◇◇◇◇◇◇◇◇◇◇

THE TRANSATLANTIC TRANSFER OF SPORTS AND THEIR CULTURES

INSTITUTIONALIZATION AND DIFFUSION

We now explore how the second globalization of sports cultures affects today's transnational political cultures and identities. We first look at soccer's development in the United States and argue that the sport's presence has indeed undergone a significant transformation over the past three decades, without its becoming part of America's hegemonic sports culture at the time of this writing. Rather, we argue, soccer in America has reached a stage of what we call "Olympianization." The game's big events—the World Cup, the European National Championships, the year-long Champions League matches, and stateside visits by the best European Superclubs such as Barcelona, Real Madrid, Chelsea, Inter and AC Milan—have indeed garnered solid attention and robust traction in America's sports topography. In stark contrast, the game's local manifestations, as notably expressed by MLS, continue a marginal existence. Even the "Beckham effect," which entails the import of a foreign bona fide superstar to help a struggling sport in a country where it has languished on its cultural margins, has its major limits.

Across the Atlantic, intra-European changes in soccer's existence have in turn been part of the game's globalization. In basketball, we discern what we have called the "Nowitzki effect," meaning that a local boy rises to superstardom in a top league of his sport and helps catapult the sport way beyond its former marginality in his home country, merely by activating a powerful synergy between national pride and the universal desire to succeed among the best. In a way, we find the "Nowitzki effect" to be much more beneficial—as well as more facile—in improving a sport's cultural standing than the "Beckham effect" by dint of the undiminished power of national and local ties in this age of globalization. American soccer enthusiasts can only hope that young American talents such as Jozy Altidore, Tim Howard, and Oguchi Onyewu—playing in Europe's top leagues—will have a similarly beneficial effect on American soccer as Nowitzki's did on basketball in Germany, or Tony Parker's in France, Drazen Petrovic's and Tony Kukoc's in Croatia, and the Gasol brothers' in Spain. For there can be no doubt about the potency of a superstar's national coattails and the beneficial effects of his exploits for his audience back home. Just think of Lance Armstrong's immense influence on having spawned a coterie of superb American bicycle racers and on having raised his sport's profile in the United States. American professional soccer, thus, is in need of a Lance Armstrong equivalent to emerge as a superstar in one of Europe's premier soccer leagues to dramatically improve its cultural role stateside.

Lastly, we concentrate on cultural transfers in artefacts such as tattoos, melodies, high fives, and baggy shorts to show that these among many others have indeed changed important ancillary items characteristic of sports cultures without, however, having altered their essence and core. Our examples bespeak a clear manifestation of cultural cosmopolitanism. Yet, its profundity remains mitigated by its being confined to the realms of mimicry and imitation. In a way, we are arguing that the diffusion of cultures is a lot easier than their institutionalization. As to why some objects are diffused whereas others are not, who the recipients and senders of these diffusions really are, why some diffused items stick while others evanesce, and when such diffusions are most likely to occur, we can offer plenty of empirically compelling examples, yet we plead theoretical ignorance.[1] This shortcoming, we hope, will nevertheless not diminish the value of our findings.

Navigating the Treacherous Waters between the Scylla of American Football and the Charybdis of English Football: American Soccer's Continued Predicament

The "Olympianization" of Soccer in America

When the United States men's national soccer team shocked the world by defeating England 1–0 in the group stage of the 1950 World Cup in Brazil,

---

[1] Even though we find Jeannette A. Colyvas and Stefan Jonsson's work fascinating and immensely helpful for our purposes, as our repeated citations of it have amply demonstrated, we believe that they, too, have not been able to offer compelling theoretical constructs for the puzzles that we just raised.

its feat was treated with nearly complete neglect from the American public and media. Though the rest of the soccer world had by then come to revere the World Cup as the premier soccer (and perhaps sports) tournament in the world, Americans were thoroughly uninterested, even when their squad was participating and actually competing with the best teams in the world.

Although soccer today occupies a boutique niche in the American sports space, as it did in 1950, the quadrennial World Cup is now embraced by the American sports media and increasingly the public with considerable attention. We will demonstrate, primarily through tallies of staff-written newspaper articles and examination of television ratings, that the stature of the World Cup in the United States has enjoyed tremendous growth from 1950 to the present. The drastic increase observed in these figures signals a new order in the American soccer world, with the World Cup clearly at the top of the heap. Although America follows the World Cup to a degree that pales in comparison to the all-out immersion seen in the traditional soccer world, the World Cup, similarly to the Olympic Games, is now greeted as a noticed and followed *event* whose prominence will only grow in the future. The game of soccer, however, remains routinely marginalized in the four years between tournaments, although here, too, some subtle but significant changes are afoot (pun fully intended). Essentially, via the World Cup, soccer has become *Olympianized* in the United States over the past half-century.

A Long and Winding Road: The Growth of the World Cup in America

When the Americans took the field against world heavyweights England in 1950, they had on their résumé a 3–1 loss to Spain four days earlier, a lackluster 1-1-2 record in World Cup qualifiers, and seven straight losses by a combined 45–2 score prior to that. The team essentially consisted of amateurs and semiprofessionals: a dishwasher, a mailman, a teacher, among others, for whom playing soccer was much more a hobby than a source of income. Simply, they were an unsuccessful team of soccer nobodies from a country that did not pay attention to the game. And since America did not care about the sport, or its own team, the 1950 World Cup was fated to obscurity in America before it even began. The print media responded appropriately, and exactly one American newspaper had a reporter on hand at the World Cup.

That paper was the *St. Louis Post-Dispatch*, whose original coverage occurred only due to the fact that its reporter, the classically named Dent McSkimming, had taken vacation time from his job at the paper and paid his own way to the tournament in Brazil.[2] So when the United States stunned England, the *Post-Dispatch*, as it did for the rest of the tournament, had the only original, staff-written coverage of this global event in the United States. While it may seem totally strange and virtually random that it was this particular paper that was the sole American publication to cover this major tournament in far-away Brazil, the fact that St. Louis has arguably been among the most soccer-oriented American cities throughout the twentieth century surely accounts for Mr. McSkimming's desire to attend this event and his employer's decision not to have him fired. Other national dailies, including the *New York Times*, the *Los Angeles Times*, the *Chicago Tribune*, and the *Washington Post*, provided exactly *zero* staff-written reporting of the tournament. Occasionally papers ran brief capsules of wire-service coverage. Such was the case when the Americans scored perhaps the greatest upset in the international history of soccer, certainly in the World Cup's history, by eliminating the heavy favorite to win the title.[3]

Losing to Chile 5–2 three days after their sensational victory over the English, the Americans returned home to the United States where nobody paid them any attention and where this event still languishes in total obscurity apart from a few historically interested soccer fans.[4] The players of that team suffered from a double dose of disrespect and inattention: that of their own country in which soccer mattered little; and that of the soccer

---

[2] Geoffrey Douglas, *The Game of Their Lives: The Untold Story of the World Cup's Biggest Upset* (New York: Perennial Currents, 1996), p. 4.

[3] It is very hard to exaggerate the magnitude of this upset but let us contextualize it: England, soccer's cradle and inventor, had repeatedly refused to participate in international tournaments such as the previous World Cups of 1930, 1934, and 1938, partly for all kinds of arcane disputes with FIFA, the global soccer federation, but also partly because England deemed itself so much better at the game than anybody else. So when the English finally consented to participate in this first World Cup held five years after the end of World War II, it was the first time in history that the English would join this global tournament. They, as did everybody else, expected to walk away with the title quite easily. So when the lowly Americans, these soccer nobodies, eliminated the mighty English from the tournament, the soccer world was shocked and remained so for years, even decades. Only North Korea's elimination of the mighty Italians from the World Cup tournament of 1966 in England comes close to the Americans' defeat of the English in its size and importance as an upset in the history of soccer's premier international event.

[4] A movie entitled *The Game of Their Lives*—eponymous with Geoffrey Douglas's book—appeared in 2005 to mixed reviews but, much more tellingly, to very little attention, let alone enthusiasm, on the part of the American movie-going audience.

world in which America mattered even less.[5] Alas, this dual burden has yet
to be fully lifted off the shoulders of America's soccer players sixty years
later.

With no American presence until the 1990 World Cup, the three subsequent tournaments—held in Switzerland (1954), Sweden (1958), and Chile
(1962), countries with little cultural profile in the United States—offered
no opportunities to raise the World Cup's standing stateside. Thus, the
next significant chance for the World Cup to gain footing in America
emerged with the 1966 tournament held in England, a country that enjoys
far and away the most prominent and positive cultural profile of any in
America. America's shared language, heritage, and history with England
rendered the tournament a compellling candidate to attract American attention. Swinging London, with all of its cultural markers (from Twiggy to
the Beatles; from miniskirts to Mini-Coopers) defining the hip zeitgeist,
already had an effect on America's cultural opinion makers.

American coverage of the 1966 World Cup, while limited, did constitute
a marked increase from the Brazil Cup sixteen years earlier which, of course,
was not televised anywhere. Perhaps the most significant inroads, though
by most measures still modest, were in the television arena, where for the
first time a World Cup match was aired in the United States. The championship game, a 4–2 extra-time victory for the host England over West Germany, was aired on tape delay on NBC. It attracted 2.4 million viewers.[6]

In print, the World Cup also made some unremarkable gains. The four
newspapers with available data combined to run nine staff-written articles.
Five were from the *Washington Post*, four from the *New York Times*, and,
consistent with their 1950 precedent, the *Chicago Tribune* and the *Los Angeles Times* produced no original content. Wire coverage, if not frequent, was
occasionally available in the four papers.

---

[5] Indeed, some of the Team USA players were consistently maligned by the English and
the rest of the dominant soccer world for not even being "real" Americans and thus imposters. To wit: the scorer of the single goal, Joe Gaetjens, was born in Haiti of a Haitian mother
and a Belgian father. He moved to New York and studied at Columbia University on a fellowship. Though he never became an American citizen, he had declared his intent to become one
prior to participating in the World Cup thus fully complying with the rules of the U.S. federation. FIFA later indicated that Gaetjens should have been ruled ineligible, but that this
could only have happened had anybody filed a protest before the beginning of the tournament. Nobody did. Gaetjens left the United States shortly after his glorious but neglected
goal and moved to France to play soccer. He returned to his native Haiti where he was killed
by the notorious Tontons Macoutes, the Duvalier family's death squad, in 1964. He was posthumously inducted into the United States Soccer Hall of Fame in 1976.

[6] "Cup Soccer, at $10 to $20, Upsets TV Viewers Here," *New York Times*, July 7, 1974.
http://www.proquest.com. Retrieved July 31, 2008.

Although the American response was underwhelming, the World Cup was so eagerly awaited and such a success in England that American business began to reevaluate the potential for domestic professional soccer. As a consequence, two new leagues were formed, the United Soccer Association (USA) and the National Professional Soccer League (NPSL). USA earned official recognition from the United States Soccer Football Association (USSFA, the top umbrella organization and adjudicating body for soccer in the United States; now known as the United States Soccer Federation [USSF][7]) as the country's top-tier professional soccer league with the antiquated American Soccer League (ASL) yielding its position to the USA.[8] Despite the optimistic climate for professional soccer in the wake of the 1966 World Cup, the precarious success and eventual failure of the new leagues indicated that the sports landscape for soccer in America was inhospitable. Tellingly, after their inaugural 1967 seasons, the USA and NPSL merged as the North American Soccer League (NASL) with many teams folding in the process.[9]

When the World Cup returned to Europe for the 1974 contest in West Germany—following the 1970 tournament in Mexico, which despite its

---

[7] Formed on April 5, 1913 as the United States of America Foot Ball Association, the governing body of U.S. soccer was among the earliest national member organizations belonging to the world's soccer federation FIFA. Not until 1945 did this institution include the word "soccer" in its name when it became the United States Soccer Football Association (USSFA). It did not divest itself of the word "football" in its title until 1974, when the organization renamed itself the United States Soccer Federation (USSF). It continues to bear this official title to this day. The battle centered on the words "football" and "soccer" in the appellation of this important organization amply reflects our earlier point how the word "football" connotes the hegemonic game played in the respective society with all other terms—"soccer" being one of them—denoting different games of less salient cultural importance. The federation in charge of soccer in America did not want to cede the term "football" to its hegemonic gridiron version until 1974, claiming sole legitimacy to this term and hence to its game, thus trying to negate reality in America where "football" had come to connote exclusively the American code of the game with hardly anybody—except some immigrant communities—associating the game of "soccer" with "football." Not until 1945 did the federation's renaming itself offer testimony to its proper assessment of conditions in American sports culture in which the "soccer" version of football clearly was secondary to its gridiron cousin. Thus, the federation realistically added the qualifier "soccer" to its name. Not until 1974 was the federation secure enough to relinquish completely the term "football" from its product, thereby creating a clear linguistic boundary in America between two formerly related games that in the course of the past 150 years had come to represent two separate entities on and off the playing fields. The game globally referred to as football had attained a safe home as soccer in America's sports culture.

[8] Steve Holroyd and Dave Litterer, "The Year in American Soccer—1966," *American Soccer History Archives* (2008). Retrieved July 31, 2008, from http://www.sover.net/~spectrum.

[9] Holroyd and Litterer, "The Year in American Soccer—1968," *American Soccer History Archives* (2008). Retrieved July 31, 2008, from http://www.sover.net/~spectrum.

geographic proximity to the United States typically generated virtually no interest among the American public—it received its first significant American attention from start to finish. This would come in the form of forty staff-written articles in *The New York Times*, with extensive reporting by dedicated soccer writer Alex Yannis, who was finally rewarded for his life-long superb reporting on soccer by being inducted into the United States Soccer Hall of Fame in 2009. The *Los Angeles Times* and *Chicago Tribune* also stepped up to the plate (to mix sport metaphors), running six and four-teen original articles respectively. Only the *Washington Post* backtracked, featuring just three staff-written articles.

While 800 million people worldwide saw the 1974 final between West Germany and the Netherlands, American audiences had to watch on closed-circuit broadcasts as NBC decided not to air the match. Such was the case for 19,600 frustrated New York City area soccer fans, who paid (sometimes reluctantly) between $10 and $20 to watch the final at Madison Square Garden on closed-circuit television.[10] Earlier Cup matches also aired on closed-circuit broadcasts.[11] This trend endured through the 1978 World Cup in Argentina, during which one of us (Markovits)—along with many Boston-area soccer fans, predominantly of non-American origin— had to watch via closed-circuit broadcast at the Boston Music Hall.[12]

In 1982, when Spain hosted the next World Cup on European soil, American papers again displayed a slight upturn in interest. With data available for six papers—the initial four plus the *Detroit Free Press* and the *Boston Globe*—a total of 106 staff-written articles appeared across the six dailies. The *New York Times* was again the leader, with thirty-five, while the more locally oriented *Free Press* ran only three. Notably, the nationally prominent *Washington Post* significantly upped its reportage, featuring twenty-eight original World Cup stories. The 1982 tournament also sig-naled a new high in American television coverage, as ABC aired the World Cup final (Italy vs. West Germany) live for the first time. While the mar-quee event was expected to attract up to 2 billion viewers worldwide, ABC's

---

[10] T. Rogers, "19,600 See TV Soccer at Garden," *New York Times*, July 8, 1974. Retrieved July 31, 2008, from http://www.proquest.com.

[11] "Cup Soccer, at $10 to $20, Upsets TV Viewers Here," *New York Times*, July 7, 1974.

[12] Markovits accompanied and chaperoned the two Miliband boys, David and Edward, whose father Ralph was then a visiting professor at Brandeis University, to the Music Hall to watch these games. He claims no causal relationship between having taken these two English boys to watch the World Cup via closed-circuit television in a run-down Boston theater, and their later becoming leading figures in British politics—with David foreign minister and Edward one of Prime Minister Gordon Brown's senior advisers at the time of this writing in 2009.

hastily arranged broadcast was having difficulty securing a camera spot as well as a commentary team up until days before the game. When it came time to show the game, ABC drew further criticism for repeatedly cutting to commercial in mid-action, thus all but butchering the game's telecast. ABC, arguably the best American network in sports broadcasting at the time, thereby fully revealed both its disregard and inexperience in presenting the most important soccer event in the world to an American audience with the care that this game so richly deserved. ABC Sports Vice President Jim Spence conceded that this event was an afterthought for ABC since the network did not expect "outstanding" ratings, but was airing the match because of the event's global prestige.[13] Spence was right. The ratings were far from outstanding. But they were not abysmal either; the broadcast attracted a nation-wide 6.6 rating. While the match lost handily in ratings to MLB games in markets like Chicago, Philadelphia, and Los Angeles, in New York it actually outdrew the Mets game 8.5 to 5.4. In San Francisco, unopposed by an MLB game, the final delivered a strong 8.8 rating.[14]

While in 1982 the World Cup was still in the midst of a healthy rise in stature in the United States, the domestic American pro soccer market was experiencing a drastic collapse. In the late 1970s the NASL had preformed surprisingly well, especially Pelé and Beckenbauer's New York Cosmos, who on occasion drew crowds in excess of 70,000 to Giants Stadium. By 1982 ten of the fourteen NASL teams were losing money, attendance was down from the previous year by 13 percent, and after four straight years of coverage, ABC decided not to air the league's annual Soccer Bowl championship game. As America grew increasingly capable of finding new space to dedicate to the World Cup spectacle every fourth year, it seemed to be growing increasingly disillusioned with watching local teams on a day-to-day basis. By 1985, the once promising NASL ceased operations.[15]

Henry Kissinger, an inveterate soccer fan since his childhood in Germany, tried his best to bring the World Cup to the United States for the 1986 tournament. As a native soccer speaker and a life-long expert of the game, he understood full well that a successful World Cup tournament was about the only thing that stood a chance of introducing soccer as a main-

---

[13] Lawrie Mifflin, "Prestige Is ABC Goal in Cup TV," *New York Times,* July 6, 1982. Retrieved July 31, 2008, from http://www.proquest.com.

[14] Jack Craig, "World Cup Telecast Didn't Overtake Baseball," *Boston Globe,* July 13, 1982. Retrieved July, 31 2008, from http://infoweb.newsbank.com.

[15] Markovits and Hellerman, *Offside,* pp. 167–68; see also "Soccer Owners Find Little to Cheer About in U.S.," *New York Times,* July 10, 1982. Retrieved July 31, 2008, from http://www.proquest.com.

stay in America's hegemonic sports culture. But even his arguably unparalleled diplomatic skills and international prestige were not able to achieve this feat, though the United States was to become the host in 1994. The 1986 World Cup was awarded to Colombia. When that South American country proved unable to organize a month-long event of such international magnitude, FIFA decided to assign the tournament to Mexico, which had organized a successful event in 1970. But as had been the case with all World Cups until then, the American media seemed even less interested in covering the tournament when it was held in Latin America, even in neighboring Mexico, instead of in Europe. This demonstrated yet again the American highbrow media's decided European bent and its comparable neglect of Latin America way beyond the world of sports and soccer.

If the 1990 World Cup was a very good opportunity for the event to gain some traction and permanence in the American sports world because it again marked a return to Europe (this time to Italy), then the fact that the American team qualified for the first time since 1950 gave the tournament the added potential to raise the Cup's profile in the United States. In step with expectations, newspapers dedicated significantly more coverage to this month-long event compared to any of its predecessors. Of the fourteen newspapers with available data, eight published over forty staff-written articles, with the *Los Angeles Times* printing the most: 152. The remaining six papers all produced fewer than ten original articles. In total, the fourteen papers printed 599 original articles; 580 of these were from the eight papers. Those eight were *USA Today* and papers from New York, L.A., Chicago, and Boston.

Cable network TNT held exclusive rights to the 1990 World Cup, and aired twenty-three of the fifty-two games played that year.[16] In contrast to the accelerating newspaper attention, TV ratings were categorically unimpressive. The early matches reached the biggest audiences because they featured the United States national team in its three group-stage games against (then still) Czechoslovakia, Austria, and host Italy—all of which the Americans lost decisively. These games averaged a 1.3 rating, which was meager at best. It meant that a mere 2 percent of households *receiving* TNT— surely not ubiquitous in American homes at that time—were tuning in for those World Cup matches.[17] The final, Argentina vs. West Germany, drew a viewing audience of only one million homes, which amounted

[16]"Networks Wary on '94 World Cup Rights," *New York Times*, July 5, 1990. Retrieved July 31, 2008, from http://www.proquest.com.
[17]"Small Audience," *New York Times*, June 27, 1990. Retrieved July 31, 2008, from http://www.proquest.com.

to a 2.2 rating.[18] Many blamed the failure of the United States to qualify for the knockout round as the reason for the dismal TV viewing figures. Regardless of the cause, the ratings were considered so bad that NBC made clear in the wake of the 1990 World Cup that it had no intention of bidding for the rights for the 1994 tournament that would be held in the United States.[19]

A Partial Breakthrough: The 1994 World Cup and its Aftermath

When the World Cup finally arrived on America's shores, it was met with heavy but mixed fanfare. Detractors often pointed to a pretournament Gallup poll showing that 66 percent of Americans were unaware that the World Cup was about to occur in their own country in three weeks' time. However, when the tournament began it was heralded with newspaper coverage vastly exceeding that of any previous Cup. Although a noted decrease in coverage coincided with the United States' exit from the tournament after the team's 0–1 loss to powerhouse and future champion Brazil at Stanford Stadium on Independence Day, reception of the competition remained strong. It set the all-time record for total attendance at any World Cup tournament ever held, a record that will remain unequalled and unbroken unless the tournament returns to the United States sometime in the future.[20] The reasons for this are legion, but two seem particularly salient to us: first, the 1994 games were played all across the United States in large stadiums, with none of the nine having a seating capacity of less than 65,000 spectators; and second, the huge enthusiasm for all the games brought to bear by the American public, who flocked in as great a number to matches contested by lesser teams as they did to those played by the game's elite squads—perhaps precisely because they were merely attracted to the tournament by dint of its being a major event, and not because they were expert soccer speakers deeply steeped in the nuances and history of the game. Television ratings were strong across the board, with the U.S. vs. Brazil match played on the Fourth of July on ABC picking up a 9.3 rating and the Brazil vs. Italy final on ABC grabbing a 9.5, a figure that has yet to be bested in the United States by any subsequent World Cup final in the men's game.[21]

[18] Richard Sandomir, "ABC Snores Its Way for 120 Minutes," *New York Times*, July 19, 1994. Retrieved July 31, 2008, from http://www.proquest.com.

[19] "Networks Wary on '94 World Cup Rights," *New York Times*, July 5, 1990. Retrieved July 31, 2008, from http://www.proquest.com.

[20] Markovits and Hellerman, *Offside*, pp. 205 and 293; 1994 FIFA World Cup, *The Official Site of U.S. Soccer*. Retrieved July 31, 2008 at http://ussoccer.com.

[21] "World Cup Final Receives Its Highest TV Rating Since 1994," *Washington Post*, July 11,

Four years later, the 1998 World Cup held in France offered a great opportunity for America's burgeoning soccer interest to run with the momentum of the 1994 Cup, which was by most measures a rousing success. Not only did the 1998 tournament mark a return of this event to Europe (and the culturally ever-present France, at that), but it also featured the United States team for the third consecutive competition.

Major print media dedicated vast coverage to this Cup: the sixteen American papers with available data combined to produce 1,327 staff-written articles. Of those, the leading nine papers together printed 1,275— an average of over 159 each. The remaining eight papers each produced ten or fewer original stories. The previously mentioned and expected major players from New York, Washington, Chicago, Boston, and Los Angeles were the most prominent. The *Los Angeles Times* led all papers with an astounding 367 original stories.

As anticipated, TV ratings were far from matching the 1994 numbers, but they were not disastrous. Entering the final match, ABC broadcasts had averaged a 3.2 rating, less than half the figure from 1994, and ESPN's numbers also were cut nearly in half. ABC closed on a relatively high note, landing a 6.9 for the France vs. Brazil final, about in line with the ratings from the 1982 West Germany vs. Italy final held in Spain, though much better than the figures from the West Germany vs. Argentina final held in Italy in 1990.[22] While moving across the Atlantic back to Europe from the United States had predictably diminished the World Cup's presence from the attention span of Americans, the newspaper and television response certainly demonstrated that the explosive popularizing effects of the 1994 World Cup were still lingering in America with the arrival of the '98 contest.

When the World Cup went to the co-hosts of Japan and Korea in 2002, it faced significant time zone and distance obstacles. This handicap, however, was soon overcome by the surprisingly solid performance of the American team, which, after a 1–1–1 group stage record, defeated archrival Mexico to advance to the quarterfinals before losing a showdown with powerhouse Germany. Spurred by Team USA's success, American papers responded with heavy coverage rivaling that from the 1998 tournament in France. In total, thirty-two papers combined to print 1,403 original World

2006. Retrieved August 1, 2008 from www.washingtonpost.com. For a discussion of the women's game and its unique television success featuring its legendary World Cup final of 1999 (held at the Rose Bowl in Pasadena), see our discussion in chapter 4.

[22] S. Gandy, "World Cup Frenzy Has No Kick for Yanks," *USA Today*, July 9, 1998. Retrieved August 1, 2008, from web.lexis-nexis.com/universe; and Rudy Martzke, "TV Ratings Fare Well," *USA Today*, July 14, 1998. Retrieved August 1, 2008, from web.lexis-nexis.com/universe.

Cup stories. The success also carried into the television market, with ESPN and ESPN2 performing especially well. ESPN's ratings increased by over 39 percent from 1998, and it earned its best ratings ever for a World Cup broadcast when the United States vs. Germany match garnered a 4.36 rating. ABC, on the other hand, did not have an impressive World Cup outing, averaging only a 1.4 average rating for its ten World Cup games. Ratings for the Brazil vs. Germany final on ABC (the network's only live broadcast) were down 25 percent from the 1998 closing game.[23]

The World Cup again returned to the friendly confines of Western Europe in 2006, this time to Germany. And while the surprising success of the United States team in 2002 seemed a major impetus for increased attention by the American television public in 2006, the media appeared content to maintain approximately the same level of coverage as in 2002. Available data for print media show that twenty-one papers produced a total of 1,191 staff-written articles. Although this represents a mean of over fifty-six articles per paper—greater than the approximately forty-four per paper in 2002—it pales compared to the nearly eighty-three per paper mean for the 1998 Cup held in France, which was a more comparable Cup than the 2002 contest because the 2006 one was also held in Europe. While part of this decline can be attributed to the presence of more locally oriented papers with small story counts, the fact that the same eight papers that combined for 1,275 stories in 1998 only produced 825 in 2006 significantly hurt the numbers. There were, however, gains in unlikely places, with the *Seattle Post-Intelligencer* jumping from two articles in 1998 to twenty-four in 2006, and the *Denver Post* similarly increasing from ten to forty-nine. The *Dallas Morning News* and the *San Diego Union-Tribune* also proved highly World Cup conscious, running ninety-one and eighty-four original articles, respectively.

Notably, coverage in the *Boston Herald* plummeted from one hundred four staff-written articles in 1998 to only nineteen in 2006. Sadly, this drastic decline coincided with the departure of dedicated soccer writer Gus Martins. For some American papers, it seems, a soccer writer is an appreciated luxury. Furthermore, coverage of soccer in a newspaper's sports section still seems to depend on the whims and idiosyncratic wishes of particular editors.

In contrast to the rather stagnant level of newspaper attention, U.S. television viewership of the 2006 World Cup achieved new highs. On ESPN, seventeen of twenty broadcasts achieved a rating over 1.0, up from

[23] Andrei S. Markovits and Steven L. Hellerman, "The 'Olympianization' of Soccer in the United States," *American Behavioral Scientist*, 46, 2003, pp. 1542–43.

seven of twenty-seven in 1998. Of those seventeen, seven attained a rating over 2.0, while only one broadcast did so in 1998.[24] ESPN2 enjoyed similar success, with early round matches drawing 1.4 percent of cable households, compared with 0.6 percent in 1998. ABC enjoyed a rebound from 2002, averaging a 1.7 entering the final game, with this match itself (Italy vs. France) garnering a 7.0—the highest single soccer broadcast rating in the United States since the tournament was played there in 1994.[25] [26] Combining ABC and Univision, the World Cup final attracted 16.9 million viewers, a figure nearly equaling that of the 2006 NCAA men's basketball championship game (17.5), and the average for the 2005 World Series (17.1). The 2006 NBA finals averaged roughly 4 million fewer viewers than the 2006 World Cup final.[27]

Still Struggling: The "Beckham Effect" and Professional Soccer at Home

With television ratings and newspaper coverage showing an unmistakably positive trend in World Cup attention in the United States, it might seem likely that the domestic soccer market would enjoy similar growth. And though top-tier matches between the best clubs in MLS—which has continued uninterrupted play since the league's founding in 1996—have given this entity much more robustness than any other soccer league had ever enjoyed in American history, MLS nonetheless remains decisively a niche league in America's sports space. On television, MLS remains all but nonexistent, and the limited growth it has enjoyed has been quite slow. Through June 1, 2008, EPSN2's nine Thursday evening MLS broadcasts averaged a miniscule 0.2 coverage area rating for the season. This was equivalent to the figure measured at the same time during the prior season, which in fact constituted a 4 percent decline from the 2006 season. The most watched 2008 game was an April 3 San Jose Earthquakes vs. L.A. Galaxy match that drew 399,000 viewers for a 0.3 coverage area rating.[28] In fact, the MLS match attaining the largest television audience ever was not

[24] Richard Sandomir, "Ratings Up, but Networks Can Improve," *New York Times*, July 11, 2006. Retrieved August 1, 2008, from web.lexis-nexis.com/universe.

[25] Michael Hiestand, "ESPN 'Amazed' at TV Ratings World Cup Draws," *USA Today*, June 15, 2006. Retrieved July 31, 2008, from web.lexis-nexis.com/universe.

[26] "World Cup Final Receives Its Highest TV Rating Since 1994," *Washington Post*, July 11, 2006. Retrieved July 31, 2008, from www.washingtonpost.com.

[27] Richard Sandomir, "Ratings Up, but Networks Can Improve," *New York Times*, July 11, 2006.

[28] "MLS Primetime Ratings Flat Through June 1," *SportsBusiness Daily*, June 4, 2008. Retrieved August 2, 2008, from www.sportsbusinessdaily.com.

even a true MLS game at all. Rather, an L.A. Galaxy vs. Chelsea FC exhibition match on ESPN (a so-called "friendly" in soccer parlance), inaugurating David Beckham's first appearance for the Galaxy and his arrival in Los Angeles, is credited as the most watched MLS game ever, garnering a modest 1.0 rating with just over 1 million viewers tuning in.[29] There can be absolutely no doubt that this relatively good rating was solely due to Beckham's presence as a globally recognized, bona fide, crossover superstar, whose every move has become fodder for the tabloids the world over. Unimpressive as these television figures are, they still constitute an improvement from those collected for MLS prior to the 2002 World Cup, when two ESPN2 broadcasts averaged a lifeless 0.09 rating. In the summer of 2002, riding the coattails of the World Cup, MLS ratings climbed over the 0.2 threshold, where they approximately remain.[30]

Grant Wahl demonstrates convincingly just how low MLS's television ratings have been: "Beckham's debut was beaten among that weekend's sports broadcasts by the British Open golf tournament (not surprising), a regular-season national baseball game (somewhat surprising), and even the IRL Honda 200 motor race (extremely surprising). Why, the final game of the Women's College World Series on ESPN2 the previous month had earned a 1.8 rating. That's right: A women's softball game outdrew Beckham's debut by nearly 2 to 1."[31] It was solely due to Beckham's celebrity status that even an injured Beckham, confined to the bench, doubled EPSN's 0.2 rating to 0.4 which was still below the Scrabble All-Star Championship that earned a 0.5 on ESPN the very same weekend.[32]

What improvements MLS experienced in viewing volume can comfortably be attributed to the ripple effect of the World Cup's burgeoning popularity and most assuredly to Beckham's presence. Furthermore, MLS has remained marginalized in print, almost never earning coverage outside of its fifteen-city market. Most tellingly, the *New York Times*, one of the most prolific reporters of World Cup soccer, does not even employ a beat writer for the New York Red Bulls, relying instead on wire services on the local team.

This would be unthinkable for any of the six New York teams representing baseball, football, and basketball; and even the three New York

---

[29] "Beckham MLS Debut Draws Record Ratings," *ESPNsoccernet*, July 24, 2008. Retrieved August 2, 2008, from soccernet.espn.go.com.

[30] Markovits and Hellerman, "The 'Olympianization' of Soccer in the United States," p. 1541.

[31] Grant Wahl, *The Beckham Experiment*, p. 64.

[32] Ibid., p. 102.

area representatives of the NHL (the Rangers, the Islanders, and the Devils) boast a much more prominent and regular coverage in the sports pages of the *New York Times* than do the Red Bulls, formerly known as the Metro Stars.

World (Cup) vs. National (MLS) Soccer

To solidify our point about the vast difference in contemporary American perception between the World Cup and MLS soccer, here is an e-mail that David Birnbaum, noted soccer expert, long-time soccer journalist and broadcaster, and New York-based inveterate soccer fan sent to us on Monday morning, November 24, 2008 following the MLS Cup championship game on Sunday between the New York Red Bulls and the Columbus Crew:

> I have a fitting testament to your overall argument about soccer's continued predicament in the United States. Unfortunately, I wasn't able to attend the MLS Cup final yesterday. I went to Fiddlesticks a West Village soccer bar, with a reservation, and with a promise that they were going to show the Red Bulls – Columbus Crew soccer championship game, only to find that when I arrived, although they had 5 TVs, all were showing the New York Jets—Tennessee Titans game. And they were not, as earlier advised and promised, going to show the MLS Cup.
>
> The place had all the trappings of a soccer bar. It didn't matter. No MLS Cup game. I then went to a couple of other spots, all sports bars . . . nada, all NFL, zero MLS championship final. I then went to the East Side, where I had once seen a regular season MLS game (it was baseball season in the midst of a very hot summer afternoon and the place was empty) and they were happy to show the Red Bulls game then, but that was in the summer and there were virtually no patrons in the bar. All these sports bars had Irish-English themes, or were European of some sort or another, Latin, etc. it did not matter yesterday. No soccer.
>
> The rule at these bars is quite clear: According to the manager of Fiddlesticks, it is English football Sunday mornings, American football in the afternoon, period. The New York Giants game against the Arizona Cardinals with a 4 PM kick-off time was shown immediately at the conclusion of the Jets game, which kicked off at 1:00 PM and concluded at 4 PM. No Red Bulls on New York television. I asked the Irish manager and bartender, what if this was the World Cup or even the World Series? They said, now THAT would be totally different. When I protested and said that this was America's version of the World

Cup-World Series, he said, "you got to be kidding me, sorry!" So, here were the Red Bulls, a New York side, playing for the MLS championship, the most important day in their 13 year history, and yet no NYC sports bars I went to would want to show the game on a single TV. "Nevada Smith", which is a place I was told to avoid because it reeked from the smell of beer and was SRO (no wonder, if no other spot is showing the match) was showing the game, and perhaps there was another place or two in Manhattan that had a TV on showing the Red Bulls in the MLS Cup final, but I had no idea where.

Basic point with this run-on diatribe is that football is still king, and will remain so for a long time, and futbol is maybe a lowly and insignificant vassal, if even that, in New York City, even when its own team is playing for the championship. So there you have it! There is soccer in America and then there is the World Cup. The two are totally different entities in the eyes of the American public, even the sports-loving and sports-following public.

The predicament of soccer's cultural presence in America and MLS's immensely hard row to hoe could not be better expressed than by that bartender at Fiddlesticks in New York City: caught between the Scylla of English football on Sunday mornings and the Charybdis of American football in the afternoons, American soccer has a very narrow and treacherous cultural space to navigate.

The *New York Times* did in fact cover the MLS championship game to a minimal degree. On the day of the game the paper ran two human-interest pieces: one on thirty-four-year-old Frankie Hejduk, a mainstay of the United States national team for many years, one of the Columbus Crew's stars, and a championship surfer.[33] The other, written by the paper's fine soccer specialist Jack Bell, focused on Danny Cepero, the Red Bulls' goalkeeper, who had become somewhat of a sensation in the world of American soccer, and even beyond, by performing a very rare feat for a goalkeeper—in fact the one and only thus far in MLS's thirteen-year history—in scoring a goal for his team, and not via a penalty but with a kick from eighty yards to boot (once again, pun intended). Cepero was also an oddity by dint of his commuting once a week to Philadelphia to finish the last course for his bachelor's degree at the University of Pennsylvania, with a senior thesis "on the British and French decolonization after World War II, and the role the United States had in manipulating the Brits and the French during the cold war."[34] It would be unimaginable for a goalkeeper in any of

[33] Billy Witz, "Soccer Field to Surfboard: A Passion to Be the Best," *New York Times*, November 24, 2008.
[34] Jack Bell, "Goalkeeper Seeks Education Only a Championship Provides," *New York Times*, November 23, 2008.

Europe's top professional leagues to commute between his university and soccer club in the midst of the season to complete his degree.

Jack Bell's article summarizing the game itself in the paper's Sports Monday section appeared on page 2 buried among the more prominent coverage accorded to both New York football teams, the Jets and the Giants, who were in the midst of enjoying an exceptionally successful streak.[35] Of the three other main New York City metro-area papers—the *New York Post*, the *Daily News*, and *Newsday*—only the first two carried an article each on Monday after the game.[36] ESPN's Sunday night SportsCenter buried its thirty-second coverage of the MLS championship game toward the end of its ninety-minute show, restricting its broadcast to the game's four goals and the joyous Columbus Crew players' lifting the cup on the victor's podium.

Quite interestingly, and tellingly, the champion Columbus Crew drew much more attention in their home city than the losing Red Bulls did in New York. In the *Columbus Dispatch*, the Crew's championship—the very first in the team's history—furnished the top story, even displacing the perennial favorite Ohio State Buckeyes football team that defeated its archrival University of Michigan Wolverines for the fifth time in a row the day before the Crew's victory, an unparalleled feat for them in their 105-year long football rivalry; this Ohio State victory led the school to claim yet another Big Ten title. So just like the Crew, the Buckeyes clinched a championship on that weekend for Columbus. In a nonrepresentative poll conducted by the *Columbus Dispatch* as to which of the two teams' respective victories were a "bigger deal" at this time, 66 percent opted for the Crew, which speaks highly of this team's acceptance and legitimacy in a football-crazed town like Columbus. On Monday, November 24, the newspaper ran six detailed and prominently placed articles on the Crew and its championship, ranging all the way from a meticulous game wrap-up to a thoughtful commentary that depicted the Crew's success as a defining moment in the city's sports history.[37]

Indeed, perhaps for the first time in Columbus's history, Ohio State's feats were relegated to second place in the Monday edition of the *Columbus*

[35] Jack Bell, "Red Bulls Squander Chances as Crew Wins M.L.S. Cup," *New York Times*, November 24, 2008.

[36] Michael Lewis, "Red Bulls Fall to Columbus Crew, 3–1, in MLS Title Game," *Daily News*, November 24, 2008; and Brian Lewis, "Red Bulls Fall to Columbus in MLS Final," *New York Post*, November 24, 2008.

[37] Michael Arace, "A Defining Moment in City's Sports History," *Columbus Dispatch*, November 24, 2008; see also Michael Arace, "Champs at Last: After 13 Years of Trying, Crew Grabs Its First Major League Soccer Title," *Columbus Dispatch*, November 24, 2008.

124

Dispatch during football season. We counted only three detailed articles on Ohio State football in that particular edition of the newspaper. The Crew's championship had achieved the unthinkable: soccer trumped football in football-mad Columbus, Ohio, if—of course—only for one day. However, highlighting the strictly local importance of the Crew to Columbus proper, our research of the *Cleveland Plain-Dealer*, arguably Ohio's most renowned and distinguished newspaper, yielded only one rather perfunctory story on the Crew and its championship in the Monday edition, even though we found extensive coverage of Ohio State football and high school sports.

Exactly one year later, Columbus's being the home to teams representing both codes of football—American and Association—would once again emerge simultaneously, perhaps even symbiotically, in one David Barclay, whose 39-yard field goal not only defeated the University of Iowa's football team in dramatic overtime but gave the Buckeyes the Big Ten title and their first trip to the Rose Bowl since 1996. Barclay, a junior walk-on kicker for Ohio State, finished his MLS career in 2005 playing for the Columbus Crew. The events of November 2008 (the Crew's MLS Championship) and November 2009 (Barclay's winning kick and his past as an MLS player) may just possibly narrow a tad the two miles separating Columbus Crew Stadium and the Horseshoe of the Ohio State University Buckeyes, whose quotidian cultures and milieus represent totally different worlds with nary a contact between each other.[38]

It is the contrast between the World Cup and MLS that is perhaps most indicative of the World Cup's position in the United States with regard to soccer in general. Considering the popularity of the NFL, NBA, MLB, NCAA football and men's basketball, NHL, and NASCAR, along with the minute-to-nonexistent American interest in international competition in the sports these leagues showcase, it would seem a foregone conclusion that domestic professional soccer would enjoy greater popularity and coverage than international competition. But with the World Cup vastly overshadowing MLS, soccer's position in the United States appears quite unique: there is strong and expanding interest for the World Cup every four years, but as MLS and the failed NASL demonstrate, America has a limited appetite for soccer on an everyday basis.

American soccer embodies a space the exact opposite to that of its Big Four competitors. In the Big Four's world, what matters to fans are domestic events, games, and championships while the international dimen-

[38] Craig Merz, "MLS Alum Kicks into Buckeyes History: Onetime Prodigy Barclay Enjoys Second Life as Collegiate Kicker," in MLSnet.com, November 17, 2009. Retrieved November 18, 2009.

sions are all but insignificant. After all, how many American basketball fans even know, let alone truly care, about the existence of the quadrennial world championships in that sport? Conversely, how many North American hockey fans worry about the annual world championships that are played alongside the Stanley Cup playoffs every spring—by players whose NHL teams had been eliminated in the Stanley Cup tournament, thus by definition not being that years' best? As to which of these two concurrently running tournaments the players themselves value more, Boston Bruins' German star player Marco Sturm had an unequivocal answer: Sturm's face lit up when he was proudly describing to a reporter the newly built Veltins-Arena in his hometown of Gelsenkirchen, host of the 2010 hockey world championship, where 65,000 spectators were going to cheer on his German national team in its contests against top national sides like the Canadians, the Russians, and the Americans. Sturm suddenly smiled and said, "'I have no interest in playing there.' 'What? Why not?' 'I intend to be in the [Stanley Cup] playoffs here, with the Bruins,'" Sturm answered.[39] Case closed: Virtually all NHL players of any nationality share Sturm's sentiment, much preferring to play in the North America–based Stanley Cup tournament rather than the world championship. Similarly, the newly instituted World Baseball Classic (first played in 2005, subsequently in 2009, and designed to be performed quadrennially a la the World Cup in soccer and the Olympics) remains marginal to the average American baseball fan; and football does not even bother to have any international competition at all.

Even marquee international events like the Summer Olympics cannot stand up to hegemonic sports in America. Tellingly, Dick Ebersol of NBC Sports had to lobby the Chinese Olympic Committee, the organizers of the Olympic Games in Beijing, China's leading politicians, and the International Olympic Committee to have the 2008 Beijing games held in August instead of the desired September. He knew that American television audiences in September would be lost to college football and the NFL, both of which commence their season right around Labor Day, not to mention the final stretch of the pennant races in baseball.[40]

Thus, the Chinese decision to begin the Olympics at 8:08 PM on 08/08/08—thus hoping that the number 8, which has auspicious connotations in Chinese culture, would serve as a good luck charm for the coun-

[39] Jeff Z. Klein, "Fenway or Gelsenkirchen? One Player's View," *New York Times*, July 16, 2009.

[40] Bill Carter, "On TV, Timing Is Everything at the Olympics," *New York Times*, August 25, 2008.

try's athletes in the competition—had less to do with satisfying Chinese superstitions and much more with accommodating NBC's (one of the Olympics' most cherished cash cows) cold calculations based on the network's well-researched preferences of the American sports-viewing public. Furthermore, while American hegemonic sports attract year-round attention, particularly to drafts, recruiting, free agency, training camps, and preseasons, the World Cup, no matter how popular, disappeared from the media within days of its conclusion in each profiled year. To invoke the Beijing Olympics yet again, even these massively popular Michael Phelps–Usain Bolt games were virtually invisible in the media within two or three days of their finish. By that time, football in its college and professional variants, and baseball's heated pennant races, had once again assumed their accustomed center stage of the American sports space.

Global Events vs. Normalcy

Even other marquee international soccer matches apart from the World Cup, like those of the quadrennial Copa América, the quadrennial Confederations Cup, the quadrennial European national championship tournament (EURO),[41] and the bi-annual Gold Cup are but a blip on the radar of the American sports consciousness. While the 2008 European national championship jointly hosted by Austria and Switzerland offered a mildly popular television presence in the United States (ESPN2 averaged a 0.5 rating through the first fifteen matches, ESPN a 0.9 through the quarterfinals, and the final drew an impressive 3.1 on ESPN—which translates into 2.4 million households), the tournament proved to be a rather unimportant event in the American print media, with twenty-nine papers combining to run only forty-nine original articles, including zero staff-written stories in soccer-friendly *USA Today*.[42]

Perhaps never as emphatically as in the summer of 2009 did the normal

---

[41] This European international competition began in 1960 as the European Nations' Cup. The name UEFA European Championship was adopted in 1968. This is still the full proper name, though since the 10th European Championship in 1996 hosted by England, the tournament has also become known, and is commonly referred to, as the "Euro." It is now presented as such in capital letters (UEFA EURO) by official UEFA sources and in the official logo. We will henceforth use "EURO" in this book. See http://europeanhistory.about .com/od/cultureartliterature/a/Uefaeuroc.htm; http://www.uefa.com/competitions/euro2012/ index.html. Retrieved November 25, 2009.

[42] Dennis Yusko, "ESPN—Extra Soccer Please Now!" *timesunion.com blogs*, June 26, 2008. Retrieved August 2, 2008, from blogs.timesunion.com. Associated Press, "Euro Final Gets 3.1 Overnight Rating on ABC," *ESPN.com*, June 30, 2008). Retrieved August 2, 2008, from www .espn.com.

dichotomy that has characterized soccer's existence in America for at least two decades become starker. In the wake of the U.S. national team's second-place finish and superb showing at the quadrennial Confederations Cup held in South Africa—in which the team defeated Spain, then the top-ranked national side in the world, and barely lost to eventual champion Brazil, always one of the very best, in a gripping final—the globe's finest club teams visited America to play local MLS teams as well as each other in a new tournament called the World Football Challenge.[43] Attendance at the tournament's six games was nothing short of sensational, the quality of the games was first-rate, and the Challenge—won by Chelsea—was an all-out success. Barely a few days after the conclusion of this immensely successful tournament, the two top Spanish teams, Barcelona and Real, descended upon the United States with all their star players in tow to play five games against MLS and a Mexican team. The biggest American soccer crowd in over fifteen years (nearly 94,000 people) watched Barcelona defeat the L.A. Galaxy by a score of 2–1 on a Saturday night in the legendary Rose Bowl in Pasadena, with David Beckham tallying the Galaxy's goal with one of his signature "bend-it-like-Beckham"-style free kicks.

Stars were out everywhere—on the field, in the stands, in the sky—and the whole event was an amazing success story for soccer in America, or was it? As Helene Elliott pointed out in her column in the *Los Angeles Times* following the game, though these attendance figures were wonderful, they had appeared before in the annals of American soccer: 97,000 fans at the Rose Bowl for the bronze medal game at the L.A. Olympics in 1984, fol-

---

[43] While we might not go as far as Paul Gardner routinely has by inveighing against America's "Eurosnobs," who constantly prefer English terminology to anything American in the world of association football (see our note 33 in chap. 1), we do believe that using the word "football" in America to denote "soccer" to establish this very game as the sole legitimate owner of this very term, will end in unnecessary frustrations and ultimate failure. The term "football" denotes a different game in America, a hugely popular and powerful one. We think it futile to establish soccer's cultural presence in America by fighting a terminological battle over an allegedly proper nomenclature, which does not exist in any case. In the same vein, we find it problematic when ESPN and Fox Soccer Channel seem to make it a habit to have most of their soccer broadcasters and color commentators speak with a British—or decidedly foreign—accent to establish their bona fide credentials to the American sports-viewing public. Far from submitting a xenophobic or countercosmopolitan argument here, in that we object to foreign-sounding announcers assuming important roles in American sports broadcasting, we do agree with Alexi Lalas that by now soccer has attained an American presence that is sui generis and that needs no hiding. Soccer in America has reached a level that places it beyond the scale in which foreign accents, particularly of the British variety, ipso facto credential the speaker to his or her audience. All of these points just confirm the validity of our language analogy in the construction of the identities of all sports cultures. (On Alexi Lalas's take on this matter, see Grant Wahl, *The Beckham Experiment*, p. 159.)

lowed by nearly 102,000 for the gold medal game in which France defeated Brazil; all eight matches played at the Rose Bowl during the World Cup tournament in 1994 drew nearly 90,000 spectators—an absolutely sensational number unparalleled at any other World Cup in its eighty-year history. More than 90,000 were present at the Rose Bowl in 1999 to witness the final game between China and the United States in the women's World Cup. Elliott then continues: "There is an audience for soccer, for the big occasions when remarkable club teams such as Barcelona visit. Yet, Saturday's crowd was about six times bigger than the average MLS crowd, which was about 15,515 in mid-July. The disconnect remains between fans who will come out in happy droves to see Barcelona or Milan play the Galaxy and the smaller crowds that file into MLS stadiums. How to turn these fans into MLS fans is [MLS Commissioner Don] Garber's biggest challenge."[44] Elliott could have mentioned another major disconnect besetting American soccer's events versus normalcy predicament: the abysmal television ratings gathered by these super clubs and super games and super tournaments. The six matches played during the World Football Challenge averaged a meager 0.3 rating for ESPN, and the much-touted Barcelona vs. Galaxy game on that starry night hailed an even lower national rating on Fox Soccer Channel.

The big-event-based success of soccer in America has not gone unnoticed among English Premier League strategists, planners and owners who have actively debated adding a 39th game to the EPL's current 38-game schedule which would then be played in the United States. But as Chris Chase astutely comments on such plans, the EPL better make sure that it not have Stoke City play Portsmouth at Giants Stadium, and that this game better feature teams with American name recognition like the big four of Manchester United, Chelsea, Arsenal, or Liverpool, preferably in a game facing each other. "A soccer equivalent of the New Orleans Saints–Miami Dolphins game (which was played in London in 2008) won't fly. . . . The EPL also wouldn't have the luxury of picking one location and sticking with it (as the NFL has done with Wembley). The game will need to rotate on a yearly basis amongst cities with big soccer followings (Los Angeles, New York, Washington/Baltimore) and places with enthusiastic hosts (as Fenway Park apparently is) to ensure freshness in new markets."[45] Soccer, so Chase, has failed in America because it has been selling the

---

[44] Helene Elliott, "The future of MLS is pinned to nights like this," *Los Angeles Times*, August 2, 2009.

[45] Chris Chase, "Can the English Premier League Succeed in the United States," *Soccer Experts Blog*, October 27, 2009. Retrieved October 29, 2009.

wrong product. The EPL could be the right one because it represents the best of the best—and the increasingly soccer-savvy American consumer knows this.

While the appeal in following hegemonic sports often lies in the sport itself, the World Cup and other soccer tournaments (and, for that matter, all other *Olympianized* events) are attractive to most American viewers primarily as an outlet for nationalistic pride. Jonathan Kay alleges that nationalism is the main, perhaps the sole, reason for the temporal popularity of most Olympianized sports. He invokes Jerry Seinfeld's classic comment that on occasions in which we cheer for sports that we otherwise do not follow, "we're essentially cheering for laundry."[46] This, of course, does not only pertain to Americans but to all nations who, just like Americans, wildly cheer for their respective compatriots performing quadrennially in sports that, between the Olympics, remain confined to niches for the rest of the time.

This burgeoning Olympianization of the World Cup signals a new facet in America's perennially puzzling soccer culture. While in the soccer-rich countries of Europe and South America, to be a soccer player means that one is almost by default a soccer viewer, no such implicit tie exists in the United States. Historically, soccer in America has been polarized; nearly 20 million people with few-to-no cultural ties to the game play recreationally, while a much smaller, distinct group of rabid enthusiasts represents America's narrow base of all-around soccer followers.[47] Now, a rather large World Cup following—a demographic whose interest in soccer essentially begins and ends with the World Cup—has emerged as America's largest swath of soccer fans. These World Cup—as opposed to soccer—fans follow this tournament decidedly not only for nationalistic reasons but primarily because it is a global event featuring the best of the best. Indeed, according to Sunil Gulati, the president of the United States Soccer Federation, "Americans are the number one ticket buyers to the World Cup" with the United States also making the largest TV rights payment of any country for that tournament.[48] With the addition of the relatively new category of World Cup followers, the traditional American dual classification of an impressive quantity of soccer players (featuring the largest number of registered active participants in the world) on the one hand and a small

---

[46] Jonathan Kay, "War in Lycra; Forget the Flim Flam about Building Global Harmony. What the Olympics Are Really about Is Petty Nationalism," *National Post*, August 12, 2008.

[47] Markovits and Hellerman, "The 'Olympianization' of Soccer in the United States," p. 1545.

[48] Jack Bell, "Gauging Progress of U.S. Soccer; 30 Seconds with Sunil Gulati," *New York Times*. November 8, 2009.

group of soccer followers on the other, has a third category—that of World Cup enthusiasts.

And nothing promises to enlarge this new category in America, and thus, perhaps, that of the soccer followers as well, than ESPN's phenomenal commitment to the forthcoming World Cups in South Africa in 2010 and in Brazil in 2014. Each year for the past six or seven, about seventy-five ESPN executives have met in a retreat to discuss the company and its challenges. The topics typically covered in these top-level meetings pertain to the network's leading priorities for the upcoming year. The World Cup in South Africa was designated just such a top priority for 2010.[49] ESPN's plans for unprecedented coverage of the World Cup was spurred by John Skipper, the network's executive vice president, who is that truly rare person on either side of the Atlantic to be fully conversant in all sports languages featured in this book. He is that rare American "who can equally negotiate the world of Craven Cottage and Ricky Craven" and whose love for and knowledge of soccer is "no Beckham-come-lately act" but hails from his devoted support for the north London club Tottenham Hotspurs.[50]

Not only will the giant network telecast all the tournament games, but it will establish two SportsCenter sets on location that will broadcast in eight languages in fourteen countries throughout the month-long World Cup. This South Africa-based SportsCenter will be airing on its own but also in hook-ups with the regular SportsCenter in Bristol, Connecticut. There will be a nightly "World Cup Live" show in which three of the network's anchors and four of its reporters will follow teams and file reports from South Africa. "One reporter will be assigned to the U.S. team in the same way ESPN reporter Ed Werder is assigned to the Dallas Cowboys. The group will collectively contribute to the majority of ESPN's planned forty-five hours of studio coverage of the World Cup."[51] And well-established broadcasting techniques hailing from such ESPN signatures as "Monday Night Football," among the longest running sports programs

[49] We are grateful to Mac Nwulu of ESPN to have shared this information in an e-mail message dated July 28, 2009.

[50] Richard Deitsch, "ESPN Planning World Cup Blowout" in SI.COM, July 1, 2009. Retreived July 1, 2009. For readers who might not be familiar with the references to either or both of the "Cravens," Craven Cottage is the home ground of the London-based football club Fulham; and Ricky Craven was a NASCAR driver perhaps best known for a spectacular crash that accorded him star status on YouTube. He is now a NASCAR analyst for various media, including ESPN. Once again, the case of John Skipper's love of a sport (in this case soccer) demonstrates how crucial in this sport's societal and cultural dissemination the role of a single dedicated individual in a position of power really is.

[51] Tripp Mickle, "Trip to South Africa? Count 'SportsCenter' in," *SportsBusiness Journal*, June 15, 2009.

and most successful shows of any kind on American television, will be brought to bear upon this World Cup coverage.

While the $100 million that ESPN will pay for the combined rights to cover the World Cups in 2010 and 2014 is rather modest compared to what NBC pays for the exclusive rights to televise the Olympics—and what the networks spend to televise major American sports events from the Super Bowl to the NBA finals, the BCS college football games, and the March Madness basketball games—the World Cup's value to a network of ESPN's importance has mightily increased. Not so long ago MLS had to pay the network to broadcast the world's premier sports tournament to the American viewing public, demonstrating prima facie soccer's weak position as a supplicant in America's hegemonic sports culture. Put succinctly, ESPN, the self-proclaimed "worldwide leader in sports," has come to take the World Cup seriously.

But more importantly, ESPN shows signs that it is beginning to take soccer seriously. Its SportsCenter anchors show soccer clips in their top-ten highlights that conclude the show daily—which are coveted by players and viewers alike. Moreover, all kinds of soccer results, from MLS, European Champions League, English Premier League, Spanish *La Liga*, Italian Serie A, German Bundesliga, and the Mexican League appear with regularity on ESPN's crawlers at the bottom of the television screen. Furthermore, ESPN entered hitherto uncharted territory in being the first American network to broadcast English Premier League games—in England. The network also acquired a package of EPL matches that it now regularly shows to American audiences on Saturday mornings and Monday nights. The consequences of ESPN's commitment to the World Cup and soccer in general will undoubted increase the game's presence in America's sports culture. Already in the summer of 2009, thirty-seven host cities were contacted by the USA Bid Committee that was formed to bring the World Cup back to the United States for 2018 or 2022. The contrast to 1994 could not have been starker. Speaking on this topic, the aforementioned Sunil Gulati says, "We are getting a receptivity that is very different than the one we had in 1986 or 1987 [regarding USA 1994]. Having been part of that effort back then, in many cases we'd have to explain what the World Cup was, when it was, how many games it was. In this case, this is a non-issue. We have got civic leaders, stadium leaders, team owners, politicians very interested in trying to bring the World Cup to their city. People understand what the World Cup is about."[52]

---

[52] "Gulati on Gold Cup, World Cup and More," *SoccerAmerica*, July 29, 2009.

"Bend It like Beckham": American Soccer Hopes between New Immigrants and Global Players

These American World Cup enthusiasts do not, of course, exist all by themselves in a vacuum. Instead, they very much represent soccer's changed gestalt in the United States and the world since the demise of the NASL in the middle of the 1980s. In a strange way, that league was ahead of its time by showcasing the New York Cosmos, perhaps the world's very first global soccer team, or arguably the first global sports team of any kind. Consistently featuring players from six countries (sometimes more), the Cosmos embodied a global team that was glamorous and played excellent soccer, but lacked any local culture and institutions to ground it and give the team, and the league in which it performed, the necessary local support that any such global venture needs in order to succeed.

But despite MLS's continued shortcomings in terms of its deficient television presence and even its still mediocre product on the field, it has become something that NASL never was and that is absolutely essential for the broad cultural success of any sport, even in (and because of) the prolific stage of our second globalization. What MLS has done is provide the presence of a local anchor, of a daily league that creates and guarantees continuity on the ground. If nothing else, this league has become the successful breeding ground for America's top male players that form the men's national team, which as we will argue later still remains perhaps the most essential piece in catapulting soccer into America's hegemonic sports culture. MLS's contribution to America's successful performance in the 2002 World Cup is exemplified by the fact that eleven of the twenty-three players in the American lineup were from that league. Eight of them were on the field during the victory over Mexico. Five of the total seven goals were scored by MLS players, and many of the team's stars, such as Landon Donovan, Claudio Reyna, Clint Mathis, Josh Wolff, Brian McBride, Cobi Jones and Eddie Pope, played for MLS teams. This essential MLS contribution to American soccer has intensified since 2002. MLS, though weak and marginal to America's contemporary sports culture, remains absolutely central to soccer's possible success in this country. It offers the grounding for American soccer that NASL never did, nor could. And let us never forget that at the point of this writing the league had just concluded its fourteenth season and the trajectory for the future shows nothing but promise and improvement. Above all, the quality of play, though still mediocre by the standards of the world's top leagues in Europe, visibly demonstrates steady improvements from season to season. MLS might still be peripheral to the world of American sports culture and global soccer; but its gradual march to the core of both—though far from guaranteed—appears quite plausible at this juncture, which it assuredly did not a decade before. The changed nature of American society and technology has massively altered much in the United States over the past two to three decades, soccer included. As part of an emerging layer of global culture, the interest in professional soccer in America has grown over time and way beyond America's borders. Quite similar to the following of the World Cup, this new dimension of soccer's presence in America jibes with the wish to see nothing but the best of the best, which in this case means the top four professional European leagues and the European superleague in the form of the Champions League. According to overnight Nielsen ratings, ESPN2 netted a 0.8 rating for its broadcast of the Chelsea vs. Manchester United Champions League final in Moscow in May 2008. It averaged 1,097,000 viewers throughout the game, which was played in the middle of the afternoon on a weekday in most of the United States and in the late morning on the West Coast. This constitutes the single highest rating for a UEFA match in ESPN's history and marks the first time in 218 UEFA broadcasts on the network that average viewership topped the 1 million mark.[53] According to Nielsen's Hispanic rating, the Spanish broadcast by ESPN Deportes was seen by 213,000 viewers, bringing the grand total of ESPN viewers to 1,310,000. With Univision's (the Spanish-language network) soccer viewership frequently surpassing ESPN's, it would not be surprising if nearly 3 million people watched this game in the United States.[54] These are still modest numbers and pale next to those attained by mega-American sports events. But such television presence for international soccer was unthinkable in the United States before the new millenium. And compa-

[53] Jeff Hash, "American TV Viewership Tops One Million," May 24, 2008; http://www .epltalk.com/american-tv-viewership-for-champions-league-final-tops-1-million/2182. Retrieved December 12, 2008. The previous record was set in the 2006 final between Barcelona and Arsenal, which got a 0.7 rating from 770,000 viewers.

[54] It is interesting to note that many English-speaking American soccer fans who do not speak Spanish prefer watching UNIVISION to ESPN because they deem the former more authentic and better purveyors of soccer culture, whereas they view ESPN as imposters and inauthentic intruders into a sport which, so these purists argue, the network's reporters do not know, understand, or appreciate. Our analogy of sports as language pertains here since one encounters precisely such exclusionist views between the speakers of one language over another. It is however noteworthy that one of Univision's soccer mainstays has now entered the American sports vernacular. Andrés Cantor, one of the networks most renowned soccer announcers, capped every one of his exultations following a goal with a very lengthy and emphatic call of "Goooooooool," a commonplace in the broadcast of soccer games in Latin America, but totally unknown to North American sports audiences until Cantor made it popular and part of sports culture here as well.

rable numbers appeared nary one month later, when 2.4 million American households watched the 2008 EURO final in which Spain defeated Germany in Vienna.[55]

But it is not only by numbers of television viewers that one can gauge a marked change of soccer's stature in contemporary quotidian American culture.

The rising presence and visibility of European soccer paraphernalia—Manchester United, Chelsea, and even AS Roma shirts—on American streets and college campuses is another indicator of this growing interest in soccer as part of global popular culture. But more importantly, due to the Internet and global media, soccer knowledge and the language of soccer are considerably more widespread in America than ever before. When Rensmann wore a sweatshirt with a tiny Roma emblem in class, an American student from Indiana asked if he was a Roma fan and engaged him in a lengthy debate about the club's fortunes, which the student knew well. Anything even vaguely similar would have been unimaginable just a decade ago. By recognizing a Roma shirt and knowing details about the club's performance and history, this young University of Michigan undergraduate demonstrated that he was a knowledgeable consumer of global soccer culture. This was quite likely independent of, parallel to, and possibly in competition with the world of MLS and American soccer. Yet, even if this student's soccer interests were confined solely to Italy's Serie A and AS Roma in particular, we believe that his acquiring of soccer language on the global stage has affected this culture's expansion in America as well.

This will most certainly be the case in the long run because any interest in soccer on any level cannot but help increase awareness on all levels. But things might be a tad more complicated in the short run. If indeed, this youngster from Indiana has time limits (which we assume he does) and if

---

[55] As mentioned before, Spain's 1–0 victory over Germany in the European Championship final got a 3.1 overnight rating on ABC. It equals a decent but not great (neither impressive nor embarrassing), rating for a TV series premiere—but surely not a bad result, considering that this was the first EURO final broadcast on U.S. network television. The rating is on level terms with ESPN's second round broadcast of the American Golf Masters, which was the most-viewed golf telecast on cable ever. This number also gives ESPN and owner Disney a reason to rejoice. At a 2.5 rating, ABC's performance for the EURO 2008 final would have equaled the national rating picked up by Univision for its American broadcast of another continental championship: 2007's CONCACAF Gold Cup final between the United States and Mexico. This shows that there is a noteworthy, if smaller, audience on American television for big-event international soccer apart from the World Cup, both with and without American teams. See Jeff Hash, "ABC Gets 3.1 Overnight Rating For Spain-Germany Final: So What's Next For ESPN?," July 1, 2008; http://www.epltalk.com/abc-gets-31-overnight-rating-for-spain-germany-final-so-whats-next-for-espn/2536. Retrieved July 1, 2008.

he opts to fill his soccer quota within these limits by watching Serie A games instead of its MLS counterparts, then we have a clear case in which the pursuit of the best crowds out products of lesser quality. The second globalization's quotidian channels of communication—mainly the ubiquity of the Internet—render time and space irrelevant, meaning that this young man can just as easily watch his beloved AS Roma in the middle of Indiana or in Rome, thus making AS Roma totally equidistant in his world to that of, say, the Chicago Fire, the closest MLS club in his conventional geographic space.

In this context, the "Beckham effect"—based on the attempt to make MLS more popular by hiring "the world's most famous athlete"[56]—offers a fascinating but also ambiguous case of global players and their impact. On the one hand, the Beckham hoopla was a rousing success. Beckham introduced to the world his new club, the L.A. Galaxy, his new league, MLS, and by extension American soccer to a degree unimaginable without him. "The number of people worldwide who were now aware of Major League Soccer and the L.A. Galaxy had multiplied dramatically. The signing of David Beckham remains one of the most important things this league has ever done," MLS commissioner Garber argued in late 2008. "We are far more recognized, far more credible, and far more popular than we ever were."[57] Moreover, solely because of Beckham's crossover star power and his unique standing as a global celebrity, no other soccer player in the world—including more brilliant ones than Beckham—would have come close to attaining such an impressive feat virtually instantaneously. Furthermore, also from an all-important "business perspective, Beckham had been a gargantuan success for the Galaxy and MLS. By the spring of 2009, 350,000 official Beckham Galaxy jerseys had been sold" in the world, "more than three times the number of NBA superstars Kobe Bryant and LeBron James (who were in the 75,000–80,000 range)."[58] Adidas sold more L. A. Galaxy shirts in 2007 (one can safely assume virtually all with Beckham's name on their back) than any of the Superclubs' that this giant sporting goods manufacturer sponsors; the L.A. Galaxy shirt outsold other Adidas clubs of the AC Milan, Real Madrid, Liverpool, Bayern Munich variety in the global market. Not bad for a middling team of an upstart league. "The Galaxy's average attendance at the Home Depot Center in 2008 was 26,009, up 24.9 percent from 2006, even though the team had raised aver-

---

[56] Thus the appropriate subtitle of Grant Wahl's book, *The Beckham Experiment*.
[57] Ibid., pp. 279, 280.
[58] Ibid., p. 166

age ticket prices from $21.50 to $32. What's more, Beckham's arrival had increased the Galaxy's sponsorship revenue by $6 million in 2007 alone."[59]

On the other hand, the Beckham saga also proved a failure. Whether the Beckham experiment is the soccer equivalent of *Ishtar* or the *Spruce Goose* on the field, as Wahl provocatively argues in his book,[60] may be a tad too harsh. Still, even though Beckham increased attendance at live Galaxy games both at home and on the road—they averaged 28,132 fans per game on the road, nearly an amazing 10,000 more than any other MLS team— his presence made virtually no difference in the League's miniscule TV ratings, "always the best measure of national impact," as Wahl states correctly.[61] But Beckham's most significant shortcomings occurred on the playing field, where he disappointed his American audience in an injury-plagued first year by his virtual absence from the game and by his pallid performance in his second. Adding insult to injury, Beckham forced a temporary transfer to AC Milan where he regained his lost brilliance and played superbly. Moreover, he repeatedly let it be known through interviews but also his body language that he would much rather have stayed in Milan to play with AC full time instead of honoring his commitment to the Galaxy and MLS. Gone were Beckham's earlier pronouncements of his wanting to be a pioneer for soccer in America by leading the sport to a greater cultural presence there.

Beckham's actions underlined two tenets of this book: 1) playing with the best matters greatly to all involved, sports producers and consumers, and even to global superstars like Beckham, who incurred a considerable financial loss (which, of course, he can easily afford) by his partial transfer to Milan and his time-sharing arrangement with the Galaxy and MLS. Being surrounded by players of comparable quality in Milan as opposed to those of lesser quality in Los Angeles surely must have increased Beckham's pleasure in playing soccer, which, though it is his livelihood, is also his passion; 2) prowess in sports ultimately remains solely anchored in output and achievement. In Beckham's case, all his glitter and pizzazz rests on his being a very fine soccer player, which the world began to doubt after the fiascos of his first two years with the Galaxy. Perhaps the most telling signs of Beckham's ultimate success in having helped transform American soccer culture at least a bit were the numerous L.A. Galaxy fans who roundly booed and jeered him during his first game with the team after his

[59] Ibid., p. 279.
[60] Ibid., p. 253. Both of these were big-budgeted, much-heralded movies that turned out to be total flops at the box office.
[61] Ibid., p. 279.

arrival from Milan. Such "European" demeanor clearly bespoke a true passion on the part of these fans, who felt slighted by Beckham's apparent lack of commitment to them and their team, and his implicitly dismissive attitude toward their game in America. But to their credit—as well as Beckham's—the player proved everybody wrong with his superb performance on the field in his third year as a member of the L.A. Galaxy. Beckham's actions once again confirmed that he was first and foremost an excellent soccer player and a serious professional who was much "more than celebrity stimulus," as a headline of a detailed story in the New York Times on David Beckham's third-year achievements with the L.A. Galaxy so aptly stated.[62] Demonstrating to himself, the L.A. Galaxy's fans, as well as MLS's and global soccer's that he remained a true champion by having led each and every one of the teams on which he played to that team's national championship or at least to a much better standing than it possessed previous to Beckham's arrival, Beckham propelled the Galaxy to the MLS Cup final in which his team succumbed to upstart Real Salt Lake in a dramatic penalty shoot out. The Beckham experiment may still prove to be an immense boon to American soccer's progress as a sport and to Beckham's stature as a player in the country's sports culture way beyond t-shirt sales and other ancillary phenomena.

Beckham's unique crosscultural appeal—he is loved by women, gays, metrosexuals, fashionistas, New Age adherents, Jews (for being one-quarter Jewish), among many other disparate constituencies—also includes the Latino community worldwide. In America's dynamic immigrant society Latinos represent a key dimension to soccer's future in the country's sports culture. Every second new American citizen is Latino.[63] Today there are some 47 million Latinos residing in the United States; 31 million of them speak Spanish. They are the fastest growing and the biggest ethnic minority, and it is projected that the Latino population will nearly triple by the year 2050, reaching 133 million. This would represent an increase from 15 to 30 percent of the total population. Latinos are dispersed throughout the entire Union without any specific pattern.[64] They play a steadily larger role in determining elections and sports culture.[65] Many of

[62] Jeré Longman, "More Than Celebrity Stimulus," New York Times, November 10, 2009.

[63] See John Branch, "Among Hispanics in America, N.F.L. Mania Hits Cultural Wall," New York Times, February 3, 2007, pp. A1, B13.

[64] See José Luis Martinez, "The Largest Minority Counts in the United States," Bulletin Safe Democracy, September 11, 2008, http://english.safe-democracy.org/2008/09/11/the-largest-counts-in-the-US. Retrieved September 11, 2008.

[65] Marie Price and Courtney Whitworth, "Soccer and Latino Cultural Space: Metropolitan Washington Fútbol Leagues," in Daniel D. Arreola, ed., Hispanic Spaces, Latino Places:

the new immigrants have strong attachments to the soccer culture in which they were socialized. They "import" soccer into the United States and instantly provide a strong base for MLS games, which have an average attendance of circa 15,000. This is a respectable figure, incidentally, that places MLS well ahead of many European countries and most Latin American ones, putting it among the top ten soccer leagues of the world, though behind the attendance of the top European leagues and the Big Four American sports.

Furthermore, according to six hundred senior level executives of the American sports industry interviewed in December 2006 by Turnkey Sports for *Sports Business Journal*, Major League Soccer does the best marketing job of all professional leagues in the Latino target group. In the long run, the still marginalized but increasingly self-assertive Latino communities may one day occupy the center of America's sports space and change the country's identity.[66]

Soccer in America—Self-Assertive at the Margins?

Soccer, the most global sports language, still has difficulties entering into America's hegemonic sports culture and the country's sports market. Yet, global pressures and the emergence of an increasingly present global soccer boom—with dedicated and powerful sponsors and investors like Rupert Murdoch and Philip Anschutz, Latin American immigration, grass-roots soccer among middle-class youths, and, as we argue, especially American successes at a number of international tournaments ("Olympianization")— have put soccer on the map. The conditions for professional soccer in today's America are markedly different than they were in the early 1990s.[67]

Community and Cultural Diversity in Contemporary America (Austin: University of Texas Press, 2004).

[66] Such "soccer migration" and diaspora communities do not have any equivalent in Europe or elsewhere, where immigrants from the Maghreb, Africa, Turkey, or the Middle East are usually socialized in the hegemonic sport. For a detailed analysis of transnational Latino soccer spaces and Hispanic soccer culture in America, see Juan Javier Pescador, "Vamos Taximaroa! Mexican/Chicano Soccer Associations and Transnational/Translocal Communities, 1967–2002," *Latino Studies* 2 (3), 2004; Juan Javier Pescador, "Los Héroés del Domingo: Soccer, Borders, and Social Spaces in Great Lakes Mexican Communities 1940–1970," in Jorge Iber and Samuel O. Regalado, eds., *Mexican Americans and Sports: A Reader on Athletics and Barrio Life* (College Station: Texas A&M University Press, 2007).

[67] "Sports are going global," *Sports Business Digest*, November 19, 2007, http://sportsbus inessdigest.com/?p=146. Retrieved December 20, 2008. As *Sports Business Digest* suggests, the "most popular sport in the world, soccer, is even gaining popularity here in America. . . .

This is also best attested to by the fact that a number of MLS teams have established close cooperative relationships with top European clubs through a mutual desire on both sides of the Atlantic. This, of course, also means that these clubs are interested in establishing footholds in America's growing soccer world. Thus, the Colorado Rapids have a relationship with Arsenal; the San Jose Earthquakes with Arsenal's main north London rival Tottenham Hotspurs; Real Salt Lake took its name from Europe's most successful club Real Madrid, as it did its all-white shorts and jerseys. The two teams enjoy very warm relations and participate in reciprocal player development. Not to be outdone by its Castilian rival, Barcelona—the pride of Catalonia—concluded a strategic partnership with MLS in April 2007. And Chivas USA, located in Los Angeles, is a direct subsidiary of Chivas from Guadalajara, one of Mexico's two most pedigreed and popular soccer clubs. Lastly, of course, there has been marketing cooperation between the New York Yankees and Manchester United since 2001. Unlike the other mentioned arrangements, this one has nothing to do with actual games of soccer or baseball, and represents a pure business venture in which the two teams share in the marketing of each other's paraphernalia in their respective home countries as well as elsewhere in the world.

As a major sign of the Europeans' respect for the quality of leadership present in American sports management, MLS included, it is noteworthy that a number of Americans and U.S.-based Europeans attained important positions in European soccer, particularly in the English Premier League, arguably the world's best: MLS deputy commissioner Ivan Gazidis was appointed as Arsenal's chief executive in late 2008; American attorney Bruce Buck is the chairman of Chelsea. It was through his work with U.S. law firm Skadden, Arps, Slate, Meagher & Flom that he advised Russian billionaire Roman Abramovich on his acquisition of Chelsea. Garry Cook, who for a long time worked in the American sporting goods manufacturing industry, is the executive chairman of Manchester City. Cook worked for Nike for many years. He was president of its Jordan brand for only four months when he was hired by City in 2008. Charles C. Krulak, the director general of Aston Villa, was previously the Commandant of the Marine Corps. He rose to the rank of general and later served as the chief admin-

---

There are actually talks of the U.S.A. holding premier league soccer matches." "I can see that happening sooner rather than later—it would be good for the game," said West Ham non-executive chairman Eggert Magnusson; see "US to host Premier League 'Soccer'?" *Footie Blog Soccer Rules!* October 26, 2007, http://footieblog.co.uk/us-to-host-premier-league-soccer. Retrieved November 20, 2008.

istrative officer for MBNA America Bank. It was his relationship with
MBNA chairman Randy Lerner that led to his work with Villa. Lerner
bought Villa in 2006.[68]

Despite all these important cross-continental shifts that bespeak genuine changes wrought by the forces of the second globalization, there is one
remaining cultural factor that still persists from the world of the first globalization. Whereas the allegiance and affinity of the regular male sports
fan, Joe Six Pack if you will, is surely nowhere near as essential and powerful as it was at the end of the nineteenth century and the beginning of the
twentieth when these hegemonic sports cultures emerged, it is equally evident that no institutionalized (and thus lasting) sports culture will emerge
anywhere even in this globalized world without at least the solid, if not
exclusive, support by this still essential social carrier of sports. All soccer
experts in America know this. And so do global companies that have been
actively marketing their soccer-related goods in every corner of the world,
including the United States. Against this background, we will let an immensely revealing advertisement by Nike, surely a major force in the world
of sports culture across the globe, speak for itself. Filling the entire back
page of the October 24, 2005 issue of *ESPN, The Magazine*—one of *the* key
American sports magazines read almost entirely by millions of American
male sports fans, dedicated almost exclusively to the American Big Four
sports, and constituting sports giant ESPN's print medium—is a Nike
commercial modeled on the Declaration of Independence of the Fourth of
July 1776. Tellingly, the whole text appears under the famous motto,
"Don't Tread on me," featuring the rattlesnake as an exclusively American
predator. The precursor for this motto and logo was developed by Benja-
min Franklin in the 1750s. However, by the beginning of the War of Independence the logo and motto together emerged as the symbol for American autonomy, resistance, patriotism, individualism, freedom, and rejection
of British rule. It has remained as a symbol of opposition and defiance in
America to this day and constitutes an icon for "red-blooded" American
patriotism that borders on the xenophobic. It most certainly signifies the
domain of American male bravado and expresses a solid dosage of unmitigated counter-cosmopolitanism:

> So Says this American Game. It is hereby stated that this game, needing only a
> ball and your feet, is no longer the whipping boy of the ignorant. The game,

[68] See Paul Kennedy, "American Influence Grows in EPL," *SoccerAmerica*, November
28, 2008; http://www.socceramerica.com/index.cfm?fuseaction=Articles.san&s=29851&Nid
=49855&p=. Retrieved on November 28, 2008.

from sea to shining sea, has swarmed America's parks and yards. Every green space and driveway is our shooting gallery. This game is now as integral to our country as hot dogs at a barbecue or turkey on Thanksgiving or fireworks on the Fourth of July. It is booming. It is exploding. Light fuse and get away.

So Says This American Game. We live in a proud nation of more than 17 million players of this game. We outnumber Holland's population. We are twice Portugal's population. By sheer numbers alone, we are going to sweep over most of the globe.

So Says This American Game. Our men's national team ranks in the top ten in the world. Less than 20 short years ago, even microscopic island nations drooled rivers at the opportunity to dribble around us; to make us wish we never gained independence from England. They laughed at us. Now, these United States are going to Germany to play on the biggest stage of all. It is our fifth consecutive qualification. Other nations do not merely scout us anymore; they toss and turn and develop digestive problems over us. And our sport is one in which you actually play other countries on your way to the championship.

So Says This American Game. A fierce, unwavering strength of this land is that it is the great American melting pot. No game has taken greater advantage of this fusion than ours. We assemble a rich roster of Hispanic, European, Asian, and African cultures, kick in a ball, stir it all up, and make the best of all worlds.

So Says This American Game. Our preeminent stars include everyone from a player who grew up in a Texas trailer home to a striker who learned to shame defenders in the projects in Florida. This sport is no longer exclusive to the children of the suburbs. The minivan is not the official vehicle of our sport.

So Says This American Game. Yes, there are still those who despise our sport—our own countrymen, in fact. But let them hate. Let them moan all they want from atop their barstools and behind their keyboards and radio booth glass; the First Amendment guarantees they can do just that. But there is no-where in that hallowed, yellowing document that says we will listen.

So Says This American Game. And no matter how France looks down on us, or Brazil doubts us, or England mocks us; no matter what the odds, or the situation, or the game, the American people have this uncanny, gloriously stubborn belief that if we want something badly enough, we will achieve it. This is the desire that coursed through the veins of our revolutionaries in 1776 and of our hockey team in 1980.[69] Our country finds a way to win.

[69] The reference here, of course, is to the famous "Miracle on Ice," when at the Winter Olympics in Lake Placid in 1980 a team of American college boys defeated the mighty Soviet Union's "Red Machine" hockey team. Then they proceeded to win the gold medal at the Games, furnishing perhaps one of the biggest upsets in any team sport's history. It also constituted one of those rare, possibly singular, moments in which Americans from coast to coast truly had the sense of rooting for a national team—which is so common to soccer culture and

So Says This American Game. This is soccer. A game for the flag-waving, tax-paying, apple-pie-eating, Star-Spangled-Banner-singing, red-blooded American.

So Says This American Game.

Here it is then, loud and clear: American soccer's declaration of independence from the Big Four American sports and a decisive challenge to them, as well as to the rest of the soccer world. Unlike the Big Four sports, whose champions all call themselves (wrongly and arrogantly) "World Champions" without ever having played anybody outside of North America, American soccer is a truly international game in which "you actually play other countries on your way to the world championship." Moreover, American soccer, so Nike alleges, is no longer the game of upper-middle-class suburban children carted around by women and soccer moms in "minivans," which are no longer "the official vehicle of our sport," but of young tough men from the white working class ("Texas trailer home")— who ride on their Harley Davidson "hogs" or in their pickup trucks presumably— and the inner-city black ghettoes ("projects") who will succeed in defying all the doubters both here at home (the Big-Four soccer haters) and abroad (the America haters). In this imagery, America's soccer world will have finally become totally "Europeanized."[70] Leave it to Nike's marketing genius to comprehend that no cosmopolitan culture's lasting success in any hegemonic sport stands a chance without the decisive support by at least a significant segment of the counter-cosmopolitan constituents. Alas, in the course of the three years that passed between this ad's appearance and our writing this book, Nike has gradually departed from its sponsorship of American soccer, leaving the field almost entirely to its erstwhile global competitor, Adidas. But many of Nike's projections and much of its wishful thinking have in the meantime become greater realities: the Amer-

---

so alien to that of the North American Big Four, with the possible exception of the Canadians' enthusiasm for Team Canada's international exploits in hockey.

[70] According to this self-confident American vision, soccer will be appropriated by the nation, while America's soccer world is fully "Europeanized." This, of course, would also be a challenge to the cherished European soccer identity, as already indicated in the suspicions and malevolence evoked by the Beckham deal. Many European fans are also alarmed by the purchase of some of their most beloved and pedigreed teams by American investors. In this realm, too, America as the hated "Mr. Big" plays a role in contemporary European politics and life. Nothing seems scarier to European soccer fans than a World Cup success by the United States men's national team (as opposed to its women's side, which merely confirms to Europeans America's strangeness and inferiority and offers them further cause to smirk about America's irrelevance in soccer) which would mean that even in the world of soccer—a key source of perceived European superiority vis-à-vis the United States—America had become a superpower.

ican men's national team has become much better, no opponent takes it for granted anymore, the quality of play in MLS has improved mightily, American soccer fans have become fixtures in the world's leading soccer venues, and the fantastic atmosphere at Seattle Sounders Football Club games rival any at the grounds of the world's top clubs—in short, while America has in no way become a soccer giant in these intervening years, it no longer is a minnow either.[71]

European Transformations: From Soccer Expansion to the Rise of NBA Basketball

The Europeanization of Soccer

Soccer has not only undergone major transformations in the United States and in European-American interactions over the past three decades, but it has also experienced a significant intra-European shift that has altered allegiances, identities and cultures. Today, soccer connoisseurs, and even average fans, know much more about teams and players from European leagues not in their own countries than they did just twenty years ago, when soccer was still primarily a national and local matter. This is a product of Europe-wide broadcasting of games, the Internet, and a general process of political and cultural Europeanization on the entire continent way beyond sports.[72] Europe has followed the television-oriented American

[71] Simon Kuper and Stefan Szymanski, just like we, present the multi-faceted nature of soccer in America that emerged during the second globalization and, again like we, point to its differences compared to soccer's structure in its European core. "The U.S. has a strong culture. It's just different from any other country's soccer culture. In particular, it doesn't require a strong domestic men's professional league. Major League Soccer is not American soccer. It's just a tiny piece of the mosaic." *Soccernomics: Why England Loses, Why Germany and Brazil Win, and Why the U.S., Japan, Australia, Turkey—and even Iraq—Are Destined to Become the Kings of the World's Most Popular Sport* (New York: Nation Books, 2009), p. 164. Our only difference with these two authors pertains to our weighting the role of MLS. Even though the league is clearly just one of many facets of America's current soccer scene, we believe quite strongly that for the game to become part of America's hegemonic sports culture, this league needs to emerge as first among equals.

[72] On European postnational identity and Europeanization, see Gerard Delanty and Chris Rumford, *Rethinking Europe: Social Theory and the Implications of Europeanization* (New York: Routledge, 2005); Paul Gillespie and Brigid Laffan, "European Identity: Theory and Empirics," in Michelle Cini and Angela K. Bourne, eds., *Palgrave Advances in European Union Studies* (New York: Palgrave Macmillan, 2006, pp. 131–50); Lars Rensmann, "Americanism and Europeanism in the Age of Globalization: Hannah Arendt's Reflections on Europe and America and Implications for a Post-National Identity of the EU Polity," *European Journal of Political Theory* 5 (2), 2006, pp. 139–70.

model—featuring spectacular sports events that have become "must-see TV" for sports fans beyond the regions of the respective teams involved—and the evolution of fan cultures that are predominantly based on "televised" events instead of actual visits to stadiums, ballparks, or arenas (think of the World Series, the NBA Finals and, of course, the king of them all, the Super Bowl). Parallel media-driven developments in Europe have made it much more common to become a fan of a "Superclub" that one watches regularly on television, even if this club's home lies at a great distance from one's own. Thus, there are now many Manchester United, Real Madrid, Barcelona, Liverpool, Milan, or Inter fans, and fan clubs in virtually every European country, which was rarely, if ever, the case twenty years ago. Making things more interesting still is the common occurrence of having fans in location X follow and adore individual players starring for teams in locations Y and Z. Thus, clubs and players have come to transcend conventional boundaries not only in the realms of commerce and marketing but also in those of genuine affection and identification.[73]

It is evident that this Europeanization of soccer has a powerful commercial component. These megateams want to market their apparel and logos to as broad an audience as they can possibly reach. And television and the Internet make this possible. In this context, we object to an ongoing devaluation of "television fans" (or viewers) as "inauthentic" as opposed to "real" fans (or spectators), who claim the mantle of authenticity by dint of attending these events in person.[74] While it is true that stadium visits (i.e., spectatorship) and television watching (i.e., viewership) furnish two different kinds of experiences, and convey different senses of what these sports and games represent, there exists absolutely no evidence that somebody who came to love AC Milan by seeing all its games on television in an apartment in Budapest (i.e., a viewer) is less authentic a fan than his Milanese counterpart who sees his Rossoneri every other weekend at San Siro (i.e., a spectator). They obviously partake in very different experiences—which, however, do not render one "better" or more authentic than the

---

[73] See Paul Gilchrist, "Local heroes and global stars," in Lincoln Allison, ed., *The Global Politics of Sport: The Role of Global Institutions in Sport* (New York: Routledge, 2005), pp. 118–39.

[74] Some scholars working on sports, such as Maarten Van Bottenburg, for example, call people experiencing sports live and at their actual venues "spectators" whereas they label those that watch on television "viewers." While we find this differentiation helpful, we have opted not to follow it systematically in our book since, we believe that the meaning of each term is clear in the context in which it is used. We also do not see a major difference in terms of the attachment to the respective sports and events that this distinction is supposed to connote.

other. AC Milan emerges for both as a very different but no less central part of their respective identities. The very nature of globalization—in this case Europeanization—entails significantly altered bonds that have expanded soccer cultures beyond their traditional local and national ties.

As Anthony King argues, the growing number of live broadcasts of Champions League games and their viewing in pubs and other public spaces is a very important social process.[75] The Champions League, and the new culture it has generated in which fans become supporters of other European clubs, "constitutes a new ritual in Europe where a virtual audience gathers to watch the same event across the entire continent. In a myriad of parallel interaction rituals which occur in living rooms and in bars across Europe, fans renegotiate their relations with each other by reference to this new transnational context."[76] Televised soccer, new media, and especially the Champions League as an institutional framework represent the new realities of European soccer and illustrate "the decisive political economic transformations which have occurred in the New Europe." The collective consumption of televised live soccer in pubs, bars, and private homes has constituted an important new way of cultural Europeanization, as King suggests. Indeed, that hitherto exclusively American institution of "sports bar," meaning a place with lots of television screens airing a bevy of sports games simultaneously, has made its successful debut across the European continent in the past decade. Whatever form European soccer takes in the future, "this ritual [of collective television viewing] is likely to constitute a key site for the expression of social solidarity and identity in Europe . . . and, in the New Europe, increasingly becoming the most important ritual in which emergent networks of social relations are affirmed."[77]

Even if King's conclusion may be a tad too far-reaching with regard to European soccer's transnational nature, he persuasively points to a new development that has no parallel with any other contemporary European phenomenon. The decided exception is the Eurovision Song Contest, which, like soccer, is a pure expression of popular culture.[78] Despite con-

---

[75] See King, *The European Ritual*, p. 257.

[76] Ibid., p. 258.

[77] Ibid., p. 258, 259.

[78] The Eurovision Song Contest (*Concours Eurovision de la Chanson*) is an annual competition held among active member countries of the European Broadcasting Union (EBU). Each member country submits a song to be performed on live television and then casts votes for the other countries' songs to determine the most popular one in the competition. Each country participates via one of its national EBU-member television stations, whose task it is to select a singer and a song to represent their country in the international competition. The

tinued counter-cosmopolitan mobilizations of local, national, and chauvinist (in both senses of that term) identities (that we will explore in chapter
5), soccer and its fan culture have become increasingly Europeanized over
the past two to three decades, especially due to new communication technologies.[79] In addition to creating a genuine base for "bridging capital"
across countries and cultures, the Europeanization of soccer, led by the
Champions League and propelled by television, has also opened the game
to a hitherto almost completely excluded clientele: women. Precisely because these megagames—such as the Champions League final, the European National Championship and, of course, the World Cup—have become mega-events, women have come to join in their consumption and
thus the consumption of soccer. By including women, a hitherto excluded
constituency, these mega-events accomplish a palpable growth in the
game's cosmopolitanism. Market researchers on both sides of the Atlantic
have long known that women are mainly drawn to watching sports through
such relatively rare spectacles rather than their routinized, quotidian presence, which still remains the predominant purview of men. Consider
NBC's "feminizing" its quadrennial coverage of the Olympics, knowing
full well that the female viewing public for those events far exceeds the
usual quotient for regular games in the Big Four. We discuss Joe Six Pack's
palpable dismay on both sides of the Atlantic with the inclusive, cosmopolitan, and "feminized" aspects of these mega-events in soccer and other
"Olympianizations" in chapter 5.

Cultural Europeanization in no way alleviates the previously extant national and local ties. Contemporary Merseysiders continue to remain fanatical Liverpool or Everton supporters just as their fathers and grandfa-
thers had been. Their love for and identification with their clubs has not
diminished one iota just because most of the players hail from outside of
the British Isles, never mind Liverpool.[80] Their clubs are now known the
world over and have fans in Romania and as far away as China who wear

contest has been broadcast every year since its inauguration in 1956 and is one of the longest-
running television programs in the world. It is also one of the most-watched nonsporting
events, with audience figures having been quoted in recent years between 100 and 600 million internationally.

[79]This new "Europeanization" is also mirrored in the small but expanding European
"ground-hopper" community that reaches well beyond the pinnacles of European soccer
such as the Champions League. It comprises soccer connoisseurs who spend their spare time
traveling to lower division local club competitions across the European continent. See Jean-
Michel de Waele and Alexandre Husting, eds., *Football et identités* (Brussels: Editions de
l'Université de Bruxelles, 2008); Oliver Leisner, *Groundhopping Informer 2007/2008* (Fuldab-
rück: Agon Sportverlag, 2007); King, *The European Ritual*. Special thanks to Cas Mudde, with
whom Rensmann had many insightful conversations on the subject.

[80]Thus, for example, there were four Spaniards playing for the English club Liverpool

their teams' jerseys and insignia with pride and joy, which might surely bespeak a different attachment to these clubs than that of their fans at home, but it is no less authentic. The global, or in this case European, does not eliminate the local and national at all: far from it. The two co-exist and interact.

Thus, detailed and regular research on European television viewership of Champions League soccer games demonstrates amply that the audience in a country's home team is often up to tenfold larger than it is in every other European country. Concretely, a Champions League quarterfinal match between Spanish side Barcelona and German team Schalke 04 in the spring of 2008 was watched by nearly six times the proportion of viewers in these two countries than elsewhere in Europe. Conversely, a match in the same quarterfinal round between English side Chelsea and Turkish team Fenerbahçe from Istanbul exhibited virtually identical proportions in terms of the difference between local viewers in Turkey and England on the one hand and other places in Europe on the other. So the local continues to dominate even this most European of venues. However, the Champions League final in 2008 played in Moscow and pitting two English teams against each other—Manchester United vs. Chelsea—was a truly European television event. Its market share of viewers that night was 34 percent in France, 28 percent in Germany, 39 percent in the Netherlands, 34 percent in Spain, and 29 percent in Italy. The United Kingdom's 46 percent of market share attained by ITV1 and an additional 7 percent via the Sky Sports 1 coverage are clearly higher than anywhere else but not to the point of marginalizing the other numbers.[81] A game between two global English clubs, one owned by an American family, the other by a Russian billionaire, played in Russia's capital for Europe's uncontested club championship, and featuring players from nine countries and three continents as well as televised all over the world, was by all measures a global affair.

Euro-Stars in the NBA

As we delineated in chapter 2, the NBA and its product have become the most successful of the Big Four North American leagues in Europe. Above all, the league has entered the quotidian and prosaic aspects of a successfully institutionalized presence. European fans in ever-increasing numbers

---

and only three Spaniards for the Spanish club Real Madrid in their European Champions League showdown on March 10, 2009 at Anfield.

[81] Results & Research, Season 2007—2008, UEFA Champions League Audience Research Data.

have come to follow the NBA's games and players apart from special events such as the All-Star game, the playoffs, and the championship finals. Thus, in contrast to the NFL and American football—whose Super Bowl has become an Olympianized event in Europe's sports space over the past decade in that the game has been televised live across the continent and folks gather in the middle of the night to watch this spectacle until the wee hours of Monday morning, but whose daily developments remain obscure and uninteresting to most European sports fans—the NBA's comings and goings have become daily fare to millions of Europeans. Baseketball is still subordinate to soccer, but present all the same, as a solid and growing second. There are two main discernable reasons for this successful institutionalization: first, as we have already mentioned, the long-time historical presence of the game in most European countries, even though it was mainly played rather than followed—an activity rather than culture. Still, there was an existing ground on which to build a new edifice, whose main architects furnished the second reason: American global icons such as Michael Jordan, Magic Johnson, and a few others of the Barcelona "Dreamers" who then spawned the evolution of players such as Tony Parker, Mehmet Okur, Hedo Türkoğlu, Toni Kukoč, Tony Fernandez, Pau and Marc Gasol, and most important of all, perhaps, Dirk Nowitzki. All of these athletes have one thing in common: They are local boys of France, Turkey, Croatia, Spain, and Germany respectively who made good in the real big time and thus became superstars back home. This would not have been possible had they succeeded in domestic leagues, which do not have the status of the NBA as being the game's global pinnacle.

The first European trailblazer who became a vanguard for the current generation of European players—and represents a link between them and the NBA superstars of the Bird-Johnson-Jordan era—was the great Croatian guard, Dražen Petrović, who died in a tragic car accident on the German Autobahn in June of 1993 and was posthumously inducted into the Naismith Basketball Hall of Fame in 2002. Petrović had another European as his NBA contemporary: the German forward Detlef Schrempf. Though roughly equivalent in the caliber of their play and enjoying a similar status of respect in the NBA and with the American basketball public, Petrović became a genuine celebrity and star in his home country while Schrempf did not. The sole reason for this discrepancy lay in the different cultural prominence and social weight accorded to basketball in Croatia, where it has steadily been a strong second to soccer. In Germany, its distance to soccer was much larger and its own standing in Germany's sports space contested by other team sports, notably team handball. This once again underlines our argument that the local remains crucial alongside the global and shapes the latter's reception in a particular culture. Nowitzki's immense achievement has been the erasing of basketball's deficit in Germany's sports space. He helped in making the game a much-followed sport on the big-event levels of the NBA, the World Championships, the European Championships, and the Olympics. Basketball's successful "Olympianization" in Germany has been an important by-product of what one could call the "Nowitzki effect," which, unlike its Schrempf and Petrović predecessors, could only flourish in the context and by the means of the second globalization.

Dirk Nowitzki does indeed have all the makings of a genuine global superstar. His basketball skills are truly unique: a seven footer, comfortable in playing all three front-court positions, but who can handle the ball like a point guard; a sensational outside shooter and an ever-present inside threat. The only average aspect of his game has been his defense. Catapulted onto the global stage of the NBA directly from his local team of DJK Würzburg of a German regional league—thus having bypassed Germany's Basketball Bundesliga (BBL), the country's top forum for professional basketball—Nowitzki became the first European and non-North American to be honored with the NBA's most valuable player award for his sensational performance in the 2006–7 season.[82] Nowitzki has developed into an icon for basketball and sports fans all over the world. We have seen youngsters wear jerseys with his name in Israel and Austria, Turkey and Canada, just as we have African Americans at The Palace of Auburn Hills when the Dallas Mavericks visited the host Detroit Pistons. And in Dallas, "Dirk" is a veritable superstar who has succeeded in making basketball a respectable second to the Cowboys and football, whose primacy will never be displaced by any star in any other sport, no matter how admired and beloved. As to Nowitzki's fame in Germany, suffice it to say, that he has become a true crossover star, meaning that he is well-known, liked, and respected by the German public well beyond the still-modest basketball community. Nowitzki promotes a number of products in Germany and enjoys every bit the public presence that the country accords its soccer stars. Every game of the Dallas Mavericks is televised in Germany, albeit the live telecasts are watched only by a small coterie of NBA devotees and insomniacs since these appear invariably in the middle of the night towards dawn in Europe. The sports pages of the major newspapers accord

[82] The only other non-U.S. born player to win this coveted award was Dirk Nowitzki's former Dallas Mavericks teammate and good personal friend Steve Nash, who is Canadian and played his college ball in the United States. Tim Duncan, the two-time MVP of the San Antonio Spurs, was born in the American Virgin Islands but spent his college career playing for Wake Forest University. He also represented the United States in the Olympics.

the NBA and the Mavericks respectable daily coverage. Much of this attention increases considerably during the NBA playoffs, and of course anytime Nowitzki plays for the German national team in an international tournament. Indeed, what we found so interesting and telling was the fact that the 2006 NBA championship final between the Dallas Mavericks and the Miami Heat, Nowitzki's first and only thus far, received major coverage in Germany despite the country's entire public space and attention occupied by the World Cup, which occurred at the very same time and in which the German team performed much better than expected.

The difference between Nowitzki's star status across much of Germany and Schrempf's virtual obscurity outside the country's basketball community is partly the result of the difference in the talent levels that these two players possess. But, perhaps more important still is the decade that separates the prime of their respective careers in which the NBA's and basketball's presence in Europe and the world has grown immensely. Put differently, Nowitzki surely would not have had the aura that he enjoys today had his prime years been between 1985 and 1995, as were Schrempf's. It may well be that by now Nowitzki's global fame has reached the stratospheric proportions of "Kaiser" Beckenbauer's and Heidi Klum's, thus making him arguably among the best-known Germans in the world.

Basketball's growth in Europe since the Dreamers wowed the world in the Barcelona Olympics in 1992 cannot be separated from hip hop and its all-encompassing youth culture of fashion, language, habits, and behavior. Unlike musical genres preceding it, like rock, blues, and jazz—with which hip hop shares the centrality of African Americans as performers and cultural leaders—sports, and basketball in particular, are central to hip hop alone. The reasons for this are way beyond the purview of this book but suffice it to say that the sight of European youngsters wearing baggy shorts and reversed baseball caps with the logos of NBA teams on them playing pickup hoops on countless playgrounds of the continent has become quite common. We turn now to a very brief presentation of these cross-Atlantic traits that, in and of themselves, are rather tangential to the sports proper yet comprise an important ingredient of the culture that accompanies them.

Odd Cultural Diffusions crossing the Atlantic: Baggy Shorts, Tattoos, High-Fives, Guitar Riffs, and Sports Paraphernalia

While the traditional *institutions* of European and American sports spaces—the hegemony of soccer in the former, the hegemonic rule of the

Big Four in the latter—have remained essentially resilient to the significant globalization of these sports, we find some striking examples of transatlantic cultural spillover in the success and recognition of international players. Differently put, while the institutions have been remarkably stable and their cultures resilient and sticky, the *actors* on the field, the *purveyors* of the very products that have tied millions to them for more than a century with such passion and love, have changed considerably throughout this process—none more so than in the course of what we have called the second globalization. But the greatest degree of inter-Atlantic diffusion has occurred in various artifacts that are ancillary to the sports themselves but yet bespeak a lively, real, and growing cultural interaction that should not be discounted. As to why these particular artifacts have "stuck" as opposed to others remains obscure to us.

Moreover, these examples do not properly answer the theoretical dilemma raised by Colyvas and Jonsson as to which objects "spread" and which ones "stick."[83] Suffice it to say that it seems quite obvious, at least in our cases, that the more innocuous, the more superficial, the more tangential, and the less threatening to the issue and structure at hand the diffused object is, the more likely its adoption will be. Entrenched institutions will not resist diffusions of objects and artifacts that they do not perceive as threatening to the core of their existence. But in addition to the lack of threat that such objects convey, their likelihood of spreading and sticking must also depend on their attraction to the "receiver" and, of course, on the degree of their simplicity in terms of their being understood and learned. All the examples to follow are a good deal easier to be mimicked, copied, followed, and enjoyed than any of the sports from which they emanated. Recall our earlier point as to why jazz and rock spread and stuck so much easier with European audiences than did baseball and basketball. The former entail a much more transportable language than the latter. Also, just like rock and jazz, almost all the ensuing examples that we will present hail from American pop culture, the world of popular music in particular. As such, they are close to hip hop and related African American creations, which—beginning with jazz in the 1920s and continuing with rock and the blues of the 1950s and 1960s—have always exerted an attraction to cosmopolitan-minded Europeans, to the horror of their counter-cosmopolitan compatriots.

Let us commence with the baggy shorts that emerged on Europe's soccer fields by the mid- to late 1990s. How did this happen? It was mainly

---

[83] Colyvas and Jonsson, "Ubiquity of Legitimacy: Disentangling Diffusion and Institutionalization," pp. 33–35.

the University of Michigan's Fab Five freshmen basketball team that came
to popularize baggy shorts in the 1991–92 season. Before that, tight, short,
and slim pants were common in both basketball in the United States and
soccer in Europe. Allegedly, so the story goes, the fad with the baggy shorts
began when University of Michigan assistant coach Brian Dutcher noticed
athletes pulling shorts down to their hips and that University of Arkansas
players already had slightly longer shorts than did those of other Division
I college teams. So he ordered shorts two to four inches longer than they
had been for the Wolverines. The players immediately liked them and
began wearing these baggy shorts regularly for all their games, together
with the black shoes and black socks that were also introduced to the hard-
woods and American culture by Michigan's Fab Five.[84] Basketball powerhouse North Carolina followed the Michigan baggy-shorts fashion in
1994, thus giving it not only much more exposure but also greater legitimacy by dint of that program's pedigreed standing in the world of American college basketball.

At the same time, North Carolina's most celebrated basketball product
and by then NBA superstar Michael Jordan, popularized the style because
he liked to tug on his shorts while playing defense and lining up alongside
the lane waiting for an opponent to shoot free throws. After this, apparel
companies began custom-making oversized shorts for basketball players
and the trend caught on throughout the NCAA as well as the NBA.[85] From
there, this fashion quickly spread across the Atlantic and changed the
sportswear not just in European basketball but also in professional soccer.
The formerly short, tight pants worn by European soccer players until this
cultural diffusion of the 1990s have long disappeared. When we now watch
films of the "short-shorts" era in European soccer, they look to us as odd
and out of place, as do similar films of the same era in American
basketball.

Whenever European soccer players greet their opponents before every
game, or a player leaves the field to be replaced by another, the standard

[84] It is amazing what a global impact these five University of Michigan freshmen had in
terms of fashion and demeanor. As far away as Australia, colleagues of ours came to learn
about American college sports—indeed American universities as a whole—by virtue of the
Fab Five. Most interesting is the fact that these players had such a lasting cultural impact even
though they lost the national championship game twice in a row. The second loss was one of
the worst mental lapses in American sports history and has become iconic for every American
sports fan and most likely prevented its culprit, Chris Webber, from proceeding to a Hall of
Fame career in the NBA, which his talent all but guaranteed. See also Pete Thamel, "On the
Cusp of Their Reunion, The Fab 5's Impact Is Still Felt," *New York Times*, April 3, 2009.

[85] See http://www.blueheavenmuseum.com/Baggy%20Look.htm; http://www.nba.com/
canada/bu_fashion.html. Retrieved July 3, 2008.

form of acknowledgment is a version of the "high five," or of a handshake popularized by African American men as a symbol of brotherhood disseminated to the world in the late 1960s and early 1970s. Both of these have entered European sports in a massive way and have through the conduit of sports spread far into other purviews of society. University of Louisville basketball player Derek Smith claims to have coined the expression "high five" during the 1979–80 season. The term then entered the dictionary in 1980 as a noun and 1981 as a verb.[86] However, the first instance of the gesture in sports is said to have occurred between Los Angeles Dodgers teammates Glenn Burke and Dusty Baker in 1977, after Baker hit a home run. The gesture was then adopted and popularized by the University of Louisville Cardinals' basketball team.[87] It received its popularity in Europe via Magic Johnson's "Showtime" Los Angeles Lakers of the 1980s and, of course, by the Dream Team's presence and performance at the 1992 Olympics in Barcelona.

Let us continue with the near ubiquity of tattoos in North American team sports and their rapid spread in European soccer. Virtually no American basketball player sported any tattoos until the middle of the 1990s, when—possibly through their high visibility and prolific presence on Dennis Rodman's body during the latter's three-year stint with the then glamorous Michael Jordan-led NBA champion Chicago Bulls, a global team if there ever was one—they emerged in short order on the bodies of a majority of NBA players to be followed by their colleagues in the NFL and, to a lesser extent, MLB. Soon thereafter tattoos appeared on the forearms of European soccer players, with the Italians at the forefront, among them such stars as Marco Materazzi, Francesco Totti, Christian Vieri, and Fabio Cannavaro. Players in other countries also began sporting tattoos and when global superstar David Beckham first tattooed himself in April 1999, the fashion attained a whole new level of legitimacy and attraction.[88] Today, tattoos on the arms of European soccer players—totally unknown until this recent diffusion begun in the mid- to late 1990s—are almost as commonplace as on their counterparts in the NBA and NFL.

On the fan side of things, the "wave"—spectators getting up and stretching their arms at certain collectively coordinated moments to create a vi-

---

[86] See Merriam-Webster's Online Dictionary: http://www.merriam-webster.com/dictio nary/high%20five. Retrieved November 11, 2009.

[87] The "high five" was originally used as a greeting in African American urban culture; see http://www.highfive.me.uk/history. Retrieved July 3, 2008.

[88] Sources: http://www.tao-of-tattoos.com/tattoos-001-soccer.html. Retrieved July 1, 2008; and http://tattoos.lovetoknow.com/David_Beckham's_Tattoos. Retrieved July 1, 2008.

sual wave—is a common global phenomenon of sports culture that evolved over the last decades coinciding with the second globalization. Allegedly, the wave began at an NHL game in Edmonton in late 1980 during a cheer led by Krazy George Henderson. Krazy George then used this idea to (purposely) start a wave on October 15, 1981 in Oakland at the American League Championship game between the local Athletics and the New York Yankees. Sixteen days later, on October 31, 1981, Rob Weller, the guest "yell-king" at the University of Washington vs. Stanford University football game in Seattle, tried to initiate a vertical wave. When this failed, students began chanting "sideways" and, after Weller realized this, he succeeded in leading this sideways wave by running around the track. The wave appeared the following week at a Seattle Seahawks NFL football game in the Kingdome. In the fall of 1983, the University of Michigan played a football game against the University of Washington in Seattle and then brought the wave back to Ann Arbor. In the ensuing spring, Wolverines fans, attending a Detroit Tigers baseball game, introduced the wave to Detroit's Tiger Stadium. For some reason, this artifact stuck over the summer and when the Tigers won the World Series that year, this odd custom attained national attention. It was also introduced beyond North America via the global broadcasts of the 1984 Olympic soccer semifinal between Brazil and Italy in Stanford Stadium. The wave's final step toward its diffusion as a ubiquitous global entity occurred when it was used by crowds at the 1986 World Cup in Mexico.[89] Thus, its most common global name, "la Ola," makes perfect sense. Independent of the particular sport or country, the wave is now widespread at sports events across the world.

The same pertains to the opening guitar riffs of the White Stripes' song "Seven Nation Army." Oddly, and surely by accident, the city of Detroit plays a leading role in the dissemination of this global artifact as well since the White Stripes and their leader Jack White hail from the metropolitan Detroit area. The band's short musical sequence was first used in American stadiums. Thus, for example, it has become a mainstay at all football games of the Penn State Nittany Lions with the band and the fans intoning it with regularity both at home and away. Then AS Roma fans adopted it and, after regular use of the riffs before every single match in the EURO 2008 tournament in Austria and Switzerland, it has become a de facto official tune for all UEFA-sanctioned games and thus a common cultural good in stadiums across Europe. With ESPN's use of it as the musical signifier in

---

[89] See www.guardian.co.uk/notesandqueries/query/0,5753,-21439,00.html. Retrieved November 20, 2009.

broadcasts of English Premier League games to American audiences, the riffs have returned full circle to America.

All these diffusions emanated from America and spread from there to Europe and the rest of the sports world. The only reverse phenomenon that we could detect was, not surprisingly, related solely to soccer where it remains hegemonic and from which it spread only sporadically to the Big Four. The most notable is the "Ole, Ole, Ole" chant by soccer fans. There also now exists more fan-led singing at American soccer games than ever before, thus mimicking their European counterparts. Lastly, the painting of faces in team colors, now relatively common in American sports venues, occurred much earlier and more prolifically in European soccer arenas. In the case of all of these objects of diffusion that characterize the culture of these games but are actually marginal to their essence, virtually none of the practitioners involved, be it players or fans, know the origins of their rituals.

International soccer paraphernalia are almost as readily spotted today on American college campuses and the streets of America's major cities as those from baseball, basketball, and football in the public sphere of every European city. Yankees hats, Michigan shirts, Lakers jerseys, and Raiders jackets have become regular apparel all over Europe; Real shirts, Liverpool jackets, Milan jerseys, and Arsenal caps have become much more frequent in America than a decade ago. Sporting these items does not turn the person into a rabid fan of the team whose colors he or she displays; nor does it imply any knowledge of the sport that the team represents. Indeed, we have seen some odd clothing combinations, such as a fellow wearing a New York Yankees t-shirt while simultaneously sporting a Boston Red Sox cap in the Vienna subway, while traveling to the Spain vs. Russia semifinal soccer match at the EURO 2008 tournament. This clearly demonstrates ignorance about the "real" world that these teams and their sport represent. Nobody would blithely mix Yankees and Red Sox symbols in their haberdashery in New York or Boston, or anywhere else in the United States. And surely no racist soccer hooligan, who had just spent much of a game sporting the Hitler salute and making monkey noises every time a black player of the opposing team touched the ball, realizes that he is engaging in behavior rendered popular by African Americans connoting racial solidarity when he high-fives his partner or offers his friend a fist bump in a gesture of approval and joy.

Even though these haphazardly diffused, media-guided, and marketing-related artifacts and customs have prima facie little to do with the sports and teams whose emblems they depict, and do not alter much in the institutionalization of existing sports cultures, we still believe that they collectively bespeak important changes and shifting conditions in which these cultures operate today. So does the precipitous growth and substantial presence of women as sports producers (i.e., players)—although not yet, to the same degree, as their consumers (i.e., fans)—over the past thirty years. It is to a discussion of women and soccer on both sides of the Atlantic that we now turn.

CHAPTER 4 ◇◇◇◇◇◇◇◇◇◇◇◇◇◇◇◇◇◇◇◇◇◇◇◇◇◇◇◇◇◇◇◇◇◇◇

A SILENT "FEMINIZATION" OF GLOBAL SPORTS CULTURES?

WOMEN AS SOCCER PLAYERS IN EUROPE AND AMERICA

We are well aware that the conventional term 'feminization" of a profession not only entails the increased presence of women in it but the concomitant departure of men from it, thus often leading to its diminished prestige and status. In the case of all sports, the growing entrance and participation of women since the early 1970s is nothing short of revolutionary. Women's boxing, for example, became a medal sport at the 2012 Olympics, with wrestling, present at the Olympics since 2004, having attained the status of a veritable old-timer. We doubt, however, that this development has led to a diminution of the prestige and status of male sports. Oddly though, the fear of such a loss is pervasive and many men resent what they perceive as women's encroachment on what some men consider one of their last uncontested domains: sports.

The revolutionary influx of women into the world of sports pertains mainly to performing and producing them; however, in terms of talking sports, the traditional gender divide remains immense, with the consumption of sports still largely a male domain.[1] As we argue in the beginning of

---

[1] In an empirical study of women sports fans, Gillian Lee Warmflash demonstrates powerfully how women speak sports differently than men. See Gillian Lee Warmflash, "In a Different Language: Female Sports Fans in America" (Senior Honors Thesis, The Committee on Degrees in Social Studies, Harvard University, 2004). This is corroborated in a study of men and women among athletes and nonathletes at the University of Michigan. Indeed, the gen-

chapter 5, the essence of manliness remains an absolute core to the self-image of many sports, certainly all hegemonic sports cultures. The cosmopolitanization of sports coincides for many men with their feminization, which these men resent.

Soccer's feminized presence is a newcomer to Europe and America. Because of the game's different standing in the two continents' respective hegemonic sports cultures, the concrete nature of this feminization assumes distinctly different characteristics in each context.

The words "women" and "soccer" make a natural pairing in American English. They roll off the tongue easily, make sense, are not contradictory, and they need little, if any, explanation or qualification. They are compatible, congruent, and even harmonious together. Contrast this situation to the dyad of "women" and "football." This pairing is profoundly incompatible and invokes tension, alienation, antagonism, and most certainly total estrangement. Tellingly, this is the case in all versions of English, be they American, Australian, British, or any other. Thus, it corroborates yet again that the term "football" connotes *the* hegemonic code of the game in a country's sports culture, whereas "soccer" does not.

We will analyze how the very fact that this game is called "soccer" in the United States constitutes an exceptional situation that renders its symbiosis with women smooth, and even "natural." However, women in the United States have remained virtually excluded as players in the world of football and continue to be subordinate to every other facet of this sport's existence with the possible exception of cheerleading.[2] Lastly, we will highlight how women in Europe had actually entered the world of their football around World War I, but remain marginal to this day. As we will soon see, though, significant shifts have happened in the course of the past thirty years on both continents.

Women and soccer, as well as women and football—different as these pairings may be—have one essential common denominator. They form an integral part of what constitutes in our mind one of the major stories of the

der gap proved greater than the difference between athletes and nonathletes in terms of the respective knowledge and usage of sports languages. See Andrei S. Markovits and David T. Smith, "Sports Culture among Undergraduates: A Study of Student-Athletes and Students at the University of Michigan," *Michigan Journal of Political Science* 2 (9), Spring 2008, pp. 5–58.

[2] We know, of course, that there are women's football teams and leagues in the United States. And we also know that the occasional young woman has assumed an important role on a high school's or even Division Three colleges' squad but, tellingly, always as a kicker, arguably the least valued and most ridiculed position in American football. "Real" football players often do not regard kickers as "real" players but as "sissies," foreigners—in short not as "real" men and as part of the game's "real" core.

second wave of feminism, namely the substantial advance of women as sports producers almost to the level of men. This is an amazing statement and bespeaks a massive shift in gender relations. At our own University of Michigan, there were for all intents and purposes no female varsity athletes as late as the early 1970s. Most certainly, women were all but nonexistent in team sports. All this has changed in the course of the past twenty to thirty years. The University of Michigan features roughly as many female varsity athletes as males—380 men, 320 women in 2009—and women compete vigorously in team sports such as basketball, volleyball, softball, soccer, and field hockey to name but a few. There still is no complete gender equality since women play a "female" version of baseball (softball) that men do not play on the varsity level. Moreover, women do not play football at Michigan or any other college, confirming yet again the aforementioned incompatibility between women and football in America. Moreover, women's massive entry into sports since the 1970s remains largely confined to the world of sports production—the "doing" of sports in the form of participation and performance—rather than in their consumption: the "following" of sports in terms of knowing their history, wallowing in their trivia, and indulging in an all-encompassing identification with them to the point of a singular passion bordering on obsession. Still, women's entrance into the world of sports production is a worldwide phenomenon that marks a significant cultural shift in gender relations on a global level.

We argue that this shift is nowhere more powerfully manifested than in the world of soccer in America and football in Europe and the rest of the world. In the United States, women entered into a soccer space that was marginal at best and managed to construct a level of excellence in it in two decades that really has few parallels in any sport practiced by either gender. By dint of their phenomenal successes and unique achievements, the American female soccer players catapulted a formerly obscure and unimportant sports language, if not quite into the middle of the American sports vernacular, then most certainly into a respectable space within it. The achievement of American women players was not so much to overcome male resistance to their entering a hitherto sacred male turf, since soccer mattered little to American males. Instead, American women proved to be pioneers in blazing the way for a hitherto little-known and ill-respected sport in America's sports culture and sports space.

In contrast, the pioneering feat of European women consisted in daring to enter a realm and play a game that was, and still is, arguably among the most male-centered sectors of European public life. If the achievement of American female soccer players was to help legitimate a sport, their European sisters' accomplishment was crashing the gates of an exclusively male club. Even though, as we will see in the next section, women's soccer existed in Europe since the early 1900s, most certainly since after World War I, we view these precursors to today's situation of women's football in Europe as virtually irrelevant other than to sports historians. The phenomenon that commenced with the late 1960s and really emerged in the 1970s and 1980s had absolutely nothing to do with its meek and obscure precursors, and owe everything to the second wave of feminism and a concomitant rethinking and reprioritizing of many aspects of social and cultural discourse in the West best known by the term "culture turn." Few, if any, female European soccer players of the 1970s and 1980s knew of or cared about players in the 1920s. Rather, the new generation's motivations, commitment, and passion for the game, and its courage in challenging this male bastion—despite repeated and constant male ridicule and hostility—emanated from the changed position and discourse surrounding women in the advanced industrial countries of what could broadly be called "the West" (i.e., member countries of the Organization for Economic Cooperation and Development [OECD]). Even though the worlds of American soccer and European football were massively different in the late 1960s to the 1980s, the two continents' respective women's movements and changed public discourse about gender were very similar, if not identical.

Of course women's soccer in America and women's football in Europe still do not belong to the core of the respective hegemonic sports cultures on the two continents. But women play this game in every advanced industrial country, and there is every indication that this will, if anything, increase in years to come. Just look at its spread in countries of Latin America, Africa, and Asia. Maybe some day women and football in Europe and the rest of the world will become as compatible as women and soccer have been in the United States since the beginning of the 1980s.

The History of Women's Soccer until the Second Wave of Feminism

Women playing association football is not a new phenomenon at all. Indeed, there is strong historical evidence that in a number of European countries women basically began to play this game soon after men did. The first recorded women's football match in the British Isles hails from 1888 in Inverness, Scotland. This was exactly the same year in which the men's game saw the establishment of the very first professional soccer league in England, thus the world. It was also precisely twenty-five years after the founding of the Football Association in 1863, and some fifty years after the game's disparate origins germinated in the exclusive world of upper-class English boys and their public schools as well as the colleges of Cambridge University. "This [match] can be interpreted as distinct from folk football, like the late eighteenth-century women's games, or mixed holiday games such as the Shrove Tuesday free-for-all in the English town of Atherstone, though it did pit the married against the single women. In the Inverness game, the two teams had uniforms, fixed goals, a fairly stable and even number of members and the game had a limited time span,"[3] all essential ingredients of the modern game of football. A match pursuant to the guidelines of the Scottish Football Association was played on Shaw-fields Ground in Glasgow in 1892.[4] By 1895, the appropriately named Nettie Honeyball, secretary of the British Ladies, organized the English North vs. South game at Crouch End in London to be followed by games in the Midlands, the North, and in Scotland—"the most significant of which was the Newcastle fixture with a crowd approaching 8,000."[5]

From its very beginning, the game became an integral part of sensitive conflicts involving class and gender in England, Scotland, and the European continent at the time. Were these females playing the game "ladies" or "women"? Was football the proper pursuit for a girl from a bourgeois home, or did this activity not behoove her station? Whatever the specifics of these socially fraught phenomena might have been, women playing the game must have caused sufficient commotion and worries for the Football Association to issue a ruling as early as 1902 preventing men's clubs from playing against "lady teams."[6]

In Germany, there are some records from 1900 of young girls kicking a ball to each other in a circle.[7] This was the year when the German soccer federation (DFB), was established though the men's game was nowhere near as popular at the time as it was in England. Still, even at this nascent stage, young women played the game in an environment in which a debate was waged as to whether girls should be permitted any physical activities at all and whether such involvement might be either detrimental to their bodies (chiefly their reproductive capabilities) or just inappropriate behav-

[3] Jean Williams, "The Fastest Growing Sport? Women's Football in England," in Fan Hong and J. A. Mangan, eds., *Soccer, Women, Sexual Liberation: Kicking Off a New Era* (London: Cass, 2004), p. 113.
[4] Ibid.
[5] Ibid.
[6] Ibid.
[7] Beate Fechtig, *Frauen und Fußball* (Ebersbach: Edition Ebersbach, 1995), p. 11.

ior for a woman. There raged controversy at this time whether women were even allowed to participate in gym classes at school. From the very beginning, women interested in playing football had to overcome the extant male prejudice of this activity being unseemly and unhealthy for women. The latter view has certainly abated in the course of the last thirty years. As to the former, while things have most definitely improved, there is still a strong male (and even female) perception in countries where football constitutes hegemonic sports culture that women who play this game are either unfeminine in their very being or are, at a minimum, engaging in an activity that should remain a man's domain.

In Sweden, Denmark, Norway, Belgium, and France women began to play football in a disorganized and rudimentary manner. But just like in Germany, these remained much less prominent than in the British Isles for obvious reasons; the men's game, too, was at this time much less well-anchored and institutionalized on the continent than in Britain, the modern game's authentic home. This was to change massively in the course of World War I. Even in the men's and the women's world of football, the Great War wrought substantial changes as it did in numerous facets of life. Many of these transformations solidified an enhanced popular participation that most certainly included women, and forced a breakdown of the old order in virtually all aspects of public life, from politics to economics, from social mores to culture. It was in the immediate pre- and post–World War I era (as we argued in chapter 2) that men's football really prospered on the European continent and became the hegemonic sports culture that we have come to know throughout the twentieth century, thus replicating the well-ensconced presence on the Continent that the game had enjoyed in England and the British Isles before the Great War. World War I also formed a watershed in the women's game. In 1917, the first women's football championships were held in France and in 1922 two football cup competitions were introduced.[8] In Sweden, the first women's football team was established in 1917. Its initial opponents were old-boys sides. One of these matches attracted 1,700 spectators. The first contest between two women's teams occurred in Stockholm in front of approximately 500 spectators.[9] Women played men in Kristiania (now Oslo) in 1919 and continued doing

---

[8] Gertrud Pfister, "The Challenges of Women's Football in East and West Germany: A Comparative Study" in Hong and Mangan, eds., *Soccer, Women, Sexual Liberation*, p. 131.

[9] Jonny Hjelm and Eva Olofsson, "A Breakthrough: Women's Football in Sweden," in ibid., p. 182.

so on a regular basis throughout the 1920s.[10] Even Germany and Austria, though much behind the Scandinavian countries, France, and most decidedly Britain in terms of women's playing football, experienced the formation of a few female football clubs. As the scholarly authorities on these two countries emphatically tell us, though, these attempts should in no way be construed as full-fledged steps toward the introduction of the women's game. In both countries there was decided resistance in having the "fairer sex" engage in any kind of male sport, particularly football.[11]

The immediate post–World War I era witnessed the blossoming of the women's game in England. Similar to the female baseball leagues in the United States during World War II—as depicted in the well-known movie, *A League of Their Own*—when women were granted a sudden space to showcase their sport with so many men at war, in England, too, women's football teams proliferated all over the country at this time. By 1921, there were 150 women's teams playing matches on regular schedules. Two teams deserve mention here: Bennets' of London and Dick, Kerr's of Lancashire.[12] During World War I, female workers of the Dick, Kerr Munitions and Engineering Works factory in Preston, Lancashire, joined apprentices who comprised the company team for football matches during lunch and tea time.[13] On one day in October 1917, a stretch during which the company team was not very successful, some of the female players boasted that they could play the game better than the men. This led to a challenge by men to play the women. The match was held and duly reported in the press, but the score was never revealed. This constituted the beginning of the Dick, Kerr Ladies, arguably the best-known female football team until the modern era. Indeed, this team continued to play for nearly fifty years. On Boxing Day in 1920, the Dick, Kerr Ladies played another team from Lancashire called the St. Helen's Ladies before a crowd

[10] Kari Fasting, "Small Country—Big Results: Women's Football in Norway," in ibid., p. 150.

[11] For Germany, see the aforementioned book by Beate Fechtig. For Austria, see Rosa Diketmüller, "Frauenfußball—Ein Paradigmenwechsel?," in Eva Kreisky and Georg Spitaler, eds., *Arena der Männlichkeit: Über das Verhältnis von Fußball und Geschlecht* (Frankfurt: Campus, 2006), pp. 347–65.

[12] Williams, "The Fastest Growing Sport?," p. 115.

[13] We owe this information, as well as all subsequent mention of the Dick, Kerr Ladies, to the pioneering work of David Litterer, one of America's foremost soccer historians. The piece from which we garnered this information is entitled, "Overview of Women's Soccer in the USA," and was shared with us via an e-mail attachment on January 22, 2002. An updated version appeared in 2005 under the slightly revised title "Women's Soccer History in the USA: An Overview," at the following link: http://www.rsssf.com/usadave/am-soc-overview-wom .html. Retrieved April 23, 2008.

of 53,000 at Goodison Park in Liverpool, the hallowed home ground of the pedigreed English club Everton. Apparently, there were another ten- to fifteen-thousand fans locked out of the completely packed stadium. Maybe it was this event, coupled with other signs of the growing popularity of the women's game in England, that mobilized the Football Association to ban all female competition from its grounds, in effect killing the women's game in its nascent stage. Ironically, this ban was not lifted until 1970, the very year that the Dick, Kerr Ladies finally folded as a team.

The Dick, Kerr Ladies not only played an absolutely key role in the early phase of women's football in Britain, but also in that of women's soccer, and soccer as a whole, in the United States. The team toured the United States in 1922. After having been snubbed by the Canadian association, the team arrived in the United States to find that there were no established women's teams for it to oppose. If anything, women's soccer in the United States was even less developed at this stage than was women's football in Britain and Europe. Women's soccer, if it existed at all, was at best confined to gym class, informal pickup games, and intramural competition at colleges—places where the game continued its meager existence until it burst onto the American sports scene with a vengeance in the late 1960s but especially the 1970s and 1980s. The Dick, Kerr Ladies were thus compelled to play men's teams. They opened with a 6–3 loss to Paterson F.C., but drew with J&P Coats, and the Fall River Marksmen, and defeated the New Bedford Whalers. All of these teams belonged to the professional American Soccer League, which at the time featured some superb players on a global scale and sported teams that could and did hold their own against fine British and European sides. Overall, the Dick, Kerr Ladies' tour record was 3 wins, 2 ties, and 2 losses, surely an impressive feat, although, as David Litterer informs us, "the men's sides were sometimes going easy on the Ladies, much to their chagrin."[14] The Dick, Kerr Ladies' overall record during their forty-eight-year existence was 758-46-24, an impressive mark by any standard. Their pioneering trail for women's football in Britain and Europe, and women's soccer in the United States, deserves much greater attention than it has hitherto received on either side of the Atlantic.

Suffice it to say that the women's game—which seemed to flourish, albeit still on a very meager level, compared to the amazing boom experienced by the men's in the 1920s and 1930s—was all but banned and officially stymied in many European countries. In some places, like in England

[14] Ibid.

with the aforementioned decision by the Football Association in 1921, there ensued official bans (e.g. in Austria in 1936) that prohibited women to play on any grounds that were under the jurisdiction of the national associations and federations. In effect, women were barred from playing football in any public and official manner. While in Germany the Nazis did not need such an official decree to ban the women's game, and it was not until 1955 that the DFB officially forbade the game on any of its grounds, women's football completely disappeared in the Germany of the 1930s and 1940s. No such official prohibitions were needed in the Scandinavian countries and in France to have the game all but vanish in the course of the late 1920s and 1930s.

The question of whether the football establishments in these countries stymied the women's game because they actively feared it as a serious competition to the men's game, or whether these outright prohibitions and unofficial suppressions occurred for other reasons, reaches beyond the purview of our project here. Nevertheless, the women's game would not reappear in any meaningful way until the 1960s and 1970s, the beginning of the so-called second wave of feminism, which—not coincidentally—has overlapped considerably with a rising cosmopolitan discourse. The second globalization, we argue, appeared as their respective facilitator, in that it heightened hitherto dormant identities and enhanced transcultural exchange. It is to this discussion that we now turn.

From Freaks and Unwelcome Intruders to a World of Marginalized Normalcy: Women's Football in Europe and Women's Soccer in the United States from the late 1960s until the Present

World War I proved a more potent force for change than did World War II in the world of women's soccer, as it did in many instances—social and cultural, though not political. As mentioned previously, women commenced to play the game in a number of European countries in a more or less organized fashion even during World War I, and most certainly right after it. And it was precisely this nascent but discernable challenge to male hegemony in sports and culture that compelled the national soccer establishments everywhere to roll back the women's game, all but ending it. No similar developments appeared during and after World War II. Women in Europe did not play football during the war and did not pick up the game after it either. Indeed, if anything, the German Federation's official banning of the game in 1955 underlined yet again how much the postwar restoration of the 1950s attempted to protect and solidify the gender status quo way beyond football. However, this blissful era of unprecedented consumption and the alleged "end of ideology" was to reach a permanent demise during the turbulent 1960s. Twenty years after the end of World War II, following a delayed reaction as it were, a cultural shift was to rock the West's bourgeois order. In essence it ended many of its key codes that were its anchor arguably from the post-Napoleonic era though certainly since the Victorian one. The history of women's football since then bespeaks some of these massive cultural and social shifts. We will first present the developments in a few European countries before we traverse the Atlantic Ocean and conclude this chapter with a detailed account of women's soccer in the United States.

England

Tellingly, it was in 1969 that the English Women's Football Association (WFA) was officially formed with forty-four affiliated teams. One year later, the Football Association (FA) lifted its ban that had kept women from its grounds for nearly half a century. The number of clubs in the WFA grew consistently on an annual basis to the point that by 1996 the teams were divided into women's teams (600) and girls' teams (750). By 2000, there were 700 registered women's teams with the girls' teams holding steady at 750. In terms of registered players, none were tallied until 1979 when the first such statistic appeared with 6,000 registered female players in England. By 2000, this had ballooned to 35,000.[15] Indeed, the WFA's success in fostering women's football in England since the late 1960s could, paradoxically, best be gauged by the fact that as of 1992 the Football Association itself assumed all responsibilities of women's football in England. Rather than an outright usurpation by the FA of the WFA, this development represented the latter's alignment with the structures of the former. Thus, for example, the WFA had inaugurated a national football league in England in 1991, which was modeled on its male counterpart and furnished the very first such permanent structure in women's football in England.

As of 1992–93, the FA Women's Premier League has had thirty-six teams competing in three divisions, which was very much akin to the pyramid format invented by English male football in 1888 and copied pretty

[15] Williams, "The Fastest Growing Sport," p. 123.

much the world over (with the notable exception of the United States). There is the Women's Premier League National Division at the top with the Northern and Southern divisions running on an equal basis underneath. The winners of these leagues each season are promoted to the top-level National Division. The terms Women's Premiership and Ladies Premiership are generally used for the National Division only. Underneath the top-flight leagues are four Combination leagues—the South West, the South East, the Midland, and the Northern Combinations. The Premiership's teams play (just like their male counterparts) for the league championship, the FA Cup, the League Cup and, since 1999–2000, the Community Shield. Arsenal has been far and away the most successful side in English women's football over these two decades, with nine league championships, eight FA Cup victories, eight League Cup triumphs, and five victories in the Community Shield. Other teams with success have been Everton, Charlton Athletic FC, Millwall FC, Wimbledon FC, and Fulham FC, all well-established teams on the men's side. England's women's national team has also made major strides in these two decades. Improving from tournament to tournament, the English team, led by the Arsenal superstar Kelly Smith, without any doubt a world-class player and among the very best of the women's game in the world, held the heavily favored and superb German team to a 0–0 tie at the Women's World Cup in China in September 2007. Thus, the English women were the only team not to succumb to the formidable Germans, who went on to repeat as World Champions with the amazing feat of not losing to any opponent and without allowing even one goal throughout the entire tournament. The English women's side also held its own against a heavily favored American team for the first half of the game before eventually succumbing to the much more experienced Americans in the second half of the quarterfinal match by a score of 3–0.

Despite these remarkable strides, women's football remains decidedly, and even officially, second class in England, arguably more so than in most other comparable advanced industrial democracies of Europe and North America. Soon after the ban on women's football was lifted, the Sex Discrimination Act of 1975 was drafted to "exempt football specifically and other contact competitive sports in general from gains in female equity, and this approach has been reinforced on more than one occasion and is still valid. . . . Women have many other qualities superior to those of men, but they have not got the strength or stamina to run, to kick or tackle, and so forth."[16] Even though the legislation was repeatedly amended over its

[16] Ibid., p. 124.

thirty-plus-year existence, the clause that limits female participation to competitive sports has endured in its original form.[17] So legally, as well as culturally and institutionally, women's football remains clearly a disadvantaged entity compared to the men's game.

While women in England have come to play football in a constantly increasing amount since the early 1970s, they still lag behind greatly in following the game. In a survey conducted by the government in 1998 that assessed the general living patterns of the British public, watching television and listening to music were at least eight times as popular as football for men and at least eighty times as popular as football for women.[18]

Germany

The all-powerful DFB, the largest national sports federation in the world, chose in 1970, like its English counterpart the Football Association, to recognize officially what it then tellingly called *Damenfußball* (ladies' football). This happened by sheer coincidence in terms of the particular event at hand, yet was anything but coincidental in the context of the rapidly changing discourse in Western liberal democracies. The reason for the federation's change of mind rested in its worries over losing control of the women's football movement that had begun gathering steam in the late 1960s. Behooving the DFB's position of having an uncontested monopoly over football's every aspect and competition level in Germany, the federation did not want to risk losing authority over an entity that its members and officials held in low esteem and on which they heaped nothing but contempt and ridicule.[19] The DFB did not want German women to play the game "in private" (meaning out of the federation's purview), but it also wanted to keep the women's game different from the men's. Initially, the DFB decreed the women's game to last only sixty minutes instead of the ninety that the men played. The women's season would commence on March 1 and end on October 31, thus entailing a "good weather" cycle. (The men's traditionally begins in late August or early September and lasts until late May or early June with only a short respite during Christmas and New Year's.[20]) Women were not to use typical football boots with studs on

[17] Ibid., p. 124.
[18] Ibid., p. 126.
[19] Fechtig, *Frauen und Fußball*, pp. 31–36; and Gertrud Pfister, "The Challenges of Women's Football in East and West Germany: A Comparative Study," pp. 133, 134.
[20] The men's game in England has no provisions for even such a short break and continues uninterrupted from late summer to late spring.

their soles but rather flat running shoes. Furthermore, due to the "female anatomy," no advertising was allowed on women's jerseys lest it would attract the spectators' prurient attention and thus become a distraction from the game. Only females were allowed to coach women's teams and all players could only begin their season after having undergone a thorough medical examination by a specialist in sports medicine. Such an exam had to be repeated within four weeks after the completion of the season. Women were not allowed to use regular footballs but, instead, were required to play their games with so-called "youth balls," which were lighter in weight and smaller in size. Lastly, women were not to play for a championship.

Most of these special rules for women simply disappeared by the 1972–73 season, which was indicative of the rapidly changing times which featured the awakening of the second women's movement in Germany and other advanced industrial democracies. All German states conducted championship rounds with home and away matches exactly like in the men's game; and the schedule soon became congruent with the men's in that the season commenced in the fall and ended in the spring. By the middle of the 1980s, women could, and did, play the game in football boots with cleats. The balls became identical to the men's. The only remaining female rule decreed by the DFB was the shorter length of the game, which in the course of the 1980s was expanded from the previous sixty minutes to eighty. It was not until the early 1990s that the women's game became completely emancipated in that it shed any and all of its "female" specialties and exceptions by henceforth playing the ninety minutes that has constituted the duration of an association football game throughout the twentieth century. Women's football in Germany changed not only "from below," that is, by dint of the ever-increasing number of young women flocking to the game, but also "from above" in that the UEFA standardized the rules and regulations of the women's game on a continent-wide basis, eliminating the country- and even region-specific rules that had guided women's football until then.

By 1971, there were 1,110 women's teams in Germany. This number had more than doubled by 1982, reaching 2,891. Many of the players came to football from the game of field handball (an outdoor version of team handball played indoors on hardwood courts), then a very popular sport for men and women in Germany as well as some of the northern European countries like Sweden, Denmark, and Norway. The first official women's football championship was witnessed in Germany in 1973. It became institutionalized since then on a yearly basis. In addition to this annual championship, German women footballers, just like their male counterparts, also participate in a parallel cup competition. As of 1980, the individual winners of the sixteen regions comprising the DFB compete in a playoff tournament whose winner then receives the country's Women's National Cup for that particular year. The final game of this play-off tournament is always played in Berlin's Olympic Stadium in early June as an opening act to the men's cup final. There can be no better measure of the immense difference between the cultural perception and social presence of women's and men's football than this event, which features matches between two excellent women's and two excellent men's teams. The stadium is at best half full when the women's game begins, with people streaming in for the impending men's game during the women's match second half. The mainly male crowd does not pay much attention to the women's game and often indulges in derision and lewd comments toward the female players on the field. Needless to say, while the ensuing men's match is played in a packed stadium and in front of millions of television viewers across Germany, the women's game has yet to attract anywhere close to a filled venue though it has been aired on television for well over a decade. Male football players— if not male spectators and fans—have over the years come to accord respect to their female counterparts and do not commence their warm-ups right along the sidelines with the women's game still in full progress, as happened well into the 1990s giving testimony yet again to the fact that athletes themselves are often less parochial and counter-cosmopolitan than fans for one simple reason: their respect for and appreciation of athletic prowess and the merit-based aspects of modern sports regardless of the ascriptive attributes of their particular practitioners.

As of 1990, German women's football also has a regularized league championship. Teams were initially divided into fourteen regional leagues and a national league with two divisions of ten teams each with the usual relegation and promotion so common to the men's game all over Europe. But, as of the 1997–98 season, "12 teams have formed a national league with a single division in an attempt to concentrate women's football on the best clubs and thus raise standards of play."[21] Starting in the middle of the 1980s, the game became "women's" as opposed to "ladies'" football (*Frauenfußball* instead of the former *Damenfußball*), perhaps the most accurate gauge for the changed perception of this sport in the male establishment's eyes.

It was in 1982 that the German national team in women's football was founded. By 1989 the team captured its first European championship; ad-

[21] Pfister, "The Challenges of Women's Football in East and West Germany: A Comparative Study," p. 135.

ditional titles followed in 1991, 1995, 1997, 2001, 2005, and 2009. Overall the German team has won seven of the ten tournaments held since their inception in 1984. This bevy of championships demonstrates decidedly that the German women footballers have become Europe's unquestioned best, even surpassing their perennial Scandinavian rivals from Norway and Sweden. The German national team's European excellence was soon to follow on the global stage. Attaining fourth place at the first official FIFA-sponsored women's football world championship in China in 1991, the Germans reached second place at the second World Cup tournament in Sweden in 1995 and then became world champions in the fourth tournament in the United States in 2003. They successfully defended their title in a most impressive manner at the fifth championship in China in the fall of 2007 and are heavy co-favorites—with the Americans—to win the next championship at home in Germany in 2011. In a matter of barely two decades, the German women had become a perennial powerhouse in the world of women's football, surpassed only by the Americans in terms of winning prestigious tournament titles.

But just like in England, excellence on the field has not translated into popularity of the women's game in Germany. Only after World Cup victories does the German team overcome the obscurity and marginalization that have become normal fare during the long years and seasons between such rare international tournaments. Then, hundreds of thousands welcome the team at a parade on Frankfurt's "Römer," one of the city's best-known public squares. The throngs appear purely for nationalistic reasons, that is, to celebrate a German victory on the world's stage rather than women's football in general. Most celebrants could not name more than two or three of the team's players, essentially confirming the public's "Olympianized" relation to this sport. The women's game in Germany will not escape the giant shadow of the men's for decades to come, if ever.

The Scandinavian Countries: Denmark, Sweden, and Norway

In a way, it is not at all surprising that the Scandinavian countries have assumed a leading role in the global development of women's football that is hugely out of proportion both with the percentage of these countries' population and with their relatively modest presence and meek results in the history of the men's game. But precisely because of the latter and the early strides that women attained in many walks of life that imbued the country with an unparalleled egalitarian ethic; women's football in Denmark, Swe-

TABLE 1
National Output of Female Football/Soccer Players in 2004

	Total	*Male*	*Female*
The world	1.00	1.00	1.00 (as a baseline)
Europe	2.46	2.71	1.13
England	3.28	3.74	0.58
Germany	3.77	3.74	4.98
Norway			11.21
Denmark		3.31	6.64
Sweden		2.91	6.55
The United States	3.09	2.12	12.31
Canada		1.60	7.68
Brazil	2.03	2.28	0.11
Asia	0.46	0.50	0.02
China	0.28	0.30	0.02
Japan	1.30	1.47	0.08
South Korea	0.55	0.60	0.06

Source: Rosa Diketmüller, "Frauenfußball—Ein Paradigmenwechsel?" in Eva Kreisky and Georg Spitaler, eds., *Arena der Männlichkeit: Über das Verhätnis von Fußball und Geschlecht* (Frankfurt: Campus Verlag, 2006), p. 355.

den, and Norway was accorded a cultural space and an early legitimacy that few other countries offered anywhere in the world. Appropriately, in all three of these countries, female soccer players not only outnumbered their male counterparts in terms of the proportional output of new players in 2004, but their gains were only exceeded by, tellingly, the proportional presence of new women soccer players in the United States.

We find table 1 useful in showing, albeit only for a single year, the proportional presence of new female soccer players compared to their male counterparts in certain key countries. It also provides some interesting intercountry comparisons. Thus, there is no doubt that the United States, not surprisingly, is the leader of the pack in terms of the disproportional entry of female players into organized soccer, closely followed by Norway as the only other country boasting a double-digit index in the women's column.

Of the three Scandinavian countries that we will briefly present here, Denmark was arguably the earliest trailblazer in the world of women's football beyond the immediate confines of the country. Almost as a lark and most certainly as an advertising gimmick, the well-known Italian beverage company Martini & Rossi organized a women's football tournament in 1970 in Italy that it called the first women's World Cup. Lacking any kind of official seal by any of the relevant institutions of football—Italian, European, or global federations—and organized completely outside of their purview, approval, and jurisdiction, one could best characterize this event as a few women's teams representing their countries in a privately organized international tournament.[22] In front of 50,000 spectators in Turin, Denmark defeated host Italy in the final by the score of 2–0.[23]

The team that won this tournament for Denmark was BK Femina, one of the best-known teams of women's football/soccer history and certainly one of the game's most prominent representatives of the pre-1970s era, almost comparable perhaps to England's Dick, Kerr Ladies. The team was founded in 1959 by a well-known Danish women's magazine called *Femina*. One of *Femina*'s male journalists, in his research on women's sports in Denmark, encountered a few women whom he encouraged to take up playing football after they had informed him that they would much rather play this game instead of team handball. The club, called Boldklubben Femina, became somewhat of a controversial sensation in Denmark. Spawning other clubs all over the country, the Danish Women's Football Union emerged in the early 1960s. Until the admission of women's football into the official Danish Football Federation (DBU) in 1972, the union organized teams to play one another in this semiofficial, semitolerated, and semiridiculed world of women's football. Of course, there were many obstacles. By 1962 the magazine *Femina* severed all relations with and financial support for BK Femina, the football club. One year later, when a few women's teams wanted to hold a tournament under the auspices of the Copenhagen Ball Games Association, their request was summarily denied with no explanations offered.

BK Femina dominated the women's game in Denmark by winning pretty much any and all titles and tournaments—and most of the games—that occurred with some, though far from established, regularity. BK Femina's first trip outside of Denmark was to Czechoslovakia, where the Danish women played the women's side of the pedigreed Czech football and sport club SK Slavia Praha. The sole Danish journalist that covered

---

[22] Fechtig, *Frauen und Fußball*, p. 31.
[23] Anne Brus and Else Trangbaek, "Asserting the Right to Play—Women's Football in Denmark," in Hong and Mangan, eds., *Soccer, Women, Sexual Liberation*, p. 104. It is interesting to note that Beate Fechtig in her important book *Frauen und Fußball* mentions the spectatorship for this game at 35,000. Whatever the correct number might be, it represents a respectable tally.

this event wrote about "hard tackling and light make-up," and the photographs accompanying the article depicted one of the BK Femina players in her football jersey followed by another picture in which she appeared in a somewhat suggestive pose by the side of a swimming pool wearing a bikini.[24] BK Femina also played a central role in the establishment of the Federation of Independent European Female Football (FIEFF), a privately financed football association that organized the first (of course completely unofficial) European championship in women's football in Italy in 1969. BK Femina represented Denmark and lost to Italy in the final, a defeat that the Danes would avenge exactly one year later in the aforementioned first world championship in the women's game. In 1971, the first genuinely national Danish team, still very much centered on BK Femina players but comprising others as well, traveled to yet another world championship tournament, this time to Mexico, where it defeated the host nation for the title by a score of 3–0. This game between Mexico and Denmark was allegedly held in the presence of 100,000 spectators; but since the final game, just like the tournament, did not occur under the auspices of a major international sports organization, these figures are at best unofficial. This attendance, if true, would have surpassed that of the final soccer matches of the 1996 Olympic Games in Athens, Georgia, and of the 1999 World Cup at the Rose Bowl in Pasadena, California (both held under the aegis of the two most potent and legitimate international sports federations in the world, the IOC and FIFA) which have conventionally been regarded as the two leading events for any women's sport—or any event, for that matter, featuring women as its sole protagonists.[25]

Perhaps as a result of these victories on an international (albeit still unofficial) stage—though much more likely due to the massively changing discourse toward women and gender in the liberal democracies of advanced capitalism at this time—the DBU finally accepted women into its fold in 1972. Interestingly, this incorporation not only led to an upgrading in the status and official presence of the women's game in Denmark, it also commenced a gradual decline of the Danish women's prominence, perhaps even pre-eminence, in the world of women's football. For nothing was more sacrosanct to the DBU than the unblemished amateurism of all its members and participants, which, as of 1972, also included all Danish fe-

---

[24] Ibid., pp. 101–3
[25] This 100,000 attendance figure for the game between the Danish and Mexican women's football teams in 1971 hails from Brus and Trangbaek.

male players and their teams. Gone were the days of sponsorships by women's magazines and Italian beverage companies.

The Danish women's national team triumphed one last time at the still unofficial European championship in 1979, but that would be the last of its successes on the international stage. Paradoxically, precisely when the women's game would finally acquire its full institutional legitimacy and its official imprimatur in the 1980s by all relevant bodies that rule over the world of Association football, the Danish women footballers became mediocre and watched their German and Scandinavian sisters in Sweden and particularly Norway surpass them as global players in the women's game.

The Swedish story follows the already well-known pattern. There were teams in Sweden in the 1910s and early 1920s, but the FA's banning of the women's game in England in 1921 was a welcome pretext for the Swedish male-dominated football establishment to do the same. In the 1950s and early 1960s there were women's games played occasionally, but they were much closer to publicity stunts than to genuine and sustained athletic activities.[26] Different from other European countries but distantly similar to the United States, Swedish universities came to play a pioneering role in the nascent establishment of modern football in Sweden which, just like everywhere else, began in the late 1960s and early 1970s. A football tournament was held at Stockholm University in 1965, and similar competitions followed at universities in Gothenburg and Lund in 1967 and 1968.[27] Even though the top office of the Swedish Football Association (SvFF) did not fully and officially incorporate women's football into its purview until 1972, two of its regional associations established women's football leagues between 1969 and 1971. Interestingly, the women's league, started by the newspaper *Arbetet* in 1969 in the southern province of Skåne (quite close to Denmark), was inspired by Danish women's football.

However, in marked contrast to any other European country mentioned, Swedish sports journalists—almost exclusively male at the time— curtailed their disdain for women having invaded this all-male domain and described women's football often in understanding tones as in:

> how women struggled against traditional attitudes regarding appropriate jobs and activities for women. . . . This does *not* mean that women's football was treated in the same manner as men's football—sexist comments such as "foot-

---

[26] Hjelm and Olofsson, "A Breakthrough: Women's Football in Sweden," in Hong and Mangan, eds., *Soccer, Women, Sexual Liberation*, pp. 184, 185.

[27] Ibid.

ball amazons" and "Valkyres" were used when talking about women footballers
. . . nor does it mean that the majority of sports journalists exhibited particularly
positive attitudes towards women's football. However, strikingly many of those
who wrote about women's football at that time, and who became "women's
football experts" for their newspapers, held a positive fundamental tone and
willingly reported on the criticism of the pioneers within women's football
aimed at SSF or at other local opposition to women's football. [28]

By 1973, Sweden fielded its very first official female national team in
football. In its inaugural game, it played to a 0–0 tie against the team from
Finland. The Swedes attained third place in the aforementioned very first
though still unofficial European Championship in 1978 in Italy, in which
the Danish women triumphed. By the end of the 1980s, there were between 37,000 and 40,000 registered female footballers in Sweden. This
level has essentially held steady since then. In the course of the 1980s and
1990s, the Swedish women have without a doubt attained a position of international excellence in women's football, perhaps only exceeded by their
Norwegian neighbors, the Germans, the Brazilians, the Chinese, and the
Americans. Sweden organized the second official FIFA-sanctioned World
Cup in 1995 in which the Norwegians won their first title. At the European Championship of 2001, the Swedish team attained second place.
Some of Sweden's female footballers became the most respected players in
the game. Thus, Pia Sundhage, perhaps the country's best female footballer of all time, followed her playing days by being a successful head
coach in the Women's United Soccer Association (WUSA) in America,
which attracted the world's best. Moreover, Sundhage was named in the
fall of 2007 to become the sixth head coach of the United States women's
national team, the first foreigner bestowed with such an honor. Barely one
year into her tenure, Sundhage led Team USA to its third Olympic gold
medal at the Beijing games in August of 2008. This success, among many
others, led to her being awarded the job at least until after the Olympic
Games in London in the summer of 2012.

The Norwegian women, with five medals (including gold in the World
Cup of 1995 and the Olympics of 2000), are well ahead of the surging Germans when gauged by the accumulation of medals at the officially sanctioned five World Cup and four Olympics tournaments in women's football since 1991. Only their American rivals, still the sole team in the
women's game to have medaled at every single one of these nine top-level
international tournaments, remain ahead of Norway in trophies and hard-

[28] Ibid, p. 187 emphasis in the original.

ware. This is not surprising since the proliferation of the women's game in Norway in relation to the men's game, weighs in a close second to the United States (as is evident in table 1). Both countries are far ahead of everybody else.

In Norway, too, the pre-1970s world of football was scattered, sporadic, and essentially unknown to most Norwegians. Indeed, the very first meaningful and generally recognized women's game was not played until 1970 when Målfrid Kuvås, representing the sport club BUL, organized a match. Not surprisingly, she has come to be called the "mother of football" in Norway.[29] In the decades of the 1970s and 1980s, like everywhere else, the women's game developed on all levels in Norway. Indeed, Kari Fasting, one of Norway's leading experts on women's sports in the country and an eminent university professor, links the game's growth and successful establishment to "the second wave of feminism." This wave commenced at the same time and featured a society-wide debate about women's rights in all aspects of public and private life that extended way beyond playing fields and athletic competitions.[30] As this chapter shows quite emphatically, this development pertained to many Western countries comparable to Norway and can thus legitimately be categorized as a global trend.

One particular act of inclusion, however, might have rendered Norway unique among its European counterparts, even comparable to the country's Scandinavian neighbors Sweden and Denmark. Once the Norwegian Football Federation (NFF) fully accepted the women's game in 1975 (actually a few years later than the other federations discussed in this chapter), the integration of women into the world of Association football began full throttle and with genuine enthusiasm, exhibiting none of the foot-dragging and reluctance that remained the case in so many of the still-predominantly male establishments in other countries. The NFF established a Women's Committee in 1976 that by 1980 placed much emphasis on the education and promotion of female managers, coaches, referees, and officials in addition, of course, to the development of female players at every level of the game. The Women's Committee and its members "systematically worked to recruit girls and women to leadership, coaching and referee positions."[31] By 1999, Karen Espelund had become the first female secretary general of the NFF and thus leader of all of Norwegian football, male and female. This was arguably the most powerful position in all of

[29] Fasting, "Small Country—Big Results: Women's Football in Norway," p. 150.
[30] Ibid., p. 151.
[31] Ibid., p. 155.

Norwegian sports, and remains to this day unique among Association football federations anywhere in the world, including the United States. At the time of this writing, Espelund remains the NFF's secretary general in addition to holding leadership positions in other major Association football bodies on an international level, including with UEFA, the game's highest body in Europe.

In addition to the prime reasons for the successful proliferation of women's football in Norway—Scandinavian egalitarianism and the power of the second wave of feminism—we would like to suggest another tradition which, yet again, makes Norway quite similar to the United States in the world of women's soccer: the relative cultural weakness and the low level of success of the men's game. Thus, it is surely not by chance that China, the United States, Japan, the two Koreas, and Norway (countries in which the men's game has historically been at best mediocre and rarely, if ever, blessed with international accolades) have furnished national teams on the women's side that consistently rank among the top seven or eight in the world. Women succeeded *precisely* in countries where soccer was not completely occupied by men, and thus did not fully constitute what we have termed "hegemonic sports culture." Put differently, the men's game did not dominate in the United States, Norway, or China at anywhere close to the level it has in the countries where it represents the absolute core of hegemonic sports culture, thus giving the women's game ample "space" to develop and flourish.

Concluding this European segment of our chapter, we can discern a virtually identical pattern in every country. The game proceeds in a semi-concealed and sporadic way—where it is little more than a marginalized curiosity, if not a freak show—to a massive opening in the 1970s and an eventual institutionalization throughout the 1980s and 1990s, which renders it at least formally equal to that of the men's. After all, the women's game is played at a continent-wide and global level in virtually the same forums as the men's: country-wide club championships, cup competitions, and international tournaments featuring national teams. The only thing still missing from the women's game that has become so central to the men's are various regularized international competitions featuring club teams instead of national ones. Thus, there still is no women's equivalent to the men's Champions League or any other comparable international club competition for one obvious reason: lack of guaranteed sizable spectatorship at the live venues and a similar paucity of television viewers.

Still, women play the game on the very same field as the men with the very same rules, number of players, and number of minutes, under the same organizational jurisdictions, and in the same formats. To arrive at this formal equality with the men's game, women footballers in Europe had to surmount a formidable hurdle in that they were compelled to enter a sacrosanct male world and contest the men in their most intimately guarded space. To do this, the women had to "gender bend," thus not only challenge the men in their encrusted domain but also counter hitherto accepted gender roles for women. Thus, it will not come as a surprise to the reader that in every single one of these European cases, women footballers are often associated by men and the male-dominated hegemonic discourse with lesbianism. After all, the perception goes, only butch lesbians can really get so passionately engaged in the macho world of soccer. At least to our knowledge, no European woman has been subjected to something called "corrective rape" and subsequently murdered for daring to be a lesbian and a soccer player, as happened to Eudy Simelane of the South African women's national soccer team, the Banyana Banyana. However, there can be no doubt that to many European men women footballers constitute something profoundly threatening, in addition to being perceived as risible and inferior.[32] The road for women's soccer in America faced equally massive hurdles, though of a very different kind. It is to the game across the Atlantic to which we now turn.

The United States

The story of women's soccer in the United States features several nuances and developments that remain particular to the sport there and bespeak soccer's unique status in the sports culture of the United States. Thus, we are reasonably certain that, with over five million known female soccer participants, the United States is at the very top of a list of countries with such athletes.[33] Indeed, during the first decade of the twenty-first century,

---

[32] "Eudy Simelane was gang-raped by four men and then wantonly stabbed many times, mostly in the face. . . . 'The crucial thing to know about Eudy is that she was gay, and that she lived her lesbian life openly. Evidently an incredibly brave thing to do in South Africa,'" writes Paul Gardner in "A shameful story from South Africa," in *Soccer America*, September 1, 2009. South Africa's Lesbian and Gay Equality Project mentioned that Eudy Simelane was subjected to "corrective rape," in which men target women to "correct" them from their "errant" ways, which, of course, to these men included lesbianism and playing soccer. Gardner rightly argues that had anything of the sort happened to a South African player of the country's male national team, the Bafana Bafana, the soccer world would have known about it far and wide. "Then again, suppose it had been a *gay* player, what then?" (emphasis in the original).

[33] U.S. Soccer Foundation, "Soccer in the USA, 2002–2003," p. 5. The exact figure for 2008 was 8,862,000. This consists of all females who have played the game at least once dur-

one third of all registered female soccer players in the whole world resided in the United States.[34] FIFA's own data hailing from 2006 corroborate our findings that nowhere is the game of Association football as female as it is in the United States. In the Confederation of North, Central American, and Caribbean Association Football (CONCACAF), FIFA's regional organization to which the United States belongs, of the 43,109,000 soccer players (both registered and unregistered), 10,038,000 (or 26 percent) were female. In UEFA, Europe's region, women hovered at just shy of 10 percent and in South America they barely reached 11 percent.[35] While these FIFA data do not specifically single out the United States, we are quite sure that this disproportionately large number of female players does not hail from Mexico, Canada, Central America, or the Caribbean in particular since other data from the same study do in fact offer helpful corroborating evidence pertaining to the United States. With its 1,670,000 registered female players, the United States Soccer Federation is the only federation in the world that has more than one million female members and thus almost doubles the runner–up—Germany's DFB with its 871,000 female members. This leadership position of the United States also pertains to youth soccer. Here, the United States bests Germany in all categories, with the gap between girls—at 1,563,000 for the United States and 237,000 for Germany—more than seven-fold.[36]

Moreover, beyond the importance of quantitative figures, it is the quality of this presence that renders the status of women's soccer in the United States so different in comparison to its position in other countries. Nowhere else is women's soccer the cultural equivalent of, or even superior to, the men's game. Where else would female players be much better known to the general public than men? After all, Julie Foudy, Mia Hamm, Brandi Chastain—to mention but three so-called crossover stars who are recognized well beyond the world of their immediate métier and are viewed as part of the general quotidian culture—are more widely known than their male equivalents in the United States, be it the generation of Alexi Lalas (1990s) or Landon Donovan (2000s). Distinguished NBC anchorman Matt Lauer would most assuredly not have mangled any of these female stars' names as he did Landon Donovan's, whom he referred to as "Langdon Donovan" in his interview with David Beckham on the *Today Show* in

---

ing the previous year. The figure for American males was 10,390,000; the combined total for both genders is 19,042,000.

   [34] Diketmüller, "Frauenfußball—Ein Paradigmenwechsel?," p. 353.
   [35] FIFA Big Count 2006: Statistical Summary Report by Gender/Category/Region.
   [36] Ibid.

July 2009. It goes without saying that Lauer would also not have committed a similar error in his mentioning any comparable star's name from the American Big Four sports, thus giving the show's viewers the plausible impression (possibly incorrectly) that Lauer was simply not familiar with Donovan, arguably the greatest—and certainly most prominent—American male soccer player of the modern era.

FIFA, on the occasion of its centenary in 2004, asked Pelé, by common consensus the greatest player the game has ever known, to compose a list of the 100 players whom he deemed the finest footballers still alive on the planet. The results are telling. Pelé could not confine himself to 100 and delivered a list of 125 players. His home country of Brazil led the way with 15 names, followed by Italy and France with 14 each, the Netherlands next at 13, Argentina and Germany with 10 each, and England with 7. The only American soccer players that made Pelé's list were Michelle Akers and Mia Hamm, who were also, of course, the only women among the 125 chosen by the legend. Many a football commentator in Latin America and Europe was outraged that the Brazilian great had dared waste two of his precious spots for American players—and women to boot. In defending his choice of including two women, Pelé said, "I confused the people I was working with but I believe that female football is very important today."[37]

Moreover, in no other country would it be possible, or even conceivable, for female players to serve as the expert (i.e., "color") commentators on national television, explaining the intricacies of the men's game to the viewing public. But this occurred with regularity in the United States during the men's World Cup tournaments in June 2002 and June 2006, as well as other important national and international soccer games. Can anybody imagine that in *any* European or Latin American country the expert commentator—the Gary Lineker in Britain , the Günter Netzer in Germany, the Herbert "Schneckerl" Prohaska in Austria—would be a woman? Unthinkable—but not in the United States, at least in the world of soccer where Julie Foudy's voice as one of the game's veteran color commentators has every bit as much authority as do those of Alexi Lalas, John Harkes, or Eric Wynalda, Foudy's generational equivalents and eminent representatives of American soccer's post-NASL incarnation. In this game, women have true authority in America, which they lack everywhere else. But in marked contrast to soccer in America, the Big Four North American sports are exclusionary of women in the same way as the world of European foot-

[37] "Pelé names top 125," http://foxsports.news.com.au/print/0,8668,8874487-23215,00 .html. March 5, 2004. Retrieved April 20, 2008.

ball—women have a meek, if any, voice there at all; they have little authority, little standing, and few interpretive powers. Thus, the Big Four color commentators' excellence as players lends them the legitimacy to enhance the telecast with their expert commentary. Ditto in European and Latin American football, where the legitimacy of the color commentator hails solely from the person's star status as an excellent former player. European and Latin American football has never featured female color commentators, and its counterparts in all hegemonic North American sports are also exclusively male. Unfortunately, most women reporters in all hegemonic sports on either side of the Atlantic are relegated to cover the "human interest" angle of the games and their protagonists, often by being confined to roaming the sidelines of the playing fields or courts where their prime responsibility is to conduct pre- and post-game interviews with players and coaches and report on injuries during the games themselves.[38]

Thus, it is *never* the inherent gestalt of the sport itself that defines its gendered identity. Rather, it is its position in the country's respective sports space and its hegemonic sports culture: simply put, if the sport—regardless of its particular form and content—has been central to these cultures and spaces, it will be heavily male and exclusive of, perhaps even hostile to, women. If the sport has not been central to them, it will be more welcoming to women.

This segment of our chapter is dedicated to an analysis of the reasons, origins, and present manifestations of this particular American sports exception. Included is the history of women's soccer in the United States, specifically the various components of the game and their development in recent years. We concentrate on the game's recreational manifestations as well as its competitive dimensions, ranging from youth league, high school, and college soccer all the way to the professional game as embodied in the defunct WUSA and its newly established successor Women's Professional

---

[38] In no way do we mean to diminish the keen sports understanding and superb sports expertise on the part of the many fine female reporters in the American media. Quite the contrary: Jackie MacMullan formerly of the *Boston Globe*, Selena Roberts at *Sports Illustrated*, Linda Cohn and Suzy Kolber at ESPN—just to pick four of the many prominent ones in the American media—are every bit as sports conversant as their male colleagues. Still, with the exception of Doris Burke, Ann Meyers, and Nancy Lieberman—all prominent former players, the latter two Hall of Fame superstars—who broadcast college and even occasional NBA games, women commentators are segregated to women's sports, particularly team sports, and rarely attain any prominence in interpreting the men's games. Even as great a former basketball player as Hall of Fame member Cheryl Miller remains largely confined to the sidelines, where she interviews players but shares little, if any, of her basketball knowledge with the viewers.

Soccer (WPS) that commenced play in the spring of 2009. Of course, we will devote some space to a discussion of the American women's national team, Team USA. We will conclude this section of our chapter with some thoughts regarding the future of women's soccer in the United States, especially pertaining to its inevitable interaction with the men's game. In particular, we will entertain the question of whether the excellence of women as sports producers could in fact change women's sports consumption and thus alter a country's sports culture. Put differently, will millions of women as a rule ever breathe, eat, sleep, hope, study, and revere sports the way men have done for well over one century?

Though women's sports in general, and women's soccer in particular, have followed a much different trajectory than that experienced by men's team sports, some similarities in their respective evolutionary paths are apparent. The Big Four in the United States (and men's soccer in most other countries) all underwent a process of "modernization"—mostly during the crucial period of 1870 to 1930—on their way to becoming primary occupants of the cultural "sports space." First, games for children and youth became the venues of recreation for adults, but initially with participation and camaraderie as their only purpose. Eventually, however, the ethos of casual games for exercise and fellowship ("playing for fun") gave way to organized competition with winning as its predominant, perhaps even sole, purpose.[39] In the United States, this transformation occurred in men's team sports at every level (including interscholastic and intercollegiate competition). This development coincided with the creation of formal organization and ongoing "rationalization" of the sport, regardless of whether or not a particular sport ever achieved a following much beyond the actual participants on the field or court.[40]

However, the history of women's team sports in general, and soccer in particular, diverges from this timeline, as participatory recreation almost always superseded the drive for competition over a long period, at least until the 1970s. This was the case particularly at those institutions that represent key facets of American sports (and constitute yet another American "exception"). It was also the case in perhaps the most important foci for the development of women's sports and women's soccer in the United States: athletic programs at colleges and universities that do not exist in

---

[39] See Warren Goldstein, *Playing for Keeps: A History of Early Baseball* (Ithaca, NY: Cornell University Press, 1989); and Markovits and Hellerman, *Offside*, pp. 13–33.

[40] See Allen Guttmann, *From Ritual to Record: The Nature of Modern Sports* (New York: Columbia University Press, 1978), and Markovits and Hellerman, *Offside*, pp. 23–33.

such fashion in any other country in the world, including Britain and its Commonwealth (see our presentation in chapter 6).[41]

Once a competitive team sport has achieved a sufficient level of "rationalization," it may attract some measure of spectatorship and following from modest numbers of enthusiasts. In the United States, sports like lacrosse and volleyball—played by both men and women at the college, semiprofessional, and (more recently) professional levels—have progressed to this point and not much further (though each has its relatively small coterie of supporters at various geographic and institutional locales).

But with men's soccer throughout most of the world and the Big Four in the United States, taking the next step proved decisive. Charismatic entrepreneurs succeeded in producing and marketing a sport, its games, and its participants while institutionalizing a structure that was accompanied by a firmly attached identification of teams in terms of geographic areas, or, in the case of college athletics, institutions. Hence, the era of professional players, managers, coaches, owners—the protagonists of modern sport culture—developed. We have noted that for a sport to have successfully penetrated a nation's cultural space, this process had to be completed by 1930.[42] However, in the case of women's soccer (and women's sports in general) in the United States, the modernization process did not really commence until the last two decades of the twentieth century, at which point the sport's evolution accelerated quite dramatically.

The Rise of Recreational Soccer in America

Any analysis regarding the proliferation of women's soccer as either a recreational activity or spectator sport requires highlighting two key milestones separated by a full generation in time. The first was the passage of Title IX of the 1972 Federal Education Amendments to the Civil Rights Act of 1964 (subsequently strengthened by Congressional legislation in 1988). The second came with the success of the 1999 women's World Cup (held in the United States) in attracting significant numbers of attendees and, more importantly, television viewers. Also crucial was the concurrent success of Team USA on the field and in garnering a wide and popular following of fans among the general public, many with little or no previous interest in soccer and/or women's sports. The years between 1972 and today witnessed the popular proliferation of soccer on college campuses

[41] See Markovits and Hellerman, *Offside*, pp. 42–44.
[42] Ibid., chapter 2.

and high schools, and as a recreational activity for boys and girls through-out the United States. This occurred particularly emphatically among middle-class and upper middle-class families, mostly through participation in organized youth leagues and scholastic athletic programs.

Much of the acceptance and popularity of recreational soccer (but not, significantly, soccer as a spectator sport, nor its attendant culture as found elsewhere in the world) was directly attributable to, and arguably the most lasting legacy of, the ill-fated North American Soccer League (NASL, 1967 to 1985). It was this league that provided legitimacy for the sport among the American professional and managerial classes who desired a game for their children that was allegedly nonconfrontational, nonviolent, multicultural, often coeducational, noncompetitive, and apart from as well as superior to what many of the upscale and educated viewed as the crass and crude milieu of the Big Four. The latter, of course, was precisely the world represented by soccer in all of Europe and much of Latin America, but its decidedly proletarian image and milieu there was immaterial to its perception in the United States. Suddenly, soccer in America allowed up-per-middle-class suburban children of cosmopolitan parents—who only drank the finest French wines, traveled to Europe repeatedly, drove Volvos and Saabs, and considered most mainstream and traditional aspects of American life, including the Big Four sports, uncultured—to participate in a newly acquired politically correct team sport. This milieu constructed a soccer that was antithetical to its existence in countries where it consti-tuted a hegemonic sports culture. Soccer became the American "antifoot-ball" that was preferred by its upper middle-class Europhile milieu that viewed American football (and the other three of the Big Four) as brutal, macho, and totally result-oriented ("winning isn't everything; it's the only thing," as coined by Vince Lombardi, the legendary coach of the champion Green Bay Packers and an icon of American sports culture).

This proliferation of recreational soccer for children "from above" placed the foci for play almost entirely in organized leagues under the aus-pices of national organizations such as the American Youth Soccer Organi-zation (AYSO), United States Youth Soccer Association (USYSA), and the Soccer Association for Youth (SAY), as well as more recently formed groups that specifically focus on developing "elite" soccer talent: the Super Y-League and U.S. Club Soccer. This path represents an obvious divergence from the ways soccer took root in nations where it represents hegemonic sports culture: "from below," as the unstructured pastime and feral passion of the masses, where kids (almost exclusively boys) play the game on their own in the streets, playgrounds, and sandlots as each of the Big Three emerged in the United States (stick ball, street ball, and hoops in drive-ways) and hockey in Canada (the frozen pond down the street, the ice-covered backyard), thus comprising the Big Four team sports of North America's hegemonic sports culture.

By nearly every measure, soccer's recreational surge in the United States has been truly impressive: In 1980, the total combined registration for the three aforementioned youth soccer leagues (AYSO, USYSA, and SAY) stood at 888,705; in 2006 it had increased to 3,907,000.[43] A breakdown of these figures according to gender shows male registration at 2,344,000 and female registration at 1,563,000.[44] An estimation of AYSO registration of six- to eighteen-year-olds for 2001–2 is approximately 348,000 registered girls and 317,000 boys.[45] According to data from the Soccer Industry Council of America (SICA) hailing from 2000, there were 17,734,000 soccer players in the United States, of whom 8,436,000 were female. The average age of all players was 15.3.[46] During the last two decades of the twentieth century, soccer became the second favorite participatory team sport in the United States, trailing only basketball (and surpassing baseball by a wide margin). And though the combined totals for baseball and its "sibling" softball remain far ahead of soccer when participants of all ages are taken into account, this is not the case regarding both the under-eighteen and under-twelve age groups, where soccer emerges slightly ahead.[47]

In terms of overall soccer participation, the increase in the number of female players has continued, while the overall number of male players in the United States has actually declined. According to the trade group Sporting Goods Manufacturers Association, there were 9.0 male and 5.4 female participants per one hundred people in 1987. In 2001 there were 8.6 male and 6.7 female participants per one hundred people (a decline of 4.4 percent, and an increase of 24.1 percent, respectively). A study released in 2006 indicates that the relevant numbers were 7.1 percent for males and

[43] FIFA report, p. 11.

[44] Ibid.

[45] John Enriquez, Registration Manager for the American Youth Soccer Organization (AYSO), personal communication, December 9, 2002. These figures represent an estimate compiled from a total of AYSO team rosters reported for either 2001 or 2002.

[46] As cited in Anson Dorrance, *The Vision of a Champion: Advise and Inspiration from the World's Most Successful Women's Soccer Coach* (Ann Arbor, MI: Huron River Press, 2002), p. 17.

[47] U.S. Soccer Foundation, "Soccer in the USA, 2002–2003," p. 15. Total participants for basketball: 38,663,000; soccer: 19,042,000; softball: 17,679,000; baseball: 11,405,000. Soccer participants in the under-eighteen age group stand at 14,972,000, compared to 6,445,000 for softball and 8,119,000 for baseball (combined: 14,564,000). The number for soccer participants under twelve years of age is 8,775,000, compared to 2,742,000 for softball and 4,731,000 for baseball (combined: 7,473,000).

3.7 percent for females.[48] The definition of "participant" included all those who had played some soccer at least once during the previous year. Among five- to twelve-year-olds, there were 4.9 million boys (a rate of 28 percent) and 2.5 million girls (23.3 percent) who fit this description. Most impressive was the increase of over 700 percent in the number of girls playing organized varsity and junior varsity soccer in high schools over a twenty-year period (from 41,119 in 1980–81 to 292,086 players in 2000–1.)[49]

The exponential rise in the number of American girls playing organized and competitive soccer in high schools and recreational leagues has provided a solid foundation for women's soccer at both the college and professional levels. This was well exemplified by the success of the American team at the inaugural Under-19 Women's World Championship in September 2002 in Edmonton, Alberta. The United States dominated by winning its first five matches (by scores of 5–1, 4–0, 6–0, 6–0, and 4–1, veritable landslides in the world of soccer) on the way to eventually defeating the host team in the final, a 1–0 overtime thriller.[50] The appearance of the newly crowned champion American women's Under-19 team on the cover of (and in a full feature article inside) *Soccer America*, the sport's premier magazine in the United States, is perhaps the greatest indicator for the relatively high levels of esteem and status attained by youth and women's soccer. It is well nigh unimaginable that a similar accomplishment by young women would ever garner such prominent exposure in a comparable publication of any European country (say, for example, *Kicker* and *Elf Freunde* in Germany; or *4-4-2* and *When Saturday Comes* in Britain, to mention just a few prominent ones).

The College Game: Essential Ingredient of Women's Soccer Success in America

The roots of women's soccer at American colleges go back much farther than the inclusion of Title IX in federal legislation, though it could be said that the "modern era" of the game commences with the 1972 law.[51] The beginning of this modern era coincided perfectly with the very years

---

[48] SGMA, 2006 Soccer Participation Report, p. 7.

[49] U.S. Soccer Foundation, "Soccer in the USA, 2002–2003," p. 16.

[50] Scott French, "Déjà vu," *SoccerAmerica*, 57 (19), September 23, 2002, pp. 8–13.

[51] Unless otherwise specified, the information for this section on women's collegiate soccer in the United States is derived from Shawn Ladda, "The Early Beginnings of Intercollegiate Women's Soccer in the United States," *Physical Educator* 57 (2), Spring 2000, pp. 106–12. Accessed through Lexis-Nexis search, Wilson Web: http://vweb.hwwilsonweb.com/cgi-bin/

1970–1973, during which women's football was finally recognized officially by the male football establishment in all of our European examples.

Physical education for girls and young women in the United States started to gain some measure of acceptance at women's colleges and girls' prep schools toward the end of the nineteenth century, though competitive sports for females were still frowned upon in many places.[52] Women played soccer on the campuses of the Seven Sisters colleges in the Northeast as part of intramural programs and at the direction of physical education departments in the early 1900s. A book entitled *Field Hockey and Soccer Rules for Women* (published by Frost and Cubberley in 1923), indicates acceptance of both sports into the physical education curriculum for girls at the elementary, middle, and high school levels, and for young women in college. Both sports originated in Europe and proliferated as recreation for females in the United States. Yet field hockey was by far the more popular and more socially valued. The United States Field Hockey Association was founded at Bryn Mawr in 1922, while women's soccer would establish no such overarching organization until the 1980s. Hence, many proponents of girls' and women's soccer during the first half of the twentieth century viewed the sport as a "forerunner for field hockey." Though soccer was played by women at colleges in earlier years, the oldest records denoting the game are from 1924 at Smith College, where the women's athletic program allowed and promoted the formation of regular teams and the playing of competitive matches at the interclass and intramural levels. Most women's athletics occurred as part of the "play days" featured as a component of an established physical education program. The vast majority of women's athletic and/or physical education departments viewed intercollegiate competition as "elitist," instead preferring its intramural variant, which these departments perceived as egalitarian participation for all for the sake of physical fitness and recreation over competitiveness (i.e., teams composed of only the best players) with winning as the goal. Heeding to this view of fostering "egalitarian" participation in lieu of "elitist" winning, most women's athletic programs banned intercollegiate competition in all team sports; Smith did so beginning in the 1940s, an exclusion that would last until 1971.

The first known intercollegiate competition involving women's soccer

---

webcl. Retrieved April 15, 2008; and Shawn Ladda, "The History of Intercollegiate Women's Soccer in the United States," Doctoral Dissertation, Columbia University, 1995.

[52] Women were playing basketball at Vassar and Smith colleges in 1892, barely a year after Dr. James Naismith had invented the game. See Bill Gutman, *The History of NCAA Basketball* (New York: Crescent Books, 1992).

occurred in the 1950s among several Vermont colleges. It is unclear which of these teams were given the status of varsity (where funding and administration of the sport and its team today originates in a school's athletic department) or were considered clubs (funded through student activities organizations). Regardless, the women playing soccer at Johnson State College, Castleton State College, and Lyndon State College (where the players did indeed receive a varsity "letter," making Lyndon State the first school in the country to do so) represent an evolution from informal recreation for its own sake to competitive contests between two organized teams from separate institutions. Additionally, women's soccer teams from the Canadian universities of Bishops, McDonald, and McGill also participated in matches against the Vermont schools. The team hosting the competition determined the rules, since specific aspects of the game were sometimes in dispute. After the match, the players from both squads usually met for a meal or snacks and beverages in the host school's dining room.[53]

By the late 1960s, the National Association for Girls and Women in Sport (NAGWS)—the organization with the most control over women's athletics in the United States at the time—had changed its philosophy to accept and promote competitive varsity programs for women. NAGWS would eventually evolve into the Association for Intercollegiate Athletics for Women (AIAW), which in turn became subsumed by NCAA in 1982. Thus, not until 1982 did almost all collegiate sports, male and female, become governed by this all-powerful body, establishing virtual numeric and status equality between male and female participation and representation in this very important world of American sports culture. Lacking social and cultural acceptance, female collegiate sports in America also remained institutionally separate from the men until 1982. As the ethos of women's sports changed to accept intercollegiate contests, the Seven Sister schools added soccer as a team sport, complete with competition among schools. However, it was Brown University in 1975 that first bestowed varsity representational status on a soccer team at the beginning of what might be considered the "modern era" of women's sports. Additionally, schools such

---

[53] The postgame socializing with meals and/or beverages is somewhat reminiscent of the milieu for the earliest baseball games between organized clubs of middle-class men in New York (circa 1845–55), and the earliest games of what would evolve into American football between students from Harvard and organized clubs in the Boston area and, more importantly, students from Harvard and McGill University (circa late 1860s through the early 1870s). In the case of these nineteenth-century contests, the postgame activities were often considered equal to or even more important than the game itself. See Markovits and Hellerman, *Offside*, pp. 55–57, 71–73.

as Castleton (which granted official status to its team the same year as Brown), Cortland State in New York, Cornell University, Colgate University, the University of Rochester, and State University of New York-Albany were fielding squads for intercollegiate matches. By 1978, the New England Intercollegiate Women's Soccer Association could count at least thirteen teams with such varsity status representing universities in the northeast, as well as an additional sixteen schools fielding teams designated as "clubs" (and eleven schools in various transitional stages between these two designations). That same year the first Ivy League Tournament was held for women's soccer. By the end of the decade the sport was played by squads with club and university status throughout the nation. The first intercollegiate national championship tournament for women's soccer, sponsored by the AIAW, occurred in 1981. Anson Dorrance, legendary coach of the University of North Carolina's "dynasty" soccer team, had nothing but praise for the AIAW and credited its open-mindedness toward soccer and its unfailing support for all women's varsity sports as the decisive agent in creating, fostering, and legitimating women's athletic activities on America's college campuses.[54] The following year in 1982, the NCAA, having expanded its domain to include women's collegiate athletics, sponsored the first National Championship Tournament for Women's Soccer.

The proliferation of women's sports on campus further accelerated in 1988 with passage by the United States Congress of the Civil Rights Restoration Act that widened the interpretation and enforcement of Title IX, making compliance with gender equity regulations a priority for most college athletic programs. Women's soccer has been a special beneficiary of Title IX. A college can include at least twenty female student-athletes on a team with a minimal level of expenses for equipment. The law demands that every college and university that receives federal funds award an equal number of athletic scholarships for women as for men. Since college football teams alone offer eighty scholarships to men, women's soccer teams have become convenient mechanisms for colleges to counterbalance the men's football teams with twenty such spots.

The growth of women's soccer as an intercollegiate sport since the early 1980s has been truly phenomenal. In 1982, 103 colleges (representing 10.2 percent of NCAA member schools) fielded varsity teams for a total of 2,743 players. In 2001, there were varsity teams from 930 colleges (78.6 percent of NCAA member schools) for a total of 21,709 players.[55] It is

---

[54] Dorrance, *The Vision of a Champion*, p. 4.
[55] U.S. Census, http://www.census.gov/compendia/statab/tables/08s1220.pdf. Retrieved April 30, 2008.

somewhat noteworthy that there were nearly 180 fewer men's varsity soccer programs (752) than women's in 2001.[56]

Women's soccer has started to outdraw men's soccer in attendance as well. Six men's teams from NCAA Division I schools averaged over 2,000 spectators in 2001, while no women's teams did so (though Texas and North Carolina both managed to average at least 1,900). Sixteen men's squads topped 1,000 in average attendance that year, compared to 12 for women's teams.[57] In 2006, two women's teams, the University of Portland and Texas A&M University, averaged over 3,000 spectators.[58] No men's soccer team attained that figure, although nine men's teams drew over 2,000 spectators while only three women's teams managed to do so. Yet the success of soccer for both genders at the college level should be kept in perspective when compared to intercollegiate football and basketball on the men's side, both significant occupants of the American cultural sports space. Whereas the men's football team of our own University of Michigan draws over 100,000 spectators every Saturday during the football season, and the men's basketball team plays its home games in an arena with a seating capacity just shy of 14,000, barely 2,000 fans attend men's and women's varsity soccer games on a good day. While some University of Michigan football, men's basketball, as well as hockey players are known all over the United States and Canada, soccer players (both male and female) are not even recognized on campus.

Additionally, women's basketball on the national level is generally much more popular and draws far more spectators on campus (and television viewers at home) than does soccer. Women's basketball programs such as the University of Connecticut, the University of Tennessee, the University of North Carolina, Duke University, Stanford University, the University of Texas, the University of Maryland, and Rutgers University—to name but the most prominent ones—have national recognition, with some of their players having become nationally known celebrities almost comparable to their male counterparts; moreover, women's intercollegiate volleyball also draws more spectators than soccer.

No presentation on women's soccer in the United States, particularly on the college level, could omit the unique role of the University of North Carolina, that legendary basketball school, whose women's soccer team

[56]"NCAA Sport-by-Sport Participation and Sponsorship: Women's Sports, 1982–2001," NCAA website: http://www.ncaa.org/index. Retrieved April 14, 2008.

[57]"2001 Division I Men's Soccer Attendance," and "Divison I Women's Attendance," NCAA website: http://www.ncaa.org/wps/portal/ncaahome?wcm_global_context=/ncaa. Retrieved April 14, 2008.

[58]NCAA Women's attendance, http://www.ncaa.org/stats/w_soccer/1/2006/2006_d1_w_soccer_attendance.pdf. Retrieved April 14, 2008.

amassed twenty-one national titles (one in the AIAW in 1981, that association's final year; and twenty in the NCAA out of a possible twenty-eight,
having reached the final four in these tournaments twenty-six times).
These incredible numbers represent a singularly stellar achievement in
any team sport, male or female, at the Division I level of college sports.
Apart from the many records achieved—winning streaks, Final Four appearances, most valuable players at NCAA tournaments, Atlantic Coast
Conference (ACC) championships, national championships—and many
other unparalleled collective and individual accolades, the Tar Heels' true
contribution to women's soccer in the United States has been their unique
and direct influence on the women's national team. The Tar Heel tally on
the United States national team includes: forty-three different Carolina
players on the roster since its inception; nine of the eighteen players that
won the first official and FIFA-sanctioned women's World Cup in 1991 in
China plus the team's coach, Anson Dorrance; eight Tar Heels players on
the victorious 1999 World Cup championship team and six Heels on the
2000 Olympic silver medal team in Sidney; and similar numbers on all
subsequent U.S. national teams that have thus far attained some sort of
medal at all Olympics and Women's World Cups. Mia Hamm—the world's
best-known female soccer player of all time, perhaps the game's single true
superstar on a global level, and a stalwart member of America's soccer successes since the early 1990s—is a UNC graduate. As a fine testimony to
Hamm's immensely respected and popular standing in soccer's global
arena way beyond the United States and the women's game, FC Barcelona
anointed her in late 2009 as the team's and its charitable foundation's am-
bassador. What follows is a brief discussion of the American national team,
which has consistently and exclusively been comprised of women who
played soccer at American colleges.

The United States National Team: The Making of Global
   Leaders in an "Un-American" Sport

With females involved in the game at the recreational, scholastic, and college level to a degree unprecedented anywhere else in the world, American
women became the very best in a sport in which its men—at least until the
2002 World Cup tournament in Japan and South Korea—had remained
largely peripheral. Unlike any other team in the world, Team USA medaled at every single one of the nine top-level global competitions in wom-
en's Association football since 1991: winner of the first World Cup in

China in 1991; bronze medalist at the second World Cup in Sweden in 1995; winner and gold medalist at the Olympics in Atlanta in 1996, the first Olympics women's soccer tournament; winner of the World Cup in the United States in 1999; silver medalist at the Olympics in Sidney in 2000; bronze medalist at the World Cup in the United States in 2003; winner and gold medalist at the Olympics in Athens in 2004; bronze medalist at the World Cup in China in 2007; and gold medalist at the Beijing Olympics in 2008.

In addition to these most prestigious competitions in women's soccer, the United States national team has also been the most successful in the Algarve Cup. This competition is a global invitational tournament for national teams. Held annually in the Algarve region of Portugal since 1994, it is one of the most prestigious women's soccer events, alongside the Women's World Cup and Women's Olympic Football. Currently, twelve teams are invited, with the top eight competing for the championship. The American women have won the tournament a record six times, followed by four championships for Norway, two for China, and one each for Germany and Sweden.

For the very first time, the game enjoyed a genuine and broad popular following among the American public at the 1999 World Cup tournament held in the United States. Four special athletes, who are charismatic individuals and unquestioned pioneers of women's soccer throughout the world—Brandi Chastain, Joy Fawcett, Julie Foudy, and Mia Hamm—led a group of young women to a special victory in front of more than 95,000 spectators and millions of television viewers. Tellingly of women's position in this gendered world beyond sports, the main thing remembered about this fabulous game against a superb Chinese team—decided by penalty kicks after the overtime did not break a 0–0 tie—was Chastain taking off her jersey after scoring the winning penalty kick for the United States and running toward her teammates in her bra, demonstrating yet again that the boundaries of women's athletic prowess and their sexualization by society remain blurred and continue to distinguish women's sports and athletes from their male counterparts.[59] Significantly, the success of the United States national team led directly to the establishment of the first venue for routinized professional women's soccer, the Women's United Soccer Association (see below). In retrospect, it can be said that the winning ways of Team USA on the field and the overall sheen of the 1999 World Cup in garnering the interest and attention of the public and media put women's

[59] Brandi Chastain, *It's Not About the Bra: How to Play Hard, Play Fair, and Put the Fun Back into Competitive Sports* (New York: HarperCollins, 2004).

soccer on the map, carving out a recognizable, though small, niche in America's sports space. While not getting anywhere near the media attention devoted to either men's sports or individual women's sports, the American national team drew decent numbers of spectators to some games prior to the 1999 tournament. A 1997 match between the United States and England in San Jose, California attracted a crowd of over seventeen thousand.[60] But it was the 1999 World Cup that engendered a newly found popularity and respect for women's soccer far beyond the confines of a recreational activity or a small number of spectator enthusiasts for the college game.

As noted above, all of the United States national team's players are products of the nation's college soccer. The fact that women playing team sports at the professional level now represents an acceptable and positive development for most Americans highlights the gender progress made in the United States. It also accentuates differences as to how women playing the game of soccer (and also participating in team sports) are perceived in the United States in comparison to most other nations, particularly where soccer and its overwhelmingly male culture dominate the sports space. Julie Foudy, former soccer great, Hall of Fame inductee, noted soccer commentator, one of the country's most respected female leaders, and perhaps the most outspoken advocate for the continued existence of Title IX as the cornerstone for women's sports and women's rights in team sports in the United States, stated the essential difference between soccer's gendered world in the United States and much of the rest of the world quite clearly: "Everyone plays soccer here [in the United States]. Girls are encouraged. But you travel abroad, and the game is considered a man's world in so many cultures. A girl is considered a freak if she plays. We've been to Spain, and jumped into a men's game and been looked at like we were crazy."[61]

Perhaps most impressive of all, Team USA attracted media coverage—which started slowly and steadily increased toward the crescendo of the final, then gradually subsided over the next two weeks—that could easily rival what is routinely directed at the Big Four. The attention given the

[60] U.S. Soccer Federation, *US Soccer Federation Media Guide*, 1998, p. 12.

[61] Harvey Araton, "A Pioneer in Her Sport and Beyond," *New York Times*, July 28, 1998, p. C23. The contrast between the perception of women's soccer in the United States on the one hand and that found in Europe and Latin America on the other was striking. Most media in the latter regions ignored the 1999 World Women's Cup or gave it marginal coverage at best. German television, for example, broadcast only the second half of the U.S. vs. China final (commencing at 11 PM local time), preferring instead to air its usual late-night Saturday soccer talk show featuring an off-season interview with the coach of a Bundesliga club, of course a man.

women soccer players in one month far surpassed all the cumulative media coverage attained by MLS in its entire three-year existence up to that time. Each night of the tournament, late-night-television talk-show host David Letterman displayed a photo of the women's national team in which all twenty players appeared to be wearing nothing but Late Show t-shirts. Letterman himself transformed the term "soccer moms" into the racier and more risqué "soccer mamas" and the openly sexualized "soccer babes," highlighting an aspect of women's team sports heretofore avoided or actually suppressed. An image of femininity and wholesome sexual appeal was conveyed in the message that "women can be both athletic and feminine in an endeavor that, in many countries, still carries the stigma that women who play are somehow unwomanly." Indeed, a side-angle photo of Team USA defender Brandi Chastain "crouched behind a soccer ball wearing only her cleats and her rippling muscles," drew the attention of journalists, pundits, and reporters, as well as many people with little previous interest in soccer.[62]

Here we are at one of the absolute key differences between men's and women's sports, namely the de rigueur sexualization of the latter. This phenomenon is best exemplified by what has come to be known as the "Anna Kournikova syndrome," in which a player who had never come close to winning a tournament on the women's professional tennis tour still became—solely by dint of her beauty and sexuality—an absolute global superstar and a household name. The obverse would be unthinkable in any men's sport: a mediocre athlete with no real achievements on the field would never mutate into a sex symbol of global proportions, attaining greater attention than many a superstar with a distinguished record between the lines.

Moreover, homosexuality among female athletes has emerged into the open to the point where there are no stigmata or sanctions attached. Times have changed since Billie Jean King lost millions of dollars in endorsements when in 1981 she admitted to having had a lesbian affair. Now there

---

[62] Jeré Longman, "Pride in Their Play, and in Their Bodies," *New York Times*, July 8, 1999, pp. D1, D4. When Chastain threw off her shirt—to reveal a sports bra—after scoring the clincher in the final's shoot-out, some speculated that this was either an act of wanton exhibitionism, an instant of "momentary insanity" (as Chastain herself claimed), a blow for gender equality (as shirt shedding by male players in celebration of a victorious moment was something of a tradition in soccer at the time, meanwhile banned), or a shrewd and calculated marketing ploy, since the sports bra in question was a Nike prototype planned for mass production. See Richard Sandomir, "Was Sports Bra Celebration Spontaneous?," *New York Times*, July 8, 1999, p. S6; and Melanie Welds and Ann Oldenburg, "Sports Bra's Flash Could Cash In," *USA Today*, July 13, 1999, p. 2A.

is near total acceptability, even celebration, of the homosexuality of Martina Navratilova in tennis, Rosie Jones in golf, but also of Sheryl Swoopes, arguably among the top-three female basketball players of all times and a huge star in America, whereas gay men are still buried deep in the sports closet. With the exception of divers, gymnasts, and figure skaters—tellingly, the least macho of sports and not associated with teams—no major athlete of the NBA, the NFL, the NHL or MLB has ever declared himself "out" as a homosexual during his days as an active player (see more on this in chapter 5).[63]

The soccer players of Team USA furnished the cover stories for *Time*, *Newsweek*, and *Sports Illustrated* the week after the final, and also graced the cover of *People* magazine (with glowing personal profiles on all eleven starters) the following week. Public appearances of the full squad after the tournament—at Disneyland, the Women's National Basketball Association (WNBA) All-Star game, on NBC television's Today Show (and outside the studio), at the White House meeting President Bill Clinton (who had attended two tournament matches, including the final), all rated high profile coverage in both the sports and main news sections of nearly all American daily newspapers and on local television news shows, as well as on the ubiquitous Cable News Network (CNN). All these developments bespoke qualities of culture that go well beyond the confines of the (mostly indifferent) public perception usually accorded to women's team sports, or soccer as a recreational or spectator activity. Indeed, the players of Team USA had achieved, at least for a few weeks, the rarity of "crossover stardom," a status attained by only a few select athletes of the Big Four.

Perhaps most significantly, the U.S. team's most prominent members—Foudy, Chastain, Hamm, Kristine Lilly, Michelle Akers, and Briana Scurry (the goalie, and the only African American member of the starting eleven)—became nationally known sports figures and heroes. They were role models for millions of young American girls who aspired to be players.

[63] There is, of course, the important memoir by British basketball player John Amaechi, who played in the NBA for five seasons with the Cleveland Cavaliers, the Orlando Magic, and the Utah Jazz. He chronicled his life as a closeted gay man in the NBA. The book, *Man in the Middle*, was published in 2007 and received some attention, especially Amaechi's chronicling of the intense hostility that he faced by the Jazz's head coach Jerry Sloan, though this was due to Sloan's disrespect for Amaechi's modest basketball abilities rather than his homophobia. Of course, Amaechi describes how the entire locker-room culture in the NBA was openly homophobic but he also gives credit to many of his fellow players who—though never explicitly acknowledging Amaechi's homosexuality—seem to have been tacitly aware of his sexual orientation. The point however remains: Amaechi was at best a role player, not anywhere near having had star status in the League, *and* he published his memoirs after his playing days were over.

Several of these Team USA participants netted lucrative sponsorship and promotional deals; Hamm, in particular, became a regular star in television commercials and magazine advertisements often featured together with Michael Jordan, the ultimate global superstar. Hamm's media presence lasted well past her retirement as an active player in 2006.

It is not an exaggeration to say that the success of the American women's national team in 1999 and the attention accorded the World Cup tournament that year provided the initial impetus for what could conceivably become a long and fruitful history of women's professional soccer in the United States and, perhaps, the world. The exceptional success of the American women's game—in notable contrast to the status of their male counterparts, with the possible exception of the 2002 World Cup—fulfills two key conditions essential to making any sport popular in the United States or, for that matter, anywhere else. The first is respect for being the very best (i.e., quality as a means). The other is respect for winning and making their fans feel proud of their national team or players in a sport where there had not been much pride and satisfaction (i.e., quality as an end). And though a successful Women's World Cup was not a sufficient condition for the establishment of a women's professional soccer league in the United States, it most definitely constituted a necessary one. Such a league was indeed established, beginning play in the spring of 2001.

The Ups and Downs of Professionalization: The Women's United Soccer Association (WUSA) and Women's Professional Soccer (WPS)

Women's soccer may present an opportunity to utilize what we have termed the "best of the best"—a key prerequisite for the successful perpetuation of any team sport and major league in the American sports space.[64] To wit, it is a given for Americans (as well as for sports fans in the rest of the world) that MLB, the NFL, the NBA, and the NHL all represent the ultimate in quality of their respective sports. Indeed, athletes in any of the Big Four from anywhere in the world must by necessity aspire to play in these North American venues if they want to compete with the best of the best because America represents the undisputed global core for

[64] See Markovits and Hellerman, *Offside*, pp. 15–61. Though another American exception, this aspect of American team sports is mostly an outgrowth of their development in relative geographic isolation in the era (1870–1930) we have identified as crucial to the establishment of modern hegemonic sports culture.

these four team sports. Yet, the situation for soccer on the men's side has been exactly the opposite. The best of the best, including a fair number of Americans, play in Europe, which is that sport's undisputed global core.

But in terms of women's soccer, a venue emerged that fulfilled this prerequisite on the left side of the Atlantic: WUSA, a league in which not only the best American players competed, but also to which the top women soccer players from all over the world migrated. Thus, WUSA could have possibly redefined how women's team sports and their participants were perceived and valued by American society (and, perhaps, by other nations as well).

WUSA was founded in the spring of 2000 by John Hendricks, chairman and chief executive officer of Discovery Communications, along with other high profile corporate investors such as Cox Communications, Time Warner Cable, and Comcast Corporation. With an initial stake of $40 million, the plan was to make the league profitable, or at least self-sufficient, within five years.[65] Like MLS, WUSA was organized and funded as a "single entity business structure." Rather than owning individual franchises linked through confederation (as found in the Big Four in North America and most professional sports leagues throughout the world), "club operators owned a financial stake in the league, not just their individual team," while player contracts were owned by the league, not the teams.[66] Prior to reaching an accommodation with MLS executives who had their own plans for a professional women's league, the brand new WUSA signed all twenty players from the world champion American national team, designating each a "founding player" awarded with equity shares in the league.[67] Player salaries in WUSA were set at a yearly minimum of $27,000 and a maximum of $85,000. The league consisted of eight teams located throughout the United States (Atlanta, Boston, Carolina, New York, Philadelphia, San Diego, San Jose, and Washington, D.C.), with each team playing a twenty-two game season from April through August. A four-team playoff culminated in the Founders Cup league championship (won by San Jose in 2001, Carolina in 2002, and Boston in 2003).[68] As noted, WUSA provided the forum for the best of women's soccer from both the United States and

[65] WUSA Communications Department, *WUSA 2002 Official Media Guide*, pp. 6, 8.

[66] Ibid, p. 21.

[67] See Markovits and Hellerman, *Offside*, pp. 180–81; and *WUSA 2002 Official Media Guide*, p. 32. Nineteen of the twenty players from Team USA's 1999 World Cup roster played in WUSA. Michelle Akers retired soon after the 1999 tournament, but was still awarded a financial stake in the league.

[68] Paul Dodson, WUSA Manager of Sports Communications, personal communication, November 19, 2002.

the rest of the world. Hence, no less than nine players from China were on WUSA rosters for 2002, while some of the league's top performers—including Hege Riise (Norway), Marinette Pichon (France), and Birgit Prinz (Germany)—hailed from outside the United States.[69] So WUSA had indeed fulfilled the requirements for attracting the best of the best, while also utilizing the public's identification with the success of American athletes on the world stage.

But playing and following soccer in the United States, and women's soccer specifically, are two completely different things. And never before was the chasm between activity (production) and culture (consumption) more pronounced than in the case of WUSA. Attendance figures at matches and television ratings declined from the league's first season to its second, as expenses far exceeded the initial $40 million seed, reportedly by close to double at the end of 2002.[70] To cut costs, WUSA reduced roster sizes from twenty to eighteen players and moved its league offices from New York to Atlanta.[71] Average attendance per match dipped from 8,104 for 2001 to 6,957 for 2002; a total of 585,374 spectators for 84 matches in 2002, with a high of 24,000 at RFK Stadium in Washington, D.C., on July 7 to a low of 4,002 at Mitchell Field in New York (Uniondale, Long Island) on July 20.[72]

With the exception of specific events such as the World Cup, the European National Championships, and the Champions League Final matches constituting the most pronounced evidence for what we have discussed in chapter 3 as the "Olympianization" of American soccer, "regular" soccer of any variety continues to be a tough sell to an American television audience. So it should be no surprise that the ratings for cable broadcasts of WUSA games were quite low, though the decline of 75 percent from the first season (0.4 on Turner Network Television and the now-defunct CNN–Sports

[69] WUSA Communications Department, *WUSA 2002 Official Media Guide*, p. 34. "Best of the Best," *SoccerAmerica* 57 (18), September 9, 2002, p. 33.

[70] Scott French, "WUSA: Profitable by 2007? Increased revenues spark hope as attendance, TV ratings decline," *SoccerAmerica* 57 (18), September 9, 2002, p. 35. Though WUSA officials said expenses had declined by 28 percent, league founder John Hendricks stated that "the league will have spent, by the end of 2002, $75 million–$80 million in total. (In addition, $24 million was spent on stadium development.)" According to Hendricks, the balance between revenues and expenses was approximately $20 million. "That would make for revenues of about $9 million in 2002 and $5.5 million in 2001. Doing the math, WUSA investors have lost about $55 million since the league's formation."

[71] Michelle Smith and Dwight Chapin, "WUSA is gearing for seconds," *San Francisco Chronicle*, April 13, 2002, p. C3.

[72] Paul Dodson, WUSA Manager of Sports Communications, personal communication, November 19, 2002.

Illustrated) to 2002 (0.1 on PAX TV) could be viewed as precipitous.[73] At
the end of 2002, the league's solvency remained contingent on the willing-
ness of Hendricks (openly and affectionately called "St. John" by WUSA
players) to provide the funds necessary to maintain operations.[74] But even
this honorific sainthood bestowed on Hendricks could not save WUSA. At
the end of the 2003 season, he called a press conference to declare the end
of this short-lived experiment. With losses close to $100 million, the league
had become untenable.

WUSA's own research revealed that 66 percent of its "fan base" (those
attending at least one game) was female in 2001 increasing to 70 percent in
2002.[75] Additionally, the league's demographic analysis also demonstrated
that nearly 30 percent of those attending its games were under the age of
fifteen, mostly girls accompanied by older family members (more than 50
percent of whom had an annual income of at least $80,000).[76] Demo-
graphic data of the television audience for the 1999 Women's World Cup
showed that prior to the final (when the television audience just about
broke even by gender), "women comprised only 34 percent of the World
Cup audience on ESPN and 35 percent on ESPN 2, compared with 39
percent for ESPN's WNBA games and 40 percent for the NCAA women's
basketball championship tournament."[77] (Indeed, these figures for wom-
en's basketball reveal something of a weakness in the female fan base for
that sport as well.) While virtually every expert agrees that WUSA was
poorly managed, especially in its insistence to remain completely separate
from the men's game and its prime purveyor of Major League Soccer, the
league's failure surely corroborates the reality of soccer's marginal presence in America's sports culture. Just because millions produce a sport does
not mean that they also will consume it. There is a major chasm between
"doing" and "following" a sport—and nowhere is this more pronounced
than among women. The way most women and girls relate to team sports
must change from the activity of recreation and participation to a culture
of spectatorship, following, and affect (if not exactly the same as what is
found in the hegemonic sports culture that is overwhelmingly male, then

[73] French, "WUSA: Profitable by 2007?," p. 35.
[74] George Vecsey, "W.U.S.A. Recognizes Its New Talent amid Thanks for 'St. John,'" *New York Times*, August 25, 2002, p. SP8.
[75] WUSA Communications Department, *WUSA 2002 Official Media Guide*, p. 170; and "The Smart Way to Reach America's Families," WUSA promotional kit, 2002.
[76] Ibid.
[77] Richard Sandomir, "Sale of Cup Merchandise Just Didn't Take Off," *New York Times*, July 13, 1999, p. D4.

some sort of variation involving significant numbers of females) to become a truly salient factor in the American sports space. In this aspect, the United States most certainly offers no exception. Indeed, this is the same in every society: women have yet to create a team sport that has even the semblance of becoming part of that society's hegemonic sports culture. Of course, this has not been the case in individual sports—such as figure skating, tennis, skiing, swimming, and track and field—where many individual women have indeed become very much a part of certain countries'(and the world's) hegemonic sports cultures: Katarina Witt, the Williams sisters, Steffi Graf, Donna de Varona, Wilma Rudolph, Jackie Joyner–Kersee, Nadia Comăneci, to mention just a few.

Still, WUSA was not all for naught. A successor league, WPS, commenced play in the spring of 2009. Fielding teams in metropolitan Boston, Chicago, Dallas, Los Angeles, New York, St. Louis, the San Francisco Bay Area, and Washington, D.C., these eight teams comprise a new professional women's soccer league that consciously and conscientiously aims to avoid WUSA's missteps. Thus, in contrast to WUSA, which employed a top-down model by relying on star players alone to earn fast profits, WPS has opted to pursue a local, grass-roots approach "from below" that emphasizes slow and steady growth. Still, some of the world's best female soccer players joined this league, arguably making it, just like WUSA before it, the very best forum for women's soccer on the globe.

Not only did WPS draft many of the top players from the United States national team and disperse them strategically among the eight participating teams, but also drafted four of the best Japanese and ten of the best Brazilian players. That included the superstar Marta, who played in Los Angeles but also returned to her native Brazil during WPS's off-season to join Pelé's old club Santos, where she was accorded the immense honor of wearing Pelé's coveted number 10 jersey and became the very first woman to play on a man's team. Even if a gimmick, it was arguably the most powerful testimony as to how far women's soccer had come in the world—that in Brazil, of all places, the Mecca of football, worshipping a macho game in a macho society, a female player would be accorded such respect and honor. Marta's countrywoman Daniela joined St. Louis and Cristiane Chicago, adding to the increasingly cosmopolitan and diverse lineups in women's soccer. The aforementioned best English female footballer and Arsenal star Kelly Smith, commenced play in Boston.

Despite careful planning and attracting all this national and international talent, by the end of the first season—in which the New York area-

202   CHAPTER 4

based Sky Blue FC won the championship—several of the league's teams lost twice as much revenue as expected, ranging between $1–2 million. This was largely due to their inability to attract local sponsors, even though global sporting goods manufacturer Puma committed itself to invest in the league. The league's average per-game attendance came to 4,500 fans, about what its executives had anticipated. Despite these uneven results, which led to the demise of the Los Angeles Sol, WPS was on track to expand to ten teams in 2010 with franchises in Atlanta and Philadelphia.[78]

Another Cosmopolitanism: Feminization and the Transnational Rise of Women's Soccer

There can be no doubt that the phenomenal rise of women's soccer is a mainstay in the altered world of sport over the past three decades. Its success evolved with the rise of feminism and in step with the second globalization and its inclusive cosmopolitan cultural effects. Both in Europe and in the United States, the trajectory of the women's game and its timeline have been nearly identical. Thanks to the massive social and cultural shifts caused by the so-called second wave of feminism in the late 1960s and early 1970s, women's soccer in the United States and women's football in Europe left their respective ghettos of semiofficial existence and transformed themselves from curiosities to mainstays on the production side of team sports.[79] Very few, if any, American and European women played this game in the late 1960s and early 1970s, but millions do today—case closed!

If the content of this change was virtually identical on both sides of the Atlantic, the form in which it happened could not have been more different. Both journeys were fraught with obstacles of a varied nature. On the one hand, American women had it much easier than their European counterparts because they blazed a trail that men had known as soccer's pioneers but had traveled lightly. Furthermore, America's sports-obsessed men were not particularly interested nor especially invested (in terms of their identity and culture) in the existence of this soccer path. Precisely because soccer has had a subordinate position in America's male-dominated hegemonic sports cultures was the road for women in this game much smoother in the United States than in Europe. Unlike their European sisters, American female soccer players did not have to enter an oc-

[78] Ken Belson, "Women's League Seeks Sponsors," *New York Times*, August 25, 2009.
[79] Feminism benefitted soccer not only in the United States, as Kuper and Szymanski correctly point out, but also in Europe. See *Soccernomics*, p. 163.

cupied space and contest it against much opposition, derision, and ridicule. On the other hand, one could also argue that the American women confronted an even more formidable task than their European counterparts in that they were pioneers in the very establishment of such a structure and language in the United States making American female soccer players not only pioneers for women but also for soccer. In contrast, European women entered a structure and learned a language that had flourished in every European culture for nearly a century. In sum, the American women became trailblazers for a sport that itself had a marginal existence in their own culture's sport history, as opposed to the European situation in which the women merely affirmed an already extant culture and language.

In comparing the different paths on these two continents with regards to their respective costs and benefits, one could possibly make the argument that the American trajectory of not having to contest with men was more beneficial in the short run, as demonstrated by the almost instant success of the women soccer players and their rise to international prominence. The reason that this least-resistance hypothesis might have some validity is best demonstrated by the fact that the women's game in China, the two Koreas, Denmark, Sweden, and Norway flourished early on as well. In none of these countries did the men ever attain any degree of sustained success in Association football, despite Sweden's second place finish at the World Cup in 1958 played in Sweden, its third place finish at the World Cup in 1994 held in the United States, and Denmark's winning the European Championship in 1992. Thus we argue that at the earliest stages of the establishment of women's soccer, a relatively meek presence of the men's game might be advantageous for the women's. However, as time passes and the women's game becomes fully institutionalized, prowess and excellence in the men's game might indeed "bleed over" into the women's. It is not by chance that the new international powers in women's football—joining the United States at the very top—are Germany and Brazil, arguably among the most pedigreed countries in the history of the men's game.

Once firmly established by the late 1970s and early 1980s on both sides of the Atlantic, it is fascinating to observe how women's soccer quickly became absorbed by the extant sports structures and cultures dominant on each of the two continents. On the European side, women's football fast became the purview of clubs, which—just like in the men's game—developed into the mainstay of the game's quotidian life. This existence ranged from regular matches and leagues to championships and tournaments, from player development, coaching and training methods, to feeding each country's national team with the best players in the land. In the United States, not surprisingly, it has been the world of college sports that assumed precisely the equivalent function. America's counterpart to England's Arsenal has been the University of North Carolina. In other words, America's international prowess in women's soccer would be unthinkable without the college game—its regular season championships, tournaments, player development, training methods, and coaching.

In many ways, the sensational proliferation and amazing growth of women's soccer over the past three decades attests to a triumph of what has come to be known as "liberal" or "equality" feminism. This is a feminism that seeks to create equality for women in structures that have been largely, if not exclusively, ruled by men. In sports (team sports in particular and soccer/football all the more), women dared enter and challenge a macho world in which they—though far from having achieved equality—have successfully attained a space of their own which simply can no longer be ignored. Tellingly, virtually all the activists in this emancipatory quest— namely the thousands, later millions, of players—rarely, if ever, perceived themselves as engaged or explicit feminists. They did not so much want to confront a male-dominated world and abolish its sexism as they desired to play the very same game of Association football as did the men: with the same rules, cleats, ball, in the same organizations, on the same grounds, and with the same teamwork, intensity, and toughness. Women wanted to enjoy competition as much as men had always done. Thus, it is not at all surprising that the intense rivalry between the American and the Norwegian national teams led the players to experience something of a mutual disdain and an antipathy for each other bordering on hatred. Foudy's realistic, indeed painful, account of how she and her teammates felt after losing to the Norwegians in the 2000 gold medal game of the Sydney Olympics, and how the Americans suffered after being publicly mocked and taunted by the Norwegian players who formed a human centipede and frolicked around on the field after defeating Team USA in the semifinals of the second women's World Cup in Sweden in 1995, reveals very little about sisterhood and women's solidarity. But it conveys all the more about competition, rivalry, the sweet sensation of victory, and bitter taste of defeat.[80] Foudy's words could have been written by any male superstar experiencing the humiliation and hurt of a major loss in a major tournament to a bitter and hated rival. Her account emphatically shows us the intense world of top-level athletes devoid of any gender. She wrote about soccer players pure and simple, not women soccer players; about top-level ath-

---

[80] Julie Foudy, "Lead On!," in Chastain, *Its Not About the Bra*, pp. 96–98.

letes at a top-level competition, not about female athletes at a female competition. And yet, public opinion on both sides of the Atlantic continues to
gauge the manifestations of female and male competition quite differently.
When the University of New Mexico defender Elizabeth Lambert el-
bowed her opponent from Brigham Young University in the back and then
threw her to the ground by pulling on her ponytail, she became "an ignominious sensation on television, the Internet and talk radio."[81] Giving
women's college soccer a level of national (and international) attention
that no Tar Heel national championship or any of the game's marquee
domestic events ever had, "the incident spurred a national debate about
sportsmanship, gender roles, double standards regarding aggressiveness
and news media coverage and the sexualized portrayal of female athletes."[82]
Put simply, no comparable act by a male soccer player at any level of the
game in the United States, or anywhere else in the world, would have attained close to the same public attention and debate as did this incident.
Case in point: The infamous head-butt by France's Zinedine Zidane of Italy's Marco Materazzi at the 2006 World Cup final with nearly one billion
television viewers as witnesses was much decried, derided, second-guessed,
lip-read, analyzed, extolled. But there were very few who viewed it as morally reprehensible and—more telling still—as profoundly dangerous to the
very essence of the game and to sports as a whole. Just like the complex
issue of sexuality continues to play a crucial role in women's soccer, indeed
all women's sports, the way it does not on the men's side, so, too, does the
level of aggressiveness which constitutes one of the last taboos for female
athletes: deep down, violence is seen as part of the men's game and is, if not
lauded and encouraged, then at least condoned, expected, and certainly
excused. For women, on the other hand, violence and physical aggressiveness remain socially unacceptable shy of satisfying some men's prurient
interest in "cat fights," which, however, pertains more to the world of por-
nography than of sports.

By becoming soccer players, women on both sides of the Atlantic entered a structure, a language, and a world that had been created and dominated by men. They appropriated this language for their very own purposes. As such, the presence of female soccer players represents no victory
for feminism if one takes that to mean the alteration of male structures or,
better yet, the creation of completely new ones devoid of any male influ-

[81] Jeré Longman, "For All the Wrong Reasons, Women's Soccer Is Noticed," *New York Times*, November 11, 2009.

[82] Ibid. See also Jeré Longman, "That Soccer Play, in Context," *New York Times*, November 18, 2009, in which Elizabeth Lambert does not condone her violent behavior but tries her best to "contextualize" it for the complete picture.

ence. And sure enough, in every country that we studied, female soccer players did indeed incur a certain irritation, if not outright wrath, on the part of feminists who reject soccer, team sports, and probably most sports as expressions of male domination and sexism. For such feminists, women players would only be acceptable had they created their own female game de novo having no relations to the conventional game of soccer whatsoever.

In a matter of three decades, women have successfully entered the male world of Association football. Though they have become the game's accomplished producers and have attained a formal equality with the men, there can be no question that women's soccer exists in a marginalized niche compared to the men's game. Above all, in the realm of following, consuming, breathing, drinking, eating, analyzing, discussing, dreaming, and debating the sport, most women still speak a different language than men. The last few decades have lent women a voice of their own in the global language of Association football. Whether that voice will ever become the equal of, or assume the qualitative weight of the men's in sheer quantity, we cannot even guess at this time. Yet, the internationalization of the game and the diversity of its female players present another new case of emerging cosmopolitan inclusion: profound social change that reaches across former cultural boundaries, altering formerly protected societal domains for good. At the same time, it also spawns defensive reactions, not least by a macho milieu whose globally present counter-cosmopolitanism manifests itself differently in Europe and America. It is to a discussion of this reactive phenomenon that we now turn.

Chapter 5 ◇◇◇◇◇◇◇◇◇◇◇◇◇◇◇◇◇◇◇◇◇◇◇◇◇◇◇◇◇◇◇◇◇

A COUNTER-COSMOPOLITAN BACKLASH?

THE POLITICS OF EXCLUSION, RACISM, AND VIOLENCE IN EUROPEAN AND AMERICAN SPORTS CULTURES

Alas, just like in most realms of human activity, so too in sports does tolerance of diversity and inclusiveness meet with resistance by forces that could best be characterized by what Kwame Anthony Appiah has so aptly termed, "counter-cosmopolitanism."[1] Newcomers, challengers, immigrants, and "alien" languages are often met with ridicule, as well as harsh, hostile, even violent reactions by the natives. Since cultural changes always imply some threat to existing identities, they are inevitably fraught with tensions and defensive responses. Nowhere is this clearer than in the world of sports, since adversity, opposition, competition, contest and thus conflict are the most essential markers of all sport identities. Without them, sport does not exist.

Cultural Resilience: Hostility against Newcomers and Global Players

One of the characteristics of any entrenched sports culture consists in its initial suspicion of and hostility toward any newcomers from within the sport itself, as well as by a rival sport. In both cases, the established sport perceives the intra- or inter-sport challenger as inferior in any number of

[1] Kwame Anthony Appiah, *Cosmopolitanism* (New York: W. W. Norton, 2007), pp. 137–53.

ways. First, that the newcomer lacks toughness, and is not sufficiently manly. For example, "true" English and Scottish football supporters perceive continental players and others hailing from outside the British Isles as weak, as "divers," as "feigning injury," in short not manly and tough as "real" footballers ought to be. Northern Europeans see Latin American and Southern European soccer players as "fakers," "frauds," and "sissies." Even the mild-mannered and worldly Franz Beckenbauer defended rough play at the World Cup 2006 in Germany by invoking proper soccer's toughness, which he contrasted derisively with the alleged softness of basketball. Or reflect on how Canadian hockey fans and self-appointed guardians of the game, even beyond the provocative showmanship of Don Cherry, have continued to belittle the skill and very presence of foreign NHL players by calling them "soft." And to millions of "manly" sports fans of the North American Big Four, soccer is basically a sport for patsies, for fakers—for women.

Here are some random but characteristic examples:

- We experienced the regular American male sports fans' views about soccer when, during a game that we attended on July 24, 2009 between the Detroit Tigers and the Chicago White Sox in Detroit's Comerica Park, the fans berated the young White Sox supertalent Gordon Beckham (no relation to David) to stop "being a woman"— to cease playacting like those patsy soccer players, after Beckham had accidentally fouled off a 95 mile-per-hour fastball onto his own foot, and fell instantly to the ground writhing in pain.
- Or take the widely viewed SONY BRAVIA NFL Sears commercial in which football and NASCAR stars sit on a dais, touting this television's quality to transmit the finest images of sports. When Peyton Manning tells the dorky-looking customer that if "football" is shot in SONY HD TV, should he not also watch it on a SONY HD TV, the customer asks Manning whether he *also* meant to include "soccer" by using the word "football"—to which Manning derisively exclaims "soccer" while he and the others on the dais break into dismissive laughter.[2] Clearly, soccer, to these hard-core manly representatives of American sports, is not to contaminate football in any way, shape, or form, by being associated with it, however marginally.
- And then there was the legendary Michigan football coach, the late Glenn Edward "Bo" Schembechler Jr., who, according to Michigan

[2] See http://www.youtube.com/watch?v=0D6TBPl6B_U. Retrieved August 21, 2009.

soccer coach Steve Burns, told him repeatedly that soccer was a wonderful game, but then you grow up.

Whereas soccer lacks in masculinity in the eyes of American sports fans,
baseball and basketball do for their European counterparts. Some European football supporters doubt the masculinity even of American football—or "gridiron," as the game has come to be labeled dismissively and
derisively in Europe—which is most certainly a brutal and violent sport by
any measure. However, to European machos, American football's alleged
"softness" consists in its players' wearing protective gear—unlike "real"
men in the related rugby games—and in its being played by freaks of nature, not real men. Football, for Europeans, more than any of the other
American sports, has also become synonymous with American power, capitalism, commercialism, and crudeness. Moreover, it has become the American sport most associated with the ills of television culture. To its European critics, American football assumes a cartoon-like quality, something
unreal and a mere by-product of America's money-making culture industry. In other words, all the threatening dimensions associated with an alleged American takeover of European culture and identity have become
associated with football. This is odd, because, as we discussed amply in
chapter 2, this sport has been the least internationally successful and globalized among the North American Big Four and has proved to be no
threat to soccer's dominance in Europe, contrary to all kinds of alarmist
and protectionist worries tinged with a fine dosage of antifootball rhetoric.[3] Behooving the strongly gendered nature of all hegenomic sports cul-

[3] Murphy, Williams, and Dunning have long expected that "soccer is a threat to gridiron
football in the country of its origin, too." While American football is the "embodiment and
display of male aggressiveness and power" and "based on sheer size and strength," in soccer
the "warlike element is less obvious, more muted and controlled." They also lament that football is "more overtly capitalistic than is the case with most professional sports in Western
Europe," and they claim that football is a "game which could only have grown up and taken
root in a society where there is considerable support for ideals of masculinity which celebrate
or at least tolerate a greater amount of overt physical violence than is considered desirable by
the dominant and majority groups in the societies of Western Europe." Lastly, the rise of
American football's popularity is situated in the context of the Vietnam War and attributed to
the concurring "brutalization of society," while the authors view the new success of soccer as
a participant sport in terms of a "civilizing process." Yet its civilizing social interventions "may
be hampered in its competition with its intrinsically more violence, but capital-packed and
superbly media-packaged North American rival." See Murphy, Williams, and Dunning, *Football on Trial*, pp. 15–19. The impressive scholarship by the Leicester School scholars on sports
and fan culture notwithstanding we are, frankly, quite baffled how knowledgeable authors
hailing from the land of such global mega clubs as Manchester United, Chelsea, Arsenal, and
Liverpool claim that European sports, in this case soccer, are less "overtly capitalistic" than

tures, the alleged absence of any requisite manliness of all rivals clearly helps to lower their legitimacy.

In addition to the perceived "unmanliness" of any newcomer to an existing sport—be it the same sport performed by outsiders (European hockey players in the NHL; Latin footballers in Europe's northern, particularly British, leagues) or a different sport (soccer coming to America; American sports going to Europe)—the establishment denigrates the challenger for being facile and aesthetically displeasing. "How hard is it really to kick a ball?" one hears the frequent criticism by America's Big Four fans leveled against soccer. "And what about any measurable statistics that convey each player's actual contribution to the game?"; and, most emphatically, "what is it with the deranged time-keeping by the referee who, in this day and age of being able to measure time with a precision to a tenth of a second—as is commonplace in three of the Big Four North American sports—decides totally arbitrarily and visible to no one else in the stadium when to end a game, not players, not coaches, not fans?" Conversely, European soccer fans grumble about the alleged facility of American sports: "how hard can it be to hit this ball with this odd stick?"; or "there is absolutely no skill to playing American football—big guys just hit each other indiscriminately and pile up on each other." And even basketball cannot be hard since it basically entails "7-foot-tall giants dunking a ball into 10-foot-high basket."

And lastly, of course, insiders invariably denigrate the new rival by labeling it boring: To millions of American sports fans, soccer is soporific by dint of the paucity of goals during a match and what they perceive as endless passing the ball in the middle of the field, apparently with little aim and all the more turnovers. Conversely, Europeans find the number-ob-

American sports, in this case football, especially since if any quasi-socialist arrangements exist anywhere in American economy, society, and culture, they have flourished in the country's four major sports leagues, the NFL included. Moreover, we are equally baffled how authors hailing from the continent that had its fair share of mass atrocities throughout its history, let alone the twentieth century, can claim a greater reticence for its culture's and population's penchant for "overt physical violence" than they allege to exist in America's. Lastly, as this chapter's topic demonstrates, violence "outside the lines"—that is, by the spectators and fans—is much more pronounced in allegedly more civilized and less macho Europe than it is in the United States. The point here is simple: We do not think it empirically accurate nor normatively desirable to attribute questionable national characteristics to the Gestalt of any particular sport. After all, the very same allegedly violent American males whose essential being some claim to be so well reflected in the bellicose game of football also delight playing and following baseball and basketball, both essentially non-contact sports, with the latter being explicitly so (and thus a consciously designed anti-football) that Europeans, including Beckenbauer, invoke derisively when they want to emphasize the legitimacy of soccer's rough manners and demeanors.

session of Americans that characterize all their sports dull, none more than baseball, which most Europeans completely fail to understand and remain unwilling to engage. On the other hand they also find basketball uninteresting by dint of its high scoring, which devalues each incremental score.

The point is clear: high scoring can be as boring to an outsider as low scoring. Both bespeak a lack of appreciation for and often irritation with the new language. Because the very same American baseball fan that categorizes soccer as boring by virtue of its lack of scoring, revels in a pitchers' duel that results in a 1–0 game, which he most assuredly found downright thrilling and aesthetically pleasing. Ditto with the reverse. A true soccer fan will rejoice in the excitement of a 0–0 draw and will dismiss American sports as boring due to an excess of scoring in basketball, paucity of action in baseball, and weird melees and seemingly uncontrolled mayhem in football.

That a different sport appears to be boring to the uninitiated makes complete sense. After all, a lecture delivered in any language in which the audience was not conversant would by definition be dull for its members. As we know from the world of languages, one needs to further denigrate any rival by diminishing its level of difficulty and beauty. Only one's own language has the requisite complexity, nuance, and aesthetics to render it incomparably superior to any other. Just like all language communities have their purists and chauvinists, whose very essence is to lord over their particular language's purity, rail against any contamination by outsiders, and tout its advantages vis-à-vis all rivals, so too do established sports cultures protect their domain against newcomers on all possible levels of contestation.

Interestingly, the counter-cosmopolitan wrath against soccer does not only hail from countries and cultures where the game has come to be seen as an intruder to the established sports culture and as a direct competitor to existing hegemonic sports. In Europe, too, there frequently emerge nationalist rages against soccer's alleged commercialization and its accompanying soullessness. Oddly enough, the telling scepter of "Americanization" is frequently invoked in these counter-cosmopolitan attacks on soccer, which is totally odd since the game is anything but American, were it not a tell-tale word used by all European opponents (left and right) whenever they depict globalization's evils.

We will briefly present an example of such a counter-cosmopolitan discourse from Germany that appeared in *Der Spiegel*, the leading German-language newsweekly akin to *Time* or *Newsweek*, and not some obscure right-wing nationalist publication. Entitled "Victory of Values: Become

Handball players," the article celebrated the German team's World Cup victory in (team) handball in 2007.[4] In his piece, the author contrasts what he perceives to be the "rooted" and "ethnic" sport of handball, performed to perfection by hard-working German men, via their "manual labor" accompanied by requisite sweat to the commercial, globalized, and thus artificial and alien sport of professional soccer. "Handball is rooted like little else. . . . No marketing-gimmicks, no fan-mile [soccer-style] hype." The author continues to extol handball's virtues and moral superiority, which he sees leading to a "victory one has fought for," unlike, presumably, in soccer, which is governed by its slovenliness with its spoiled prima donnas for whom victory just materializes out of thin air. The author then invokes Prussian virtues such as subordination to the collective and obedience to authority, which he contrasts favorably to such ills as individualism, creative play, intellectual activity, and wealth. He then extols the "stoic" handball coach, Heiner Brand, as a heroic ideal. Brand embodies the "prototype of the German handball player. He does not haggle or philosophize but offers 'honest labor': no advertizing contracts which are worth millions, no loud contract haggling, no esoteric philosophy, no film and photo sessions, no overpowering personality cult. No geniuses but men as little cogs in a big wheel." The article then explicitly praises team handball as a locally rooted sport "of original German nature," the "core values" of which will eventually surpass international, Americanized soccer: "The coach and his boys personify German core values. They do so much more than soccer's pop business. . . . They play in Flensburg or Göppingen, in Kiel or Magdeburg [midsized German towns as opposed to teaming cosmopolitan me-

[4] "Handball" in this case refers to the sport Americans know, if at all, under the term "team handball." The sport known to Americans, especially urban denizens such as those of New York City, as "handball" is unknown to Europeans. "Team Handball" involves two teams that play against each other by scoring the ball into the opponent's goal. The game is kind of a soccer played with hands instead of feet. "Handball" as known to Americans is a sport in which a hard rubber ball is propelled against walls by one player with his opponent having to reach the rebound and hit the ball thereafter. This game is akin to squash and racquetball, though played with bare hands both indoors and outdoors. All of the ensuing quotations hail from Achim Achilles, "Sieg der Werte: Werdet Handballer!," *Der Spiegel*, February 4, 2007; www.spiegel.de/sport/sonst/0,1518,464225,00.html. Retrieved December 30, 2008. It is striking that this decidedly nationalistic, countercosmopolitan essay was not published in *Der Spiegel*'s English online edition. Here is an English translation of the German title: Victory of Values: Become Handballers! In a previous article, the editorial columnist Achilles described Italian men and soccer players as "parasitic": "The Italian man, let's call him Luigi," writes Achilles, "is a parasitic life form." "It [sic!] cannot live without a host animal 'from which it sucks all it can.'" "Luigi," according to Achilles, "is perennially engaged in demonstrating his need for help." Quoted in *La Repubblica*, June 27, 2006. After protests by Italians, *Der Spiegel* removed the article from its website.

tropolises where alien soccer rules]. They are neither dependent on Russian millionaires nor on Italian silk scarves. The local small construction entrepreneur is still this sport's main sponsor. Handball players do not try to imitate the easygoing and ridiculous American professional mentality . . . . Handball, in its rootedness, is a sport true to its original German nature." In handball, according to the author, we presumably find "honest fans," "honest insults," and "real sport of devotion and fighting spirit, at times even brutish. No Brazilian, Argentinean, or Italian can keep up with that." In contrast to glamorous soccer players, the author claims, the tough handball playing regular Joes from the periphery do not care about outward appearances, unlike the "metro-sexual style terror of urban pantywaists." Note once again the appropriation of strength and manliness to legitimate this sport and contrast it with the feminized and spoiled ways of its rival, in this case soccer.

Such voices combine resentments against modern urban life, cosmopolitanism, and pluralism, and bespeak a nationalistic disposition that opposes German and European soccer's recent internationalization. The overtly displayed disgust against modern, cosmopolitan, and globalized soccer is intimately linked to the stereotypical construction of national identity, claiming the superiority of the German-dominated (and European) sport of handball over the "Americanization" of soccer and life in general. While we picked a German example to illustrate such a counter-cosmopolitan attack against the alleged evils of contemporary soccer, such expressions continue to flourish in every European country. These inveigh against the evils of a commercialized sports world (European soccer, American everything) that has allegedly steamrolled the local.

Hatred against "Others": Racism, Hooliganism, and Violence

Counter-cosmopolitanism's ugliest expression is resilient racism and random violence against "others." It is no coincidence that radical counter-cosmopolitan sentiments and activities frequently exhibit pronounced anti-Semitism: traditionally, Jews have been identified with cosmopolitanism in Europe, and anti-Semites have always seen cosmopolitanism as their enemy because (like Jews) it presumably undermines the rootedness of the local and traditional, especially as manifested by the *Volk*.[5] Since the 1980s,

[5] Appiah, *Cosmopolitanism*, p. xvi; Seyla Benhabib and Raluca Eddon, "From Anti-Semitism to the 'Right to Have Rights': The Jewish Roots of Hannah Arendt's Cosmopolitanism," *Babylon* 22, 2007, pp. 44–61.

counter-cosmopolitan extreme right groups and movements have re-emerged across Europe. Over the last two decades, new radical parties featuring counter-cosmopolitan agendas have enjoyed significant inroads in the public spheres and political landscapes of Western and Eastern Europe.[6]

Some hooligan and extreme right groups deliberately target the sports arena in which to exhibit their racist prejudices, committing violent acts and agitating for the politics of exclusion. The quantity and quality of such counter-cosmopolitan activities varies over time and space. Indeed, one of this chapter's tasks is to show how such counter-cosmopolitan trends arise, who their major carriers are, what constitutes their context and characteristics, but also how they peak and abate, if, alas, not quite disappear completely. After all, the very nature of sports is competition, where one favors one's own side as best one can while at the same time attempting to fluster and impede one's opponent to the best of one's abilities. Since shaking an opponent's confidence will remain an integral part of sports, it is safe to assume that taunting (trash talking; getting into the opponent's head; getting under the adversary's skin) will never disappear from any competitive sport. Indeed, it is the power of such taunting, of distracting, unnerving, and intimidating, which is meant to impede the effectiveness of the opponent's efforts, that comprises one of *the* most cherished ingredients of all sports: home-field (or court) advantage, the power of the sixth man in basketball, of the seventh man in hockey, or that of the twelfth man in football and soccer.[7] And as we know from all sports, this advantage is huge, constant and ubiquitous! Winning away from home, on the opponent's field, court, gym, is arguably one of the most daunting tasks in any team sport. Human beings, even well-paid megastars, prefer playing in front of thousands of adoring fans who desperately want them to succeed, instead of thousands of ill-wishers who delight in their failures and will do everything in their power to foster such. Thus, it is more than understandable that in the Big Four North American team sports, teams spend an entire regular season playing for little else but home-field or court advantage in the all-important playoffs, the so-called second season. Needless to say, we

[6] For an overview on the European extreme right see, Cas Mudde, *Radical Right Populist Parties in Europe* (Cambridge: Cambridge University Press, 2007); and Lars Rensmann, "The New Politics of Prejudice: Comparative Perspectives on Extreme Right Parties in European Democracies," *German Politics & Society* 21 (4), 2003, pp. 93–123.

[7] There are a number of studies in soccer and in the Big Four American sports which demonstrate, however tenuously, that referees favor the home teams in their calls. It is unclear as to the reasons for such actions, but most likely referees, too, being human, fear abuse and threats.

know that many factors apart from the crowd's vociferous support of its beloved team contribute to the powerful boost called "home field advantage": the field's (court's, rink's) texture intimately known to the home team and strange to the visitors; the visiting team's arduous travels, its staying in hotels, all the inconveniences associated with "being on the road"; and even some evidence that referees and umpires favor home teams in their calls if not intentionally than precisely because they are human, which in this case means that they are influenced, if not downright intimidated, by the home crowd's demeanor.

Taunting the opponent is arguably the most effective arsenal for any team's supporters, and indeed belongs to their very identity and quotidian vocabulary. "Fan," after all, is short for "fanatic" and thus implies at the very least enthusiasm and passion, if not zealotry and fanaticism.[8] It always involves the extolling of one's own as heroes and the vilification of the others as bums. In each and every case, for example, baseball's stars accused of doping have remained untouchable idols with their home fans whereas fans everywhere else have vilified them as scoundrels and worse. And just think how supporters of teams opposing Manchester United regularly raise their arms to impersonate an airplane's crashing thus invoking joyously the tragedy of February 6, 1958 that decimated that talented team known as the "Busby Babes"; or how fans opposing Liverpool raise their hands in front of their faces thereby imitating a cage-like contraption that killed nearly one hundred, mostly Liverpool supporters, in the tragedy of Hillsborough in 1989. And the frequent extolling of the destruction of the Twin Towers on 9/11 by many a team's fans opposing the United States men's national team also constitutes a commonly deployed measure of creating insecurity, anger, distraction—all designed to weaken the opponent and strengthen one's own team. Since winning matters much more in these ultracompetitive team sports than mutual understanding and fairness, taunting will always be an essential ingredient to any kind of fandom.

But the content of this taunting has varied widely and continues so to this day. Thus, as our chapter will show, there is perhaps no greater difference between American and European hegemonic sports cultures today than in the expression of counter-cosmopolitanism in these. While in America, overtly racist taunts accompanied by violent acts against players and viewers have all but disappeared and lack any kind of legitimacy in

---

[8] For a fine book on fans and fandom in North America and Europe, see Pierre D. Bognon, *The Anatomy of Sports Fans: Reflections on Fans and Fanatics* (N.p.: Editions Bognon, 2008).

contemporary sports, this, alas, is not the case in Europe. As the bulk of our chapter will highlight, soccer grounds have become perhaps the last bastion in Europe in which the worst kind of racist, sexist, anti-Semitic, xenophobic—in short, counter-cosmopolitan—language and behavior have not only been tolerated but actually extolled. We offer our own extensive bicontinental experiences as cases in point. Between the two of us, we have attended many hundred baseball, basketball, football, and hockey games on virtually all levels in the United States since 1960. While we have encountered the occasional incident of ugly taunting, often of the sexist and homophobic variety, at the high school and college, though rarely at the top professional level, we have never experienced overt racism and anti-Semitism at any of these events. Nor have we witnessed major acts of violence among the spectators beyond the occasional beer-fueled fistfight between two fans that invariably was stopped very quickly either by people in the immediate surrounding or by the stadium authorities, most often both.

Alas, this is not the case with our European experiences where—especially beginning in the mid-1970s—our numerous visits to soccer grounds from Germany to England, from Austria to Spain, from Italy to Holland were regularly marred by overt racist and anti-Semitic language as well as behavior. Worse still, whenever either one of us, or others, tried to quell these ugly outbursts, we (and others) were met either with total indifference or indignation, sometimes with outright hostility, that we dared to challenge the norm and rock the boat. Groups such as the Berlin-based "Roter Stern Nordost," among others, have repeatedly attempted to fight the pervasive racism in Germany's soccer stadiums with a variety of actions designed to render this scourge unacceptable. They have thus far met with open hostility by the police, various security agencies, and, most tellingly, the vast majority of the fans. No one wants to stand out in the crowd, or dare challenge the loud and violent minority, and too few seem sufficiently offended by this counter-cosmopolitan behavior and discourse in their stadiums to counter it effectively. In other words, it is not so much the activities of a committed minority that differentiates the European case from the American but rather their de facto approval by the majority. However as our chapter will show, in Europe too, there are discernable changes for the better.

We will discuss cases of radical and violent counter-cosmopolitan manifestations in recent and contemporary European soccer from Italy, Spain, Poland, Holland, Austria, and Hungary to demonstrate the continent-wide existence of this ill. We will then discuss England and Germany in which these hostilities have most certainly not disappeared but in which there have been important structural changes that have at least contained and displaced them from the center of soccer's stage to its peripheries. We will offer a few tentative explanations as to why these ugly sides of soccer have emerged and discuss the many intercountry similarities but also the extant, though less numerous, intercountry differences. And lastly, we will provide a brief overview of the American situation in which we perceive substantial differences to Europe, not so much in that American sports fans have overcome their counter-cosmopolitan feelings and attitudes but that the larger public's construction of acceptable behavior and discourse has succeeded in containing these hostilities.

Racism and Violence: European Soccer's Ugly Underbelly

Let us commence with an important clarification before we proceed to present our cases. As our examples will amply demonstrate, racism, anti-Semitism, and violence in soccer stadiums are closely connected phenomena.[9] Yet they are also distinct and, in part, have different origins. "Hooliganism" is defined as a militant, violence-seeking fan group culture, whose behavior is primarily directed against other fan groups or rival teams.[10] It embodies mainly violence for violence's sake and is first and foremost a demonstration of male power and aggression. It is frequently characterized by arbitrary, even random, violence. Not all hooligans are racist and, most decidedly, most racists are not hooligans. Moreover, hooliganism need not be right-wing extremist per se, although hooligan violence in practice is indeed frequently directed against various "others," and hooliganism has proven to be receptive to antiegalitarian, racist, anti-Semitic, and extreme right ideologies and organizations.

The same applies to the "ultras," the highly organized, passionate, and often militant fan groups that spread across Europe over the last three-to-four decades. Founded in Italy in 1968, the first "ultras" took their name

[9] For an overview of racism in European soccer, see Christos Kassimeris, *European Football in Black and White: Tackling Racism in Football* (Lanham, MD: Lexington Books, 2007).
[10] There are several theories about the origin of the word "hooliganism." *The Compact Oxford English Dictionary* states that the word may originate from the surname of a fictional rowdy Irish family in a song of the 1890s. Clarence Rook, in his 1899 book *Hooligan Nights* (New York: Henry Holt and Company), claimed that the word came from Patrick Hoolihan (or Hooligan), an Irish bouncer and thief who lived in London. There have also been references made to a nineteenth-century rural Irish family with the surname Houlihan who were known for their wild lifestyle. Another theory is that the term came from a street gang in Islington called *Hooley*. Yet another theory is that the term is based on an Irish word, *houlie*, which means a wild, spirited party.

from left-wing politics. Today, however, ultras' political affiliations range
from the far right to the far left[11] though it should be stated clearly that in
practice the ultra groups adhering to the right far outweigh those following a left-wing agenda. There also exist ultra groups that are neither extremist nor racist. Moreover, some "ultra" groups are not prone to violence. However, the very fact that these fans label themselves "ultras"
denotes an uncompromising fanaticism in support of their respective
teams, which, in turn, lends itself to a ready predisposition for violence,
exclusion, and intolerance of any "other," be it a team, a race, a neighborhood, a nation, or a gender.

When we use the terms "ultras" and "hooligans" in our presentation, we
mean them to denote the specific cases that we describe and not pertain to
the larger and murky topic of "hooliganism." So when we speak of hooligans having committed murder or engaging in a particular act of violence,
we use the word "hooligans" in its common usage of the vernacular, tantamount to terms such as "violent individuals" instead of the technical term
that hooligan has come to connote, though with no extant agreement as to
whom it depicts with accuracy and precision. Rather than engage in fruit-
less definitional debates as to what exactly constitutes "hooliganism" and
"ultras," we merely want to present events that highlight the presence of
counter-cosmopolitan discourses and agents in Europe's soccer stadiums.
However, we do differentiate between racist sentiments and attitudes
shared among average spectators on the one hand, and organized extreme
right and "ultra" groups that use the stadium as a public space to display a
certain political ideology on the other.[12]

We are also perfectly aware of the fact that forms of collective violence
have occurred in virtually all countries in which athletic competition has
been performed in the presence of large viewing audiences. After all, these
performances elicit passion that, in turn, can lead to violence among the
viewers and between viewers and performers. We are also well aware of the
fact that—as Eric Dunning has persuasively demonstrated—hooliganism

---

[11] Katherine Sutherland and Katharine Jones, "Unite Against Racism, Unite Around Nation: Political Impulses at EURO 2008." Paper presented at the annual convention of the
North American Society of Sports Sociology (NASSS), Denver, Colorado; November 7,
2008.

[12] Anthony King distinguishes broadly between "organic" racial discrimination in the
stands and "instrumental" racism promoted by extreme right groups; see King, *The European
Ritual*, pp. 232–37. This terminology, however, is somewhat misleading. We distinguish between informal or nondeliberate forms, on one hand, and organized or deliberate ones, on
the other. See also on these distinctions, Udo Merkel and Walter Tokarski, eds., *Racism and
Xenophobia in European Football* (Aachen: Meyer & Meyer, 2003).

and ultraism are not solely linked to soccer and Europe but occur on a global scale featuring other sports as well.[13] Indeed, the end of Uruguay's 2008 regular championship round had to be suspended for two weeks due to an egregiously violent riot on the field following the top-of-the-table match between Danubio and Nacional.[14] In neighboring Argentina, the death toll linked to soccer games exceeded 230 for that calendar year. This datum only includes fatalities that occurred inside Argentinian soccer stadiums and "ignores victims in clashes outside the stadiums, which are crimes that of course have everything to do with football."[15] Thus Europe most assuredly has company in terms of its violence associated with soccer fandom.

In the case of fan violence, too, America, once again, appears to be a tad different. As we will show in this chapter's last section, American fans can also be physically unruly and have of course engaged in violent acts at major sporting events. Yet there is a huge difference between the kind of purposive and premeditated violence anchored in a deeply racist, xenophobic, and anti-Semitic worldview as has happened all across European soccer for decades, and what Dunning properly calls "celebratory rioting"[16] in American team sports in which fans in the United States engage—tellingly and oddly—after their team has attained its ultimate triumph such as winning the World Series, the Super Bowl, the NBA championship, or a national title in college football or basketball. These incidents, though ugly and often violent, are of a completely different texture and content than the violence in Europe's stadiums to which we now turn.

The Italian Case: The Avoidable Triumph of Extreme Right Politics and "Ultra" Violence

In Italy, just like in all European countries that we discuss in this chapter, violence connected to soccer is nothing new and hails from the game's proliferation into mass culture in the 1920s. The problem of political violence and racism infecting Italian soccer reaches back to this decade and

---

[13] Eric Dunning, "Football Hooliganism as a Global Problem," *International House of Japan Bulletin* 21 (2), Autumn 2001, pp. 1–20.

[14] Reuters, "Uruguayan Championship Resumes amid Controversy," *SoccerAmerica*, December 4, 2008.

[15] Mónica Nizzardo, an Argentinian lawyer who works with the organization Salvemos al fútbol (Let's Save Football), as quoted by Joel Richards, "More important than life and death: the escalating violence in Argentine football" in the *Guardian*, republished as "Murder And Mayhem in Argentine Soccer," in *SoccerAmerica*, December 4, 2008.

[16] Dunning, "Football Hooliganism as a Global Problem," p. 10.

the 1930s, when fascist fans of Bologna FC attacked the left-wing supporters of Genoa FC, and when the brutalities between left-wing Roma and
right-wing Lazio fans escalated in Italy's capital.[17] However, as Birgit
Schönau points out, until the 1980s Italian fan and "ultra" culture served in
many ways as a positive model for fans across Europe. For instance, the
manifesto of the left-leaning and antiviolent *Commando Ultra Curva Sud*
(CUCS), which was founded in 1977, impressed fans across the continent.
These original Roma "ultras" were among the first to display an entire
choreography of colorful flags, songs, anthems, candles, and witty slogans.
The Roma "ultras" occasionally surprised their Lazio opponents with a
gigantic *Ti amo* ("I love you") song in the stadium, and built alliances with
other left-wing fans in Bologna, Milan, Florence, and Perugia.[18] Residues
of this inclusive cosmopolitan culture lingered until the 1990s.

Alas, those days are long gone. Formerly colorful bright spots have
largely been displaced by racists and right-wing extremists, who do not shy
away from violence. The progressive CUCS became powerless in the face
of the violence deployed by extreme right groups and dissolved itself in
1999.[19] Since then, Italy's soccer stands came to be dominated by a far-
right and racist culture in opposition to an increasingly globalized and cosmopolitan game and society. A few clubs with left-leaning identities still
exist, such as AS Livorno, at home in the city in which the Italian Communist Party (PCI) was founded in 1921. Smallish clubs in provincial
places like Siena, Cagliari, Lecce, and Verona also still exist that sport politically neutral "ultras." But that this benign formation constitutes an increasingly insignificant minority among the onslaught of right-wing extremism is best demonstrated by the fact that in Verona it used to pertain
to Chievo, whereas its crosstown rival Hellas had long been dominated by
fans and club members who exhibited their xenophobia by opposing the
hiring of any black players.

Even in Bologna, where left-wing fans annually host the "anti-fascist
soccer World Cup" of peaceful soccer fan clubs, supporters are now divided. Major clubs like the initially "internationalist" *Internazionale* (Inter)

---

[17] See Simon Martin, *Football and Fascism: The National Game under Mussolini* (Oxford:
Berg, 2004).

[18] See Birgit Schönau, *Calcio: Die Italiener und ihr Fußball* (Cologne: Kiepenheuer &
Witsch, 2005), p. 144.

[19] In contrast to the traditionally right-wing club Lazio, Associazone Sportiva Roma,
founded in 1927 by the Roma Jew Renato Sacerdoti, was for the longest time a left-wing,
working-class club. By now, many Roma fans are almost as many of the infamous Lazio supporters, and among the most radical in Italy. Some Roma "ultras" are also tied to the anti-
Semitic extreme right party, Forza Nuova. See Schönau, Calcio, pp. 144–48.

Milan have been confronted with a broad extreme right and often violent "ultra" fan base, even though many soccer intellectuals from Milan, who despise the powerful right-wing billionaire and Prime Minister Silvio Berlusconi (owner of Inter's bitter crosstown rival AC) still live in denial about this.[20] Inter's core fans are linked to the *Azione Skinhead*, which welcomes visitors to their website with "Heil Hitler." The situation at AC Milan or Juventus is hardly better, though the fans at Inter games voice far more racist chants.[21] Over time, most of the newly formed "ultra" fan groups in Italy of the 1970s adopted an increasingly and decidedly right-wing extremist and racist outlook.

This rightward drift in Italian soccer's fan culture has found active support by extreme right political agents and parties: banned from public demonstrations, the neo-fascist *Movimento Sociale Italiano* (MSI)—together with the Austrian Freedom Party (FPÖ), arguably the most successful postwar far right party among West European democracies—utilized young male soccer fans to create prominent ultra groups. In Milan, MSI's youth section founded the "Inter Boys," while a large number of middle-aged extreme right militants motivated and recruited Lazio fans.[22] According to police statistics, of the 80,000 Italian ultra fans in the country's premier soccer division (Serie A), roughly a quarter belong to political organizations that explicitly locate themselves on the radical right.[23] Though parties have changed, the initial marriage between the ultra fan milieus and extreme right political parties has continued to spread to this day. This symbiosis is embedded in a larger context of what might be termed "informal" or "unintentional" racism and a growing predisposition to violent behavior among larger groups of Italian soccer fans.

Let us mention just some of this milieu's violent acts resulting in homicides. In 1979, a Lazio fan died during the violent clashes in the Roman derby (rivalry game) between Lazio and Roma. In 1989, a Roma fan was killed at the gates of the city of Milan's San Siro Stadium (shared by AC and Inter); in 1995, AC Milan fans murdered a Genoa CFC fan during the match between the clubs.[24] This terrible event was the first to cause an

---

[20] Tommaso Pellizzari's "No Milan" manifest, an adaptation of Naomi Klein's antiglobalization manifest "No Logo," is just one example; quoted in Franklin Foer, *How Soccer Explains the World: An Unlikely Theory of Globalization* (New York: Harper, 2004), pp. 187–88.

[21] Foer, *How Soccer Explains the World*, p. 190.

[22] See King, *The European Ritual*, p. 231; Carlo Podaliri and Carlo Balestri, "Racism and Football Culture in Italy," in Adam Brown, ed., *Fanatics: Power, Identity and Fandom in Football* (London: Routledge, 1998).

[23] See Schönau, *Calcio*, p. 156.

[24] Steve Wilson, "Calcio Chaos: A History of Violence," *Calcio Italia*, March 2007, p. 11.

outcry among the Italian public, as well as soccer club and federation officials concerning the widespread presence of violence in Italy's favored pastime. Yet, nothing of any significance happened in response. Even the increasing numbers of murders and violent clashes in stadiums during the
1990s did not end the tacit tolerance toward what was nothing short of a
takeover of Italy's soccer arenas by hooligans and right-wing radicals.

The series of violent incidents has continued since 1995, and many of
Italy's premier sports venues have become totally off-limits for immigrants,
fans accompanying the visiting team, families, and Jews. "Unfortunately,
due to this climate Jewish fans in Rome no longer go into the stadium,"
said Riccardo Pacifici, speaker for the Jewish community in Rome and
himself an ardent Roma fan.[25] In Juventus Turin's home ground, the Stadio
delle Alpi, ultras regularly display a banner on April 25 labeling it the "holiday of the traitors," thus agreeing with those on the Italian far right who
have come to depict Liberation Day, the holiday commemorating Italy's
liberation from Nazi rule and fascism, as an act of betrayal and shame.[26]

Apart from the upsurge of violence that has led to the exclusion of spectators and the playing of games in empty venues in Italy's professional soccer in the last few seasons, racist slogans by ultra fan groups have become a
common experience in Italian stadiums. The insults against Marc André
Zoro, a player from the Ivory Coast who played for ACR Messina, in this
particular case by Inter Milan fans, is only one of many examples. Large
sections of the stadium imitated monkey sounds when Zoro touched the
ball, an all too common fan reaction to black players across Europe; others
shouted "dirty nigger."[27] Swastika flags and anti-Semitic banners remain a
common occurrence in the Stadio Olimpico in Rome (among other
places), where they are hoisted by the notorious *Irriducibili* (the "unbend-
ing"), a 7,000-member-strong Lazio ultra organization. Their most infamous banner was sixty-feet long and displayed the slogan, "Auschwitz is
your home, the ovens are your house."[28] The former Lazio star and Mus-

[25] Quoted in Schönau, *Calcio*, p. 151.

[26] Ibid., p. 156.

[27] Yves Pallade, Christoph Villinger, and Deidre Berger, *Antisemitism and Racism in European Soccer* (Berlin: American Jewish Committee Berlin Office/Ramer Center for German-
Jewish Relations, 2007), p. 7. As a first symbolic, albeit ineffective response to the incident,
the following week all Italian soccer league games postponed their kickoff by five minutes by
order of the sport's governing body to allow players to demonstrate against racism by holding
up banners with the caption, "No racism." In addition, Inter was fined 25,000 Euros by a
sports court. The incident marked the beginning of an awareness campaign and helped to
create some public attention for the problem of racism in Italian soccer, according to the antiracism campaign *Progetto Ultra*.

[28] Quoted in ibid., p. 8. As recently as 2006, Roma fans—once enjoying a rather left-wing,

solini admirer Paolo Di Canio, the ultras' darling, was suspended twice after repeatedly saluting fans in the stadium with an outstretched arm, the so-called *saluto romano* or "Hitler salute."[29] In 2005, Lazio displayed a huge banner stating, "Rome is fascist."[30] Moreover, the most radical and militant of Italy's extreme-right parties, the profoundly anti-Semitic *Forza Nuova*, has successfully turned Italian fan culture into its stomping ground and major recruitment source.

By and large, this has been tolerated as an unfortunate but inevitable part of Italian soccer. The clubs and the national federation *Federcalcio* (FIGC) alike have looked away for decades and employed a laissez-fair attitude, despite the fact that spectatorship in Italian soccer stadiums has suffered a dramatic decline since the 1990s, with considerable economic consequences for the clubs. The numbers are drastic and represent a countertrend to soccer's increasing popularity elsewhere in Europe, in good part due to a substantial rise of female attendance in stadiums as of the 1990s. From the 2005–6 to the 2006–7 season, Italy's flagship league *Serie A* lost over one million spectators, from 8,129,671 to 7,049,945. Whereas 39,000 spectators on average attended first division soccer in 1986–87, only 18,552 did so in 2006–7. Professional soccer in Italy lost more than half of its spectators in the country's stadiums in the two decades.[31] Italy's middle-class and families have largely deserted the country's crumbling stadiums, thus making it possible for young male far rightists to take control of this emptied space.

Two incidents occurred in 2007 that signaled a new low in the history of Italian soccer. During the Sicilian rivalry match between Catania Calcio and US Palermo on February 2, 2007, Catania hooligans deliberately killed police officer Filippo Raciti near the stadium during escalating riots

---

progressive working-class reputation—unfurled a large banner attacking Livorno also by alluding to Auschwitz and the extermination of the European Jews: "Lazio-Livorno, stessa iniziale, stesso forno" (Lazio-Livorno, same initial, same oven); www.theglobalgame.com/blog/2006/02/semantics-are-fascist-footballers-also-racists. Retrieved October 25, 2008. Prior to World War II, Livorno was home to a large Jewish community. Today, some players (rather than fans or club officials), like Roma's soccer hero "il capitano" Francesco Totti, confront the problem by supporting antiracist campaigns.

[29] See Alexander Smoltczyk, "The Fascist Soccer Star and the Auschwitz Survivor," www.spiegel.de/international/spiegel, February 27, 2006. Retrieved October 25, 2008. The national federation penalized Di Canio, while his club Lazio did not take any measure. Di Canio had to pay 10,000 Euros, whereas Cristiano Lucarelli, a forward and leftist from AS Livorno, was forced to pay 30,000 Euros for showing a clenched left fist, the Communist salute.

[30] Schönau, *Calcio*, p. 147.

[31] See *La Gazzetta dello Sport*, May 31, 2007, p. 3.

and violent clashes among fans and police forces.[32] The Italian sports daily *Tuttosport* proclaimed in light of the event that "soccer in Italy died yesterday."[33] Just the weekend before, an official of the low division team of San Martino was kicked to death during an amateur match.[34] Whether these two tragic events will have finally constituted the turning point for the Italian authorities to begin a decisive counteroffensive against the pernicious forces of violence and destruction that have come to dominate the core of Italian soccer, still remains to be seen at the time of this writing, more than two years after these senseless murders. Perhaps the much more important question remains as to when Italian public opinion will decide not to countenance such behavior and the atmosphere that legitimates it. Alas, the evidence for substantial improvement is not very encouraging. Racist incidents continue to shape Italian soccer culture. For instance, the black Italian striker Mario Balotelli, a star of the national under-21 team who also plays for Inter, is frequently exposed to racial slurs. Although in 2009 Juventus had to play a game in its emptied stadium after chants by Juve fans that were directed against Balotelli, and even though the city of Naples subsequently honored him with an antiracism award, he is continuously subjected to racist invectives in Italian stadiums.[35] Yet the emerging public debates about such incidents may also rep-

[32] Catanias Homepage stated after the game: "Sorry, but it appears absurd to us to write about soccer in these hours. Our thoughts are exclusively with the family members of police officer Raciti, who lost his life to guarantee public safety—at a soccer match." (Cataniacalcio. it., retrieved on February 3, 2007).

[33] Excerpts from daily newspapers on the day after (February 3, 2007) display the scope of the shock after the murder, which initiated a broader public debate on violence. The *Gazzetta dello Sport*, the highest circulation daily paper in Italy, observed that soccer has become "powerless and tired" because the "deepest meaning of this sport is lost. Italy, we have a problem, which does not just affect soccer fandom. It is not only about public safety but about the deep matrix of this country, its administrators, schools, our families. . . . You can only feel sad about what we have become." *La Stampa* diagnosed: "Murderous soccer. One casualty per week. This is the shocking rhythm of horror which we still call soccer. We are a country seized by hooligans." The leading liberal paper, *La Repubblica*, added: "War in the stadium. Italy should stop thinking about the EURO 2012 and should instead seriously think about the barbarians who frequent these stadiums. We cannot be surprised that the stadiums are more and more empty. It is right to suspend the championship if you consider that these stadiums are the most dangerous and nevertheless the most expensive in Europe." The newspaper of the Vatican, *L'Osservatore Romano*, perceived "madness" and even demanded a year-long suspension of professional soccer: "Soccer has turned into a sport which is in the hands of criminals, indeed even of murderers. In spite of strong economic interests one has to have the courage to stop this ungovernable circus for at least a year because it is dominated by scandals and the violence committed by vandals and criminals."

[34] See Wilson, "Calcio Chaos: A History of Violence," p.13.

[35] See http://www.goal.com/en/news/10/italy/2009/04/26/1230419/city-of-naples-ho nour-inter-striker-mario-balotelli-in-anti-raci. Retrieved November 20, 2009. To be sure,

resent a sign of change toward less public tolerance for racism in Italy's favorite pastime.

The Spanish Case: Racism, Failing Authorities, and a Culture of Denial

The lack of understanding of racism and the culture of its denial in Spain, and in Spanish sports, can best be exemplified by a scandal caused in 2008 by the country's Olympic men's and women's basketball teams.[36] Before the Olympic tournament in Beijing, both teams posed for pictures in which they used their fingers to pull back their facial skin around their eyes to render them slanted and have them look Chinese. The ensuing photos appeared in a commercial featuring a Spanish courier company and were published in a full-page advertisement in the national sports daily *Marca*.[37] Apparently, both the company and many of the participating basketball players perceived this pose as humorous and innocuous. Nobody viewed it as racist or controversial in any shape or form. Initially, there was no public criticism of this commercial in Spain. But it soon became an international scandal in which the Spanish basketball players were viewed as insensitive and offensive, if not deliberately hurtful and overtly racist. Reflecting the generally obdurate climate in Spain pertaining to racism, Pau Gasol, the country's premier basketball player and superstar center of the Los Angeles Lakers, defended the ad by characterizing the whole thing as "funny"— not trying to be "offensive in any way." Point guard José Manuel Calderón, of the Toronto Raptors, went even further by saying that "we felt it was something appropriate, and that it would be interpreted as an affectionate gesture." Topping things off, Juan Antonio Villanueva, the communications director for Madrid's 2016 Olympic bid, was "surprised," adding with unbridled confidence that "Spain is not a racist country—quite the opposite."[38] There have been few signs of public outrage towards and criticisms of racism in Spain's sports culture. Tellingly, much of the Spanish

---

some argue that the slurs against Balotelli are not racially motivated. For example, Milan midfielder Clarence Seedorf, a black Dutchman, insists that these insults are a response to Balotelli's provocative behavior on the field. See http://www.goal.com/en/news/10/italy/2009/11/26/1648716/clarence-seedorf-chants-against-inter-star-mario-balotelli. Retrieved November 26, 2009.

[36] "Racist? Spanish Basketball Player Defends Controversial Photo," *welt-online*, August 15, 2008, www.welt.de/english-news/article2311278/Spanish-basketball-player-defends-controversial-photo. Retrieved November 8, 2008.

[37] Pete Thamel, "Questions of Racism for Spanish Basketball," *New York Times*, August 13, 2008, p. C15.

[38] All quotes from "Racist? Spanish Basketball Player Defends Controversial Photo," *welt-online*. August 15, 2008.

public commentary and reaction concerning the international outcry about this pre-Olympic photo viewed its criticism as unfair attacks on, and insults of, the Spanish nation.

This lack of sensitivity among a wide swath of the Spanish public manifests itself in a continued denial of racism as a problem, or the minimizing of its importance. Thus, even after significant UEFA penalties against Spain for repeated racist offenses at its soccer matches and in its stadiums, Spanish officials and famous soccer players like goalkeeper José Manuel Reina insisted against all evidence that "there is no problem, and there has never been a problem" of racism in Spanish soccer and society. "I can guarantee that Spain is not a racist country."[39] It should not come as a surprise, then, that Spanish soccer fans have exhibited racist behavior at a number of instances. During a match between Spain and England at Real Madrid's Bernabéu stadium in 2004, Shaun Wright-Phillips, Ashley Cole, Rio Ferdinand, Jermain Defoe, and Jermaine Jenas—England's black players on that squad—were all verbally abused and greeted with monkey noises. [40] The Spanish Football Federation (RFEF), usually inactive in such matters, was eventually fined £45,000 by UEFA. Apart from Barcelona's Camp Nou stadium, racist chants arose all over Spain with regularity against Samuel Eto'o from Cameroon, at the time one of Barcelona's stars.

But even in Barça's allegedly enlightened milieu, racist chants have been commonplace. What makes this case all the more telling about the general insensitivity to racism in Spanish sports and football is the fact that such incidents occur in the Catalan club's well-known history of opposition to Franco's fascist regime[41] and its proud embrace of cosmopolitanism by displaying UNICEF on its players' jerseys instead of any number of multinational corporations that grace the shirts of virtually every soccer club in the world and that would only be too happy to have their name appear on the uniforms of the star players representing this immensely popular club admired and loved the world over.[42]

---

[39] See www.teamtalk.com/football/story. Retrieved November 1, 2008.

[40] Thamel, "Questions of Racism for Spanish Basketball," p. C15.

[41] It is noteworthy that the Franco regime even insisted on changing "Football Club Barcelona" to "Club de Football Barcelona," the translation of the team's name into Castilian Spanish. Franco sought an ideological transformation of the club but faced fierce opposition. Thus, Barça's correct name is "FC Barcelona." See Foer, *How Soccer Explains the World*, pp. 203–4.

[42] While we do not want to minimize Barça's antifascist and anti-Francist credentials, it still remains unclear whether the club opposed the Franco regime in its very essence and thus disdained fascism as a whole, or whether Barça's opposition hailed mainly from the club's unwavering identification with Catalan nationalism which, of course, Franco's Castilian centrism repressed quite brutally.

Racism is common to all aspects of Spanish soccer, both on the level of club games and international competition. Ultra hooligans dominate the fan scene, just like in Italy, and have established themselves as a proto-fascist subculture with considerable political force over the years. Today, all kinds of racist slurs and other expressions of racial hatred are everyday occurrences in many of the *Primera Division*'s soccer stadiums in what is arguably one of the best, most professional, and most culturally diverse leagues of the world.

Alas, the media often instigate hostility toward foreigners by being a tad too cavalier in their depictions of foreign cultures with stereotypes that are less than flattering. For instance, during EURO 2008—the European tournament won by the Spanish national team, celebrating its first international title since 1964—the public climate repeatedly turned hostile against nationals belonging to Spain's opponents. The television station *Cuatro*, broadcaster of the Spanish games, advertised the respective matches with "jokes" about other countries that few people but Spaniards found funny. For example, before the game against Italy *Cuatro* showed a pizza that was quickly eaten, bite by bite, while the television ad proclaimed "we will eat you." Before Spain's game against Russia, a Russian doll was smashed, while the ad insisted that "we will destroy you."[43]

Too often, official responses to racism have been less than rigorous. For example, then national coach Luis Aragonés, who led Spain to the 2008 European Championship, had called the French forward Thierry Henry (at the time playing for Arsenal, now scoring for Barcelona) "a black shit."[44] Aragones never apologized, nor was he penalized by the Spanish soccer federation; only many months later was he made to pay a small fine of $3,000.[45] Amazingly, the newly established government-run Anti-Violence Commission, created to address violence and racism in Spain, and soccer in particular, protested the fine to the Disciplinary Court of Spanish Sport, though without success. In the end, it was the global soccer authority,

---

[43] The advertisement campaign by Canal Cuatro was called "podemos," "We can." See http://www.youtube.com/results?search_query=publicidad+superheroes+eurocopa+2008 +cuatro; http://www.youtube.com/results?search_query=publicidad+cuatro+eurocopa&search _type=&aq=f. Retrieved November 26, 2009. Special thanks to Samira Klingenberg and Cosimo Ligorio for this information.

[44] Indeed, fans of the Dutch club PSV Eindhoven also heaped racist abuse on this stellar player in a Champions League match without incurring any penalties for their vile actions.

[45] "Aragones Fined for Henry Remarks," www.bbc.co.uk/sport2/hi/foofball/internatio nals/4055395, March 1, 2005; retrieved November 1, 2008. Aragones said he had "a very clear conscience" because he never intended to offend anyone. The European antiracist initiative Kick it Out commented: "We expected very little from the Spanish Football Association and are not surprised by this pitiful fine. The only positive is there's finally been a recognition that what Aragones said was racist, despite his protests."

FIFA, that imposed a severe fine of $87,340 on the Spanish soccer federation, threatening, in the case of such racist recurrences, to sentence the Spanish national team to play in empty stadiums without spectators or to expel the team entirely from all international (FIFA-sanctioned) competitions.[46] In 2005, Málaga CF player Paulo Wanchope was attacked by a mob of Málaga fans during warm-ups. He was called "black shit"—the same expression that Aragonés had used to insult Henry—and then physically assaulted.[47]

In clubs like Franco's erstwhile favorite Real Madrid, its crosstown rival Atletico Madrid, and Real Zaragoza, antidemocratic groups have spread and far right traditions have survived despite many of these clubs' best players hailing from all corners of the world. Especially in Real Madrid's case, this internationalism has a fifty-year tradition ever since such greats as Alfredo Di Stéfano from Argentina, Ferenc Puskás from Hungary, Raymond Kopa from France, and José Santamaria from Uruguay led the team to five consecutive European club championships in the late 1950s. Then again, it is quite certain that even today, let alone in the 1950s, Spaniards hardly regard Spanish-speaking Argentinians and Uruguayans as foreigners. As to Frenchmen and Hungarians, the tally might be quite different but here, too, both of these players were bona fide white Europeans, thus far less irksome to xenophobes and racists than contemporary Africans and other nonwhite players. Like in Italy, clubs tend to support their radical hooligans precisely because they view them as their teams' most loyal supporters and their most reliable—and intimidating—twelfth men both at home and on the road. At Real Madrid, for instance, the board gives away free tickets to the politically extremist "Ultra Slurs," and even at allegedly anti-fascist Barcelona the former president Josep Núñez tolerated the emergence of racist skinhead gangs such as "el Boixos Nois" and invited its members to travel with the team.[48] Clubs remain reluctant to place any limits on the support of their most loyal fans, no matter how vile their voices and reprehensible their actions.

Whereas extreme right-wing organizations have remained marginalized[49] in Spain's political spectrum since the fall of the Franco dictatorship, they and their sympathizers have found fertile ground and safe havens in

---

[46] Quoted in Pallade, Villinger, and Berger, *Antisemitism and Racism in European Soccer,* p. 9. It is noteworthy that there are no minority representatives in the commission.

[47] Ibid., p. 10.

[48] See King, *The European Ritual,* p. 242.

[49] Although groups like the neo-Nazi *Circulo Español de Amigos de Europa* (CEDADE) continue to exist, they have attracted minimal attention.

the country's soccer fan culture. The belated establishment of an Anti-Violence Commission represents a step forward as does the fact that the penalties it metes out, though not mandatory and enforceable, have by and large been viewed as acceptable by international football authorities and the offended parties. Still, the continued lenience toward racism (including the downplaying of violent acts instigated by such racism) exhibited by Spain's governmental authorities, its sports and soccer establishments, as well as its civil society, remains a serious shortcoming in this country's lively democracy.

The Polish Case: Anti-Semitism and Unchallenged Neo-Nazi Hooliganism

Widespread tolerance of prejudice and hatred toward all things perceived as foreign on the soccer field and beyond characterizes the Polish situation. This has fostered and consolidated a flourishing skinhead culture and hooligan scene that is strongly tied to the country's extreme right, and well represented in all of the country's soccer divisions.

In fact, an important segment of the most violence-prone and significant neo-Nazi subculture in Poland hails from soccer hooligan circles. Tomasz Drogowski, the editor of the popular hooligan publication *Szalikowcy*, speaks openly in an interview with a neo-Nazi fanzine: "Fascism is not a horrible idea. I think National Socialism is the necessary and only means of purifying the ranks of some groups from Gypsies, punks, and Negroes. From everywhere I hear it is more and more welcomed at stadiums."[50] Anti-Semitic chants such as, "We will do what Hitler did to the Jews,"[51] have been popular in the stands of Poland's major soccer clubs as well as in the minor leagues. This is not at all surprising, since anti-Semitism remains pervasive in virtually all right-wing movements and parties in Poland.

Recurring fights among rival gangs, fans, and police, though solidly present on Poland's soccer grounds, are actually not Polish soccer's biggest problem. Instead, the game arguably provides the most effective public arena for the informal recruitment and articulation of right-wing extremism and neo-Nazism in the country. Successfully infiltrating skinhead groups since the 1980s, organizations like National Rebirth of Poland (*Narodowe Odrodzenie Polski* [NOP]) with its five hundred core activists re-

---

[50] Quoted in Rafael Pankowski and Marian Kornak, "Poland," in Cas Mudde, ed., *Racist Extremism in Central and Eastern Europe* (London: Routledge, 2005), pp. 169–70.

[51] See ibid, p. 170.

cruit primarily in soccer stadiums without being hindered by the authorities.

The NOP is one of the country's most dynamic extreme-right organizations operating "on the street" and "in the stadium." Its stated programmatic goal in politics is the overthrow of democracy via a "national revolution." Apart from adhering to the standard staple of European-wide right-wing politics such as opposition to NATO and the EU, the disdain of all foreigners, and a blatantly nationalist view of the world that often features racist themes; the NOP is also decidedly and explicitly anti-Semitic. Thus, Holocaust denial is paired with the exceptionally blatant declaration that, in the words of the NOP leader Adam Gmurczyk, "anti-Semitism is a virtue that we must cultivate with great care."[52] The group established international contacts via alliances with the anti-Semitic *Forza Nuova* in Italy and its German equivalent, the *Nationaldemokratische Partei Deutschlands* (NPD). The NOP, however, constitutes just one example of the well-organized, radical right-wing groups that draw their strength "from the anti-Semitic culture that dominates many sports stadiums in Poland, with rival gangs routinely calling each other's clubs 'Jewish' as a term of abuse."[53] At games of Widzew Łódź, a club with a particularly strong and violent hooligan following, anti-Semitic and racist chants are consistent fare in the stadiums. It is in the ranks of this Łódź-based club that the NOP has its largest organizational base.

In Warsaw, the enormous banner sporting Nazi symbols of the ultra-hooligan gang, "White Legion," remains widely visible at every home game of the capital's Legia soccer club, certainly one of the country's most internationally known. One of the gang's leaders, Damian Mikulski, served a long jail sentence for brutally murdering a teenage boy because his hippie-like clothes incurred Mikulski's wrath.[54] Across the country, extreme right-wing nationalist groups overlap with hooligan communities and also express their views in numerous hooligan magazines.

While in some European countries like Germany attendance at professional soccer games has steadily increased over the past few years, attendance in Poland has declined. Polish soccer clubs and their stadiums are in bad shape. This development coincides with a drop in the quality of play on the field as well as the growing power and relevance of violence-prone hooligans in the stands. In fact, all three phenomena—the decline in attendance, the drop in quality of play, and the rising relevance of hooligans—appear to be mutually interrelated and self-perpetuating. Low-

[52] Quoted in ibid, p. 161.
[53] Ibid, p. 161.
[54] Pankowski and Kornak, "Poland," p. 170.

quality play leads to fewer viewers, which in turn expedites an extremist minority's ability to occupy an increasingly empty space and rule it to its liking. Soccer stadiums in Poland have basically become protected public spaces for hooligans where they and their activities have met with very little, if any, opposition by any of the relevant authorities—be they representatives of the state (i.e., the police), of the soccer establishment (i.e., club owners and the Polish soccer federation), or of civil society (i.e., offended public opinion). As in Spain, Polish politicians, the authorities, media, and public figures consistently downplay the problem, if indeed they ever address it publicly at all.[55] The club managements' continued unwillingness even to admit the prominent existence of hooliganism and neo-Nazism in soccer remains especially striking.

Furthermore, racism is also a problem among the players themselves. While Polish clubs cannot pay foreign players the money that would attract high-profile global stars, "those who have joined Polish clubs since the mid-1990s have been increasingly affected by racism. According to the Cameroon-borne Polish league player Frankline Mudoh, players in many teams put pressure on the coach not to include black players in the line up."[56]

But there is a bright light on the horizon. Poland and the Ukraine have been chosen as cohosts for the European nations' soccer championship in 2012. It is more than likely that both countries will do everything in their power not to have racism tarnish an event of such global magnitude that also bestows much national pride on any successful organizer. Perhaps the preparation for and the hosting of such an internationally prestigious tournament will force Polish soccer to rid itself of the egregious expressions of xenophobia, anti-Semitism, and right-wing hooliganism that have ruled Poland's stadiums for years. Were this to happen, it would furnish us with yet more evidence that an increase in internationalism and the demands of modernization enhance the forces of cosmopolitanism and the discourse of tolerance.

The Austrian and the Hungarian Case: Resurgent Legacies of Anti-Semitism

Austrian soccer, the first on Europe's continent to introduce a professional league in 1924, was arguably among the world's best in the 1920s and 1930s. The famed "Danube football," played by Austria's national side and

[55] Pallade, Villinger, and Berger, *Antisemitism and Racism in European Soccer*, p. 8.
[56] Ibid., p. 9.

232   CHAPTER 5

its top club teams, all of which were located in a Vienna that—with Buenos
Aires and London—had the greatest density of major-league soccer teams
anywhere in the world, featured as much elegance and fluidity on the field
as it did rivalries, animosities, and even violence in the stands. It was interwar Austria's blatantly public anti-Semitism that informed the country's
soccer partisanship, which was voiced most virulently against the country's
(and Vienna's) two "Jewish" teams: Hakoah, which was indeed an all-Jew-
ish club—from leadership to membership, from players to fans—that won
the Austrian soccer championship in 1924 before its players disbanded all
over the world (to the United States, and New York in particular), fully
cognizant of the fact that their days as Jewish athletes in Central Europe
were numbered;[57] and FK Austria, a club with no Jewish players but a few,
occasionally prominent though largely assimilated, Jews in its management and a fan base anchored in the city's professional class that, until the
Anschluß in 1938, was heavily Jewish, and perceived as such by an increasingly hostile gentile world. In an article on anti-Semitism in Austrian
sports during the post-1945 Second Republic, Michael John and Matthias
Marschik give a fine account of its massive presence throughout the 1950s
on the soccer grounds of this new political entity. This demonstrated convincingly that the continuity, at least concerning the public presence and
acceptability of anti-Semitism, to the First Republic and the Nazi era was
solid and far from ruptured as the country's official myth and self-exculpat-
ing ideology had succeeded in conveying to itself and the rest of the
world.[58] Thus, in the realm of soccer as well, the much-touted "zero hour"
(*Stunde Null*) that was alleged to have abruptly separated the "new" Germany and Austria from their ignominious predecessors appeared to be
much closer to a self-legitimizing whitewash than to actual reality. After a
raucous 1950s and a relatively quiet 1960s, a vocally aggressive anti-Semitism and racism became commonplace on Austria's soccer fields from the
early 1980s until today.[59] Thus, a report in *Kurier*, one of Austria's leading

[57] The two best books on Hakoah are John Bunzl, ed., *Hoppauf Hakoah: Jüdischer Sport in
Österreich. Von den Anfängen bis in die Gegenwart* (Vienna: Junius Verlag, 1987); and Susanne
Helene Betz, Monika Löschner, Pia Schölnberger, eds., . . . *mehr als ein Sportverein: Die ersten
100 Jahre Hakoah Wien 1909–2009* (Innsbruck: Studienverlag, 2009).

[58] Michael John and Matthias Marschik, "Ortswechsel: Antisemitismus im österreichi-
schen Sport nach 1945," in Heinz P. Wassermann, ed., *Antisemitismus in Österreich nach 1945*
(Innsbruck: Studienverlag, 2002), pp. 188–215.

[59] Markovits, who lived in Vienna in his teenage years in the 1960s and was a regular on
the city's soccer grounds every weekend, experienced much verbal hostility and adverse body
language that could easily have been interpreted as anti-Semitic. But only once, as a visible
supporter of "Austria," was he subjected to outright anti-Semitic curses by fans of "Rapid" on
its home ground of the *Pfarrwiese* in Vienna's Hütteldorf region. Andrei S. Markovits, "The
Ancient Hatred: Postwar Austrian Anti-Semitism," in Günter Bischof and Anton Pelinka,

dailies, detailed that the outbreaks of violence and racist incidents on Austria's football fields were never worse than during the 2008–9 season.[60]

That FK Austria and its fans have been constantly subjected to anti-Semitic attacks does not come as a surprise since this club, as already mentioned, has been viewed as the "Jew Club" since well before World War II, a tradition that continues unabated.[61] And that it is particularly fans of FK Austria's archrival SK Rapid that are the most vocal in these anti-Semitic denunciations also does not qualify as unexpected. However, much more telling of how generally pejorative—how universalized—the term *Jude* has become is the fact that whichever opponents one does not like for whatever reason quickly become saddled with this most vicious expletive. Opponents of the working class club SK Vöest from Linz, which never had any connections to anybody or anything Jewish, regularly deride the club and its supporters as "SK VAU–Judensau" (SK V–Jew Pig, which rhymes in German). Notable in this anti-Semitic discourse in Austria's soccer stadiums is its unmitigated aggression that naturally invokes tropes from the Nazis, the Holocaust, and other ills befalling the Jewish people. The ubiquity of such hate speech has grown over the years and proliferated well beyond the expressions of any particular club's fans. The Austrian soccer magazine *Ballesterer* documented that younger FK Austria fans, who do not know anything about their club's historically close identification with Jews, have come to deride their opponents—and anybody they dislike, including certain journalists—as "Jew boys" or worse epithets most of which are steeped in profoundly anti-Semitic lore.[62] In Austria, too, just as in many other continental countries, the usage of the term "Jew" as an epithet

---

eds., "The Americanization/Westernization of Austria," *Contemporary Austrian Studies*, 12, 2004, p. 261. See also Markovits, "Wiener Fußball ganz persönlich: Die kakanische Welt eines sportbegeisterten und sportkundigen amerikanischen Sozialwissenschaftlers," in Wolfgang Maderthaner, Alfred Pfoser, Roman Horak, eds., *Die Eleganz des runden Leders* (Göttingen: Verlag Die Werkstatt, 2008), pp. 180–92.

[60] Peter Grolik, "Extreme Gewaltsteigerung: Abpfiff für Fußballrowdys," in *Kurier*, July 11, 2009.

[61] Thus, for example, fans of the Dutch club "Feyenoord Rotterdam" invariably invoke chants about Auschwitz (including a hissing sound that is to replicate the release of Zyklon B that murdered Jews in Auschwitz's showers), Hammas, and gas (rhymes with Hammas) when their team plays its major rival "Ajax Amsterdam," which—together with "Bayern München," "AS Roma," "FK Austria " of Vienna "MTK Hungaria" of Budapest and the North London club "Tottenham Hotspurs"—comprises the so-called "Jew clubs" in Europe. Most of these clubs' identification with Jews hails from Europe's interwar period when Jews were in some fashion—as fans and/or owners and/or officials and/or managers and/or denizens of the clubs' neighborhoods—linked to these clubs. Even though in most of the cases any connection to Jews had long been severed in the post-1945 period, these teams have not been able to shed their stigma as "Jew clubs" to the very present.

[62] Jakob Rosenberg, "'Judenschweine gegen grüne Parasiten,'" in *Ballesterer*, 40, March 3, 2009.

has become universalized in the discourse of European soccer fandom to denote one's disliked opponent. "Jew" has mutated into an equal opportunity insult on Europe's football grounds.

The most radical expressions of pervasive and consistent anti-Semitism, however, arguably belong to the fans of the Budapest club Ferencváros. The club's fans

wrap banners around their bodies and conceal them beneath their clothes. Before games they unfurl the sheets so that they extend over entire rows. One begins, "The trains are leaving . . . " The second concludes, " . . . for Auschwitz." This slogan is pretty much all you need to know about the atmosphere in the arena. But what makes Ferencváros so impressive isn't just the depth of their hatred; it's the breath of it. They have an unending array of Dr. Mengele-inspired songs and chants. Lyrics typical of the genre include, "Dirty Jews, dirty Jews, gas chambers, gas chambers." Another set repeats the mantra, "Soap, bones." As if the death camp imagery wasn't clear enough, Ferencváros fans press their tongues into their palates to produce a hissing that mimics the release of Zyklon B. For a time in the nineties, they would punctuate the celebration of goals with an extension of the arm into a Nürnberg-style salute.[63]

While Ferencváros fans deploy this Nazi-style behavior against any of their team's opponents, it reaches its most frenzied expressions when the club plays its crosstown Budapest rival MTK Hungária, one of Europe's already noted "Jew clubs." In fairness to Ferencváros fans, we would be remiss to omit the fact that MTK Hungária's appearance at any of its games in Hungary is greeted with similarly hateful invectives by the fans of this club's opponents.

What is amply clear in all of this is the fact that a vocal and often violent segment of young European men (this milieu is almost totally male) have appropriated the soccer stadium as a locus where anti-Semitism as a cultural code can be openly expressed without it however becoming public and part of the larger society. Anti-Semitism has thus remained—or once again become—very much part of Europe's real discourse in soccer stadiums, the local bar, the neighborhood café, and private dinner parties. It is open without being public, real without being acceptable. Under the guise of "boys will be boys," and the cover of "fool's freedom," the reality is such that the vilest form of anti-Semitism and the usage of "Jew" as a universalized pejorative have become acceptable in the world of European soccer stadiums where they might not have remained as contained and confined

---

[63] Foer, *How Soccer Explains the World*, p. 86.

as European elites would have us believe. The magnitude of its "bleeding over" into society may not yet be clear, but we fear that such a process has long been happening and is far from abating.

The German Case: Neo-Nazi Hooliganism—Return of the Repressed?

Despite a rise in informal right-wing extremism, especially in soccer venues located in the former East Germany, and recurring incidents of violent hooliganism in and around stadiums, the situation in Europe's biggest country has become, comparatively speaking, less grim in the past decade than it was in the 1980s and 1990s. This situation pertains especially to Germany's top-flight professional league, the Bundesliga. In the 1980s a neo-Nazi fringe culture had emerged in German soccer that had spread to most clubs, rendering the vilest racist slurs such as monkey chants directed at black players the norm on every weekend during the soccer season. However, such incidents have diminished at Bundesliga games in the course of the first decade of the new century, though they have far from disappeared.

This relatively auspicious development is partly due to a change in soccer culture, which in turn reflects a growth in cosmopolitan inclusiveness in the sport as well as a greater degree of cosmopolitanism in German society, particularly in the former West Germany. Such transformation commenced in West Germany's urban centers throughout the 1970s, preceding similar developments in Eastern and Southern Europe by a good two decades. Major political battles and social conflicts over issues of inclusion of immigrants into Germany's polity, economy, and society informed much of the 1980s and 1990s with various degrees of xenophobic opposition constant, occasionally even violent. However, these counter-cosmopolitan sentiments faced the social reality of an increasingly diverse and growing immigrant society. The eventual recognition by the political establishment across parties that the country needed immigration, coupled with a change in government in 1998 to one comprising the Social Democrats and Greens, led to the introduction of a new immigration law that substantially increased immigrants' rights and made it possible (though still difficult) for immigrants to obtain German citizenship. Still, until today, there is virtually no representation of minorities in German politics, big business, or the judiciary.[64]

---

[64] In a country of 82 million citizens there were just five visible minorities in the 613-seat German national parliament, the *Bundestag* in 2008. See Jennifer Miller and Lars Rensmann, "Ethnic Minority Outreach among Conservative Parties in European Democracies: Com-

The internationalization of professional soccer since the 1980s initially encountered a rise of right-wing activity in West Germany. By the 1990s, however, clubs like Borussia Dortmund began featuring key immigrant players, such as the aforementioned Júlio César, a skillful black Brazilian central defender, with whom Borussia won the European Champions League in 1997 and who became one of the locals' most beloved players. Decisive steps by club leadership and in some cases protests by fans in favor of their very own black player—though they were rarely against racism in football and society as a whole—helped to facilitate a more inclusive atmosphere among many West German clubs. In Borussia's case, for example, club officials actively combated the extreme right-wing fan group "Borussenfront," which was infamous for its neo-Nazi activities in the stadium's southern curve.[65] Officials banned the front's entry into the stadium. In doing so, the club gathered and found support among local fan clubs.

The gradual change in German professional soccer is also the result of more rigorous measures jointly designed and implemented by the national soccer federation and the federal government between 2000 and 2010. Following the World Cup in France in 1998 and in preparation of playing host to the tournament in 2006, the DFB, supported by FIFA, commenced to take serious measures in its fight against right-wing hooliganism in the German game.[66] Symbolic politics and antiracist campaigns were com-

---

paring Germany, Great Britain, and France," Paper Presented at the 104th American Political Science Association Annual Meeting, Boston, August 27–31, 2008.

[65] As a regular at many German sports venues, Rensmann has witnessed the changes in West Germany's stadium culture—and particularly in Dortmund's *Westfalenstadion*—from the early 1980s to the present. Two decades ago racist chants were everyday normalcy in the stands, especially in Dortmund's "southern stands." The neo-Nazi group *Borussenfront* was constantly present there. Racist chants, alternating with monkey sounds, mocked the few black players from the visiting teams whenever they touched the ball. This was simply part of the "experience" if one attended a game. While racism has by no means fully dissipated, the situation has changed significantly since then. This is to some extent due to active antiracist fan initiatives and campaigns that have been supported by the club. Moreover, the stadium has become more family friendly and now draws a larger, ever-growing female audience that is—even though not necessarily less racist—less likely to chant racist slurs. However, the improvement is also, and more importantly, quite clearly a consequence of an increasingly diverse squad with which the crowd identifies. Until the 1980s, there were few international players in Borussia Dortmund's lineup, and even fewer who became identified with the club's historical success. Few players have epitomized the club's resurgence over the last two decades and have helped change its culture as the two "global players," Julio César and Dedé. Displaying strong local ties and an obvious love for the club, César in the 1990s and Dedé in the 2000s turned into ultimate fan favorites. This rendered racist manifestations largely illegitimate and served to marginalize racism in the stands.

[66] However, the DFB's disciplinary code still provides considerable leeway and remained quite vague, often leaving the imposition of sanctions to the discretion of sports functionaries and local officials. Only after riots during a game between Dynamo Dresden and Erzgebirge Aue in 2007, and subsequent court trials against the culprits, did the DFB initiate amend-

bined with increasing federation, governmental, and team support of grass-roots activities by antiracist fans and their clubs. Such spirit of cooperation, along with effective police tactics and special unit operations that hindered the right-wing activists in a myriad of ways, led to significant improvements in and around Germany's soccer stadiums.[67]

Even though these measures have had significant success, progress remains contested, largely limited to the western part of the country, and confined to the Bundesliga, the top tier of German soccer.[68] Germany may no longer be *the* hotbed of racism and violent hooliganism on the European continent, as it was in the 1990s when German thugs brutally assaulted the French policeman Daniel Nivel during the World Cup held in 1998 in France.[69] Yet neo-Nazi hooliganism, extreme right activity, and racism remain a constant threat in the world of German football.

---

ments to the articles of association that now entitle the federation to penalize directly all clubs in all competitions at its own uncontested discretion. See *Westdeutsche Allgemeine Zeitung*, June 14, 2007.

[67] And Saxony's minister of the interior, in charge of all police matters of this East German state, assured his listeners in an interview in November of 2008 that increased police presence at soccer games in Saxony (home to Dresden and Aue)—as well as in Germany at large—have come to show first steps of demonstrable progress in reducing violence, racist language, and general aggressiveness that have rendered German soccer stadiums outright dangerous and most certainly unpleasant places. See "Gegen rechtsextreme Parolen auf deutschen Plätzen[.] Sachsens Innenminister Buttolo: Höhere Polizeipräsenz bei Fußballspielen zeigt erste Erfolge[.]Albrecht Buttolo im Gespräch mit Elke Durak." http://www.dradio.de/dlf/sendungen/interview_dlf/879303/,21.11.08.

[68] See Ronny Blaschke, *Im Schatten des Spiels: Rassismus und Randale im Fußball* (Göttingen: Die Werkstatt, 2007). Until recently, the German national team did not feature any ethnic diversity. Today, it is still a world apart from a truly multiethnic team, although finally some visible minority players like Patrick Owomoyela and Gerald Asamoah made it onto the team, a fact against which right-wing extremists mobilized before the World Cup 2006. For decades, the ethnically homogenous national soccer team had reflected and regenerated the German collective self-image of ethnic homogeneity, its *ius sanguinis* citizenship, and the mistrust against minorities that accompanies such views of citizenship and self. Consequently, many good immigrant players decided to play for national teams to which they had ethnic ties; see Sebastian Edathy and Bernd Sommer, "Alle auf den Platz," *Berliner Republik* 3, 2006, pp. 40–43. Even though prejudices against nonethnic German players continue among many German fans—most assuredly those of right-wing bent—the campaign denouncing Owomoyela and Asamoah as non-German undesirables failed miserably on account of the solidarity extended to them by ethnic German members of the national team as well as the general German public's rejection of such overt racism.

[69] In June 1998, after a World Cup match in Lens between Germany and the then Yugoslavia, German thugs repeatedly kicked and hit Nivel with a weapon during violent clashes between French police and German hooligans. Some of these latter had gathered in Germany that morning with the explicit purpose to beat up a French policeman. Following the incident in Lens, German football hooligans were warned to stay away from Germany's next match in the tournament against Mexico in Montpellier. German police contacted many of the more than 2,000 known German hooligans to warn them that they would be arrested if they traveled to France. Police were concerned that neo-Nazi groups would try to cause

Thus, some of the German national team's most active fans continue to be linked to far right groups. This makes sense since, as we delineated in chapter two, the sole reason to support a national team is an identification with the nation that the team represents. Even during the much-celebrated World Cup tournament in Germany in 2006, which on the whole show-cased a peaceful, joyous, open-minded, and even a postnational, cosmopolitan German soccer culture, hooligan violence erupted. When Germany beat Poland in a World Cup match in Dortmund, the game was marred by violent clashes between German and Polish fans, with more than three hundred hooligans from both countries arrested. Moreover, there were ugly incidents in the so-called "fan miles," open-air public areas in many German cities in which fans watched games on huge television screens. After Germany's quarterfinal victory against Argentina, Argentinian fans dressed in their team's colors of pale blue and white ("albi-celeste") were assaulted in various Berlin subway stations and trains. A chant by German fans that exhorted all Germans to stand up in the stadium led to occasional verbal and physical assaults on those—German or otherwise—who chose to remain seated. Two years later, during the European national championship held in neighboring Austria and Switzerland in 2008, German fans chanted slogans such as, "All Poles must wear a yellow star," and "Germans, defend yourselves, don't buy from Poles" before, during and after the match between Germany and Poland in Klagenfurt. Of course, some German fans indulged in their usual Nazi salute at their team's games at both tournaments, though it must be said in fairness to the German team's fans that, especially during the EURO 2008 tournament, Italian, Croatian, Austrian, Russian, Spanish, and even Swiss fans were all reported to have performed Nazi salutes on a regular basis, yelled racial slurs, or raised far-right banners before, during, and after games—once again underlining the cross-national dimensions and pan-European appeals of this counter-cosmopolitan discourse in the world of soccer.[70]

Though racism and violent counter-cosmopolitanism have decidedly

---

trouble in Montpellier. As a result of the incident in Lens, Andre Zawacki was arrested in July 1998 and charged with attempted murder and causing serious bodily harm. In November 1999, four more Germans were convicted for their part in the beating of the French police-man, who had barely survived this vicious, unprovoked, and premeditated attack in which he incurred life-long brain injuries. The main defendant, Zawacki, was found guilty of attempted murder and sentenced to ten years in jail. See "Hools and Thugs: Germany's Hooligans 3 of 3," www.video/aol.com/video-detail/hools-and-thugs-germanys-hooligans-3-of-3/761732452. Retrieved November 9, 2008.

[70] Sutherland and Jones, "Unite Against Racism, Unite Around Nation: Conflicting Political Impulses at EURO 2008."

abated in German soccer's showcase Bundesliga, the ghosts of the past have not yet been vanquished in any of the lower rungs of Germany's eleven-tiered soccer pyramid featuring the vast majority of the country's 26,000 federation-registered teams. Alas, even in the Bundesliga, outright racism and neo-Nazi symbolism have not yet disappeared. A special case is the capital's club, Hertha BSC Berlin, which is supported by many Turkish immigrants in the multicultural capital. However, it also has a strong core of the so-called "Hertha frogs," who are dominated by neo-Nazis. Representing the team's most rabid followers, they regularly invoke SS slogans, and sing with relish "We build a subway to Auschwitz" on the subway ride to the Olympic stadium, which was built by the Nazi regime for the Berlin Olympics in 1936. Some of Hertha BSC Berlin's fans, seated in the Olympic Stadium's northern end zone, regularly regale their club's corner and free kicks, as well as any exciting situations during the club's home games, with Nazi-tinged chants and exhortations.[71] Club authorities waited a long time to confront the neo-Nazis and extreme right party activities in front of the stadium. With Hertha's successes on the field leading to the club's greater international exposure and, more important still, attracting a much broader and diverse public beyond its hard-core fans, the club launched major public campaigns against racism that are still unthinkable among many clubs in Germany's East.[72] Hertha, like many other Bundesliga teams, have come to sport since the new millenium a bevy of trailers denouncing racism surrounding the field. But it is still rare for the club's officials to denounce racism in an unequivocal tone and with the true conviction that would unmistakably convey to the public—and most important, the team's die-hard fans who indulge in much of the repulsive behavior—that the club will henceforth not condone any kind of aggression and will prosecute such to the full extent of the law. Again, as we already mentioned, the teams' leaders are extremely reticent to offend their teams most devoted supporters, whom they deem indispensable for the teams' successes in an increasingly competitive domestic and international arena.

Lastly, there is evidence that the situation has not at all improved in the country's lower divisions and its youth and children's leagues. This is par-

[71] We are especially grateful for this information that Wolf-Dietrich Junghanns, Lecturer at Stanford University in Berlin, and a regular in Berlin's Olympic Stadium at Hertha BSC Berlin games for nearly two decades, provided to us in a confirming e-mail on January 5, 2009, after he recounted his experiences to Markovits during a lengthy meeting at the Center for Advanced Study in the Behavioral Sciences (CASBS) of Stanford University on December 18, 2008.

[72] Steffen Dobbert and Christoph Ruf, "Nazis im Spiel: Rechtsradikale übernehmen immer mehr deutsche Klubs," *Rund: Das Fußballmagazin* 19 (2), 2007, pp. 20–31, here p. 22.

ticularly the case in Germany's eastern regions, the former German Democratic Republic. In this area, an informal right-wing extremist movement and violent adolescent subculture evolved more or less unhampered in the first years after unification and even the waning years of the old Communist regime.[73] This proto-fascist milieu has flourished in many mid-sized towns of the former East and consolidated its power and legitimacy to the point where its adherents have usurped public spaces such as town squares and, of course, soccer grounds where anybody perceived as "foreign" or simply "different" is in danger of being physically attacked, even killed. This environment has provided a haven for all kinds of right-wing movements and supported the creation of what could arguably be viewed as one of the most radical and self-assured neo-Nazi movements in Central Europe. It attracts young voters and activists, many of whom are now members of the NPD, the oldest extant German neo-Nazi party hailing from its foundation in the former West Germany in the 1960s. The party found the situation in the former East Germany so auspicious for its modus operandi that it moved its national headquarters from the former West Germany to Dresden in the country's eastern state of Saxony. And sure enough, this move was rewarded by the party's successful entry into Saxony's legislature.[74] With its young and dedicated members,[75] the NPD has overcome its image of being a sclerotic organization of irrelevant old Nazis, and found a robust grass-roots base among young people in the East.

Many of the party's 5,300 members are active in the fight against "Judeo-American globalization" and multinational capitalism on the soccer

[73] See Lars Rensmann, "From High Hopes to On-Going Defeat: The New Extreme Right's Political Mobilization and its National Electoral Failure in Germany," in *German Politics & Society* 24 (2), 2006, pp. 67–92.

[74] Founded in 1964, it almost disappeared after its initial successes in the late 1960s and its defeat in 1969. By the 1990s the NPD had become largely an "irrelevant force comprising competing and opposing wings within the party." See Lee McGowan, *The Radical Right in Germany: 1870 to the Present* (London: Longman, 2002), p. 177. Today the NPD proclaims to fight a "battle over people's minds" (ideological influence and cultural hegemony), "battle on the streets" (mobilization of extreme right social movements and cooperation with militants), and a "battle for voters" (participation in the electoral process), and it does so quite successfully in Eastern Germany. Among other things, the party entered Mecklenburg-Vorpommern's state legislature in 2006 with 7.3 percent of the vote. And it received an impressive 9.2 percent of the vote in the 2004 state election in Saxony. Due to internal quarrels the party lost votes in the subsequent election in Saxony in 2009. Yet it still obtained 5.6 percent of the vote, thus surmounting the 5 percent electoral threshold needed as a minimum in Germany for parliamentary representation. The NPD therefore remains a relevant force in Saxony's parliament and beyond; http://wahlarchiv.tagesschau.de/wahlen/2009-08-30-LT-DE-SN/index.shtml. Retrieved on August 30, 2009.

[75] The members' average age is thirty-seven, which is much younger than that in catch-all parties; see Toralf Staud, "Vormarsch in der Provinz," *Die Zeit*, July 28, 2005.

fields and beyond. This organized group of counter-cosmopolitans interacts with an aggressive neo-Nazi hooliganism that originated in the East already during the GDR years. In the 1980s, East German soccer stadiums were the central place in which the extreme right seized a public space for its own purposes in the socialist republic.[76] Since then, this milieu's ranks have expanded, especially surrounding such teams as SG Dynamo Dresden and FC Sachsen Leipzig, which were once prominent clubs under the old regime but have since been relegated to lower divisions where they derive much counter-cosmopolitan capital and considerable local support while having become largely irrelevant to Germany's national soccer scene.

In fact, one might argue that to some extent public pressure has succeeded in pushing violent behavior and overt racism out of the stadiums of the Bundesliga only to have become more salient and entrenched in the minors. Here the public does not pay much attention to such occurrences, and referees as well as officials are much less skilled (and/or willing) to respond to racist provocations and acts of fan violence.[77] Especially in these lower divisions—to which most of East German soccer has been relegated—the game remains an important medium for extreme right agitation and racist attacks against players belonging to ethnic minorities. Chemnitzer FC, for instance, has become nationally known not for its success on the field but on account of its particularly violence-prone and brutal hooligan group *HoNaRa* (*Hooligans-Nazis-Racists*), which identifies openly with Nazism and racism. The group has had major influence on the club itself and even served as its temporary security service. Today the ultra youth group NS-Boys has gained ground in the club's ranks, and few of its supporters or officials seem to object to their ever-present "Out with the Jews" chants during games. On April 1, 2006, Chemnitz fans accompanied their team to a match against Hamburg's FC St. Pauli, which rightly or not is widely perceived as German football's most cosmopolitan and xenophile club. Sure enough, the visiting Chemnitz fans attacked Turkish-owned stores and displayed red flags with white circles though with no swastika in

<hr/>

[76] Our colleague Dariusz Wojtaszyn from the Willy Brandt Center for German and European Studies at the University of Wrocław has been engaged in a detailed empirical study on soccer fans in the German Democratic Republic (GDR) called "Kibice piłkarscy w NRD." He has found ample evidence how these football grounds became crucial loci of right-wing mobilization in the GDR beginning in the middle of the 1980s. Interestingly, Wojtaszyn's work shows that prior to that time these fan groups were anything but right-radical and resembled rather spontaneous and unorganized revolts by some fans against the state and its security apparatus. As will be recalled from our previous discussion of the Italian case, there, too, the early "ultras" were not right radical at all.

[77] See Pallade, Villinger, and Berger, *Antisemitism and Racism in European Soccer*, p. 3.

their midst, still leaving little to the imagination as to which political movement had captured their fancy. About two hundred Chemnitz hooligans shouted, "We are building a subway to Auschwitz," and called St. Pauli officials "Jewish pigs."[78]

Just a month before, the Nigerian player Adebowale Ogungbure, who played for FC Sachsen Leipzig, had faced racist slurs and physical attacks by fans of the Hallescher FC. In response, the German sports court imposed a lenient punishment by fining the Halle club a meager 1,100 Euros.[79] In the second division match between the East German clubs FC Dynamo Dresden and FC Energie Cottbus in December 2005, Cottbus fans displayed a banner with the word "Jews," flanked by two stars of David referring to the Dresden team's emblem. The banner, shown on television, was neither confiscated by the police nor the club's security guards. And no soccer or league officials imposed penalties on the Cottbus club, even though the incident was widely publicized in the media.[80]

In a youth game in the Saxon town of Wurzen, players and spectators attacked the visiting team with slurs such as "foreigner pig" and "Jewish pig, f*** your mother because she is Jewish." No officials of the host team acted against the slander; instead, one official warned those present to desist from filing any report to any authorities pertaining to these vile occurrences. Such incidents remain common on German soccer's local level.[81] On November 12, 2008, Sachsen Leipzig fans tried to gain access to the stadium's opposing sector populated by supporters of Türkiyemspor, a Berlin club, featuring mainly players of Turkish descent. While unable to gain entry and thus physically attack the Türkiyemspor fans, the Sachsen Leipzig supporters indulged in persistent chants of the vilest sort featuring nationalist, racist, and anti-Semitic themes: "Out with the Jews"; "Türkiyemspor are Jews in Berlin, Jews in Berlin, Jews in Berlin"; "Germany belongs to Germans"; and "shitty Turkish pigs."[82]

The NPD has enjoyed especially high support in towns like Wurzen, creating a climate of legitimacy for racism and anti-Semitism in public spaces, which include the soccer grounds. In other towns, the Hitler salute appears commonly as an opening act accompanying the kickoff of soccer

[78] Quoted in ibid., p.2.
[79] See ibid., p. 5.
[80] Ibid.
[81] See Heike Baldauf, "Neonazis im Osten: Judenhass in der Kinderliga," *Der Spiegel*, May 31, 2007; Heike Baldauf, "'You Jewish Pig': Severe Anti-Semitism Hits Youth Football in Germany," www.spiegel.de/international/germany, June 1, 2007. Retrieved June 1, 2007.
[82] Pressesprecher des Roten Stern Nordost Berlin e.V. "Pressemitteilung – Inland – Sport, http://www.roter-stern-berlin.de. Retrieved on December 20, 2008.

games.[83] Extreme right groups have also founded their own local soccer teams, usurped existing ones, become active within the soccer associations, and initiated so-called "national tournaments" in which only like-minded teams of the "movement" have been permitted to participate.[84] Soccer on the local level hereby serves both as a recruitment arena and as a bridge for the extreme right into the center of society. All of these incidents—and there have been many more—show that virulent right-wing activity, anti-Semitism, and racial prejudice have become an integral part of soccer's fabric in Germany's Eastern *Länder*. They also show that the putative measures against these groups have remained insufficient and ineffective. Officials at various levels of the soccer world—be it on that of the local village club or even on that of the mid-level regional association—remain reluctant to take any action, legal or otherwise, to oppose the presence of this vile world of violence and hatred. The fact that much of the local population has yet to see these attitudes and behaviors as unacceptable and illegitimate surely helps perpetuate the inactivity on the part of the game's officials which, in turn, further encourages the continued presence, even growth, that these right-wing racist groups have enjoyed for decades. And there seems to be no end to this in Germany's east and in its minor leagues even though the successes that we mentioned in the Bundesliga need to be acknowledged.

The English Case: An Unlikely Success Story from Pariah to Model?

The origins of soccer hooliganism can be traced to nineteenth-century England, the cradle of the game itself.[85] Throughout the game's storied existence there, as well as elsewhere where it embodied hegemonic sports culture, occasional acts of disorder, mayhem, and violence emerged. Yet, it was especially in the England of the 1970s in which fan groups emerged that seemed more intent on committing violence than on following the game or even supporting their team, subsequently turning the stadium, entire city squares, streets, and railway stations, into veritable battlefields. England's, and to a lesser extent Scotland's, soccer spaces were emblematic for hooliganism in the 1970s and 1980s, years that also were the heyday of open displays of racism at soccer games, although such incidents were not widely reported by the media.[86] It was in England that the merger between

---

[83] Dobbert and Ruf, "Nazis im Spiel," p. 22.

[84] Ibid., p. 25.

[85] See Rogan Taylor, *Football and Its Fans* (New York: St. Martin's Press, 1992).

[86] See Pallade, Villinger, and Berger, *Antisemitism and Racism in European Soccer*, p. 3.

soccer violence and hooliganism on the one hand, and right-wing extremism and racism on the other hand, celebrated its ignominious debut. The National Front in particular, which in the course of the 1970s emerged as the country's most visible counter-cosmopolitan political force, discovered the standing-room-only terraces on England's increasingly dilapidated football grounds as fertile recruiting territory for its cause. This xenophobic milieu of the late 1970s and early 1980s formed the core from which soccer hooliganism spread to the rest of Europe. By the mid-1980s, many British clubs and their supporters mutated into unwelcome pariahs of the soccer world, outcasts known for riots, violence, and chauvinism in all senses of that word.[87]

We will mention merely two incidents very briefly not only because of their egregiousness but because we believe that they led to a substantial turn-around of English football to the point where over the past ten years it has mutated from the pariah of European football to its model. On May 29, 1985, violent hooligans supporting Liverpool clashed with fans of Juventus Turin one hour before the scheduled kick-off for the match between these two teams contesting the European Champions final in Brussels's Heysel stadium. Thirty-nine Italian and Belgian spectators were killed and more than four hundred injured.[88] The Heysel disaster had serious repercussions for English soccer. For the first time in its history, the European soccer federation UEFA acted swiftly and applied serious penalties. Initially, it banned all English clubs indefinitely from participating in any European competitions, a restriction that was gradually lifted after five

---

[87] British hooliganism generated a vast amount of academic and popular literature and research over the last two decades. Among others, Bill Buford, *Among the Thugs* (New York: Vintage, 1993); Clifford Scott, *Football "Hooliganism," Policing, and the War on the "English Disease"* (London: Pennant, 2007). Some initial works downplayed the violence by attributing hooliganism to some harmless, ritualistic "aggro," as in the work by Peter Marsh, *Aggro: The Illusion of Violence* (London: Dent, 1979). Particularly influential are the studies by the Leicester School, who took a comparative orientation and focused on the social conditions and contexts of hooliganism, and were among the first to point out that hooliganism is not just a problem with English fans. Accordingly, hooliganism is complex and multifaceted, entails variables such as (1) the degree of match-related violence, (2) the varying intensity and forms of violence, (3) the manner to which hooliganism is organized and disruptive behavior is planned, and (4) the fashion in which heterogeneous values unrelated to soccer are expressed; see Eric Dunning, Patrick Murphy, and John Williams, *The Roots of Football Hooliganism* (London: Routledge, 1988); Williams, Dunning, Murphy, *Hooliganism Abroad* (London: Routledge, 1989); and Murphy, Williams, and Dunning, *Football on Trial: Spectator Violence and Development in the Football World* (London: Routledge, 1990); on the Leicester school see Alan Bairner, "The Leicester School and the Study of Football Hooliganism," *Sport in Society* 9 (4), 2006, pp. 583–98.

[88] "Heysel" is the French word for this stadium in Brussels, while "Heizel" is its Flemish-Dutch designation. We opted for "Heysel," which is the commonly used term in English.

years.[89] Until then, there had been trouble at almost every game in England, to a lesser degree in Scotland as well. Against the backdrop of this ongoing and escalating violence, Heysel was a catastrophe waiting to happen. Soccer stadiums had turned into public spaces where street gangs and disenfranchised adolescents engaged in ritualized and routine violence every weekend, befitting their station as representatives of an "anti-intellectual, non-cosmopolitan and divided Britain."[90]

Two factors played a major role in the decline of violence that started in the aftermath of Brussels. First, slowly but surely nonviolent fans raised their voices, trying to take back their clubs from the grip of this ubiquitous scourge that drove them away from their beloved teams and game. Second, the club officials realized that the loss of a substantial revenue stream that they now had to forego on account of being banned from international competition was serious and detrimental to their clubs. So, a coalition of fans and club officials came to the game's rescue by commencing to oppose hooliganism and violence at the football grounds. But enter a third factor: the structural reconstitution of Britain's century-old football venues with their ancient terraces and other features that fostered violence and became inimical to the modern game, apart from being lethally dangerous to spectators and players alike.

And it was precisely such a venue that featured the site of the second incident, which led to the absolute nadir of English football and to reforms that were to transform it for the better. A catastrophe of hitherto unprecedented proportions—following the Heysel disaster—occurred during an FA Cup semifinal match between Liverpool and Nottingham Forest held on the neutral ground of Sheffield Wednesday FC's Hillsborough stadium on April 15, 1989. A human crush resulted in the death of ninety-seven spectators, most of them Liverpool supporters.[91] This was largely the re-

[89] See "The Heysel Disaster," BBC News, May 29, 2000, http://news.bbc.co.uk/2/hi/uk_ news/768380.stm. Retrieved November 1, 2008.

[90] Murphy, Williams, and Dunning, *Football on Trial*, p. 21.

[91] As terrible as these casualty numbers from Heysel and Hillsborough really are, they are not unique in the annals of soccer violence. Eric Dunning in his fine essay "Football Hooliganism as a Global Problem" *International House of Japan Bulletin* 21 (2), Autumn, 2001, p. 8, lists the following preceding incidents: In 1968 there were 74 deaths and 150 injuries in the Buenos Aires rivalry match (derby) between Boca Juniors and River Plate. In 1982, there were 22 deaths and 200 injuries in Colombia during a game between Deportivo Cali and Club Argentina. The most costly violence occurred in Lima, Peru, in 1964 during a match between host Peru and Argentina when the Uruguayan referee disallowed Peru's equalizing goal: 318 people were killed and 500 injured. In the same year, 44 fans were killed and 600 injured in a match between Kayseri and Sivas in Turkey. Lastly, in the former Soviet Union, 69 people were killed and 100 injured in a match between Spartak Moscow and the visiting Dutch side Haarlem in 1982.

sult of a tragically lethal confluence of a dilapidated stadium's inadequate facilities, barriers around the field that resembled cages from which there was no possibility to escape, and a complete failure by security personnel and police in crowd control leading to late-arriving fans crushing others up against the iron cages, thus suffocating them.

The post-Hillsborough climate provided new opportunities and led to new actions by all parties involved: club owners and leaders, fans, police, security personnel, the FA, the British government, and the British public. It took the tragedies of Heysel and Hillsborough to transform the Association game in the British Isles. Economic interests pushed the Premier League clubs, but also their lower division counterparts, to eliminate the standing-room-only terraces that defined soccer venues in Britain until then and transform their arenas into family friendly places with seats for all. The overall modernization of the stadiums also saw the removal of all barriers at the front of the stands that had created "cages" for fans. These steps, of course, exacted higher ticket prices for games, which, in turn, began to attract a more mixed and upscale crowd instead of the male, blue-collar workers that had dominated spectatorship of the English game for over one hundred years. Needless to say, these changes also had their costs. English and Scottish soccer were long embedded in and dominated by working-class culture and strong local ties. Soccer was the leisure passion of the male proletariat. These old conditions however, had allowed violence-prone hooligans and racist counter-cosmopolitans to seize soccer stadiums for their own purposes.[92] Today's tickets for a Premier League club are largely unaffordable for blue-collar workers without undue economic hardship. It is thus not surprising that many working-class fans opposed the modernization measures that transformed English soccer in the wake of the Hillsborough and Heysel tragedies. Yet the implemented reforms created a spectatorship whose social composition by and large spurned violence. Along with the introduction of a binding customer charter and new cooperative security strategies addressing the needs of supporters, there can be no question that commercialization of English football had its share in keeping hooliganism at bay.

The diminution—if not total disappearance—of hooliganism, racism, and violence in England's soccer stadiums resulted without any doubt via a beneficial synthesis of the concerted actions by the FA and its officials, club

---

[92] It is important to note with the Leicester School, however, that class-related social frustration cannot fully explain or account for hooliganism. The violent hooligan deviance from social norms also expresses forms of atavistic pleasure-seeking—a hedonistic quest for enjoyable excitement—independent from class divisions; see Dunning, Murphy, Williams, *The Roots of Football Hooliganism*.

managers, and owners, and, most important, the fans themselves. In addition to the committed agency on the part of these crucial actors, the altered nature of Britain's economy, society, and culture provided an auspicious structure and framework wherein this tangible improvement in England's soccer world became a reality. Indeed, conditions had improved so markedly that Steve McLaren, the England team's ex-manager, believed that for countries on the Continent, like Italy, whose soccer culture in and around the stadiums was deeply marred by violence, there was "a lot to learn"[93] from the English model.

However, Britain, too, still has a long way to go. Although parliamentary representation of ethnic minorities is higher than anywhere else in Europe, it is still far below the proportion that these minorities comprise in British society.[94] In an increasingly multiethnic and cosmopolitan Britain, a black prime minister is still unthinkable. "If Barack Obama were British, racism would keep him from becoming prime minister," argues the head of Britain's Equalities and Human Rights Commission, Trevor Phillips.[95]

Like elsewhere in Europe, foreign and minority soccer players have embodied a vanguard of cultural globalization and cosmopolitanism, mobilizing broader support for nonwhite British people and migrants. Yet racism and anti-Semitism are of far greater complexity than simply containing hooligan violence.[96] Racist and anti-Jewish incidents continue to occur frequently in the stands, in spite of greater public awareness and recent efforts to cope with such slurs and other verbal abuse. Clubs on the British Isles are still confronted with a broad cluster of fans who revel in shouting xenophobic and anti-Semitic resentments near the field. Furthermore, the lack of minority representation in political institutions is matched by a discriminating lack of such presence and participation in the power structure of British soccer. For instance, whereas there are many black players in the English Premier League and the other top leagues in Britain, there are very few black managers. Moreover, the membership of all relevant boards, clubs, and federations, as well as virtually all football officials, remains practically all white.[97]

Though challenged by more cosmopolitan fans of the game, racism and

[93] Quoted in *Gazzetta dello Sport*, February 3, 2007.

[94] See Miller and Rensmann, "Ethnic Minority Outreach among Conservative Parties in European Democracies."

[95] http://Bbc.co.uk/1/hi/uk_politics/7717149, November 8, 2008. Retrieved November 8, 2008.

[96] See Dougie Brimson, *Kicking Off: Why Hooliganism and Racism Are Killing Football* (London: Headline, 2007).

[97] See Pallade, Villinger, and Berger, *Antisemitism and Racism in European Soccer*, p. 11.

anti-Semitism have not disappeared from English soccer and remain an integral part of its fan culture. Tottenham Hotspurs' fans proudly revel in calling themselves "Yiddos," and some hard-core Spurs fans have "Yiddo" sown on the back of their jackets and/or tattooed on their forearms. This is a fascinating aspect of European soccer and fan culture, since virtually none of the people who proudly call themselves "Yiddo" ("Yid," "Yid Army," "Yids," "Yid 4 Life," and many variants thereof) are Jewish, nor ever wish to become so. And while this in-your-face Jewishness has in the meantime developed into a common expression by fans of Europe's other "Jewish" clubs, most notably Ajax Amsterdam, it hails, of course, from the constant and still persisting anti-Semitic abuse that opposing teams' fans heap on Tottenham Hotspurs (and Ajax Amsterdam) supporters—as in "Gas a Jew, Jew, Jew, put him in the oven, cook him through,"[98] a regularly incanted chant by Chelsea supporters on their home ground of Stamford Bridge when Chelsea host Spurs.[99]

Tottenham fans have simply turned a vile racial epithet directed at them for years into a conscious, even proud, expression of their collective identity, as documented in the popular homage to the blond German—and decidedly non-Jewish—striker Jürgen Klinsmann, one of Spurs' most successful and beloved players: "Chim-Chiminee, chim-chiminee, chim-chim churoo, Jürgen was a German, but now he is a Jew!"[100] The Jew as warrior,

[98] Quoted in Foer, *How Soccer Explains the World*, pp. 79–80.

[99] For the most complete analysis of this fascinating phenomenon, see John Efron, "When Is a Yid Not a Jew? The Strange Case of Supporter Identity at Tottenham Hotspurs," in Michael Brenner and Gideon Reuveni, eds., *Emancipation through Muscles: Jews and Sports in Europe* (Lincoln: University of Nebraska Press, 2006), pp. 235–56. Here are two particularly telling chants by Chelsea fans taunting their London crosstown rival Tottenham Hotspurs: "Spurs are on their way to Auschwitz; Hitler's gonna gas 'em again; We can't stop them; The yids from Tottenham; The yids from White Hart Lane." And "Good old Adolf Hitler; He was a Chelsea fan; One day he went to White Hart Lane; And all the Jew Boys ran; At last he got a few of them; Up against the wall; At first he laughed a little bit; And then he gassed them all: hahahahahahaahhhhh; hohohohohohoohhhh; hahahahahahaahhhh, etc.," pp. 247–48.

[100] By now claims of Jewish identity have become part and parcel of Tottenham's political culture. Similar to Ajax Amsterdam's fans, Spurs supporters use the Israeli flag as a symbol of their identity and struggle. To a more limited extent, such a self-identification can also be observed among fans of Bayern Munich. Moreover, Glasgow Rangers fans, deeply anchored in the symbols of Scottish Protestantism, have resorted to displaying the Israeli flag in support of their color blue in direct opposition to the flaunting of the Palestinian flag, which features the color green, by their green-clad cross-city rival Celtic, a living symbol of Gaelic and Catholic pride. That things are far from linear and simple regarding this matter is best attested to by the fact that a few years ago a Rangers fan sporting a t-shirt that insulted the Pope—a common costume adorning Rangers fans at "Old Firm" contests—ran across the pitch waving a Palestinian flag. The man was arrested and the club had to pay a penalty. And Celtic fans resisted en masse an exhortation by the Scottish Trade Union Congress (STUC) to wave 10,000 Palestinian flags that the Congress hoped to distribute to Celtic supporters

not as Yeshiva bocher, has developed into an icon for these fans, though, one should never forget the origins of this development. This hails not so much from a positive identification with Jewish culture but rather from the desire to mutate abuse and derision—such as the term "Yid" has clearly connoted in London, as well as elsewhere in Europe—into pride and honor. Thus, it has parallels with homosexuals turning the formerly pejorative "gay," and the even more discriminatory and abusive "queer," which were commonly used to deride and humiliate them, into expressions of a proud and open self-identification in a largely heterosexual and still homophobic society. There are even parallels to the usage of the "n-word" on the part of African American rappers.

Thus, to conclude our section on England, immense improvements that were consciously executed by institutional leadership and changed societal mores have almost purged soccer from the scourge of violence that was so endemic to it for twenty years, roughly between the early 1970s until the early 1990s. Flare-ups, alas, still occur from time to time, as they did on August 25, 2009 before an English League Cup game between Millwall FC and West Ham United at the latter's Upton Park ground in London. Supporters of the two clubs engaged in large-scale violence that led to injuries and a stabbing. And barely two months later, on October 27th, there was ugly crowd violence, also in an English League Cup match, between Barnsley FC and Manchester United. Eight fans were arrested, a food kiosk was looted, property was seriously damaged, police in heavy riot gear with dogs (pelted with bottles by angry fans) had to be deployed to restore order, and fans even jumped onto the railway tracks in a bid to stop the Barnsley to Sheffield train before it had started moving. Such events, once the norm in English soccer, have become quite rare while openly racist taunts and vulgar language continue unabated.[101]

when their team hosted the Israeli club Hapoel Tel Aviv in early December of 2009. The club's leadership and the vast majority of its fans refused to participate in this action, which they found particularly misplaced and distasteful since Hapoel Tel Aviv is one of Israel's most left-leaning clubs with fans that are among the most peace-motivated citizens of Israel and—like all the country's Hapoel teams—hails directly from the trade union movement. See Martin Krauss, "Fahne schwenken für Palastina" in Zeit-Online, December 4, 2009, http://community.zeit.de/user/martin-krau%C3%9F (retrieved on December 7, 2009).

[101] Thus, for example, Markovits attended the quarterfinal World Cup match between Portugal and England in Gelsenkirchen in July of 2006. Sitting in a section mainly with England supporters, he experienced 120 minutes of nonstop profane language, the booing of the Portuguese national anthem, and the derision of England captain David Beckham when he—just like his Portuguese counterpart, Luis Figo—read a broad and rather innocuous statement before kickoff in which FIFA expressed its desire to ban racism from global football. This was met with sneers, boos, and a few choice words by many England supporters in this particular section of the stadium. Of course, whenever a Portuguese player touched the ball, these fans

A 2009 study of racism and ethnic discrimination in European sports, comprising data from all twenty-seven of the European Union's member states, delves into what its authors call "open racism" (or "racist incidents") by which they mean "the racist abuse of migrant or ethnic-religious minority athletes by spectators, other athletes, coaches or officials, on the field, in the dressing rooms, on the training ground or in other areas of sporting practices"; and "structural discrimination," which for them includes open as well as hidden norms, attitudes, rules, regulations, and behavior that impede players and athletes belonging to ethnic, racial, and/or religious minorities from participating in their sports on an equal footing with those belonging to the majority.[102] The study's overall findings pertaining to soccer (just one of many sports considered in this research) corroborate our own analysis: that the higher and more international the organizations, the more they have programs and policies in place to counter these counter-cosmopolitan developments. Thus, the EU, FIFA, and UEFA are much more explicit and pro-active in fighting racism than are most country-level federations; and as to the latter, the more prominent the league, the greater the endeavor to oppose racism. The researchers confirm our findings that "right-wing extremism in Germany and Italy" has begun to abate in soccer's top professional leagues but has emerged with a vengeance in the minors and amateur leagues.[103] Severe and frequent racist incidents are confirmed for men's amateur football in all twenty-seven member states of the European Union most of which, the authors note, have federations that proudly display their antiracist language and antidiscriminatory statutes. Alas, their actual enforcement is a totally different matter with the study demonstrating how the scourge of

---

launched a tirade of vulgar invectives. The same pertained to most decisions by the refereeing team. Almost inexplicably, and lending credence to the notion that the stadium is the last space in advanced industrial societies that allows men simply to behave badly with no sanctions and no stigma, these fans also derided their own players, even before England eventually lost yet another important game in a penalty shootout. After the game, Markovits milled about on the stadium's perimeter, talking to people, when all of a sudden a tirade of the most vulgar invectives rained down on a group of young, well-clad and very attractive women who, it turns out, were the (in)famous WAGS, the wives and girlfriends of the England players, on their way to the team bus. None of these instances were the least bit dangerous or close to anything violent. But they sure were very offensive and quite aggressive, even beyond their obvious verbal meaning.

[102] Elisabeth Kotvojs, Salomé Marivoet, Georg Spitaler, *Beyond the Game: Racism and Ethnic Discrimination in Sport in the EU and Preventive Initiatives' Comparative Report* (Vienna: European Fundamental Rights Agency, 2010); pp. 5, 6. The report available to us was dated November 13, 2009. The published version, to appear in 2010, might possibly have a different title than the report which we cite here.

[103] Ibid., p. 8.

racism and all its accompanying ills are still not viewed with a real urgency by the pertinent institutions that have the power to improve the situation. However, in soccer's professional game, the more prominent the league, the greater is the awareness on the part of its leaders that racism poses a serious problem to the league's and the game's legitimacy and that appropriate measures need to be taken to fight this blemish. Tellingly, it has been the world of professional soccer that, by dint of its Europeanization and globalization, has emerged as perhaps the most vocal opponent and potent agent in fighting a flourishing counter-cosmopolitanism all over Europe's sports fields and stadiums. In other words, the greater the prevalence of global players as cosmopolitan actors, the greater is the likelihood of racism's marginalization, if not—alas—its total elimination.

The study also confirms our presentation of anti-Semitism's continued presence, even proliferation, on Europe's soccer grounds. The authors find the following items particularly pervasive:[104] Insults of opposing fans, no matter if these are Jewish or not, with anti-Semitic invectives featuring the word "Jew" and "Jewish" in a derogatory manner; anti-Semitic slander and chants directed at the fans and players of clubs that have (or once had) some kind of Jewish background or roots in the Jewish community like Ajax Amsterdam, FK Austria in Vienna, and Tottenham Hotspurs in England;[105] references to the Holocaust in graffiti, chants and on banners directed at fans and players of opposing teams; and anti-Semitic references in connection with the conflict between Israel and the Palestinians.

What Happened in the United States? The Disappearing Specter of Racism and Violence in American Sports Culture

By contrast to all of these European cases, violence is a very marginal occurrence in present-day American sports culture, and open racism is practically taboo and socially unacceptable in the stands and among players. University of Texas football coach Mack Brown summarily expelled center Buck Burnette from the University of Texas's football roster because Burnette had posted threatening and racially offensive remarks on his Facebook page about President-elect Barack Obama. Such reactions are common both in college and professional sports, and they indicate that while

---

[104] Ibid., pp. 67, 68.
[105] Interestingly, the authors do not mention in their study the anti-Semitic invectives hurled at fans and players of MTK-Hungaria Budapest.

discrimination and racism undoubtedly remain major issues in American sports and society, explicitly worded overt racism has for all intents and purposes been banned from contemporary American sports.[106] In fact, any of the racist remarks and gestures that remain commonplace in many European stadiums—even where fan violence has been successfully contained if not completely eliminated over the last few years, such as in England—have virtually disappeared from all major league and college-level sports venues in the United States. Moreover, the rare cases of fan violence that have existed in America—and will always remain in any context in which large numbers of people gather for emotionally charged events in a relatively small and confined space—have had a completely different substance and tone from their European counterparts. Thus, violence at American sports venues has almost never been a premeditated, organized activity, implemented by a small group of well-trained street fighters whose primary, perhaps sole, purpose is to engage in fights and cause havoc rather than to watch the game.

Sports and Violence in America

Much of the fan violence surrounding American sports has been random, unstructured, and quite spontaneous. Most important, it is mainly fueled by alcohol abuse on the part of fans getting into fights with other drunken fans. Some baseball stadiums still keep their traditional jail cells—often established in the rougher early days of the game when fights among fans were much more common—to "store" their drunken fans and separate them from the game while their alcohol level decreases. The Philadelphia Eagles have a magistrate on hand at their stadium to book unruly fans right then and there. However, already more than forty years ago Philip Goodhart and Christopher Chataway observed that in America, "a land so often characterized as a land bubbling with violence, sporting hooliganism, apart from racial disturbances, seems to be largely unknown."[107] Riots be-

---

[106] Reid Cherner and Tom Weir, "Longhorn Cut because of Obama Slur," http://blogs .usatoday.com/gameon/2008/11/longhorn-cut-be.html. Retrieved November 8, 2008. Bernette wrote: "All the hunters gather up, we have a Nigger in the White House."

[107] Philip Goodhart and Christopher Chataway, *War without Weapons* (London: W. H. Allen, 1968), p. 144. The "racial disturbances" to which Goodhart and Chataway refer are the fights between black and white youths that led to a temporary ban on high school night matches in parts of the United States. In an early, yet methodologically controversial study, Jerry Lewis observed 312 incidents he classified as "riots" at American sports events between 1960 and 1972; 97 in baseball, 66 in football, 55 in basketball, and 39 in hockey; quoted in Allen Guttmann, *Sports Spectators* (New York: Columbia University Press, 1986), p. 119. The scale and seriousness of these incidents, however, are not weighted, measured or elaborated.

fore and after games have occurred upon occasion; however, even such incidents have been on the decline for decades. While some scholars had observed a temporary rise in sports-related fan violence at American venues in the 1970s and 1980s—to some extent due to more extensive media coverage and public sensitivity towards the issue[108]—occurrences since then have become few and far between.

In April 1988, Pete Rose's altercation with umpire Dave Pallone in which Rose claimed that Pallone had scratched him in the face during the argument and Rose, in arguing his point vehemently, clearly made physical contact with the umpire, caused a near-riot at Cincinnati's Riverfront Stadium with the fans littering the field with debris and throwing unopened beer cans and whiskey bottles.[109] In 2004, at the end of an NBA basketball game between the Indiana Pacers and the Detroit Pistons at The Palace in Auburn Hills, Michigan, a physical confrontation between Ben Wallace and Ron Artest erupted into violence between Pacers players and Pistons fans.[110] It happened on live television and made big news thereafter leading to all kinds of soul-searching within the NBA, basketball, and American society and culture. But the incident was hardly noteworthy compared to the levels and frequency of violence that remain constant and regular fare in European stadiums. Similarly, local violence problems might occasionally have ramifications for sports events; for example, fear of gang violence forced authorities to postpone a high school football game between Belleville High School and Ypsilanti High School in Michigan after rival gangs planned to use the game for a fight.[111]

[108] See Jerry M. Lewis, *Sports Fan Violence in North America* (Lanham, MD: Rowman & Littlefield, 2007); Harry Edwards and Van Rackages, "The Dynamics of Violence in American Sport," *Journal of Sport and Social Issues* 7 (2), 1977, pp. 3–31; "Why Are There No Equivalents of Soccer Hooliganism in the United States?," in Murphy, Williams, and Dunning, *Football on Trial*, pp. 194–212, here pp. 200 and 203. Murphy, Williams, and Dunning cite an example of massive forms of disorderly conduct and assault during a Monday Night Football game between the New England Patriots and the New York Jets in 1977, leading to several arrests, while eighteen people had to be taken to the hospital.

[109] See O. Johnson, "Sports and Suds," *Sports Illustrated*, August 8, 1988, pp. 70–72.

[110] Shouting and physical confrontation had died down, a fan in the stands threw a cup of ice-cold soda at the prone Ron Artest, who then climbed four rows into the stands to confront the fan. After pushing between Artest and Pistons fans, several of Artest's teammates followed him into the stands, trying to protect him. As the players finally returned to the court, other fans confronted them and the fighting continued. When the Pacers players left the arena they were assaulted by cups of beer, soda bottles, and screaming fans. A chair was thrown, and several fans were injured as the police and security seemed incapable of controlling this altercation.

[111] See Marjorie Kauth-Kajala, "Belleville Moves Basketball Game to Deter Violence," *Ann Arbor News*, January 10, 2008.

By far the most prevalent forms of violence in connection with any sports in America belong to the category best captured by the terms "celebratory violence" or "celebratory riots." Typically, this involves unruly, and often rather inebriated, fans celebrating their team's victory by rioting in the streets, burning cars, turning over and igniting garbage cans, and fighting the police that are dispatched to quell the disturbance. Interestingly, it is exclusively fans of the winning teams that engage in such behavior, never the losing teams. This was the case following the Tigers' World Series triumph in Detroit in October of 1984; in Chicago after the Bulls' championship victory in June of 1992; in Los Angeles after the Lakers regained their title in June of 2008; in October of 2004 in Boston when the hometown Red Sox overcame a three-game deficit to beat their hated long-term tormentor New York Yankees in the series by 4 games to 3; in November of 2002 in Columbus, Ohio, when Ohio State fans stormed the field of the Horseshoe after their team had defeated archrival Michigan on the last play of the game. In each of these cases, the victories released much pent-up frustration by the winners' fans. The Boston Red Sox had not only won their series in a manner never achieved by any sports team in the history of major league baseball, professional football, and basketball (down three games to none in a best-of-seven series and winning it by triumphing in four must-win games in a row) but they did so against the very team that had constantly outshined them and was their ever-present nemesis since 1918, the last time the Red Sox had won the World Series.[112] Ohio State had been dominated by Michigan throughout much of the 1990s and the Buckeyes had just concluded an entire "Beat Michigan week" on campus that preceded the game and catapulted much of the student body into a frenzied state of mind. But even in these instances, one needs to differentiate between the "celebratory riots" that occurred immediately following these victories, largely in and around the venues themselves, and subsequent physical assaults and lootings, that were only loosely, if at all, connected to the sports events and were only convenient pretexts to engage in violent acts.[113] Moreover, unlike in Europe, where virtually all of the violence in the stadiums is premeditated, prepared, and designed well before the actual games, "celebratory violence" at American venues occurs spon-

---

[112] The Toronto Maple Leafs of 1942 and the New York Islanders of 1975 in the National Hockey League were both down by three games to none in a best-of-seven series and still managed to win. These were the only times in North American major team sports that such an amazing feat had been accomplished prior to the Boston Red Sox's defeat of the New York Yankees in 2004.

[113] See "Violence amid Celebration," *New York Times*, June 15, 1992.

taneously and in an improvised and ad-hoc fashion. Above all, these riots are not directed against the fans of the opposing teams, as much as they are random acts of destruction against whatever constitutes their immediate surroundings. In perhaps the greatest contrast to its European counterparts, these American instances of fan violence had not been accompanied by racial hatred, anti-Semitism, or any discourse or activity directed against a particular minority. Jeering the New York Yankees and deriding the Michigan Wolverines with vulgar language might not be pretty, but it surely is in a whole different category than spewing hatred and venom against Jews, blacks, and other nonwhite minorities as has remained commonplace in Europe's stadiums since the 1970s. Jerry M. Lewis, author of one of the most comprehensive studies of fan violence in North American sports, summarizes the situation: "For North America, and particularly the United States, the data on fan violence at the collegiate and professional levels of competition are clear. The typical rioter is likely to be a young, white male celebrating a victory after a championship or an important game or match."[114]

While we in no way mean to downplay the ugliness of occasional fan violence in the United States caused by these "celebratory riots"—after all, a young Emerson College journalism student lost her life totally senselessly and tragically in the mayhem following the Red Sox's defeat of the Yankees—and certainly see its occurrence as detrimental to American sports and society, it is noteworthy that European-style violence and hooligan-type riots have never emerged at American sport venues and events. Why has this been the case? Why has fan violence largely been absent from American team sports, when by any measure the United States suffers from a much higher level of violence in virtually every other aspect of its society than does any country in Europe?

Less Favorable Conditions: Size, Rivalries, Cultural Multiplicity

There have been many rather speculative scholarly responses to this puzzle in the social sciences. For example, the Leicester School on hooliganism, which has often provided first-rate studies and interpretations of this phenomenon in Britain and Europe, argues that in "welfare state" Europe sections of the working class were more fully integrated into the overall "consensus" of society. Thus, these welfare states incorporated workers more fully into sports than has been the case in the United States. In con-

[114] Lewis, *Sports Fan Violence in North America*, p. 69.

trast, according to the Leicester School, America's free-market principles and "federal and state policies based to a greater degree on laissez-faire values may have resulted in a greater proportion of the lower classes being less incorporated into dominant values and, consequently, less integrated into sports. In its turn, a consequence of this may have been to insulate American sports to a greater degree from the lower-class pattern of gang fighting."[115]

The authors rightly conclude that in contrast to the European cases, where violent street gangs have conquered soccer stands in many places, gangs also exist in America but have not chosen to make sports the loci in which to fight and act out their aggression.[116] Yet we disagree emphatically with the Leicester School's interpretation on two counts: first, that fighting and hooliganism are somehow the (possibly exclusive) purview of the working classes; and second, that the American working class has been excluded from the world of American sports. That is factually incorrect and hails from a widely held view by many left-leaning European intellectuals that the people of the United States are deficient in their class politics compared to Europe—being generally less "deep" and "authentic" than Europe and thus not having had the benefit of a "real" working class for the country's political and social development, instead having to make do with a commercialized amalgam of disparate individuals whose politics and social demeanor had to be therefore conformist, if not reactionary. Yet, any reading of baseball's history, not to mention the early days of the NFL, basketball's ubiquitous reach into playing and following, as well as hockey's attraction to the industrial working classes of large Canadian cities and those of the Midwest and Northeast of the United States, reveals a massive inclusion of workers into these cultural forums. Football was a way of life for the coal miners and steel workers of the Ohio Valley and western Pennsylvania and had every bit the equivalent socializing function as Rugby League and soccer did in England's Yorkshire and Lancashire. To the Italian, Irish, Polish, and Jewish workers of New York, Boston, Chicago, Detroit, and Cleveland, their baseball (and football) teams had the same cultural meaning and social importance as did the soccer teams to their English and continental comrades. But by dint of ethnicity superseding class as a major signifier of collective identity in the United States, one might think of class as less important to America's sports culture than to Europe's. After all, people perceive Hank Greenberg's exploits or Joe

---

[115] See Murphy, Williams, and Dunning, "Why Are There No Equivalents of Soccer Hooliganism in the United States?," p. 208.

[116] See ibid., p. 207.

DiMaggio's feats as having helped Jews and Italians respectively to integrate into America's mainstream culture. Few note the modest social milieu from which these two American icons arose and what they meant to Jewish and Italian workers. American sports have emerged over time into a particularly powerful medium for broadly inclusive cultural, social, and national integration that cuts across class divisions and increasingly transcends ethnic conflicts. In doing so, American sports have functioned as an integrative substitute for other forms of social (welfare) mechanisms. With the disproportionate success of minority athletes in America's hegemonic sports culture, sports have turned into a major model that facilitates exposure to cosmopolitan diversity and enhances broader recognition of ethnic and cultural multiplicity in American immigrant society.

Before we return to the question of a wider and deeper "social consensus" and the integrative function of sports in the United States compared to Europe, we want to address conditions in American sports that we see as less favorable for sport-related hooliganism and collective violence than they have been in Europe. America is a country of continental proportions. The long distances inhibit travel to accompany one's team for an away game.[117] In addition, there is less of a tradition in following one's team across the country for a regular season or even play-off game than in Europe. Only year-end bowl games in college football, traditionally played on neutral sites, and the March Madness tournament in men's college basketball also played in neutral arenas strewn across the country, witness American sports fans traveling in large numbers to follow their teams. Rivalry games (or derbies, to use soccer parlance)—Auburn vs. Alabama, USC vs. UCLA, Ohio State vs. Michigan, Florida vs. Florida State, Stanford vs. California, Duke vs. North Carolina, Yankees vs. Red Sox—constitute exceptions to the American norm. And sure enough these emotionally charged encounters do on occasion yield fan violence before and after the games in bars and streets near the relevant stadiums, and sometimes even during the games themselves, particularly in the bleacher seats. These altercations are invariably quelled quickly by surrounding spectators, and the authorities are also at hand to nip things in the bud. But fights do happen at these emotionally charged games. With the exception of the rivalry games, however, American sports venues feature few visible "enemies" or outsiders. This drastically reduces the chance of clashes between large groups of opposing fans. By contrast, European soccer matches are more local affairs, and there is a tradition of clubs traveling with a large coterie

---

[117] See ibid., p. 209.

of fans even to distant games. Geographic proximity in team sports breeds rivalries, which in turn foster contempt and hatred that then increase the likelihood of violence.

Many European cities have had a long-standing tradition of featuring a number of clubs in close proximity, which intensifies rivalries and mutual hatreds: Vienna once furnished ten soccer clubs in Austria's top-level league of twelve teams well into the 1960s and continues to have three or four to this day; Budapest has had six; Bucharest, Istanbul, and Moscow four; London still boasts five clubs in the English Premier League's 2009–10 campaign; and many cities have at least two. Because American sports teams began as businesses with their owners explicitly disallowing the establishment of any rivals in their territory, no cities other than New York, Chicago, and Los Angeles have more than one team per sport. And in those rare cases where cities have multiple teams per sport, they originated in different leagues (as in baseball) and led parallel but rarely overlapping existences. Or, they arose at vastly disparate time periods (as in basketball and hockey), both of which mitigated rivalries. But let us recall that the intense mutual dislike on the part of Giants and Dodgers fans in baseball hails precisely from their proximate histories in New York City, where they played each other repeatedly in the very same league. Their antipathy stems not from their post-1958 West Coast incarnation, representing NorCal and SoCal respectively. The bad blood between New York Rangers fans and their counterpart supporters of the New York Islanders and the New Jersey Devils in hockey also attests to the ubiquitous phenomenon in all competitive team sports that proximity breeds competition and hatred, not respect and harmony. Distance may not foster affection but it most certainly decreases the acerbity of conflict. And the larger distances of America's spaces—sports and geography—contribute considerably to a less-violent atmosphere in American sports compared to their European counterparts.

In contrast to European clubs, many of which to this day sport strong political identities, sports teams in the United States—tellingly called franchises—do very little of this. In Europe, clubs are often close to political parties or movements, which in turn reflect often bitter social, economic, religious, ethnic, and linguistic cleavages that divide people. And thus *any* contest, even a football match, between a club identified as representing a "red" (i.e., socialist) subculture confronting a rival club seen as the embodiment of a "black" (i.e., Catholic-conservative) subculture, attains a vicarious dimension. The actual events on the field stand for something completely different, alas usually something divisive, precisely because these games are inherently contested between a clear "us" vs. "them."[118]

Crucially, American sports have virtually no national dimension to them. There are no national baseball, basketball, football, and hockey teams that represent the country on a regular basis in constant contests with neighboring countries. Americans are not familiar with the emotionally charged identification with a national team commensurate to what the Brazilians experience for their *Seleção*, Germans for their *Nationalmannschaft*, Italians for their *squaddra azzurra*, or Argentinians for their *Albiceleste*. Of course, there are "Team USAs" participating in quadrennial global competitions such as world championships and the Olympics, but these are far away and few in number and have virtually no relevance for Americans' emotional investment in their sports and teams. American sports and the accompanying emotions are completely inner-directed and insular, in that they exist in an intercity and intracountry environment in which international dimensions are secondary at best. Only once did Americans from coast to coast receive anything near the emotional charge from one of their national teams that Europeans (and Latin Americans) experience on a regular basis: the "Miracle on Ice" victory by a motley crew of inexperienced collegians representing the United States Olympic hockey squad over the mighty Soviet "Red Machine," and the subsequent gold-medal run by Team USA at the Lake Placid winter Olympics in 1980. At this time relations between the United States and the Soviet Union had

---

[118] In his regularly taught sports and society class, which attracts 150 University of Michigan undergraduates, Markovits always asks his students the day before Michigan's game against Ohio State how high their antipathy towards Ohio State is. It is quite clear from the answers, that, not surprisingly, there is little love lost for the Buckeyes among his students. Then Markovits informs the students that there is virtually no difference between University of Michigan undergraduates and their Ohio State counterparts, with the exception of a few points on various tests and grade averages—no serious religious, political, social, or economic differences worthy of mention. And then he tells the students to imagine their animosity for Ohio State were Michigan a predominantly Protestant school with students hailing from a wealthy East Coast social background voting largely for the Republican Party (perish the thought for most contemporary Michigan students, we are sure) as opposed to Ohio State being largely a Catholic university whose student body was mainly working class that voted heavily for the Democrats. In other words, what would happen if there were *real* differences between these student bodies? How much more intense would their enmity be towards Ohio State? And would not the upcoming contest stand for much more than just a standard rivalry game between two very similar American institutions of higher education? That exactly is the situation in parts of European soccer. In fact, Markovits's advisee Andrew K. Watkins wrote a senior honors thesis precisely on this topic, highlighting the deep enmities of local soccer rivalries in Europe. See his "Same City, Different Worlds: The Manifestation of Intra-City Divisions in Soccer" (Princeton University, 2004).

just deteriorated precipitously following the latter's invasion of Afghani-
stan. Tellingly, in the world of American soccer, where the national teams—
both on the women's and the men's side—play an integral, indeed leading
role in that sport's presence in the country, there have developed intense
rivalries with the Mexicans on the men's side and the Norwegians, Brazilians, and Germans on the women's. These could, possibly, slip into some
sort of violent altercations between opposing fans at future contests,
though this is unlikely, especially in women's soccer.

Furthermore, in contrast to the high emotional investment in soccer's
dominant monoculture in Europe, the multiplicity of America's hegemonic
sports languages tends to spread a fan's emotional involvement and allegiances over three, possibly four, teams, thus easing the pain and frustration accompanying a lost game or, God forbid, an entire season. If, as a
New Englander, one is (very likely) a passionate Red Sox fan, and a season
goes badly, there are always the New England Patriots, the Celtics, and the
Bruins to hope for. Ditto in many American cities and regions in which a
multiplicity of teams representing the Big Four of American sports culture
split loyalties to some degree, thereby lowering passions and fanaticism for
one. This is less the case in sparsely populated areas with no major professional teams, where a single college or even high-school team assumes a
fan base of quasi-European proportions, as we will discuss in the next
chapter. Indeed, being a Cornhusker fan in Nebraska is more similar in its
intensity and commitment to being a European soccer club's supporter
than that of an American professional team (at the risk of slighting the
legendary devotion by Oakland Raiders' fans populating the team's famed
Black Hole). While sports as a whole are much more popular and prevalent in American than European culture, the distinct history of soccer's
club and national team cultures in Europe have, as a rule, created deeper
ties and long-term local attachments by communities with "their" clubs
than exists between American franchises and their fans. For one thing,
American teams have regularly moved from location to location, even
from league to league, unthinkable in the European context. On average,
contests between two American teams connote proxy battles between two
rival communities on a much feebler scale than has been the case in
Europe.[119]

Professional leagues, club authorities, and owners in American sports
have increasingly assumed major responsibility in violence prevention and
commonly play an active role in an effective, spectator-friendly security

[119] See ibid, pp. 208–9.

system[120] that comprises programs to eliminate hostility among fans. As we discussed, such measures were until recently largely absent in European soccer. To wit, American venues never included the creation of virtual cages in which fans in Europe had been perilously confined. The constant modernization of facilities in America, a priori in better condition than their European counterparts, and the reshaping of the sports themselves that renders a stadium visit a more congenial experience to the general public, coincides with the search for new solutions to minimize fan violence in the United States. With excessive alcohol consumption posing the biggest problem in terms of fan violence and unruliness, many arenas have come to stop the sale of beer either in its entirety or after a certain period in the game, such as the seventh inning in baseball.[121]

Racism vs. Classism

If violence does occur among fans of the North American Big Four, it is not articulated in racist language and activities. Lest we be misunderstood here, we are *not* arguing that racism has disappeared from American sports, let alone among spectators, culture, and society. Far from it! Alas, it is alive and well. What we are saying, however, is that overt racist taunts have become completely unacceptable in the vocabulary of American sports in the major leagues and on the college level. The reason for this, we are convinced, lies in the fact that in sports and other realms of public life, "the United States has worked harder and gone farther than any other advanced majority-white nation in confronting and righting the wrongs of its racist past."[122]

This is much less the case with "classism." Thus, in American sports, various "classist" taunts continue to flourish with "ho, ho; hey, hey; you will work for us some day" being on the milder side; nor have misogynist slurs disappeared, though they too have become rarer as the number of women as athletes, spectators, and viewers has consistently increased since the 1980s. Any offensive language, let alone action, directed toward a collec-

[120] Stephen J. Dubner, "Why Aren't U.S. Sports Fans More Violent?," Freakonomics blog, February 9, 2007, http://freakonomics.blogs.nytimes.com/2007/02/09/why-arent-us-sports-fans. Retrieved October 30, 2008.

[121] Major League Baseball and the National Basketball Association participate in TEAM (Techniques for Effective Alcohol Management), which is a program for training everyone from vendors to ushers in handling people who have had too much to drink. See www.teamcoalition.org.

[122] Orlando Patterson, "Race and Diversity in the Age of Obama," *New York Times Book Review*, August 26, 2009. Patterson has argued this point emphatically in some of his scholarly work as well.

tive that is perceived to be disempowered and/or a minority—be they blacks, Latinos, or women—has been effectively banned from American sports at the top levels, with racism having become a total taboo.

In college sports, for example, each conference and association has in its bylaws a requirement that a "crowd control statement" must be read over a public announcement system. Or, a printed version of the statement must be distributed to fans. Different variants of the crowd control statement are permitted, as long as there is a statement of some kind made at the event. Here is the NCAA's boilerplate version that many colleges follow at all their sporting events:

> The NCAA promotes good sportsmanship by student-athletes, coaches and spectators. We request your cooperation by supporting the participants and officials in a positive manner. Profanity, racial comments, sexist language or other intimidating actions directed at officials, student-athletes, coaches or team representatives will not be tolerated and are grounds for removal from the site of competition. Also, consumption or possession of alcoholic beverages is prohibited.[123]

Telling of the state of public discourse at American sporting venues, everything but the prohibition of alcohol is largely followed and accepted as legitimate.

Of course, personalized slights directed at individual players continue to flourish, be it about habits, posture, demeanor, language, or friends and associates. Deriding a player for making a mistake and continuing to irk him/her about it, sometimes in aggressive, if not necessarily vulgar, language, also continues unabated in American arenas. Again, as we have repeatedly stated throughout this chapter, such taunts and "trash talk" will always remain part of competitive sports. But it is telling that even foul language, the usage of four-letter curse words, has become quite rare in the stadiums of major league teams. It is not uncommon to have spectators reprimand a fan for repeated usage of foul language, usually with statements like, "Hey, my kids are here, as is my wife: cool it with the swearing!" These types of interactions were witnessed by both of us together and independently at many baseball, football, basketball, and hockey games. It is also not unusual at American venues to have the public announcer declare before the beginning of the game that "foul language"

---

[123] See www.ncaa.org/wps/wcm/connect/resources/file/eb046e46e2d926a/CROWD%2520 CONTROL%2520STATEMENT.doc%3FMOD%3DAJPERES%26attachment%3Dtrue +%22crowd+control+statement%22&hl=en&ct=clnk&cd=2&gl=us&client=firefox-a. Retrieved August 25, 2008.

will not be tolerated and its usage might lead to being expelled from the venue. Racist songs, slogans, and banners, let alone Nazi salutes—that are still commonplace in Europe's football stadiums—are unthinkable in contemporary American sports. It is not only because the authorities would not allow such behavior and punish it promptly and severely, but much more important, because the fans would never countenance it. We regard such massive change in language and behavior in contemporary America—including its male-dominated sports culture—as one of the many success stories that the civilizing agents of the 1960s and early 1970s (mostly, of course, the women's and the civil rights movements) attained to enhance institutional and cultural inclusiveness and thus augment the democratic cosmopolitanism of sports.

Moreover, size matters! When there were few black players on the sports fields and in the stands, racist language and behavior flourished. The same pertains to Latinos, when only a few of them plied their trade in baseball's major leagues in the 1950s and 1960s. But with the proliferation of both among the ranks of top-level players—to the point where African Americans comprise nearly 80 percent of all NBA players and close to 70 percent of the NFL's; and when Latinos exceed 30 percent of major league baseball players—racism by necessity fades into the background.

Lastly, in notable contrast to Europe, in which most countries until recently had few, if any, sizable nonwhite populations, it was American sports that played a vanguard role in the progress toward racial equality and color-blindness in the country.[124] Beginning with Jackie Robinson's integrating America's pastime in 1947 by joining the roster of the National League's Brooklyn Dodgers (followed eleven weeks later by the oft-forgotten Larry Doby in the American League), the changes toward more inclusion and diversity in America's sports world regularly preceded and anticipated similarly inclusive changes in other cultural, social, and politi-

---

[124] In basketball and football, where the universities took the lead, African Americans found earlier access than in the commercially controlled, and stubborn world of baseball. It took racial slurs by the New York Yankees outfielder Jake Powell in 1938 to lay bare the game's racism and break the silence that protected segregated baseball until then; see Chris Lamb, "Public Slur in 1938 Laid Bare a Game's Racism," *New York Times*, July 27, 2008, Sports section, p. 5. The first African American football player was active for the University of Michigan in the 1890s. And virtually all Jewish football stars had their breakthrough because they attended a college: for instance, Benny Friedman and Harry Newman at the University of Michigan, Sid Gillman at Ohio State University, Marshall Goldberg at the University of Pittsburgh, Charles Goldenberg at the University of Wisconsin, Sigmund Harris at the University of Minnesota, Benny Lom at the University of California at Berkeley, Sid Luckman at Columbia University, Ron Mix at the University of Southern California, and Edward Newman at Duke University.

cal spheres. Integration in sports commenced not because of the enlightened and egalitarian inclination of its practitioners but rather due to the inherently meritocratic, competitive, result-oriented, and profit-seeking nature of major-league professional team sports, where winning wasn't everything but the only thing. Today, the stardom of African Americans in the sports world, as exemplified by basketball stars like Magic Johnson and Michael Jordan or golf legend Tiger Woods, helped expand the social acceptance of blacks and thus constituted the precursors to Colin Powell, Condoleezza Rice, and eventually Barack Obama. Though racial discrimination in American sports has certainly not disappeared—a quick glance at the paucity of black team owners, front-office leadership, coaches, as well as managers will corroborate this point—the environment for racism has become socially taboo. And initiatives like the NFL's Rooney Rule are long overdue and much-needed institutionally mandated policies to increase the presence of African Americans among the top football league's head coaches. Though still woeful in the scarcity of their numbers—as is that of black head coaches in the country's Football Bowl Subdivision (FBS), formerly known as Division I-A college programs—the seed for improvement has been planted with a modicum of success more than likely in the not-too-distant future. Black athletes, as well as some coaches, have become widely respected heroes of these hegemonic sports and via them in American society as a whole. It is now much harder for the exclusionary counter-cosmopolitans, who have most certainly not vanished from American society and sport, to spew their racist venom openly. Above all, their surroundings no longer countenance it. We agree with Orlando Patterson that the remaining pernicious racial divide in contemporary America pertains much more to our private than our public lives.

Globalization and Its Discontents: The Counter-Cosmopolitan Challenge

To varying degrees, xenophobia, anti-Semitism, and hooliganism comprise an integral part of Europe's contemporary soccer topography. Racist and violent fans, who oppose the cosmopolitan modernization that has occurred in and around the game, have turned many stadiums into their political battlegrounds. In spite of increased public attention and more robust institutional responses over the past few years—including FIFA's campaign against racism at the 2006 World Cup tournament in Germany and UEFA's parallel endeavor at the European national championship two years later in Switzerland and Austria—the fight against hooliganism and racism remains far from won.[125] Unfortunately, the situation has improved only gradually, and at the game's top events, over the past several years. In fact, racism in European soccer remains so rampant that the latest efforts to curb this ill have transferred to soccer-featuring video games, in which the statement "Say no to racism" remains posted on the screen throughout the game. Alas, there exists evidence that this message goes unnoticed by Europeans playing on their video screens.[126]

In several ways, soccer in Europe continues to serve as a significant conduit for right-wing counter-cosmopolitans to express their "resistance to globalization"[127] and cultural change. The game constitutes a crucial arena for this cultural conflict, and its main protagonists—the ever-visible

---

[125] We have included the FIFA and UEFA statements and programs on these matters in this footnote.

First, here are the statements and plans by FIFA for World Cup 2006:

Before each World Cup match, the center circle of the field is covered by a light blue tarp. On it are the tournament's two mottos: "A time to make friends" and "Say no to racism." Shortly before kickoff, a crew of blue-clad volunteers runs onto the field, picks up the tarp and carries it away. Before the national anthems are played, the team captains recite a statement drafted by FIFA officials which condemns racism and rejects discrimination. As decided by FIFA's Executive Committee, all 64 matches of the 2006 FIFA World Cup were marked by a visible element sending a clear message against racism to the world. On 28 June 2006, FIFA organised a media conference at the Stadium Media Centre in Berlin to launch the FIFA Anti-Discrimination Days and show support—through football personalities and world leaders—to the fight against racism. The conference—moderated by FIFA's Director of Communications, Markus Siegler—was attended by FIFA President, Joseph S. Blatter; Local Organizing Committee President, Franz Beckenbauer; UNICEF Executive Director, Ann Veneman; German Minister of Interior, Dr Wolfgang Schäuble; FIFPro President, Philippe Piat, and South African human rights activist, Tokyo Sexwale.

Then, here are the details for the UEFA EURO Tournament 2008:

The Unite Against Racism programme, run by the Football Against Racism in Europe (FARE) network with UEFA's backing, will include an advertising spot broadcast at every game, pitch-side boards and activities with fans, culminating in high-profile activities on the field at the semi-finals in Basel and Vienna on 25 and 26 June. Messages of anti-racism will be delivered from the pitch by the captains of both teams at the semi-finals.

The statement made by the captains states: "I and my teammates wish to make clear that we stand against all forms of discrimination. We have seen over the last three weeks how football can bring people together to enjoy our common passion whatever our religion, nationality or skin color. Please join us to Unite Against Racism." UEFA vice-president Şenes Erzik will also address guests before the premier of the advertising spot, Different Languages, One Goal: No To Racism, which was shown at every UEFA EURO 2008™ game.

[126] "Obama, Europe and Racism in Football—The Audacity of Superficiality," http://shapingdebate.blogspot.com. Retrieved on December 18, 2007.

[127] Bairner, *Sport, Nationalism, and Globalization*, p. 16.

global players that embody cosmopolitan progress—furnish a ready target for such contestation. It is also no accident, we believe, that in literally every single instance that we encountered in our research—from Spain to Germany, from Hungary to Holland, from Austria to Italy—anti-Semitism assumes a central role for soccer hooligans, at least in their rhetoric if not necessarily their actions. Making matters worse is the vile enmity that many visiting Israeli teams (in soccer, basketball, tennis, and other sports) experience in their trips virtually everywhere in Europe, from Spain to Turkey, from Russia to Sweden. While the iconography and vocabulary of the insults and invectives heaped on the Israeli athletes is nothing short of blatantly anti-Semitic, we chose to omit all such incidents from our study lest their anti-Semitism be disputed and exculpated as legitimate protests against Israel's policies.[128]

We realize that the ultimate trash talk in the postwar European public sphere, the most egregious expression of rebellion and nonconformity, is denying the Holocaust, making it the butt of jokes, showing irreverence to it, and thus to its main victims, the Jews. So young males bonding together in the closed confines of a stadium trying to intimidate the opposing team and its fans, and competing with each other as to who can surpass whom in being outrageous, will surely resort to Jew-baiting, anti-Semitic chants and language that ridicules Auschwitz. But there is a bit more at work here than the old adage of "boys will be boys." Throughout modern European history, nothing and nobody seems to have been more potently (and perniciously) associated with the ills of modernization and cosmopolitanism than the Jew. And while conventional tropes of anti-Semitism have by and large become illegitimate in contemporary European discourse, they most decidedly did not disappear from counter-cosmopolitan thought and language where, if anything, they have experienced a certain renaissance. Soccer hooligans instinctively feel and heartily voice their feelings en masse in Europe's stadiums knowing full well that they will not face serious social sanctions by the rest of society for their transgression. This "longest ha-

[128] For an excellent account of all the discriminations experienced by Israeli teams and athletes in many sports in Europe and beyond, see Alex Feuerherdt, "Geschichte der Boykotte gegen Israels Sportler" (lecture delivered at the Deutsch Israelische Gesellschaft Berlin on July 6, 2009). http://www.digberlin.de/seite/feuerherdt.php[8]. On anti-Jewish discrimination and double standards in international sports see also http://www.robinshepherdonline .com/kick-racism-out-of-sportunless-the-victims-a-jew-is-this-the-new-mantra-of-internat ional-sports-and-athletics-bodies/#more-1678. Retrieved November 28, 2009. And yet, there is hope. Recall from footnote 100 of this chapter how Celtic Glasgow's supporters massively resisted and successfully refused the exhortations by the Scottish Trades Union Congress to wave Palestinian flags when Hapoel Tel Aviv traveled to tradition-laden Celtic Park to face host Celtic in an important international club competition.

tred," to use Robert Wistrich's apt characterization of anti-Semitism, has found a new outlet across Europe's soccer world, independent of the paucity—indeed, virtual nonexistence—of Jewish players, owners, even fans, demonstrating once again that anti-Semitism in Europe, though related to racism and xenophobia, embodies a construct all its own, thus reinforcing the old adage that anti-Semitism needs no Jews.

Despite all these ugly occurrences, there is nothing inevitable about the rise of counter-cosmopolitan language and behavior in European soccer stadiums. They can be countered, contained, perhaps even defeated if certain institutional responses are brought to bear in the context of a changing sociocultural environment.

First and foremost, there is the institutional response on the part of clubs, federations, municipalities, regional governmental structures, the national government, and the European Union. As our German and English cases demonstrate, once these institutions resolved that something had to be done about hooliganism in their respective countries, they were quite successful at least in containing its most heinous manifestations in the top leagues, though they still proved unable to eliminate vile and violent behavior altogether.

Of course, these institutional responses do not occur in a vacuum, but are embedded in underlying social and cultural changes that define acceptable behavior. We have witnessed more positive effects against racism and a marked dissipation of public resentment against players of color in countries in which the presence of a modicum of cultural diversity and cosmopolitanism has some historical legacy by dint of a multiethnic understanding of citizenship. Thus, in postcolonial Britain and France, counter-cosmopolitan reactions, though clearly extant, became more powerfully contested in soccer and beyond.

Resistance against inclusion of ethnically different players tends to be stronger in countries that have had a more "homogenous" self-perception in terms of national identity and where immigration has been a relatively new but rapidly expanding phenomenon, as has been the case in Spain, Italy, and Eastern Europe. In these places, soccer provides the battleground for struggles over society's cosmopolitan challenges to a greater degree than in countries belonging to the previous group.

And numbers matter. Thus, the bevy of superb black players such as Ruud Gullit, Frank Rijkaard, Patrick Kluivert, Edgar Davids, and Clarence Seedorf, among many others, have legitimated the presence of nonwhite superstars in Dutch football and society as a whole. Ditto the case in England, where Rio Ferdinand, Shaun Wright-Phillips, Sol Campbell, and a number of other black soccer players have heightened the profiles of non-whites in English soccer, culture, and society. In France, the broad enthusiasm for Zinedine Zidane—for years France's most popular citizen—and the success of the culturally diverse 1998 World Cup championship team featuring such global superstars as Thierry Henry, David Trezeguet, and Lilian Thuram, offered powerful rebuttals to counter-cosmopolitanism.

Even in the ethnic composition of European national teams, by definition bastions of a political exclusivity, there are movements afoot that are hopeful harbingers for greater tolerance and a more inclusive concept of who can represent the nation in international competition. Once again, it is the desire to win that spurred such inclusive reforms, where special laws were created in many countries that facilitate the nationalization of sports stars who can then enhance the nation's profiles with victories. Slovenia, Bahrain, and Qatar have been the most proactive in granting citizenship to top athletes to represent them in international competition. But even Switzerland—a country with one of the most restrictive notions of citizenship—has lowered its threshold for the acquisition of citizenship for athletes, so much so that nine of its eleven players in the 2005 Under-20-Year-Old World Cup soccer competition in the Netherlands were of foreign origin.[129] The point is clear: a critical mass of such players eventually renders them the norm and thus leads to their acceptance by the larger public that in turn will lead to a greater tolerance, if not full appreciation, of diversity.

Just as in matters of diversity and racial integration in sports, so, too, has America been ahead of Europe in terms of the presence of women as spectators at major sporting events. With the presence of women hovering around 40 percent of spectatorship in American stadiums, and reaching 50 percent in college sports, the threat of violence has been substantially reduced. More important still, women and families constituting a significant percentage of spectators in American sports has raised the threshold of shame for exhibiting violent behavior and voicing racially offensive language in sports venues across the board. Though England's and Germany's top soccer leagues have not yet experienced the influx of women that has reached American proportions, there is now such a critical mass that the acceptability of fights and other acts of physical violence has declined. The role of women as civilizing agents, as active carriers of cosmopolitan thought and behavior, of curtailing men from behaving badly, should not

---

[129] Poli, "The Denationalization of Sport," p. 652.

be underestimated as major contributors to the reduction of violence at soccer matches.[130]

There is one remaining fault line that neither the United States nor Europe has been able to reduce, let alone eliminate, from its respective hegemonic sports cultures: homophobia. Not only are homophobe taunts by spectators still acceptable on both sides of the Atlantic, but no prominent active player in any of these sports has openly admitted to being gay. The stigma of this is still so great that when rumors arose about Mike Piazza, a certain first-ballot Hall of Fame baseball star, being gay, he promptly proceeded to call a news conference to dispel them and assert his heterosexuality by subsequently being conspicuously photographed in the company of attractive young women.[131] Shortly after concluding his stellar career, Piazza got married.

To end this chapter on a positive note, we believe that the comparative study of sports-related racism and violence confirms and reinforces our broader argument that hegemonic sports constitute an important force within popular culture and do in fact facilitate cosmopolitan change. Com-

---

[130] Markovits experienced a particularly poignant instance where the presence of women most definitely prevented a tense situation from mutating into a violent one. At the end of the Croatia vs. Turkey quarterfinal match at the European National Championship in Vienna's Ernst-Happel Stadium, Croatian fans in the section where Markovits sat, were taunting and insulting the victorious Turkish players. They had come to greet their supporters a few rows in front of the irate Croatian fans, whose team had just lost the game in a real heartbreaker. Things were getting heated and turning quite ugly when a particularly distraught Croatian fan appeared ready to descend to the Turks and escalate the confrontation. At that point, one of the women among the Croatian fans just placed her hand on this man's shoulder, gesturing to him to cool down, to desist, giving him a pat and indicating to him to just let it go, that it was painful for the Croatians to lose but not worth commencing a fight with all its adverse consequences. And sure enough, the man—still hurt and irate and upset about his team's loss—did just that. He and his friends simply walked away. Had the situation not been such a major event—in which women in Europe have come to attend in greater numbers over the past few years—and had this contest been a regular club game, to which this man's girlfriend or wife or sister would have been much less likely to go since such games still attract mainly male fans, things could have easily (and quite likely would have) escalated into violence. Rensmann can recount many similar examples from German and Italian soccer venues. These observations are especially relevant in light of the fact that since the 1980s there is a significant rise in female spectatorship in European soccer stadiums.

[131] For a superb account of the (in)famous Fowler – Le Saux incident in English football concerning homophobia and its related ramifications, see Georg Spitaler, "'Lads' vs. Metrosexuals'—Fußball als maskulines Melodrama am Beispiel des Fowler-Le Saux Zwischenfalls," in Birgit Sauer and Eva-Maria Knoll, eds., Ritualisierungen von Geschlecht (Vienna: Facultas Universitätsverlag, 2006), pp. 163–80. And recount our mentioning the John Amaechi case in the previous chapter as an example of a journeyman NBA player's coming out of the closet after his active days in the league.

pared to other social spheres, hegemonic sports provide relatively easy access to (and for) immigrants and ethnic minorities in the global age. In the long run, ethnic minorities are able to enhance their visibility, gain respect and social recognition through sports in increasingly multiethnic postindustrial societies. Despite the continued threat by counter-cosmopolitans in countries in which immigrant sports heroes have acquired considerable standing over time, sports' merit-based cosmopolitanism has furthered progressive developments in culture, society, and politics.

CHAPTER 6 ◇◇◇◇◇◇◇◇◇◇◇◇◇◇◇◇◇◇◇◇◇◇◇◇◇◇◇◇

THE LIMITS OF GLOBALIZATION

LOCAL IDENTITY AND COLLEGE SPORTS' UNIQUELY AMERICAN SYMBIOSIS OF ACADEMICS AND ATHLETICS

Much of this book centers on comparisons between Europe and the United States as, arguably, the most important players in the two globalization eras that comprise the framework of our study. America and Europe are quite similar to each other, yet also different.[1] One difference pertains to a historical phenomenon that has puzzled so many European observers of America: why the United States constitutes the only advanced industrial democracy with no large-scale socialist and/or social democratic and/or communist parties and movements co-defining its politics, society, economy, and culture from the onset of industrialization. As Werner Sombart asks, Why there is no socialism in the United States?[2] Markovits then extended the Sombartian question to the world of soccer, asking why the United States, that most sports-obsessed of all societies, never had soccer develop as its main sports language as did so many countries in the world.[3] Of course, socialist, social democratic, and communist parties have indeed

---

[1] Of course these differences pale when both—or either—of these two continents is compared to the rest of the world. Viewed on a global scale, the gaps between Europe and America comprise a wonderful example of what Freud so presciently called the narcissism of small differences.

[2] Werner Sombart, *Why Is There No Socialism in the United States?* (White Plains, NY: International Arts and Sciences Press, 1976).

[3] Andrei S. Markovits "The Other 'American Exceptionalism': Why Is There No Soccer in the United States?," *International Journal for the History of Sports* 7 (2), Fall 1990, pp. 230–64.

existed in the United States, as has soccer. But both of these constructs never attained the importance that their counterparts did in Europe. From there, both began their successful global journeys, which never quite included the United States. Thus, while both socialism and soccer remained marginal in America, it would be erroneous to construe their respective "exceptions" as exclusions. Pursuant to the previously mentioned framework of institutionalization and diffusion, soccer in the United States became readily "accepted" in terms of its institutionalization though never "prevalently diffused" in its culture, whereas socialism remained "uncommon" and "inappropriate" both in its institutionalization and its diffusion.[4]

But there exists in fact an exception in contemporary American culture that is truly unique and unparalleled anywhere in the world—way beyond Europe, originator of socialism, social democracy, and communism on the one hand and soccer on the other. This American uniqueness centers on the phenomenon of college sports, featuring three team games in particular: football, men's basketball, and, to a much lesser extent and regionally limited, men's hockey, the three "revenue" sports. Their presence has become integral to America's sports space. They constitute such an essential part of American culture well beyond the playing fields and television screens that life without them in America is almost unthinkable.

More than any aspect of American sports and culture, it is the world of college sports that finds absolutely no parallels anywhere on earth, Oxford and Cambridge included. Indeed, America's singular successes at the Olympic Games over more than a 110-year period, which have amassed 2,514 medals (1,000 more than the runner-up Russian Empire/Soviet Union/Russia) originate from the world of college sports. Whereas other nations create their Olympians via centralized plans designed and administered by state-run sports ministries, a network of sports clubs covering the entire country (the aforementioned Vereine in the German-speaking world), and usually a combination of the two, the primary source for American Olympians is college sports. American colleges have often provided the athletic home for Olympians representing a bevy of countries other than the United States. Thus, for example, Stanford University featured a total of forty-eight enrolled and former students at the 2008 Beijing Olympics, which amounted to a number greater than that of any university in the United States, quite likely the world.[5] Representing eight

---

[4] See Colyvas and Jonsson, "Ubiquity and Legitimacy: Disentangling Diffusion and Institutionalization."

[5] "Stanford's Deep Bench: Thinking about Playing," *Stanford Report* 41 (9), November 19, 2008, p. 10.

countries, these athletes took home 25 medals, which would have placed Stanford, were it a country, at number 12 in the rankings of medal winners, behind the Ukraine's 27 but well ahead of the Netherlands's 16 demonstrating yet again how colleges in American sports assume very similar roles and identities to clubs in Europe.

Recall, as we mentioned in chapter 2, how the two Milanese clubs, Inter and AC, were hosts to a bevy of international players—all of whom represented their home countries in the World Cup, professional soccer's equivalent to the Olympics. If anything, the trend of student-athletes from around the world availing themselves of the sports facilities and athletic opportunities offered by American colleges has increased over the past few years and shows all signs of becoming even more prominent in the future, as we will see at the conclusion of this chapter. In short, no country in the world has combined first-rate athletics and academics for the past 150 years the way the United States has. While this unique synthesis and symbiosis is most certainly not always as brilliant and exemplary as Hans Ulrich ("Sepp") Gumbrecht claims it to be, at least in the case of his beloved Stanford University—which he believes embodies an institution that offers a singular unity between intellectual and physical pursuits not witnessed anywhere since ancient Athens[6]—we do not view college sports as an inherent corruption of the educational mission and the venal undermining of the very essence of American universities as so many of our colleagues have.[7] Big-time sports have been part and parcel of American universities—and *only* American universities—for more than a century. They show no signs of disappearing anytime soon nor, do we believe, should they.

We will start this chapter by presenting data to demonstrate the sheer size of college sports in America, particularly (though not exclusively) the Big Two of men's basketball and football. Bespeaking the immense, indeed revolutionary, change over the past three decades in terms of women's ad-

---

[6] See his wonderful book, *In Praise of Athletic Beauty* (Cambridge, MA: Harvard University Press, 2006).

[7] While there are many books and even more articles berating the evils of college sports for American higher education, we will list only those that we found the most interesting: Andrew Zimbalist, *Unpaid Professionals: Commercialism and Conflict in Big-Time College Sports* (Princeton: Princeton University Press, 2001); Murray Sperber, *Beer and Circus: How Big-Time College Sports Has Crippled Undergraduate Education* (New York: Holt, 2001); James J. Duderstadt, *Intercollegiate Athletics and the American University; A University President's Perspective* (Ann Arbor: University of Michigan Press, 2003); James L. Shulman and William G. Bowen, *The Game of Life: College Sports and Educational Values* (Princeton: Princeton University Press, 2002); and William G. Bowen, Sarah A. Levin, James L. Shulman, and Colin G. Campbell, *Reclaiming the Game: College Sports and Educational Values* (Princeton: Princeton University Press, 2005).

vances in virtually all aspects of public life in the United States, a word about women's basketball at Division I colleges is in order. It sure seems worlds away that little Immaculata College of Pennsylvania, a Catholic women's school, won the first three national women's collegiate basketball championships in the late 1970s playing under the aegis of the long-defunct AIAW, which we encountered in our chapter on women's soccer. Of course, the NCAA did not even recognize women's collegiate basketball until 1982. In the three ensuing decades, the women's game has come to draw nearly 20,000 spectators when basketball powerhouses like the Lady Vols of the University of Tennessee, the Lady Huskies of the University of Connecticut, and standouts such as Stanford, North Carolina, Duke, and Maryland play at home as well as on the road. The bitter rivalry between the University of Tennessee and the University of Connecticut—far and away the two most successful programs in women's college basketball over the past two decades—has in the meantime become one of the classic rivalries (derbies) in all of American college sports, and perhaps well beyond that. The antipathy between the two coaches, Pat Summitt of Tennessee and Geno Auriemma of Connecticut, is well-known to all conversant with American sports—once again demonstrating the immense rise in the importance of women's sports over the past two to three decades. Every game of the women's championship tournament in March has been regularly televised by ESPN. In notable contrast to women's Division I soccer, which we discussed in chapter 4, women's collegiate basketball has indeed become a noticeable player in the contemporary world of American college sports and thus the larger construct of American sports culture. Despite these amazing gains, the women's game is still nowhere close to the two giants of men's college basketball and football, which are really sui generis in every conceivable and measurable dimension.

It will become obvious merely by virtue of our data on the value of the top teams, the advertising revenue that these teams and their sports generate, the number of viewers both in the stadiums and on television that they attract, and select other items that are an integral part of contemporary American culture and society, what huge players these two college sports have become in America's sports space. In order to highlight the uniqueness of the construct called American college sports, we will also introduce data from Canada and Britain. These are two countries in which college sports exist in a meaningful way beyond informal arrangements among university students, yet remain totally unnoticed by anybody but the participants themselves and have absolutely no importance in the rest of society and culture. Such constructs are present, of course, in arguably every country in the world. For instance, university games have been held on a regular basis for decades, and the Germans celebrated national university Olympics in the 1920s. Bespeaking the unimportance of these events in contrast to their American counterparts, these university sports remain understudied.

Our comparison of American college sports with those in Canada and Britain (which, with its Oxford and Cambridge universities, played a crucial role in inventing and establishing this genre in the first place) will serve to delineate how unique a culture and construct American college sports really are in the English-speaking world, let alone the world at large. In the subsequent segment of this chapter, we will provide a very brief account as to the reasons and historical developments that rendered college sports in America so crucial to its sports culture and culture in general. We will then conclude our chapter with an observation that corroborates the overall argument of our book: American college sports have in recent years become magnates for foreign students, who arrive in the United States to participate as student-athletes and thus help perpetuate and enrich this unique phenomenon.

The point is that even this most local of cultural constructs—American college sports—that exists nowhere else in the world, remains subject to the forces of globalization and thus is contained within the world of global languages while at the same time reveling in its localized traditions. College sports have also become glocalized in the wake of the second globalization.

The Behemoth of American College Sports: A Powerful Cultural Force All Its Own

There were more than 380,000 NCAA-registered college athletes in the United States in 2007. (The number grows to 430,000 if we include those that play under the umbrella of the much smaller National Association of Intercollegiate Athletics.) These student-athletes participated in 17,625 officially registered, NCAA-accredited varsity teams including men's, women's, and coed combined sports. Of these, 6,213 teams belonged to Division I schools representing men's, women's, and coed combined sports. There were 1,033 so-called "active members" in the NCAA, denoting all institutions of postsecondary education in the country that were allowed to compete for NCAA championships at all three divisional levels. Of these, 329 institutions represented Division I active members. Total NCAA membership, which includes all active members in addition to all provisional members, conferences, and other voting members, consisted of 1,281 institutions.[8]

The vast majority of these 380,000 student-athletes, their sports, and their teams have continued to operate from the very beginning of their discipline's college-level history as amateurs in the purest sense of this nineteenth century, upper-class concept. This means that these student-athletes commit to their sport in a purely Kantian manner—for the sheer pleasure of performing it, for no ulterior motives, with no extraneous interests, and with the process of participation far outweighing the achieved results in importance to all, that is, themselves, their competitors, spectators, and institutions. Much of this world remains totally confined to the participants and activists themselves, far from any public recognition and involvement and with virtually no spectatorship of any significance. In a very real sense, the vast majority of American college sports still conforms to that nineteenth-century ideal of *mens sana in corpore sano* (a healthy mind in a healthy body), a true amateurism in which "doing" and "participating" far outweigh "following" and "spectating" and where the sport continues to be defined by its practitioners and not its spectators and followers. Above all, these student-athletes derive no monetary remuneration of any kind for their performance in their sports at their institutions. One might, of course, argue that varsity athletes are not "real" amateurs in the strictest sense of that term since they are "paid" by their respective universities (excepting those comprising the Ivy League and a few others)[9] in the form of "athletic scholarships" to perform a certain task representing the university and that the true amateurs are only those college students who engage in intercollegiate club sports that are not supported by their universities, receive no athletic scholarships, do not play to adoring crowds, and organize their practices, games, schedules, leagues, and travel themselves with minimal, if any, "adult" leadership and help. While the club phenomenon is actually growing in the world of American college culture and thus constitutes part and parcel of America's sports exception related to college sports, we do not include club sports in our presentation of college sports and confine ourselves solely to its varsity variant.[10]

[8] Composition & Sport Sponsorship of the NCAA. http://www1.ncaa.orgmembership/membership_svcs/membership_breakdown.html#sponsorship. Retrieved August 30, 2008.

[9] And in the Ivies, too, being good at sports and able to play them at a varsity level, has very tangible, if not monetary, benefits in that such abilities much enhance the probability of acceptance by these desired institutions.

[10] Bill Pennington, "Rapid Rise in College Club Teams Creates a Whole New Level of Success," *New York Times*, December 2, 2008: "College club sports are swiftly rising in popu-

Like the world of soccer in America (which, of course, has been a main-stay of college sports in the United States throughout the twentieth century, exhibiting all the features of this phenomenon that we just delineated), some college sports have also experienced their quadrennial "Olympianization," and actually become featured venues at the Olympic Games. Thus, during every Olympics, college swimmers, track and field athletes, and gymnasts in particular attain an importance and recognition that reaches well beyond the confines of their campuses and their specific sports. But they do so not by dint of the popularity of their discipline as a spectator sport, but by virtue of representing the United States or, as already mentioned, increasingly other countries as well, in the crucial international competition that the Olympics have become. In other words, these athletes gain a temporal attention by a wider audience because it says "USA" on their jerseys, essentially because of their laundry, to use Jerry Seinfeld's apt characterization. But with the Olympic Games over, even medal-winning swimmers, track and field athletes, and gymnasts revert to their pre-Olympics obscurity and recede to the bounded world of their college sport. An NCAA Public Service Announcement best characterizes the participation-driven, profoundly amateur-natured world of American college athletics by stating: "There are more than 380,000 student-athletes and just about all of them go pro in something other than sports."[11] One can also add, "and just about all of these athletes will never be famous, even on their own college campuses, let alone the country or the world."

In addition to this just-depicted world of college athletics, in which the values of nineteenth-century amateurism continue to thrive and remain hegemonic, there exists a different world that, in a way, has only a tangential relationship to the former. There are two sports in particular that have emerged as sui generis in the unique world of college sports: football and men's basketball. Interestingly, the third major sport of the American Big Four in popular sports culture, baseball, has rapidly gained importance in college sports in the past twenty to thirty years. In a sense it has regained some of the significance that it once possessed in the 1850s through

---

larity, a largely unnoticed phenomenon sweeping across campuses nationwide. These are not intramural sports but expertly organized, highly skilled teams that often belong to regional conferences and play for national collegiate championships.... An estimated two million college students play competitive club sports compared with about 430,000 involved in athletics governed by the National Collegiate Athletic Association and the National Association of Intercollegiate Athletics."

[11] Myles Brand, "Celebrating the Student-Athlete Provides Motivation to Excel." *The NCAA News*, January 2006. http://www.ncaa.org/wps/ncaa?ContentID=1189. Retrieved August 30, 2008.

1870s—before it lost its position of prominence to the rapid onslaught of football on campus. We will give some data from college baseball just as we will from college hockey, which, though regional in its presence on college campuses, has played a culturally important role well beyond the confines of college life in the New England states, New York, Ohio, Michigan, Minnesota, Wisconsin, North Dakota, Colorado and Alaska.[12]

"Amateurs" and Serious Money

Sports-related revenues for the 123 colleges and universities listed as Division I-A by the Department of Education amounted to nearly $5 billion in 2007. Of this sum, college football alone brought in over $2 billion in 2007–8, with men's basketball accounting for over $600 million in the same season. Baseball weighed in at almost $65 million, more than double hockey's still very respectable $25 million.[13] There were 242 Division I football teams in 2007–8 (combining the 123 Division I-A teams, now belonging to FBS with the 119 Division I-AA teams now placed in the Football Championship Subdivision [FCS]) and 341 Division I basketball teams.[14]

Forbes Magazine has begun to compile some interesting statistics on the valuation of college football teams. It is based on what these football programs contributed in 2007 to four important beneficiaries: their university (the value of contributions from football to the institution for academic purposes, including scholarship payments for football players); athletic department (the net profit generated by the football program ultimately retained by the department); conference (the distribution of bowl game revenue); and local communities with a vested interest in the team (incremental spending in the county during home-game weekends). The top-five college football programs weigh in as follows:

1. Notre Dame   Value: $101 million   Profit: $45.80 million
2. Texas   Value: $92 million   Profit: $46.20 million
3. Georgia   Value: $90 million   Profit: $43.50 million
4. Michigan   Value: $85 million   Profit: $36.20 million
5. Florida   Value: $84 million   Profit: $38.20 million

[12] We would be remiss not to mention in this context the fascinating case of the "Chargers" of the University of Alabama in Huntsville who have represented this school as solid participants in Division I men's ice hockey for years and have competed on an equal footing with the very best college teams in the country on a regular basis.

[13] http://ope.ed.gov/athletics/screen_detail.asp. Retrieved July 24, 2008.

[14] NCAA Sports Sponsorship. *NCAA.* http://web1.ncaa.org/onlineDir/exec/sponsorship?sortOrder=0&division=1&sport=MBB. Retrieved August 30, 2008.

The overall value of the top-twenty college football teams amounts to $2.8 billion. The total profit for the same top-twenty programs tallies at a hefty $515 million.[15]

Revenue received by American colleges whose football teams participated in the thirty-two bowls concluding the 2007–8 season amounted to an estimated $225 million.[16]

Following the exact same four-headed beneficiary formula that *Forbes* developed to measure the valuation of the top-twenty college football teams, the magazine devised a parallel scale for the top-twenty college men's basketball programs. As expected, the numbers are far smaller than in football, but still considerable. The top-five programs are:[17]

1. North Carolina $ 26.0 million
2. Kentucky $ 24.9 million
3. Louisville $ 24.4 million
4. Arizona $ 22.7 million
5. Duke $ 12.6 million

In terms of revenue from merchandising, which is almost exclusively due to a university's prowess in its two flagship sports of football and men's basketball, college sports generate $3 billion annually.[18] The University of Texas led the way in 2005–6 with $8.2 million in merchandise sales.[19] Texas maintained its lead in 2006–7 but was closely followed by Notre Dame, Florida, Michigan, Georgia, and North Carolina comprising, of course, not by coincidence, the top-five schools of *Forbes*'s football list followed by its basketball leader, North Carolina.

In the summer of 2008, The University of Michigan began an eight-year contract with Adidas. For the duration of the contract, Adidas will provide the university with $7.5 million annually in cash and equipment, putting the total value of the contract at $60 million.[20] This is the largest contract that Adidas has signed with any American university's varsity

[15] "Notre Dame Football Program Ranked Most Valuable In College Football, http://und.cstv.com/sports/m-footbl/spec-rel/112007aag.html. Retrieved August 30, 2008.

[16] *NCAA Football.com*. http://www.ncaafootball.com/index.php?s=&url_channel_id=348url_article_id=119948change_well_id=2. Retrieved July 27, 2007.

[17] "Terrapin Basketball Among Nation's Most Valuable Programs," http://umterps.cstv.com/sports/m-baskbl/spec-rel/010308aab.html. Retrieved August 30, 2008.

[18] Anthony Clark, "UF to Make Cool Cash Off Hot Sports Merchandise," *Gainesville Sun*, January 2007. www.gainesville.com. Retrieved August 30, 2008

[19] Bill Sullivan, "Top Universities by Merchandise Sales," *Get Listy*, June 2008. http://www.getlisty.com/top-universities-by-merchandise-sales/. Retrieved August 30, 2008.

[20] http://www.press.adidas.com/DesktopDefault.aspx/tabid-11/16_read-8081%20retrieved%20on%20July%2030. Retrieved July 30, 2008.

sports teams. And barely a few weeks after this arrangement with Adidas went into effect, the world learned that the international sports marketing and media giant IMG signed a twelve-year contract with the University of Michigan in which IMG will pay $86 million to permit the company to run the University's game-day radio broadcasts, the coaches' television and radio shows, and all Internet-related activities connected to its sports teams, hospitality, and corporate sponsorships.[21]

College football and men's basketball's magnitude in American culture as measured by television-based advertising revenues has been nothing short of astounding. Lest we bore the reader with too many numbers, we have placed some helpful data corroborating this point into a footnote.[22]

[21] John Heuser, "U-M OKs Marketing Deal: IMG to Pay $86 Million for 12 Years." *Ann Arbor News*, August 5, 2008.

[22] In 2006, advertisers had to pay $2.5 million for a thirty-second spot in Super Bowl XL. For the championship game in the NCAA men's basketball tournament, a thirty-second commercial cost $1.1 million, the only event on American television other than the Super Bowl that reached over the $1 million mark. The semifinal games exacted $653 thousand for a thirty-second spot—less than such time slots during the NFL's AFC and NFC Championship games ($900–$956 thousand) but more than the NFL Divisional Playoff games ($547–$600 thousand). Thirty-second ads during college football's BCS Bowl games covered the relatively large spread between $268 thousand and $530 thousand, depending on the importance of each game's outcome for the national championship. That year, the NBA finals pulled in $359 thousand and the MLB World Series landed $400 thousand per thirty-second commercials. In other words, college basketball and football games during the final stages of their respective seasons exact a higher price from television advertisers than do anything else on television (sports related or not) other than the NFL's Super Bowl and its AFC and NFC Championship games. By 2007, men's college basketball surpassed the Super Bowl and the World Series for the very first time in terms of total revenue obtained from television advertising. Whereas the Super Bowl garnered $151.5 million and the four World Series games a total of $156.6 million, the three final-four games attained a total of $168.4 million. This is lofty company indeed.

The total postseason advertising revenue garnered by the NCAA Men's basketball in 2006 ($497 million, increasing to $519.6 million one year later) exceeded that of the NBA's postseason that same year ($424 million), the NFL's including the Super Bowl ($423 million), and MLB's fall playoffs and World Series ($382 million). The $662 million obtained by men's college basketball for the entire 2005–6 season surpassed that of college football's $506 million and only trails the NFL's $2,041 million. There are many more college basketball than college football games, a factor which almost certainly accounts for that particular discrepancy. It is also interesting that in the case of college basketball, the NCAA tournament accounts for 75 percent of these revenues, with the postseason bowl games in college football only comprising 22 percent of the seasonal total. The NFL's postseason also weighs in at 21 percent (the Super Bowl alone counts for 8 percent). These numbers demonstrate emphatically that for both footballs—college and professional—regular season games are much more valued than in college basketball. Figures for the NBA are quite comparable to those of the college game. With an eleven- to twelve-game season in college football and a sixteen-game season in the NFL—compared to a thirty-plus-game season in college basketball and an eighty-two-game season in the NBA—the value in advertising per game corresponds remarkably well to each game's value for the season's eventual outcome and final standings. "TNS

Live spectatorship for both sports has been equally impressive and continues to grow consistently. In 2008, the Men's Division I Basketball Tournament (better known as March Madness) boasted a live attendance of 763,607—an average spectatorship of 21,817 per game. These data represented an increase from the 2007 total live audience of 696,992, an average per game attendance of 19,914. The small but steady annual increase in the spectatorship of this tournament has been a reliable phenomenon for decades. During the 2006–7 regular season, Division I men's basketball attained a total attendance of almost 28 million for an average of nearly 6,000 fans per game.[23]

Division I football saw a total attendance of over 43 million fans in the 2007 season, amounting to nearly 15 percent of the entire population of the United States.[24] The overall attendance at all thirty-two bowl games for the 2007–8 season was 1.7 million. To underline the sheer magnitude of college football as part of America's sports culture, indeed its culture as a whole, it might be helpful to mention the staggering numbers attained by leading football programs in every single one of their team's completely sold-out home games over decades. It is telling of college football's popularity that the numbers for each of the venues to follow are averages that are equal to their total capacities, or actually surpass them. First and foremost, there is the University of Michigan's Michigan Stadium (the "Big House"), which officially seats 107,501 spectators. Attendance almost always swells beyond that, particularly in marquee games against archrivals Ohio State, Michigan State, and Notre Dame. Three further stadiums seat more than 100,000 spectators: Penn State's Beaver Stadium with an official seating capacity of 107,282; Tennessee's Neyland Stadium with 104,079; and Ohio State's Ohio Stadium, the "Horseshoe" with 101,568.[25] Venues for five colleges (Georgia, LSU, Alabama, USC, and Florida) accommodate more than 90,000 spectators; and three more (Texas, Auburn, and Nebraska) seat over 85,000.

To place these numbers into proper comparisons, none of the NFL's venues exceed an 80,000 capacity, and Europe's largest stadium, the venerable Camp Nou in Barcelona, weighs in at 98,772. Only five others have a

Media Intelligence Releases March Madness Advertising Trends Report," *TNS MediaIntelligence*, March 2007. http://www.adscope.com/news/03062007.htm. Retrieved August 30, 2008.

[23] "Men's Basketball Attendance." *NCAA*. http://www.ncaa.org/wps/ncaa?ContentID=1093. Retrieved August 30, 2008.

[24] *NCAA.org*. http://www.ncaa.org/wps/wcm/connect/resources/file/eb04d809ac57460/2007/FBattendance.pdf?MOD=AJPERE. Retrieved July 31, 2008.

[25] "100,000+ Stadiums," http://www.worldstadiums.com/stadium_menu/stadium_list/100000.shtml. Retrieved August 30, 2008.

capacity beyond 80,000. Among the top-ten stadiums in the world, four feature American college football, and among the top twenty, ten belong to this uniquely American institution. Only the Rungrado May Day Stadium in Pyongyang, North Korea (capacity of 150,000), and the Salt Lake Stadium in Kolkata, India (120,000), surpass the University of Michigan's Big House. The size of these college football venues, and the fact that they are consistently sold out for every game, provides ample testimony for the immense popularity of this sport.[26] But perhaps nothing bespeaks the cultural power of college football more emphatically than the fact that each April millions of fans go to these stadiums to watch their beloved teams engage in a meaningless practice game—with 90,000 at the Horseshoe and 60,000 at the Big House being the norm.

A brief presentation of television data demonstrates the immense popularity enjoyed by these two college sports. College basketball's attraction on television has been spectacular since the late 1960s. Much of this started with the legendary UCLA dynasty anchored by Lew Alcindor (better known, perhaps, by his later name of Kareem Abdul-Jabbar). Indeed, it was the so-called "Game of the Century" between the undefeated UCLA Bruins led by Alcindor and the equally undefeated University of Houston Cougars featuring Elvin Hayes on January 30, 1968, that was the very first NCAA regular season basketball game telecast nationwide in prime time. It also established college basketball as a first-class television sports attraction across the United States and paved the way for the modern "March Madness" television success.

In addition to drawing 52,629 to Houston's Astrodome for this venue's very first basketball game, the showdown attracted a vast television audience and catapulted men's college basketball into the premier ranks of American television programs way beyond sports. To wit, men's college basketball has since that time regularly outperformed the NBA's television presence with the exception of the latter's Celtics vs. Lakers showdowns of the 1980s and the Michael Jordan-led Chicago Bulls finals of the 1990s, both of which attained immense ratings successes. Since 1975 the average television viewership for the March Madness championship game never fell below 22 million and reached as high as 35 million. The 1979 championship game between Michigan State, led by the inimitable Earvin "Magic" Johnson, and Indiana State, featuring the equally superb Larry Bird, at-

---

[26] Pierre Gottschlich, "Michigan Stadium—Eine Pilgerstätte des College Football," lecture delivered at the Institut für Verwaltungswissenschaften, University of Rostock, Germany (January 22, 2008).

tracted 35.11 million television viewers. That figure set a record for viewers of any basketball game—college, professional or otherwise—on American television that continues to remain intact to this very day.[27] Without citing similar data for the regular season, we can still conclude that men's college basketball has embodied a very eminent, and consistently growing, role in American sports culture.[28]

If anything, college football on television is more prominent still. One-hundred-twenty-nine million households tuned in to watch the thirty-two bowl games concluding the 2007–8 college football season. The average number of households watching a bowl game on ESPN was 2,866,410. On ESPN2, 1,502,134 households viewed bowl games at the end of this season. ESPN on ABC—arguably the most important network on American television showing college football—featured the Rose Bowl and the Capital One Bowl, which attracted viewerships of 12,531,880 and 10,301,679 households respectively.

The national championship game played in New Orleans and televised by Fox attracted 16,291,263 households. During the regular season, ESPN and ABC averaged 4,364,148 households per game. The equivalent number for ESPN on its own was 2,013,687 and for ESPN2 it was 1,027,368. CBS, the main outlet for the South Eastern Conference's (SEC) football games, received an average national household rating/share of 3.5/8, meaning that 3.5 percent of all televisions in America and 8 percent of televisions turned on at the time watched these SEC broadcasts. The most watched game of the season, the November 24th Missouri vs. Kansas showdown, landed 10,960,755 viewers. One week later, the Oklahoma vs. Missouri contest attained 10,841,849 viewers.[29] The Michigan vs. Ohio

[27] In the years since that UCLA vs. Houston regular season game in 1968, which was reprised with an equal amount of public interest and attention in the March tournament of that very season, there have been a number of NCAA finals beyond the just-mentioned Michigan State vs. Indiana State game that have attracted 30 million plus viewers on national television. UCLA vs. Kentucky in 1975; North Carolina vs. Georgetown in 1982; North Carolina State vs. Houston in 1983; Villanova vs. Georgetown in 1985; Michigan vs. Seton Hall in 1989; Duke vs. Michigan in 1992; North Carolina vs. Michigan in 1993; and Arkansas vs. Duke in 1994.
[28] Here are the viewing totals from the first round tournament games through the regional finals from 2001 to 2007: 2001 – 8.0 million; 2002 – 8.5 million; 2003 – 7.2 million; 2004 – 8.4 million; 2005 – 9.7 million; 2006 – 8.8 million; and 2007 – 8.3 million. Bill Gorman, "NCAA Men's Basketball TV Ratings, 1975-2008," *TV by the Numbers*, April 15, 2008. http://tvbythenumbers.com/2008/04/15/ncaa-mens-basketball-tv-ratings-1975-2007/2844. Retrieved August 30, 2008.
[29] *NCAA Football.com*. http://www.ncaafootball.com/index.php?s=&url_channel_id=348url_article_id=119948change_well_id=2. Retrieved July 27, 2008.

State game in 2006 was viewed by nearly 15 million households nationwide,[30] and the University of Miami vs. Notre Dame game in 1989 attracted nearly 14 million American households. In 1993, Notre Dame vs. Florida State drew over 16 million households to their television sets.[31] The Texas vs. USC Rose Bowl contest of 2006 attained an astounding 21.7 rating. This game was only surpassed in television viewership by the 1987 Fiesta Bowl between Penn State and Miami, which gained a 25.1 rating. The1986 Rose Bowl contest between UCLA and Iowa received a 22.7 rating,[32] and the Ohio State vs. USC Rose Bowl of 1980 garnered a 28.6 rating.[33]

These ratings are truly impressive and bespeak the immense popularity of major college football games, particularly at the all-important year-end bowls. With the notable exception of the Super Bowls, virtually no other sports programming on American television—most assuredly neither the World Series nor the NBA Finals (never mind the Stanley Cup championship round)—has surpassed the massive television audiences consistently garnered by the year-end tournaments in men's college basketball and football.[34]

Not in the Same League: Sports at Canadian and British Universities

Let us conclude this section with a very brief presentation of the Canadian and British cases to highlight the uniqueness of college sports in America.[35]

[30] Associated Press, "UM-OSU Most-Watched Regular Season Game since '93," November 19, 2006, *ESPN.com* http://sports.espn.go.com/ncf/news/story?id=2668704. Retrieved August 30, 2008.

[31] Richard Sandomir, "TV SPORTS: Rating To Match Football Rankings," *New York Times*, November 16, 1993. http://query.nytimes.com/gst/fullpage.html?res=9F0CE1D9143 AF935A25752C1A965958260. Retrieved August 30, 2008.

[32] Associated Press, "Rose Bowl Gets Top TV Rating." *New York Times*, January 6, 2006. http://www.nytimes.com/2006/01/06/sports/ncaafootball/06ratings.html?_r=2&oref=slogin &oref=slogin. Retrieved August 30, 2008.

[33] "Fiesta Bowl Sets Record for TV," *New York Times*, January 6, 1987. http://query.ny-times.com/gst/fullpage.html?res=9B0DE7DA123CF935A35752C0A961948260. Retrieved August 30, 2008.

[34] In November 2008, ESPN successfully outbid FOX to air college football's Bowl Championship games from 2011 to 2014 for a reported sum of $125 million a year, which exceeds by $45 million what FOX had been paying yearly for the right to televise these games from 2007 to 2010. The new agreement with ESPN covers the Fiesta, Orange, and Sugar bowls each year and the BCS title game from 2011 to 2013. The Rose Bowl will continue to be televised on ESPN's broadcast partner ABC through 2014 under a separate, previous contract. Rachel Cohen, "Bowl Championship Series Games Will Move to ESPN Starting in January 2011," Associated Press, November 18, 2008.

[35] In our attempt to ascertain the uniqueness of American college sports, even in the con-

The Canadian Interuniversity Sport (CIS) program (Canada's equivalent of the NCAA) has twenty-six participating universities in football, forty-three in men's basketball, and thirty-three in men's hockey.[36] It should be noted that Canadian universities play, of course, the Canadian version of football, which is similar to its American variant though not identical to it. Thus, by mere quantity, the Canadian participation is much smaller than the American. But by any other measure of importance as well, Canadian college sports assume a lesser role than their American equivalents.

Take Canada's national sport, hockey. The thirty-three men's college programs do not come close in popular importance and media coverage to the many junior hockey leagues and other venues wherein this game is played, not to mention its presence in the National Hockey League. Indeed, the country's best hockey players rarely, if ever, reach the NHL via hockey at Canadian universities. Instead, Canada's top hockey talent eschews going to university and enters the NHL via junior hockey and—increasingly and tellingly—through playing college hockey at American universities. College hockey in Canada remains a low-key pastime for its participants, who represent their respective universities barely noticed by the world outside the campus walls. And even on campus, there is virtually no involvement with a university's hockey team on the part of that university's students, alumni, and alumnae. Hockey, which constitutes Canada's national passion and identity much beyond a mere sport, has a meek and all but irrelevant existence at the nation's colleges and universities.[37]

---

text of university life and culture in other English-speaking democracies, we also looked at Australia, where we noticed the following situation: the University of Sydney actually fields cricket and rugby teams but has to do so in local club competitions precisely because there is no other university that can produce a team. Needless to say, the clubs against which the University of Sydney competes are strictly amateur and Sydney-based. No more than fifty or sixty people attend any of the University's cricket games and rugby matches, with the possibility of a few hundred appearing for a final. When the University won the Sydney club cricket championship in 2004, which is a considerable achievement since it affirmed the university's team as the best amateur cricket club in this large city, the achievement was not publicized anywhere on campus and interested parties had to turn to the *Sydney Morning Herald* to learn more about it. In fact, the competition in rugby union and rowing between elite private secondary schools in Sydney gets more spectators and more media attention than university sports. The situation is no different in Melbourne or any other large Australian city. We owe many thanks to David Smith for his helpful insights in this matter.

[36] "CIS News," *Canadian Interuniversity Sport*. http://www.universitysport.ca/e/index.cfm. Retrieved August 2, 2008.

[37] We gratefully acknowledge Jason Botterill's expertise on this topic. Assistant General Manager for the Pittsburgh Penguins, Botterill spent all his life in the world of hockey. His trajectory and career confirms our point. He grew up in Winnipeg in the province of Manitoba, and excelled at junior hockey there. Then he attended the University of Michigan on an athletic scholarship, where he helped the Wolverines win an NCAA Division I men's hockey

The same pertains to college football. When the Vancouver-based crosstown rivals Simon Fraser University and the University of British Columbia played in the Shrum Bowl (the city's derby so to speak) in 2001, the attendance was about 2,500, barely filling half of Swangard Stadium's capacity of 4,972. Meanwhile, south of the border on the very same day, 72,500 spectators packed Husky Stadium in Seattle (the official capacity of the stadium is listed at 72,469) rooting for their beloved University of Washington Huskies against their cross-state rivals, the Cougars of Washington State. Later that year, Canadian college football's premier event, the Vanier Cup, between the Huskies of St. Mary's University and the Bisons of the University of Manitoba, attracted 19,000 spectators—where they all but disappeared in Toronto's cavernous Skydome, featuring a seating capacity of 50,516. The same day, the University of Miami played against the University of Nebraska in the Rose Bowl for the unofficial United States men's college football national championship title in front of more than 93,000 spectators in the stadium and millions of television viewers across the land. "The winner of the Rose Bowl gets between 12 and 15 million dollars to their university and that's big money. Up here in Canada we don't even see a $1.50! There isn't a lot of money being generated by the programs. There doesn't seem to be much interest amongst the student population. The major difference is that one [the American college football program] makes money for the university and the other [the Canadian college football program] is just part of university life."[38] No contests between Canadian universities in any sport attract any attention beyond the confines of the two contestants' institutions. Even there, they also languish and generate little, if any, interest among the students. Whereas college sports in the United States, in particular football and men's basketball, form the core of America's sports culture, their Canadian counterparts are more or less irrelevant.

This is also the case in Britain, where university sports have remained restricted to the colleges of Cambridge and Oxford universities and the

national championship in 1996. After his graduation from the University of Michigan, Botterill played for ten years with a number of teams in the National Hockey League before he returned to his alma mater to obtain a Masters degree in business administration. Upon receiving his MBA, Botterill rejoined the NHL in a managerial position with the Pittsburgh Penguins. Jason Botterill is the older brother of Jennifer Botterill, arguably Canada's best-known female hockey player and a genuine national star. Tellingly, she attended Harvard University (where she honed her hockey skills), not a Canadian institution of higher learning. (Interview with Jason Botterill on July 25, 2008 in Ann Arbor, Michigan.)

[38] Karl Yu, "Sport Speak: Contrasting College Football," e.Peak, January 2002. http://www.peak.sfu.ca/the-peak/2002-1/issue1/sp-speak.html. Retrieved August 30, 2008.

varsity competitions between the two. While, as we will briefly see in the next section of this chapter, the sports world of Oxford and Cambridge were the distant, albeit important, precursors of America's college sports, their sporting rivalry has had virtually no significance for the larger domain of British sports culture, with two exceptions. The first is the famed annual Varsity Match played between Oxford and Cambridge at Rugby Football Union's hallowed home ground, Twickenham Stadium, in London. Between 40,000 and 50,000 spectators attend the game with the 41,000 present in 2006 fairly typical for this event.[39] The match is nationally televised and in 2005 it attracted more than one million viewers.[40] The print media cover it as well, and by any measure of public attention and involvement, the Varsity Match, first played between these two tradition-laden universities in 1872, constitutes a significant part of British sports as well as general culture.

The second event is, of course, the annual "Boat Race," the rowing regatta held between the "blue boats" of the Cambridge University Boat Club (light blue) and the Oxford University Boat Club (dark blue) on the river Thames between Putney and Mortlake. The first race occurred in 1829 and the annual event has continued without interruption since 1856, with the exception of the cancelled races during the two world wars.[41] This boat race is popular well beyond the alumni, students, and communities of these two pedigreed universities. Typically, an estimated quarter of a million people watch the race live from the banks of the river, and around seven to nine million viewers follow the event on television in the United Kingdom. The overseas television audience has been estimated by the Boat Race Company to be around 120 million,[42] while other approximations place the international audience below 20 million.[43] Whatever the exact numbers might be, there is no doubt that this event plays a noticeable role in Britain and reaches well beyond the confines of the two con-

[39] "Thursday Is the New Friday!," http://www.rfu.com/microsites/varsity/twickenham/index.cfm?StoryID=17186. Retrieved August 30, 2008.

[40] "History," *Oxford University Rugby Football Club*. http://www.ourfc.org/history/index.asp. Retrieved August 30, 2008.

[41] The finest book on the Oxford vs. Cambridge boat race is by David and James Livingston, *Blood Over Water: Oxford Versus Cambridge. One Race, Two Brothers, Only One Winner.* (London: Bloomsbury, 2009).

[42] "Frequently Asked Questions," *The Oxford & Cambridge Boat Race.* http://www.theboatrace.org/article/introduction/faqs. Retrieved September 6, 2008.

[43] Stephen Brook, "Euro Final Tops TV Sports League," December 23, 2004, *guardian.co.uk.* http://www.guardian.co.uk/media/2004/dec/23/broadcasting. Retrieved September 6, 2008.

testing universities. It thus comprises a tangible component of British, even global, sports culture.

Now that we have presented the contours of the impressive dimensions of American college sports, particularly as embodied by its two main representatives of football and men's basketball, we will delineate the main highlights of the uniquely American causes that created this formidable construct of sports and popular culture.

How, Why, and When Did College Sports in America Become What They Are Today?

While a genuinely proper answer to this complex issue would be way beyond the scope of our task at hand, we would like to frame our analysis in terms of these three vectors:

(1) The British origins of American universities and the central influence of Oxford and Cambridge upon key institutions of higher learning on America's East Coast, most notably Harvard and Yale.

(2) Harvard and Yale (and to a lesser extent its entourage of East Coast elite colleges) as the absolutely decisive loci of forging within less than fifty years (between 1852 and the beginning of the twentieth century) virtually every single aspect and quality that continues to define big-time American college sport to this very day.

(3) The decisive difference of Harvard and Yale's structural presence in the topography of American higher education and society, compared to that of Oxford and Cambridge in Britain's and that of other European universities' on the Continent.

Elite Education and Early Contests across the Atlantic

When Henry Dunster introduced the Cambridge University classical curriculum to Harvard in 1640, he established an educational structure that was the first to dominate—more or less uncontested—the curricula of all nine colonial colleges (i.e., those institutions of higher learning that were chartered in the American Colonies before the American Revolution[44])

---

[44]The nine colonial colleges were in the order of their founding: Harvard College, the College of William and Mary, Collegiate School (Yale University), Academy of Philadelphia (University of Pennsylvania), College of New Jersey (Princeton University), King's College (Columbia University in the city of New York), College of Rhode Island (Brown University), Queen's College (Rutgers, the State University of New Jersey), and Dartmouth College.

and nearly all universities and colleges in the United States well into the middle of the nineteenth century, at least until the Morrill Act introduced a much more practically minded curriculum for the Land Grant colleges in 1862. The establishment of Johns Hopkins University in 1876, based on the German model propagated by Alexander von Humboldt, emphasized the primacy of research over teaching as the key identity of a university. This further altered the status quo.

Much of student life in the eighteenth- and early to mid nineteenth-century universities of the "New World" centered on going to mass, sometimes as often as fourteen times a week, and on memorizing lengthy Greek and Latin texts that then had to be recited in class. Dominated by a repressive faculty whose main purpose was to instill discipline in the students and to rule every aspect of their lives in loco parentis, American universities—most of which were tied to some kind of religious denomination—were not exactly fun-filled places, nor were they loci of real intellectual activities or scholarly pursuits. Indeed, at probably no time in the history of American higher education were universities so beset by student rebellions and violence both against the faculty and administrative authorities as well as against the students themselves as in the eighteenth and early nineteenth centuries.

The first extracurricular activities that the students controlled and harnessed for themselves were various literary societies and debating clubs. Of course, the students also engaged in various types of unorganized and spontaneous physical activities that could best be called games and play, but they were certainly nowhere close to anything related to what we today would categorize as sports. These forms of play included various bat and ball games, some of which resembled precursors to latter-day baseball. Others involved running with, kicking, and throwing a ball-like object that was to become a forerunner to the modern variants of football (Association, Rugby, and American).

A number of these American colleges also engaged in various so-called "Bloody Monday" contests in which, on the first Monday of the fall semester, the freshmen played a "football game" against the sophomores. It amounted to little else than an often rather brutal hazing with the junior and senior classes occasionally joining the melee for good measure. In-

---

Seven of these nine colleges came to compose the eight-member Ivy League athletic conference founded in 1954, with Cornell University (established in 1865) joining these seven institutions of the seventeenth and eighteenth centuries. The two colonial colleges not in the Ivy League are the College of William and Mary and Rutgers University, both of which are public institutions of higher learning.

deed, at Harvard University, this annual frosh-soph battle assumed such destructive dimensions that the faculty outlawed it in 1860, largely because of the many injuries incurred by the kicks against shins and other parts of the body. The Harvard sophomores buried the ball that they used in an elaborate funeral-like ceremony while the faculty's strong antipathy to kicking was to prove perhaps a decisive element in Association football's failure to enter America's sports culture the way it did elsewhere in many parts of the world.

Across the Atlantic in Britain, the post-Napoleonic era fostered a concept of education in which young boys of the country's elite and the Empire's future leaders and key administrators were to develop a healthy mind in a healthy body. This notion of *mens sana in corpore sano* soon dominated the curricula of the so-called public schools, in which young English schoolboys at places like Eton, Harrow, Westminster, Winchester, Rugby, Cheltenham, among others, engaged in all kinds of sports-related activities. Rowing, cricket, and local variants of football were the most common. Arguably the most important representative of this educational approach was the headmaster of Rugby School, Dr. Thomas Arnold. Via his depiction in Thomas Hughes's important book, *Tom Brown's School Days*, published in 1857, he became an iconic figure who was to influence the upbringing of millions of upper- and upper-middle-class young boys in the English-speaking world, including the United States, through much of the nineteenth century and well into the twentieth.[45]

The graduates of these exclusive private secondary schools proceeded to the colleges of Oxford and Cambridge Universities where they continued with their athletic activities and commenced doing so in a more systematic and rationalized manner that was to allow interuniversity competition. When Charles Wordsworth, nephew of British poet laureate William Wordsworth and an Oxford student and Harrow graduate, organized a cricket match between Oxford and Cambridge at London's venerable Lord's Cricket Ground in 1827, intercollegiate athletics was born.[46] Two years later, at Henley-on-Thames, these two universities met in a boat race attended by more than 20,000 spectators. By the 1850s when these two British universities established this contest as a yearly event, Harvard and Yale, who had their own boat clubs as early as the 1840s, were to change the nature of American intercollegiate athletics.

[45] In 1861, Thomas Hughes published a sequel to *Tom Brown's Schooldays*, fittingly called *Tom Brown at Oxford*.

[46] Ronald A. Smith, *Sports and Freedom: The Rise of Big-Time College Athletics* (New York: Oxford University Press, 1988), p. 6. We rely on Ronald Smith's superb work in the next few pages.

Harvard and Yale competed in a boat race of their own on August 3 of 1852—harnessing the newly introduced railroad that proved a decisive facilitator to all modern athletics in Britain and the United States, intercollegiate contests included—on the Winnipesaukee River at the junction where it enters Lake Winnipesaukee, New Hampshire's largest body of water. Financed by a railroad magnate who conceived of this race as a fine advertisement for his railroad and the lake as an excellent destination for vacationers, the Harvard and Yale crews thought of the whole thing as a "jolly lark," since they were offered free rail transportation to an all-expenses-paid, eight-day vacation with fine food and good lodging on this gorgeous lake. Thus, tellingly, it was a purely commercial endeavor that conceived, promoted, organized, and implemented from start to finish America's very first intercollegiate sports contest. Harvard's victory in the race was quite incidental to the whole event, for which neither of the teams was prepared and neither of the crews had trained. This was to change in a hurry.

Already before this race, Yale was upset by the fact that the Harvard coxswain, who had already graduated from that university, participated in the contest at all. But Yale had no recourse in the matter and no external body existed to which it could direct its grievance, since the whole affair was totally student-controlled and student-run and had no prearranged rules or organizing authorities of any kind.[47] But Yale's complaint and worry introduced the issue of eligibility into American college competition's very first event in 1852.

This important matter as to who was allowed to represent which college at what time and under what conditions was to remain an absolutely central concern and debate in college sports to this day. Very soon, the desire to win became so important to the students at both universities that they began to systematize their preparations for the contests. Thus, in 1864 Yale hired William Wood, a New York City gymnastics and physical education instructor, to train the team. Wood became the very first professional trainer of an American college team. Four weeks before the race, Wood had the Yale boys get up at 6AM to run and walk three to five miles in heavy flannels before breakfast. Later in the morning, the team would row four miles at racing speed. They did the same in the afternoon, and also worked out with weights in the gymnasium.[48]

Yale defeated Harvard by more than forty seconds in their meeting that

[47] John A. Lucas and Ronald A. Smith, *Saga of American Sport* (Philadelphia: Lea & Febiger, 1978), p. 198.

[48] Smith, *Sports and Freedom*, p. 35.

year. The race was accorded greater publicity on the campuses of both universities than General Sherman's approaching Atlanta and General Grant's pressuring the Confederacy around Richmond and Petersburg.[49] Harvard, in turn, had to respond with its own training methods, which consisted of running, walking, and the throwing of twelve-pound canon balls inside the gymnasium. The training regime also included a rigid dietary dimension in which the Harvard rowers ate "rare beef and mutton, stale bread, oatmeal gruel, only small quantities of milk and water, and no fruit or vegetables."[50] Whether this was to the benefit or detriment of the Harvard rowers remains unclear, but it was all justified in the name of "scientific" training, which had become de rigueur in the newly established world of college athletics.

Harvard was to fulfill its dream by taking a trip to England in the summer of 1869 to challenge Oxford University in its home waters on the River Thames, where it had raced Cambridge University for years and proven to be the better of the two at the time. Over 750,000 people, possibly one million, attended the Oxford vs. Harvard race with the Prince of Wales, the newly elected Prime Minister William Gladstone, the writer Charles Dickens, and other notables in attendance. The aforementioned author and Member of Parliament Thomas Hughes was the umpire of the race. The media in both countries extolled this contest in fierce nationalist terms, touting the advantages of their own system of education and culture over the other.

For both, it was more than a boat race. The event pitted Great Britain, far and away the most powerful nation on earth at the time, against its ever-growing offspring and overseas creation, the upstart United States. However, the latter was already well on its way by this time to challenging Britain's global hegemony. This race was arguably the very first event in a chain of many to come in which a sport contest became the vicarious expression of national rivalries.[51] Oxford won the race by only three lengths, according to Harvard crew adviser (though not yet official coach) William Blaikie, solely on account of Harvard's sportsmanship. The Americans refused to take Oxford's water even though the opportunity arose, likely eschewing victory.[52] But gentlemen were not to do such "foul" things at this

---

[49] Ibid.

[50] Ibid.

[51] For a detailed account of this race and its importance for the establishment of sports at Harvard, see Samuel Whiston Spirn, "A Scientific Sport Fit For Gentlemen: Why Rugby Supplanted Soccer in the Early History of American Football, 1860—1877" (Honors Thesis for the degree of Bachelor of Arts, Department of History, Harvard University, March 2003).

[52] Smith, *Sports and Freedom*, p. 41.

time merely for a victory over their social equals. Winning was on its way to becoming everything, but it was not yet the only thing (to paraphrase Vince Lombardi's famous dictum).

A disagreement between Harvard and Yale over the acceptability of sliding seats—which Yale used in its boat for the first time in a decisive victory over Harvard—caused Yale to withdraw from the annual competition in 1871 and Harvard to invite other colleges in Yale's place. This broadening, perhaps even democratization, of crew, no matter how inadvertent, created the Rowing Association of American Colleges. It included a number of renowned East Coast schools such as Brown, Columbia, Cornell, Dartmouth, Trinity, Wesleyan, Williams, Amherst, and Bowdoin, but also the Massachusetts Agricultural College of Amherst, the forerunner of what later became the University of Massachusetts at Amherst.

In the 1871 race, the Massachusetts Aggies defeated Harvard by fourteen lengths and Brown by twenty. The dam had been broken, a major social barrier removed: sons of simple Massachusetts farmers decisively defeated the sons of America's elite in head-to-head competition. While the Aggies failed to repeat their victory the next year, Harvard and Yale's mystique of invincibility had been banished once and for all. Sport as a vehicle for meritocracy had gained its first foothold in the topography of American college culture.

Most important, the annual regatta on Lake Saratoga became a prestigious event for schools to win. Even the president of such a pedigreed institution as Columbia University engaged in ecstatic panegyrics when Columbia's crew won the race in 1874. Among other things, President Frederick Barnard said the following: "I congratulate you most heartily upon the splendid victory you have won, and the luster you have shed upon the name of Columbia College. . . . I thank you for the Faculty of the College, for the manifest service you have done to this institution. . . . I am convinced that in one day or in one summer, you have done more to make Columbia College known than all your predecessors have done since the foundation of the college by this, your great triumph." Barnard then proceeded to mention that the telegraph had carried the name of Columbia, solely due to this triumph by its crew on Lake Saratoga, to far-away places like Paris, London, Hong Kong, and Kolkata. He concluded his praise with the following thought: "I assure you in the name of the Faculty and the Board of trustees, whom I represent, that whatever you ask in the future you will be likely to receive."[53]

[53] As quoted in ibid., p. 46.

That Barnard was far from unusual could best be gauged by words uttered by his colleague at Cornell University, President Andrew White, who one year after Barnard's praise for the Columbia rowers, offered the following laudatory words upon Cornell's victories in the varsity and freshmen races on Lake Saratoga: "The University-chimes are ringing, flag flying and canons firing. Present hearty congratulations to both victorious crews."[54] This was the very same president who, barely two years before, when students from the University of Michigan invited their counterparts from Cornell to play a football game in neutral and equidistant Cleveland, responded in the following inimitable manner: "I will not permit thirty men to travel four hundred miles merely to agitate a bag of wind."[55]

Here we have a fine example of the power of prestige and its all-important presence in the creation of the behemoth of American college sports. Rowing at this time enjoyed a much higher esteem than football, and the Eastern colleges were much more prestigious than the University of Michigan. Cornell president White was only too happy to see his students triumph in rowing among the former and decline permission for participating in football with the latter. But football's low prestige was to evaporate by the end of the 1870s and the beginning of the 1880s. In a matter of decades, it would reach heights, widths, depths, and breaths over the entire continent of which rowing or any other college sport could not even dream.

Harvard Has Its Way: Localism and Anglophilia on the Charles River

Chronologically speaking, football was to become the fourth organized intercollegiate sport in America following crew, baseball, and cricket. Cricket never much appealed to American college students outside the Philadelphia area, where the game was played quite prolifically among people of English descent and recent British origins. The first collegiate cricket game occurred on May 7, 1864 between Haverford and Penn, two prestigious and prominent Philadelphia-area schools. The first baseball game between colleges happened on July 1, 1859 when Amherst and Williams played each other, with the former beating the latter by a score of 73 to

---

[54] As quoted in Lucas and Smith, *Saga of American Sport*, p. 218.
[55] Howard H. Peckham, *The Making of the University of Michigan, 1817–1992* (Ann Arbor: University of Michigan Press, 1994), p. 85.

32.[56] Unlike cricket, baseball did indeed become quite popular at a number of colleges, Harvard and Yale included.[57] The colleges did not only compete against each other but also against baseball teams outside the universities, which as of 1869 also included professional teams such as Albert Spalding's aforementioned Cincinnati Red Stockings, the world's first professional sports team of any kind. The Red Stockings barnstormed from coast to coast and amassed a perfect 58-0 won-lost record, which also included a 30-11 victory against Harvard.[58] Yale played nearly twice as many games against professional baseball teams from 1865 to 1875 as it did against colleges.[59] When the National League was formed in 1876, college teams continued to play these top professional teams now and then, even winning against them on occasion. A number of college baseball players played the game at such a high level that they could, and sometimes did, in fact play for professional teams in the summer between school years. But this became increasingly untenable as colleges created and enforced eligibility rules, which disallowed such practices.

Despite the rise of amateurism as a legitimating ideal of college sports in the course of the latter decades of the nineteenth century, which we will discuss later in this chapter, college-based baseball players continued to receive payment for their off-campus summer services well into the twentieth century. But it was clear well before then that the rise of professional baseball in post–Civil War America, and the game's proliferation from coast to coast as the single-most dominant sport for the masses, made it unquestionably America's "people's game." Due to its summer schedule, the fall- and winter-bound college campuses of the northeastern United States were not going to be the major purveyors of this crucial sport. Baseball, though consistently played *at* and *in* colleges, was never really *of* them. The exact opposite was to befall football.

---

[56] The game played on that Sunday bore very little resemblance to what we have come to associate with baseball today. One of the last games to be played under the so-called "Massachusetts Rules" instead of the "New York Rules" that were already in ascendance throughout the 1850s and were to become the only ones constituting the game of baseball, the Amherst vs. Williams "base ball" contest (as the game was then called) had a number of oddities from our current vantage point: Thus, for example, it was played on a square instead of a diamond, by teams of 13 players each, with no "foul" territory confining any hit ball, and a team having to score at least 65 runs to win the contest. This particular game lasted 25 innings.

[57] We found *The H Book of Harvard Athletics: 1852–1922*, edited by John A. Blanchard and published by the Harvard Varsity Club in 1923, an indispensable source for descriptions of the crucial founding period of rowing, baseball, track, and, most important, football at Harvard University.

[58] Smith, *Sports and Freedom*, p. 57.

[59] Ibid.

In America, men played various versions of unorganized and localized ballgames on village greens, town squares, and near taverns that could be classified as forerunners of football. However, the most prominent loci of these unruly and rule-less games occurred at colleges where they were occasions for the upperclassmen, mainly the sophomores, to haze the incoming freshmen during the first Monday of the fall term. These "Bloody Monday" incidents, though particularly prominent at Harvard—where they led the faculty to outlaw the game of football, as previously mentioned—had parallels at other Eastern schools. Throughout the 1860s, however, America's college students became aware of the game's transformation in England and expressed interest in adopting it on their campuses. While the split between the "handling" and the "dribbling" games was well underway in England, this schism did not happen overnight and thus any game of football, even in England at the time, still possessed elements of both. When Princeton and Rutgers met for the very first official intercollegiate football game in America's history on November 6, 1869 in New Brunswick, New Jersey, they played a game that was much closer to the Association version of football than to its rugby cousin. In a sense, then, the very first football game in American history was much closer to a soccer match than to what later became American football. This, of course, made sense since the players at these two colleges adopted the code that developed as the dominant and official one of the Football Association since December 1863. Rutgers and Princeton liked the contest so much that they commenced a rivalry in football that was to last more than a century. Other prominent Eastern schools came to play this game, with the Yale vs. Columbia match in the fall of 1872 being perhaps the most significant. The Yale victory, in its very first intercollegiate football contest, debuted what was to become America's most successful and most important college football program throughout the nineteenth century. By mid October 1873, interest in the game had progressed sufficiently to have Yale, Princeton, and Rutgers draw up common rules with the thought of forming a league. But this did not happen for one simple reason: Harvard's conspicuous absence.

Put crudely but, we believe, correctly, had Harvard joined Yale and the other private East Coast colleges in forming a football league in 1873 (that would have continued to feature the Association game which all these colleges already played), college soccer, not college football, would have become the passion of many millions of American sports fans over the past 150 years and the country would have developed into one of the premier soccer powers of the world.

Why did Harvard reject the Association game that its main rival, Yale, and its somewhat lesser rivals Princeton and Columbia, had already embraced and played? Moreover, why did Harvard eschew the "dribbling" code of football? Surely there must have been students, perhaps even faculty, on campus who were aware of the fact that this code emanated from Eton and Harrow, the absolute crème de la crème of British public schools, rather than from the somewhat less prestigious Rugby, whose code Harvard students were to embrace so passionately barely one year later.

The answer lies in a combination of localism, reaction to past events, haughtiness, the belief in "science" as a preferred modus operandi, and a great dosage of Anglophilia. Pertaining to localism, Harvard students had become quite enamored with the so-called "Boston Game," which was played prolifically throughout the 1860s on the Boston Common by students of its two finest secondary schools, Latin and Dixwell's. Both schools sent many of their top graduates across the Charles River for their college studies. Indeed, Harvard's president at the time, Charles Eliot, was an "Old Boston Boy" himself, had taught at Dixwell's School, and was a fan of the Oneida Football Club founded in 1861 in Boston. Oneida was the first organized football team of any kind to play this game in the United States and was undefeated between 1862 and 1867, when the team folded. The club played many of its games on the Boston Common, where a plaque commemorates them. It played matches against pickup teams throughout the Boston collegiate community and thus had a strong connection to Harvard. When the Harvard faculty and President Eliot consented to having football restored at Harvard in 1871 after its eleven-year ban—dating from 1860 and instituted on account of the violence associated with "Bloody Monday"—it was this "Boston Game" that became the venue for the newly founded Harvard University Foot-Ball Club in 1872.

The Club played some intramural games on nearby Cambridge Common in the spring of 1872 and began to revive interest for football among the Harvard undergraduate population. As this happened, there soon developed the desire to introduce this game on an intercollegiate level, thereby adding it to the already existing sports of crew and baseball. But Henry Grant, captain of the Harvard University Foot-Ball Club, remained wary about participating in the soccer-style game then already played by Yale, Princeton, Columbia, Rutgers, and others of Harvard's college competitors. He worried that the soccer-style game would be too akin to the uncontrolled kicking and violence of the Bloody Monday incidents and thus insisted that Harvard's version of football—basically a somewhat tamed variant of the Boston game—was much more "scientific" than the game played by Yale and the others. The Harvard faculty concurred.

With science having played such a crucial role in legitimating training methods and other dimensions of boat racing at the time, its introduction into justifying one code of football over another was an effective way to buttress an argument even if it was met with derision by commentaries in the *Yale Record*. Adding insult to injury, members of the Harvard Foot-Ball Club and its captain Grant invoked the ideal of British amateurism by extolling on-campus interclass and intraschool matches (which Harvard had come to pursue in the early 1870s) as morally superior to intercollegiate contests. Harvard's football-playing students admired the in-school rugby games described so colorfully in Hughes's *Tom Brown's Schooldays*, claiming that Harvard's Boston game was "of a kind that did not depend upon intercollegiate rivalry."[60]

But such a parochial policy proved untenable due to the student body's excitement on account of the Harvard vs. Oxford regatta of 1869, and the various boat races against Harvard's archrival Yale. Intercollegiate competition had already by this time become part of student culture in the world of East Coast institutions of higher learning. And thus, it was with great delight that the Harvard football players accepted a challenge from Canada's McGill University in the spring of 1874 to compete in the game of football. There was just one problem: the two teams played different games. While Harvard played the Boston Game, McGill played the rugby code of football. The teams reached a compromise whereby the first game was to be played according to Harvard's Boston-Game rules and the second pursuant to McGill's rugby union rules. The games were played in Cambridge on May 14 and 15. Harvard won the first game easily, as the Canadians had never played the Boston Game before.

But then something crucial happened on the next day. The Harvard team held the McGill squad to a scoreless tie, which the former rightly interpreted as a major achievement since none of the Harvard boys had ever played rugby before this encounter. This favorable result instantly excited the entire Harvard community to the point where the players and their entourage quickly began to tout the rugby code's advantage over the Boston Game. The rugby game appeared to the Harvard men to be quicker, more challenging, and just more exciting than their own Boston version of football.

But there was another reason for this instant attraction to McGill's rugby game on the part of the Harvard students: the profoundly British

[60] Spirn, "A Scientific Sport Fit for Gentlemen," pp. 51, 52.

nature of McGill's entire appearance. The Harvard *Magenta*'s account of the two-day event focused as much on the British aura of the McGill team, whose players were "dressed in the English foot-ball suits," as it did on the games. The newspaper derided the Harvard players' "dilapidated appearance," which it contrasted mockingly to the McGill team's elegance. "The *Magenta* further insulted the dress of Harvard's players, relating one instance when a Harvard player had nearly reached the McGill goal, but was pulled down by one of his trailing rags of clothing."[61]

Suffice it to say that the Harvard players made it absolutely certain to wear proper uniforms for the two rematches held in Montreal in October of that year. To the team's surprise, the Harvard faculty allowed the players to travel to Montreal even though the games were held in the class period of the fall semester. The Harvard men were accorded an exceedingly warm welcome by their hosts—replete with lavish dinners, late night drinking, sightseeing tours of Montreal, and temporary memberships in the exclusive Metropolitan and City Clubs. All the privileges and amenities delighted and honored the Harvard boys no end, but the real clincher in wooing the visitors was the fox hunts. The hunts impressed the Harvard guests precisely because they witnessed for the first time in real life an actual event whose scenes adorned many of their dormitory rooms back in Cambridge and held pride of place as perhaps the most "thoroughly English" of all sports. Of course, it was a "sport" that—to continue with Anthony Trollope's characterization of fox hunting in his book on English sports published in 1868—"does more to make Englishmen what they are, and keep to them as they are."[62] Oh yes, and there were also two games to be played, this time in reverse order from the Cambridge event, with the rugby code game to precede the Boston version. When Harvard defeated McGill at its own game on its own field by scoring three unanswered touchdowns, the conversion of the Harvard players and their entourage to the rugby game was so complete that the two teams did not even bother to play next day's match, thus in effect burying then and there the Boston Game's fate for good.

The fact that Harvard had refused to play Yale because the latter played a game close to the Association code and Harvard indulged in its Boston Game variant—in other words, because of the incompatibility of the respective footballs that these two schools were playing at the time—does not hold up, since McGill also played a game that was not Harvard's. Instead, all indications seem to point to Harvard's being much more accept-

[61] Ibid., p. 54.
[62] Anthony Trollope, *British Sports and Pastimes* (London: Virtue & Co., 1868), pp. 70–71.

ing, indeed solicitous, of a school's game if it perceived both the game and the school as being English, and thus superior. McGill had mutated for all intents and purposes into a North American Oxford, which was merely a few hundred miles from Cambridge, Massachusetts instead of thousands across a mighty body of water. Put bluntly, Harvard students looked up to Oxford and its culture, which they wanted to emulate, even in its McGill guise. They most assuredly did not look up to Yale.

Harvard returned home from its encounters with McGill totally converted to the rugby code. The team beat nearby Tufts College in June of 1875 in the very first organized college football game in the United States contested via the rugby code. But none of this mattered as long as Yale remained outside of Harvard's purview. In the fall of that year, Yale extended once again an invitation to Harvard to have it join the already existing association of soccer-playing schools. Once again, Harvard refused. But as sports historian Ronald A. Smith so aptly put it, "Yale needed Harvard more than Harvard needed Yale."[63] Indeed, Yale seemed to need Harvard so much that it all but abandoned its sister schools in the soccer-style football association merely to play its erstwhile rival. So in the fall of 1875, Harvard and Yale agreed to play a game of football guided by so-called "concessionary rules," which ostensibly represented a compromise, a synthesis, between the two different codes then played by the two rivals. In actual fact, Harvard prevailed decisively, since Yale all but agreed to a game basically guided by rugby rules. On November 13, 1875, the first Harvard vs. Yale football game was played in New Haven. Harvard, as expected, won easily since the Yale men contested a game that they had never played before.

More important than the game's actual outcome was the fact that 150 Harvard undergraduates, sensing the significance of this occasion, accompanied their football team to New Haven. "Coverage of the game occupied three pages in the *Advocate* and provided further evidence that football had arrived as a popular sport at the college."[64] The interest on Yale's side was, if anything, even more prominent. Yale used its loss to Harvard to abandon the kicking game and devote full attention to the new rugby code, which it would soon come to master superbly.

In short order, Yale began to defeat Harvard on a regular basis and, most important of all, transform rugby into what, less than a decade later, had mutated into a code all its own: American football. Initially, Princeton, the self-proclaimed collegiate champion of the kicking game (soccer),

[63] Smith, *Sports and Freedom*, p. 76.
[64] Spirn, "A Scientific Sport Fit for Gentlemen," p. 60.

stuck by its code and wanted to maintain playing in its association of like-minded schools. But by the fall of 1876, Princeton's entire student body gathered after chapel to discuss whether or not to begin playing football under the rugby code. Very soon, a motion passed unanimously to drop soccer in favor of rugby. The third in the perennial troika of America's most venerable colleges and most pedigreed institutions of higher learning, Princeton simply could not resist the pull exerted by Harvard and Yale. Two years later, all of America's colleges had abandoned the soccer code for its rugby rival. On May 30th, 1878, a team from the University of Michigan defeated Racine College from Wisconsin in a game in Chicago, the very first organized football game west of the Allegheny Mountains. Tellingly, this game featured the rugby code, which banned the soccer version to the margins of American sports culture where, barring some recent promising developments, it continues to linger 150 years later.

This fascinating story makes clear that Harvard had unique prestige, reputation, cultural capital, and thus power among all American colleges at the time, and probably still does today. For had it been any of the other universities that chose to abstain from playing the dribbling code, it would not have mattered one bit. The code would have become the hegemonic version of football among all American colleges just as long as Harvard had adopted it. Whereas Harvard looked eastward, and in the McGill case northward, to follow models that it deemed worthy of emulating, Yale and Princeton looked to Harvard. The rest of the country's universities, in turn, followed the venerable threesome of Harvard, Yale, and Princeton.

The Ultimate Rise of College Football

The tracks had been set and the freight train of college football was on its way to becoming the American propertied classes' autumnal pastime. Yale, led by Walter Camp, often called the George Washington and Father of American Football, transformed the rugby game that it had learned from Harvard into the new code. By the early 1880s the annual Thanksgiving game played on New York City's Polo Grounds—mostly between Yale and Princeton, both of whom were Harvard's superior in football by then—attracted more than 10,000 cheering spectators. Among them were New York and East Coast social elites like Mrs. William Whitney and Mrs. Douglas Stewart. The 1887 Thanksgiving Day game between Harvard and Princeton attracted 24,000 spectators to the Polo Grounds. "By the mid-1890s, it was estimated that 5,000 football games, involving 120,000 athletes, were played on Thanksgiving Day. Many of these games, of course, involved athletic clubs and high schools, but the traditional game [invented, developed and perpetuated by America's pedigreed East Coast colleges] had spread to all parts of America."[65]

It was around this time that Harvard, Yale, and Princeton decided to withdraw from playing their games on Thanksgiving in far-away New York on somebody else's grounds, since they could now attract thousands of spectators closer to home by building major concrete-based arenas on their campuses. Harvard's horseshoe-shaped Stadium, completed in 1903 with seating of over 30,000 spectators, was the first such edifice and was soon to become a model for many colleges far and wide.

In a matter of less than twenty-five years, virtually all features that were to characterize the entity "college football" in America's sports space and culture throughout the twentieth century were firmly in place:

- the game came to be much more important than the actual play on the field;
- it assumed iconic dimensions for all of the university's constituents: certainly students, alumni, administrators, presidents, perhaps even faculty, though they remained decidedly the most critical of it;
- financial favors to sub-freshmen recruits commenced;
- intensive training before, during and after the season, became the norm;
- constant violations of eligibility rules emerged;
- questionable ethics were used;
- payment of professional coaches well beyond faculty salaries (with Yale leading the way by being the first university to professionalize its coaching staff completely) was established;
- bowing to alumni interests and those of outside boosters of all sorts became commonplace;
- construction of large stadiums for the public well beyond the immediate purview of the universities emerged not only as a sign of the game's arrival in the midst of America's middle-class culture but also constituted a fine source of considerable revenue;
- income from the game and budgets for programs far exceeded those of large departments and even entire schools (thus, for example, Yale's income from football in 1903 equaled the combined budgets of the law, divinity, and medical schools)

[65] Smith, *Sports and Freedom*, p. 81.

What had started as a completely student-run pastime in the late 1860s and early 1870s, had mutated in a few years into a massive entity in which students lost total control and autonomy to a thoroughly professionalized endeavor ruled by a network of coaches, university administrators, and, as of 1905, even a supracollegiate body later called the National Collegiate Athletic Association. Indeed, the only amateurs left in the fully profession-alized and commercialized entity of American college football have been the players on the teams. So-called student athletes, they have remained the only constituents who must abide by a strict code of amateurism con-jured up by English aristocrats in the early to middle decades of the nine-teenth century to keep their "pure" sports free from the working and com-mercial classes. These aristocrats and gentlemen of comfortable financial means and good social standing legitimated the notion of amateurism by falsely attributing it to ancient Greek athletes, who were anything but am-ateur in that they were handsomely rewarded by prizes and remunerations of various kinds, including material goods, for their athletic efforts and victories.

College football thus provides us with a solid case for what Arthur Stinchcombe so aptly called "organizational imprinting."[66] Stinchcombe differentiates between what he labels "influential" and "reproductive" im-printing with the former denoting the importance of the founding events on the identity, character, and inertia of an institution. The latter high-lights the maintenance and changes derived from such processes in the continued viability of these institutions. In the college football story, Har-vard clearly offered the necessary influential imprinting whereas Yale, and the state universities a few years later, played the leading role in this insti-tution's reproductive imprinting. Both proved necessary for the eventual success and cultural staying power of college football as an icon of Ameri-can culture.[67]

[66] Arthur Stinchcombe, "Social Structure and Organizations," in James G. March, ed., *Handbook of Organizations* (New York: Rand McNally, 1965), pp. 142–93.

[67] We are grateful to our University of Michigan colleague Victoria Johnson for alerting us to the relevance of Arthur Stinchcombe's work to ours at hand. Above all, we would like to take this opportunity to draw the reader's attention to Johnson's own superb scholarship on "organizational imprinting," particularly her fine book *Backstage at the Revolution: How the Royal Paris Opera Survived the End of the Old Regime* (Chicago: University of Chicago Press, 2008), which is a masterful analysis highlighting how the "organizational imprinting" of the Paris Opera hailing from the middle of the seventeenth century and the reign of Louis XIV not only survived the French Revolution but was made to thrive by the revolutionaries even though the Opera was so deeply identified with the Ancien Regime. See also Victoria John-son, "What Is Organizational Imprinting? Cultural Entrepreneurship in the Founding of the

College Sports as Product Differentiation in a Competitive Environment

Why have college sports in England remained confined to the quaint bailiwick of Oxbridge amateurism of the nineteenth century and why, in contrast, did they depart from this world across the Atlantic already by the last two decades of that century and become the behemoth that we came to know throughout the twentieth? Put differently, why did Harvard and Yale depart so drastically in sports from the ways of their beloved English models, which they were so keen to emulate in other aspects? The answer lies in America's quintessential bourgeois being, which neither created nor abided a genuine aristocratic class comparable to Britain's and the European Continent's. It emphasized instead the [white male] individual's equal opportunities in economy, culture, and society. Moreover, the rise of American college sports to prominence rests with the multiplicity of universities and thus their different social worth in America, compared to the monopoly in postsecondary education exerted by Oxford and Cambridge universities well into the second half of the nineteenth century. Of course, with this multiplicity came the accompanying necessity of competition among these American universities for students, prestige, status, and every other thinkable social and cultural capital. Put crudely, college sports, and football in particular, served both as important agents of product differentiation and of equalization among a multitude of American universities with vastly distinct social profiles.

Recall President Frederick Barnard's unmitigated pride and joy about how Columbia's victory in a regatta on Lake Saratoga had enhanced the university's name recognition beyond any of its previous (most likely) academic achievements. And remember Cornell President Andrew White's similar delight in the victory of his university's rowers. "When 'Siwash College' or the state university won an important athletic contest, people everywhere could read about it in the newspapers and rejoice in the recognition it brought to their locale and institution. People generally had no idea what was occurring in the college philosophy or geology class, but they could easily relate to the institution through a visible athletic program."[68]

Sports programs, particularly as represented by a college's football team, lent universities their distinct markers and gave them a brand identity that

---

Paris Opera," *American Journal of Sociology* 113 (1), July 2007, pp. 97–127; and Victoria Johnson, "What Makes Organizational Imprints Stick? Identity Persistence at the Paris Opera from Louis XIV to the French Revolution" (forthcoming).
[68] Lucas and Smith, *Saga of American Sport*, p. 218.

none of their other activities could even vaguely approximate. A lasting alliance among students, alumni, local and state denizens, and school administrators emerged that, often at odds with and to the outright chagrin of the universities' faculties, fostered the prominence of college football as a key vehicle for the institution's identity and visibility. In the crowded place of American institutions of higher learning—which, after all, also invented that highly American practice of ranking universities, departments, professors, and, of course, college football and basketball teams—any means to attain prestige, and social and cultural capital was warmly welcomed. None proved more effective to all relevant constituents—prospective, current and past students, administrators, politicians, donors, and the public at large—than successful college sports programs, led by college football.

Even venerable Harvard and Yale were not exempt from this measure of public prestige. "That Harvard had by the early twentieth century led the nation with forty endowed professorships was no less important, only less well known, than that it had built the first concrete stadium in America. At Yale, the establishment in 1890 of the Yale Alumni Fund drive and its national leadership in alumni giving added to its prestige, just as having Walter Camp lead Yale in athletics enhanced Yale's visibility."[69] Oxford and Cambridge did not need their visibility enhanced in England's topography of higher education, where the so-called "red brick" universities were about to get founded precisely when sports became institutionalized as mass culture in the latter half of the nineteenth century. Oxford and Cambridge were key loci of sport's invention, proliferation, and development and both universities enjoyed an advantage of more than half a millennium over their newly constituted upstart rivals with whom neither one had to compete anyplace in British society—be it the lecture halls or the sports fields—for any kind of name recognition, product differentiation, or cultural and social capital.[70]

[69] Smith, *Sport and Freedom*, p. 218.

[70] We, of course, in no way mean to shortchange the academic excellence of the superb Scottish universities of St. Andrews, Aberdeen, Glasgow, and Edinburgh, as well as the University of Durham in England and Dublin's Trinity College that clearly contributed to British intellectual, cultural, and professional life alongside Oxford and Cambridge. But none of them came close in terms of enjoying the sheer prestige that these two dowagers of British postsecondary education did, and still do. As to the term "Red Brick (or "redbrick") universities, it refers to the six so-called "civic" British institutions of higher learning that were founded in the major industrial centers of Victorian England and achieved university status before World War II. They are the University of Birmingham, the University of Bristol, the University of Leeds, the University of Liverpool, the University of Sheffield, and the Manchester Institute of Science and Technology, which mutated into the University of Manchester. While all these institutions did not receive their official royal charters until the first de-

College Sports as Democratizing Agents

In addition to being central in giving America's universities prestige and general visibility, college sports also offered a key venue for leveling social inequalities. Student athletes from schools of lesser prestige and station could compete with, and defeat, their counterparts from institutions of wealth and pedigree. Recall when five sons of Massachusetts farmers and a Portland, Maine resident representing Massachusetts Agricultural College of Amherst defeated a Harvard boat by fourteen lengths and a Brown boat by twenty in a rowing competition in 1871. It was clear that in the world of sports at least, the playing field for America's elites and its regular folk was, if not level, then certainly a good deal less skewed than in just about any other aspect of American public life.[71] In no other imaginable venue besides college sports would students of institutions with such disparate amounts of status and prestige have met in those days, let alone experienced the reality of students with less prestige and status publicly defeating, well-nigh humiliating, their counterparts from institutions with higher status and prestige. College sports, led almost exclusively by football from the1880s, had not only become the most efficient prestige-making machine for America's institutions of higher learning, it also developed at the same time into its most potent equalizing agent.

Two government interventions in particular came to alter—and democratize—the topography of higher education in America, distinguishing it thoroughly from that in Britain as well as the European continent. We mean, of course, the Northwest Ordinance of July 13, 1787 and the first Morrill Land-Grant Act signed into law by President Abraham Lincoln on July 2, 1862. Both, in their own way, though separated by seventy-five years and embodying different concepts of a university's curricular content and educational mission, created a bevy of institutions of higher learning. Most of these changes came to be located in far-away places that emerged totally sui generis for the sole purpose of housing these new institutions.[72]

---

cade of the twentieth century, their precursors existed throughout much of the second half of the nineteenth.

[71] Smith, *Sports and Freedom*, pp. 42, 43.

[72] We found Jurgen Herbst's analysis of the Northwest Ordinance's impact on the development of American higher education particularly enlightening. See Jurgen Herbst, "The Development of Public Universities in the Old Northwest," in Frederick D. Williams, ed., *Northwest Ordinance: Essays on Its Formulation, Provisions and Legacy* (East Lansing: Michigan State University Press, 1988), pp. 97–117. Whereas institutions—such as the University of Michigan first in Detroit and then in Ann Arbor, Ohio University in Athens, Ohio, and Indi-

Thus emerged the American college town across the country, where the university came to be if not the sole then certainly the most dominant political, social, economic, and cultural institution. Indeed, these college towns were, structurally speaking, not that different from company towns that arose at the same time. Just like companies that developed all kinds of recreational facilities, sports included, to pacify workers and provide them with distractions but also to facilitate the population's identity with the company, so too did college towns come to foster and identify with "their" teams by rallying around college sports, football in particular.

There are *Universitätsstädte* in Germany like Tübingen, Göttingen, Freiburg, Marburg, Münster, and Heidelberg, and few towns are more university-dominated than Oxford and Cambridge. But with the exception of the latter two, the norm for European university students is to live at home and commute to the local university or if living away from home, to live in town but not on campus or "in college." Most European universities, even the traditional ones, are in large cities such as Vienna, Paris, Rome, Madrid, London, Berlin, Budapest, and Prague with "college towns" being the exception. This is not the case in the United States, particularly with the establishment of the all-important state-based public universities that were essentially created out of thin air away from large population centers. From Ann Arbor to Bloomington, from West Lafayette to East Lansing, from Urbana-Champaign to Madison, from Stillwater to Boulder, from Corvallis to Athens, from Amherst (home of the aforementioned Massachusetts Agricultural College and an institution of the Morrill Land-Grant Act) to Lincoln, from Fayetteville to Gainesville; American state universities were built in sparsely inhabited areas, thus becoming de facto boarding schools and closed communities. It is in this context that universities assumed responsibilities in lieu of the students' parents, thus maintaining the key concept of "in loco parentis" that they inherited from their institutional predecessors of the eighteenth century, as we mentioned above, and that still dominates American undergraduate life but is com-

---

ana Seminary, later to become Indiana University, in Bloomington—were part of the first wave of these public institutions and an outgrowth of the Northwest Ordinance, such mainstays of American higher education as the University of Arizona, the University of California at Berkeley, the University of Connecticut, the University of Delaware, the University of Florida, the University of Georgia, the University of Illinois at Urbana-Champaign, the University of Minnesota, Pennsylvania State University, and the University of Wisconsin at Madison were among the 106 land-grant institutions that would come to democratize American higher education. As an interesting aside, our neighbor, Michigan State University, founded in 1855 and established in East Lansing, was the pioneer land-grant institution and served as a model for the Morrill Act of 1862.

pletely antithetical to its European counterpart. The popularity of college sports grew in this closed milieu, not only to foster institutional loyalty and create a communal spirit between town and gown, but also to channel potentially problematic behavior such as student revelry into socially more acceptable and controllable venues.

Bespeaking America's true bourgeois ethos, the country developed a concept of education that emphasized the inclusion of large numbers on all levels, even that of the postsecondary colleges and universities. In Britain and the Old World—and parts of the quasi-aristocratic and traditional establishment of the wannabe-British private universities of America's eastern states—higher education remained the preserve of a privileged few until the education explosion of the late 1960s and early 1970s. In contrast, higher education in the United States rapidly developed into a mass structure with the establishment of public universities that had the clear mission of educating the country's growing middle class. Already by the Civil War, but most certainly in its wake, the United States had a large network of universities and colleges that by the eve of World War I were attainable goals to a degree unparalleled anywhere else in the world. Higher education and its institutions developed into an integral part of American middle-class culture well before it did so in Europe and elsewhere. By analyzing detailed historical data from countries including Belgium, Denmark, Holland, France, Great Britain, Germany, Switzerland, Sweden, Italy, Austria, Japan, Canada, and the United States, Joseph Ben-David convincingly demonstrates that the system of higher education in the United States has been far and away the most egalitarian of all comparable structures in the advanced industrial world. It is crucial to note that Ben-David dates this egalitarian development in American higher education with the end of the Civil War and thus with the massive expansion of the public university system anchored in the individual states.[73] Needless to say, this expansion coincides perfectly not only with the establishment and proliferation of college sports as part of American culture, but with all sports in general and fits solidly into our period of the first globalization.

Town and Gown Unite as Fans of Their "State U"

The role of higher education in the development and institutionalization of sports as a mass phenomenon in America has been part and parcel of the same basic tenet: that of the early and thorough bourgeoisification of

[73] Joseph Ben-David, "The Growth of the Professions and the Class System," in Reinhard Bendix and Seymour Martin Lipset, eds., *Class, Status, and Power: Social Stratification in Comparative Perspective* (New York: Free Press, 1966.)

American public life and culture. Indeed, the fact that to this day a larger percentage of the American population attends institutions of postsecondary education than anywhere else in the world dates back to the Jeffersonian initiatives of the early nineteenth century and their subsequent massive expansion between 1865 and the beginning of the twentieth century. Particularly in the world of public institutions, these universities evolved into the primary foci of state and local pride, becoming the leading producers of the respective state's professionals, bureaucrats, notables, and other holders of high-status positions. Since these institutions often existed in states with few large cities and thus in areas where the presence of professional sports made no economic sense, universities and their teams soon became the sole purveyors of first-class sport on a meaningful competitive level for large areas of this continent-spanning country. By the early twentieth century, these large state universities derived their fan base from three sources: undergraduate students on campus, alumni (meaning former students who became life-long fans during their four-year studentship at the university), and, absolutely crucial, state residents and other "regular" nonuniversity affiliated locals. The latter never aspired to attend these universities, and most likely would never have succeeded in passing their rigorous entrance requirements or their four-year courses of study. There emerged a unique situation in which millions of people came to forge life-long emotional bonds with universities exclusively via their sports teams thus in effect replicating the relationship between a European club and its followers.

It is in this aspect of the fan base in which private colleges differ so markedly from public ones, particularly the large state universities of the Midwest, the West, and the South. Private colleges never aspired, nor could ever claim, to include in their fan base citizens from the area in which the colleges existed. After all, their very distinction and identity was that of being private, of being exclusive in notable contrast to the public institutions that derived much of their legitimacy from being the jewel of their state. To give examples, very few in Cambridge, Massachusetts, let alone in the larger Boston area or the state as a whole, would ever become Harvard fans without having been students there. Equally few in New York City, let alone the state of New York, ever became Columbia fans without having attended that institution. And non-Yalies from New Haven and Connecticut seldom harbor any love for Yale and its teams. If anything, quite the opposite might be the case. The town-gown cleavage has always divided private universities from their larger surroundings. As in everything, there exist exceptions that prove the rule: The University of Notre Dame, clearly a private institution, varies from this model and resembles that of the public schools' (which we will discuss momentarily) in that the fandom of its sports teams—particularly its football team—reaches way beyond the world of the immediate Notre Dame community of students, faculty, and alumni. Indeed, by capturing the affection and loyalty of millions of mainly Catholic sports fans all across America, Notre Dame's following constitutes without any doubt one of the most nationwide fan bases in all of American sports.

Things are different for public universities. In the entire state of Nebraska, breathing, eating, following, and fretting about the University of Nebraska's beloved "Cornhuskers" is every bit the equivalent of being a Barça fan for Catalans in Barcelona or a Rangers fan for Protestant Glaswegians. In states with two major public institutions, the rivalries are nearly every bit as intense as the Old Firm between Celtic and Rangers in Glasgow. They divide families, factories, offices, streets, and towns in the state: the Sooners of the University of Oklahoma vs. the Cowboys of Oklahoma State; the Longhorns of the University of Texas vs. the Aggies of Texas A&M University; the Wolverines of the University of Michigan vs. the Spartans of Michigan State University; the Tigers of Auburn University vs. the Crimson Tide of the University of Alabama. Whereas a non-Harvard citizen of Cambridge might likely wish the Harvard teams nothing but ill if he even cares about the Crimson's athletic endeavors in any way, his non–University of Michigan counterpart from Ann Arbor will quite possibly be an even more rabid Michigan fan than many an out of state student attending the university.

Above all, college football and basketball flourished mainly in small towns surrounded by large geographic areas (mostly states) that were almost always devoid of any competition from major-league professional sports. Thus, in terms of intellectual interest (i.e., following) and emotional involvement (i.e., identifying with), these college teams became, for all intents and purposes, surrogates for all the emotional, cultural, and economic capital exacted and provided by top-level professional teams in America's big urban centers. The football and basketball teams of these public universities resemble European and Latin American soccer clubs in one further important detail. Just like them, and unlike franchises in North America's professional leagues, college teams remain geographically immobile and immutable, solidly anchored in their traditional setting for perpetuity. The likelihood of the University of Michigan's Wolverines closing up shop in Ann Arbor, no matter how abysmal their season or low the attendance at their games may be, and moving to Arizona remains as unthinkable as any European soccer club's relocation to a different city.

College teams in America also resemble continental Europe's clubs) in that their "ownership" consists of an amorphous yet also well-defined agglomeration of their members—in this case students, alumni, faculty, administrators, in short a large and disparate group whose sole common bond is belonging to the entity (club) of Harvard, Michigan, Nebraska, Stanford, whatever. Moreover, market forces neither define the essence of European clubs nor that of American universities, though neither can afford to remain impervious to them. In notable contrast to the potency of this school-tied identity that is so essential to the culture of American post-secondary education (indeed American culture as a whole), few European universities (with the notable exception of Oxford and Cambridge) exhibit any such strong life-long bonds.

The Marginalization of Baseball on Campus

Why have football and basketball dominated collegiate sports culture in the United States, with baseball, after all still called "America's pastime," playing a marginal role at best? The answer lies once again in the social position of the institutions and structures that created these sports and became their early purveyors. American football emerged from the hallowed grounds of America's oldest and most prestigious academic institutions, particularly Harvard and Yale, and soon migrated to other universities in the East and the Midwest. The South and West's institutions of higher learning were soon to follow. Well before football even began to emerge as a professional game in the early years of the twentieth century, it had already become a hegemonic icon of America's middle-class culture solely by dint of its collegiate incarnation. Indeed, the professional side of football remained largely secondary to America's sports culture until that New York Giants vs. Baltimore Colts NFL Championship game on December 28, 1958—the "greatest game ever played." Television then began to dominate the game's public presence and propelled professional football to the pinnacle of American sports culture in the course of the 1960s, where it safely resides to this day.

Whereas basketball was not invented until 1891, by which time football had become a staple of American college life and sports culture, it, too, emerged from educational institutions. In this case they were not universities but Young Men's Christian Associations (YMCAs) that were eager to purvey what they called "Muscular Christianity," that was in some way an anti-football. With college football having gotten brutally violent, indeed lethal, Christian educators believed that young men, though in need of serious physical activity, had to be lured away from this game that had gotten out of hand. Moreover, these reformers realized that football required large open spaces, expensive equipment, and the pedigreed world of colleges. None of these requirements were readily accessible to millions of young men, particularly in the rapidly growing population centers of the East Coast such as New York, Philadelphia, and Boston. And thus basketball emerged as the anti-football! Featuring finesse instead of strength, no contact instead of head-on collisions, and indoor play in the winter instead of outdoor play in the fall, the differences were obvious. From its beginning, basketball—played in high schools, clubs, fairs, dances, barges, and town halls—became a much more ubiquitous sport than football, which remained anchored mainly in the colleges. However, basketball too was warmly embraced by colleges and was soundly ensconced in college sports culture by the beginning of the twentieth century. Indeed, as the only one of the Big Four American sports, basketball was played by women on America's college campuses from the game's very origins in the late 1890s. Suffice it to say that both sports, basketball and football, emerged from the world of education (high school and college in particular), where they remain ensconced to the present.

Baseball, in contrast to both football and basketball, emanated from a world that had nothing to do with any form or level of education. It mutated from a street game played in colonial and postcolonial America to an organized city game governed by clubs comprised of bank tellers, firemen, policemen, and small shopkeepers—in short, what is best described as the lower middle class. Even before the Civil War, baseball began a process of professionalization that culminated in the creation of the Cincinnati Red Stockings in 1869. With the establishment of the world's first purely professional sports league in 1876—the National League of Professional Base Ball Clubs—baseball by the early 1880s had become the world of the lower middle and working class. It was the "people's" game, the purview of the common man. Of course it existed at universities as we discussed, and still does. But played in that structure, it has always remained subordinate to its professional version outside the walls of academia and to football and basketball inside it.

We are in no position to offer solid answers as to why football and basketball displaced rowing as America's number one college sport by the 1880s at the very latest. However, we are reasonably certain that their identities as team sports played in modern venues such as large stadiums and indoor arenas—thereby facilitating repeated and regular spectatorship on a large scale and having entrance fees assures stable and solid revenue—had a lot to do with it.

The World Joins America's College Sports

If anything, college sports have continued to grow in recent decades. Most important by far has been the massive inclusion of women in this world in the wake of the federally mandated reforms anchored in Title IX of the 1972 Federal Education Amendments to the 1964 Civil Rights Act. This measure—in our opinion arguably one of the most decisive and effective democratizing endeavors enacted in modern American history—completely changed the topography of college sports on its production side. With the notable exception of football, virtually all other sports have witnessed a complete opening to female athletes, who now regularly furnish around 50 percent of student athletes at pretty much every institution of higher learning in the United States that fields a varsity team on any level.

In the last few years, college sports have begun to experience an equally interesting transformation that has not yet attained the extent of the inclusion and integration of female athletes but which is anything but negligible. It is constantly growing and bespeaks an essential characteristic of our times: the globalization of college sports, which, like the participation of women, is transforming this construct on its supply and production side—among its athletes, activists, and "doers," if not yet among its consumers, followers, and fans. In this respect, even this most local and "nested" structure of American sports is in the process of becoming increasingly global and cosmopolitan.

The number of foreign players in many Division I sports has doubled since the beginning of 2000. "In tennis, 30 percent of the male players were from outside the United States in 2005–6, as were 23 percent of male ice-hockey players [mostly from Canada] 14 percent of female golfers, 13 percent of all skiers, and 10 percent of male soccer players. And although the numbers are not as high, they are growing fast in basketball, gymnastics, swimming, and track. Some teams are even made up entirely of foreign players. The athletes come from all over the world: Africa, Australia, Europe, and South America are the most common places, but it is hard to find a country that has not sent players to the United States. One thing is clear: The number of foreign players will continue to rise. Ross Greenstein is the chief executive of Scholarship for Athletes, a company that helps American and foreign students land scholarships. "'The number of international athletes is going to grow and grow,' he predicts, 'until they're the majority.'"[74] Thus, for instance, college soccer's connections to the interna-

[74] Robin Wilson and Brad Wolverton, "The New Face of College Sports," *Chronicle of Higher Education*, January 11, 2008.

tional game have grown considerably in multiple ways over the last few years. Four women's teams and three men's at the 2008 Beijing Olympics featured current or former players from colleges based in the United States.

There has emerged an interesting symbiosis in terms of fusing the uniquely American construct of college sports with an increasingly global clientele on the players' side. With the pressure to win becoming ever more important in the world of college sports—well beyond the two giants of football and men's basketball—colleges have eagerly expanded their recruiting horizons outside the North American continent. This desire has met fortuitously with the unique fact that the United States represents the only country in the world where students can get a first-rate education for free by competing in their sport of choice. Everywhere else, "athletes must choose between higher education and pursuing their sport professionally. Amateur athletes abroad have no access to the kind of high-level coaching, training facilities, and competition that exist on campuses in the United States."[75]

The land-grant colleges in the latter half of the nineteenth century democratized American higher education by making it more inclusive of children of the middle classes, farmers, and other non-elite segments of the American population. College sports leveled, at least to some degree, the distance between these schools and their elite East Coast predecessors. So, too, does an opening of college sports to foreign students potentially diminish the gap between schools of different reputation and resources. In 2007 the University of Texas at El Paso (UTEP) had no American citizen on its men and women's track teams, whose combined forty athletes hailed from twelve countries, many from Africa. This meant that UTEP's track team was in a much better position to beat the likes of the University of Texas—the state's flagship university which, by dint of its elite status, has had much greater access to attract star American athletes than a regional school like UTEP—in head-to-head competition than if UTEP could only rely on its local clientele from El Paso County (home to more than 80 percent of the institution's student body).[76] That the presence of foreign students coming to American universities to play sports and get an education with the help of athletic scholarships has become a major issue, can best be gauged by the fact that the NCAA announced a new policy in 2007.

[75] Ibid.
[76] Robin Wilson, "A Texas Team Loads Up on All-American Talent, With No Americans," *Chronicle of Higher Education*, January 11, 2008.

It regulates the eligibility of all international players, stripping colleges from this responsibility, which they had previously enjoyed. And sure enough, the NCAA's rigid definitions of amateurism guide the two-page questionnaire that all international athletes must complete to qualify for college sports in the United States.[77]

Still, despite the continued internationalization and growing cosmo-politanism of college sports in terms of the participating athletes (i.e., their producers and "doers"), their consumers (i.e., "followers") remain, with the exception of fringe groups and small "diaspora" communities across the globe, almost exclusively American. The players in college sports are be-coming increasingly global,[78] yet their fans stay almost exclusively local with no indication of any changes in the latter in spite of all the globalizing forces that have altered so much in many facets of culture in America, Eu-rope, and elsewhere in the world. However, local in no way means paro-chial since by rooting for his/her beloved State U—featuring players from all corners of the world—Joe and Jane College fan fosters a cosmopolitan identity.

---

[77] "Controversy Surrounds NCAA's Certification of International Athletes," *Chronicle of Higher Education,* January 11, 2008.

[78] A wonderful case of this globalization and its impact on football is the Polynesian foot-ball immigration to California and Utah. Polynesians, whose presence at all levels of football is already disproportionately high compared to their percentage of the U.S. population con-tinue to increase their participation as players in the game (as has previously occurred in Rugby League and Rugby Union in Australia). Polynesians are disproportionately members of the Church of Jesus Christ of Latter-day Saints. Brigham Young University (BYU) in par-ticular (as *the* national *and* international Mormon university) thus has an excellent recruiting advantage, which is being reflected in star players like Harvey Unga. Not surprisingly, Brigham Young has been unusually successful in recent years. This advantage is likely to in-crease, partly because adherence to the Church of Jesus Christ of Latter-day Saints will keep growing in the Pacific Islands, thus giving BYU a recruiting base beyond the United States; the other important favorable factors are proximity to the traditional Polynesian-American recruiting base in California (which is why the University of Southern California also has a lot of excellent Polynesian players) and to a Polynesian coaching staff (Norm Chow, who has worked for both BYU and USC, was a stellar recruiter of Polynesian players for both univer-sities). Because of its Mormon ties, BYU then, is better placed than any other university to be able to draw Polynesian players in the global age. We gratefully acknowledge this informa-tion to David Smith. See also "American Samoa: Football Island," http://www.cbsnews.com/stories/2010/01/14/60minutes/main6097706_page6.shtml

CONCLUSION ◇◇◇◇◇◇◇◇◇◇◇◇◇◇◇◇◇◇◇◇◇◇◇◇◇◇◇◇◇◇◇◇◇◇◇◇◇◇

In his singularly impressive and important work, Jared Diamond demonstrates more convincingly than anybody in our opinion why Europe "won," or put differently, why it was this relatively small archipelago, appended to a huge Asian landmass thumbing into the Atlantic Ocean, that created the preconditions and the fundamentals for a system of society, governance, warfare, economy, and culture that was to conquer the rest of the world.[1] Best known under the term "capitalism," the search for and analysis of its origins and nature gave rise to virtually every discipline of what we have come to know as the social sciences. And capitalism's trials and tribulations continue to nurture them. In his own magnum opus, Immanuel Wallerstein analyzes capitalism's rise to a "world system" by assigning it a core, a semiperiphery, and also a periphery.[2] To no one's surprise, capitalism's core rests in the northwestern part of the Atlantic Ocean anchored in the Low Countries and, most important, Great Britain.

Few, if any, items have confirmed Wallerstein's conceptual framework more powerfully and lastingly than the world of sports, with the possible exception of the English language's becoming the global lingua franca. By transforming previously local and disorganized games into rule-driven and institution-bound novel entities, and by exporting this to its empire's (and the world's) semiperipheries and peripheries, sports developed into one of Britain's most lasting contributions to our global civilization. Of the many sports that Britain bequeathed to the world, none became more globally successful than the game of Association football. Soccer's success can best be gauged by the following three developments: first, the game penetrated the globe's most distant peripheries and is played literally everywhere on

---

[1] Jared Diamond, *Guns, Germs and Steel: The Fates of Human Societies* (New York: W. W. Norton, 1999).

[2] Immanuel Wallerstein, *The Modern World-System I: Capitalist Agriculture and the Origins of the European World-Economy in the Sixteenth Century* (San Diego, CA: Academic Press, 1976).

earth; second, that one of its semiperipheries, meaning continental Europe, soon joined the motherland in becoming the core of this game, where it continues to reside to this day; and third, that the other semiperiphery, namely Latin America, developed decidedly into the core's equal as far as the quality of its game and players have been concerned, yet simply never attained a level of capitalism to compete with Europe's becoming the unquestioned core of global soccer. Thus, not by chance, hundreds of Latin American players, led by the continent's superstars, ply their trade in Europe with virtually no European of any significance playing in Latin America.

One of Britain's former semiperipheries was to emerge as a burgeoning core in its own right in the course of the nineteenth century, precisely the era when Britain introduced sports to the world. But as a semiperiphery that had successfully surpassed the British core and that busily and self-consciously was forging itself into a bigger and more powerful one, the United States remained largely impervious to Britain's sports exports. Still, America accepted them briefly only to convert them into its self-contained systems where they developed into languages all their own. Of course, these American sports continued to share essential commonalities with their British relatives in that both featured all the essential attributes of being profoundly modern constructs. Moreover, in the first and the second globalization, the sports worlds across the Atlantic helped create forms of "cosmopolitan citizenship." They developed new transnational bonds and languages reaching far beyond their respective shores. The "best of the best" evolved into popular icons that enjoy global recognition. Still, while the deeper structures of the two sports worlds on either side of the Atlantic share great similarities in form and content, and both have spawned global players, their actual expressions and their hegemonic manifestations—their languages—remain divergent for good.

Our book primarily depicts the world of these two cores: on the one hand Europe-centered soccer; on the other hand the America-centered Big Four of baseball, football, basketball, and hockey. What matters most to us, however, is capturing the interaction of these cores in their personae as semiperipheries (even peripheries), which is exactly what their relationship has been in the realm of sports cultures for more than one hundred years. America has been peripheral to Europe's core in soccer and continues to exhibit every aspect of such a relationship, as amply depicted by Wallerstein and other "dependency" theorists. The best American players have to go to Europe to play at the highest level of the game and to make the most money because the best teams and the best leagues are in Europe, as is the highest remuneration for players. Simply put, the greatest weight of the game, its core, its best-of-the best, remains firmly in Europe.

The exact obverse pertains to the Big Four. The very best basketball players come to America, as do the very best hockey players. The best leagues are in America, and the most money is there as well. Again, there is no doubt that the greatest weight of these games, their core, their best of the best, continues to reside in America. America, of course, furnishes the uncontested core in baseball, with Japan, the Caribbean, South Korea, Taiwan, Australia, and a few other countries assuming the role of semiperiphery. Much of Europe is relegated to the game's periphery although Holland, Italy, and Russia have made recent strides possibly qualifying them as members of the "more advanced" semiperiphery. American football, as we argue in the book, constitutes the lone outlier among these sports in that it enjoys no meaningful concentric circles outside the United States in terms of the game's production side, though it most certainly has both ample semiperipheries and peripheries in the successful consumption of its American-based products—ranging from its jerseys to its televised games, with the Super Bowl having actually developed into a globally followed television event. Thus, there is no question that the semiperipheral roles of Europe in American sports and America in Europe's have substantially gained in stature in the course of what we have come to call the second globalization. And there can also be no question that each side will do its best to succeed in the other's core. Moreover, in our brief mention of the situation in China and other "new" areas currently "in play," there is little doubt that the two cores have entered the contest to attain major footholds in these open spaces and have assigned substantial resources to render these places—with China being the real prize—into a semiperiphery beholden to their particular core. But pursuant to the immense changes wrought by the second globalization, it would not be surprising to witness the mutation of formerly peripheral and semiperipheral regions into core ones. For example, in the world of soccer, countries that until the new global age were on the fringes of the game's periphery, such as Australia, Japan, the two Koreas and China, have with little doubt made major progress that puts them well on the road to enter the game's core in the next two-to-three decades.[3]

One need not be a committed Marxist to realize that the two most powerful capitalist entities of this world, North America and Europe, battle

[3] Kuper and Szymanski, *Soccernomics*, pp. 297–306. The authors argue that a country's entrance to soccer's global core depends on the following three variables: a sizeable population, economic strength, and experience in soccer.

each other in their own backyards just as they do in these newly available spaces. Moreover, it is quite evident that money has played a very important role in the increasing commercialization of these sports cultures on the global level. Thus, *SportsBusiness Journal* estimates that the annual organized global sports industry is as large as $213 billion. This figure includes all economic activities that are ancillary to sports themselves, such as advertising, media contracts, gambling facilities, construction projects, operating expenses, transportation, and lodging.[4] Taking slightly less encompassing categories into consideration, the accounting firm Deloitte & Touche estimates that the entire English Premier League, far and away the richest soccer league in the world, received revenue in excess of $2.3 billion in 2006–7 (with its debt being much higher). Reports by MLB Commissioner Bud Selig had Major League Baseball enjoying over $6 billion in revenue in 2007. The NFL's annual revenue for 2005 was nearly $6 billion as well. And let us recall Andrew Zimbalist's figure mentioned in chapter 1 that the annual revenue of all the Big Four North American sports amounts to around $15 billion. Furthermore, the nearly $2 billion price tag for teams like the New York Yankees, the Dallas Cowboys, the Washington Redskins, Manchester United, and Real Madrid, is anything but trivial and has grown precipitously during the era of the second globalization. Thus, Takeo Spikes, the eloquent linebacker for the San Francisco 49ers, was spot on when he said, "I always tell today's young quarterbacks who enter our League that with their arm and brain and legs, they are actually in charge of a one billion dollar plus corporation. Because it is clear that any professional football team's ultimate worth is decided by its quarterback's overall performance, quarterbacks in essence have the fate of their team's value on their shoulders."[5]

We need not belabor the fact that global players plying their trade in the top leagues on both sides of the Atlantic have reached heights in their remuneration that were unimaginable only two decades ago, let alone five, when, for example, most players contesting that legendary Baltimore Colts vs. New York Giants NFL championship game on December 28, 1958 had to tend to their "regular" day jobs during the off-season to supplement their income from football, which only paid very few stars the kind of

---

[4] "Sports Industry Growth Trend," *SportsBusiness Journal*, as presented in Kenneth C. Teed, Lisa Delpy-Neirotti, Scott R. Johnson, and Benoit Seguin, "The Marketing of a NHL Hockey team," *International Journal of Sport Management and Marketing*, 5 (1–2), 2009, pp. 226–46.

[5] "Takeo Spikes on Sport-Sunday Late Edition," NBC Bay Area News, November 23, 2008.

money that accorded them a comfortable lifestyle. Identical patterns pertained to basketball, baseball, and hockey in America as in European soccer. There were a few rich individual sports stars prior to the second globalization—for example, Babe Ruth, who made more money than the
president of the United States, at least for one season. But collectively,
players in top leagues have only attained anything resembling wealth in
recent decades.

Let us not forget that these much-maligned megasalaries of our era also
bespeak the victory of a merit-based cosmopolitanism that rewards the
very best performances completely irrespective of their producers' social
backgrounds.[6] These new player migrants are not only expressions of the
second globalization. They also help create transnational publics and cosmopolitan communications beyond the confines of the nation-state. And
they are instrumental in promoting diversity and cultural cosmopolitanism
"from below," that is cultural change and diversity accepted by "the
masses."[7] We witness this on the local level. Over time, players who make
their team better, no matter their origins, are loved even by a team's most
ardent "localist" fan community and, at least if they succeed, are seen to be
"worth every penny." If a player's performance pleases a team's fans, than
the alleged exorbitance of his salary bears no adverse sentiments whatsoever. Ditto with doping, best demonstrated by the fact that fans readily
forgave self-admitted or suspected culprits provided their performance
helped the team win on the field, ultimately the only measure that truly
matters to sports fans the world over. Just think how Alex Rodriguez (one
of the highest-paid athletes in the world and an admitted user of perfor-
mance-enhancing drugs) mutated from pariah to hero for Yankee fans in a
matter of months solely by virtue of his accomplishments on the baseball
diamond that contributed to the Yankees' winning their 27th World
Championship.[8] Rodriguez and culturally diverse players exhibiting rare

---

[6] Mika LaVaque-Manty offers a compelling theoretical account of the competing ideals of
equality and excellence in modern democratic society by looking at the example of sports.
LaVaque-Manty argues that sports provide a significant arena for resolving the tensions between these two co-existing ideals. In fact, for LaVaque-Manty, modern sports illustrate the
interdependence between excellence and equality, between autonomy and egalitarianism. We
situate this argument in the broader context of the egalitarian and cosmopolitan impact of
sports. See Mika LaVaque-Manty, *The Playing Fields of Eton: Equality and Excellence in Modern
Meritocracy* (Ann Arbor: The University of Michigan Press, 2009).

[7] See Fuyuki Kurasawa, "A Cosmopolitanism from Below: Alternative Globalization and
the Creation of Solidarity without Bounds," *European Journal of Sociology* 45(2), 2004, pp.
233–55.

[8] Truth be told, fans ultimately do not much worry about the money that the players make
or the type of substances that they inject or ingest as long as these players perform to the best

and much-appreciated skill levels comparable to his in other sports have rendered different communities around the world ever more inclusive. Thus, the handsome reward of top achievement entails a socially inclusive dimension that sports share with few other venues, since the clear-cut criteria of good and bad, successful and unsuccessful, and winning and losing that lie at the very heart of modern sports are much less clear-cut in other endeavors.[9]

With all this said, megasports still remain puny in their economic dimensions compared to many other industries and commercial activities. We looked at the Fortune 500 largest U.S. corporations and the Global 500 as well. Neither of them lists any sports team. Indeed, on the latter ranking, the last company listed, Fluor, had roughly $17 billion revenue in 2007, which exceeds by $2 billion the entire annual revenue generated by the Big Four sports in America according to the Zimbalist data. On the domestic U.S. list, all of the revenue generated by the Big Four would have weighed in at 170, between the Paccar Company in Bellevue, Washington and Computer Sciences in Falls Church, Virginia. "Even the biggest teams, such as the Yankees, generate revenues of $300 million per year or less. While this is a lot of money, it is only comparable to a large department store. In a typical big league city, a business like this hardly is a blip in the economy. . . . In 2005, the combined revenues that year of the Seahawks . . . the Mariners, and Sonics"—the three top-league professional teams of the Seattle-Tacoma community, the fifteenth largest U.S. metropolitan area comprising a $182 billion economy—"accounted for $449 million—less than one quarter of one percent of total economic activity in the metro area."[10] Even the Green Bay Packers—representing a virtually unique situation in big-league American sports in that this top-notch, arguably most

of their abilities and—most important—thus help their teams win; ditto with all the strikes, lock outs, and corruption scandals that have occurred with constancy on both sides of the Atlantic. The scenario is always identical: Fans are up in arms whenever these disruptions commence and their cause becomes public. But in due course, fans forgive and forget, their passion takes over and fully restores the status quo in which they once again are glued to the issue at hand—following their beloved game and hoping (even against hope) that their team wins in every contest in which it performs.

[9] The clear-cut nature of sports, the dichotomy between winning and losing, seems to be a major reason for sports' attractiveness to men. In a brilliant scene in the film *White Men Can't Jump*, the character played by Woody Harrelson describes to his girlfriend (played by Rosie Perez) why he loves to play street basketball for money: at the end of every game, there is a clear winner and a clear loser—no ambiguities, no complexities, nothing left unclear. Needless to say, the girlfriend disagrees and tells him that sometimes the winners are losers and vice versa, in other words that reality—even in sports—is much murkier than apparent at first. Of course, the couple splits up.

[10] Kevin G. Quinn, *Sports and Their Fans: The History, Economics and Culture of the Relation-*

pedigreed, team in professional football calls a community of less than 250,000 its home—have a marginal economic effect. "The team's $194 million revenues represent only 1.5 percent of the surrounding area's $13 billion economy."[11] And let us recall from chapter 1 that owners of sports teams do not gauge their investment in terms of monetary rewards but almost solely in the social status and prestige that such ownership and association bestows on them, their entourage, and their community large and small.

We realize that number games of this kind are fraught with inaccuracies and need to be gauged with extreme caution. Still, our point is simple. Sports' most important capital is cultural, political and social, not economic. The power and global attractiveness of their teams and actors have little to do with the wealth and the money involved. Rather, these entities speak to emotions that create a bevy of "bridging" and "bonding" capital that are often competing, yet both are important in the creation and maintenance of key collective identities. As such, sports are much more akin to museums or operas and similar kinds of cultural institutions than to major international corporations, to which they have come to be compared in recent times.

We believe that the disapproval of, even anger toward, the money involved in these global sports—of which the players (rarely, if ever the team owners, agents or others earning millions off the players' excellence) get the brunt though notably not so much by the fans themselves for whom, as we just argued, winning is the only thing that matters but by the public at large—has much to do with their immense popularity and imagined simplicity since, after all, sport is a form of play, and child's play to boot. Whereas millions upon millions of hitherto mainly men have engaged in these sports primarily as children and youngsters, they thus deem themselves experts at something that, after all, cannot be that difficult since not too long ago, they, too, practiced it. Thus, the public on both sides of the Atlantic is much more likely to begrudge sports its commercialization, and global players their huge incomes, as compared to, say, musicians, actors, or any other professionals rewarded for excelling at a métier that appears less facile and common than sports. After all, how difficult can it really be to kick or throw a ball for a living? Indeed, the alleged simplicity of sports serves to discredit them as needing special physical and mental skills. Rarely are sports' exceptional practitioners accorded the honor and esteem

---

ship Between Spectator and Sport (Jefferson, NC: McFarland & Company, Inc., Publishers, 2009), p. 26. Emphasis in the original.
    [11] Ibid.

bestowed on highly skilled workers, artisans, and artists who deserve to have their labor and product rewarded by whatever the market bears. Our experience in the academy convinces us that it is this perceived lack of sophistication that renders so many of our colleagues so studiedly ignorant of popular sports.

The put-down of sports as "simple" is also common in the ever-extant intersport competition that has heated up between America and Europe, and across the globe, in the course of the second globalization. As we discussed at the beginning of chapter 5, the discrediting of a foreign rival is often coupled with the newcomer's being boring and not manly enough. How often have we heard all three of these negatives—simple, boring, not tough enough—from fans of the Big Four in their resistance to soccer? Conversely, European soccer fans disparage the Big Four American sports for their lack of toughness—yes, including collision-based American football which, to "real" men, would be played with no padding, like rugby—and, of course, disdain "feminized" American soccer. The powerful attraction of manliness, coupled with a defiant localism that spurns all forms of outside intrusion as "female," "weak," "commodified," and "foreign" provide constant challenges to the "sportization" of sports. Thus, for example, as Maarten Van Bottenburg and Johan Heilbron perceptively demonstrate in their research on "ultimate fighting" and other so-called "No Holds Barred Events," these sports arose precisely as local oppositions to the overruled, overregulated (i.e., overly "sportized" and cosmopolitan) pugilist venues such as boxing, wrestling, and the martial arts.[12] Men wanted to find out who was the last guy standing after a fight with virtually no rules, who was the best of the best so to speak in a ruleless (i.e., "de-sportized") context not dictated by any outside (i.e., global) authority or any distant bureaucratic federation. They wanted to ascertain who is the best fighter, period, not the best wrestler or boxer or judoka. But once these local contests proved to be popular, they soon became "re-sportized" in that they spread all over the world which, of course, meant that they acquired rules, regulations, venues, television contracts—once again demonstrating that in our contemporary world, with its speedy and ubiquitous channels of communication, even the most local of discourses quickly attain global dimensions, thus they emerge as glocal.

There exists absolutely no compelling reason for the global topography of sports to remain essentially unchanged, since its establishment in the

[12] Maarten Van Bottenburg and Johan Heilbron, "De-Sportization of Fighting Contests: The Origins of No Holds Barred Events and the Theory of Sportization," *International Review for the Sociology of Sport*, 41 (3–4), 2006, pp. 259–82.

mid to late nineteenth century. After all, why should a world created by English students in elite public schools and at Oxbridge, and the industrial working class of the Midlands, as well as that of their social counterparts in the United States established pretty much at the same time, last forever? Indeed, by extending one of our book's main arguments, there exists every reason for the best basketball players to hail from China in, say 2040. And, the Italians and the Dutch might lead the world of baseball by then, and Americans might become the globe's best soccer players after having won the World Cup repeatedly. One could go even further and argue that these very sports languages, which were, after all, creations of a specific time and space, and are thus random, need not persevere forever. Who knows, maybe the real global game will be Quidditch in centuries to come. After all, we have already had the first Quidditch World Cup video game in which the United States, England, France, Germany, and Scandinavia united as the Nordic Team and played against a joint squad comprising Japan, Spain, Australia, and Bulgaria.[13]

But note, even in this Quidditch World Cup, long-established entities called nation-states formed the key organizational core of the players. Thus, our book also demonstrates the immense cultural resilience and social stamina of this bizarre world established 150 years ago called modern sports. We agree with Simon Kuper and Stefan Szymanski that by virtue of the second globalization American soccer fans have come to follow and identify with the European core's mega clubs just like British football fans have become totally conversant with the NFL. In a globalized world, real fans follow the best of the best regardless of time and space. But this development has not eliminated affection for and identification with local variants of these top performers such as MLS or even United Soccer League (USL) teams for American soccer fans, and "some bunch of no-hopers playing on a converted rugby field a few miles from your house" in the case of British fans of American football.[14] Far from "crowding out" the second or third-rate local, the best of the best global in fact fosters such developments by giving fans a real live experience to practice and hone their newly acquired language as participants and spectators that they would otherwise only enjoy as television viewers. Thus, for a soccer-loving resident of Utah, being a Real Madrid fan does not obviate one's passion for Real Salt Lake. Instead, the two reinforce each other. Ditto for American football fans in

[13] Indeed there exists a widely-circulated *Intercollegiate Quidditch Rules and Guidebook*, http://sites.google.com/site/savannahquidditchleague/IQARulebook.

[14] Kuper and Szymanski, *Soccernomics*, pp. 177, 178.

Vienna whose love for the Minnesota Vikings does not displace their affection for the Vienna Vikings but, if anything, strengthens it. The Metropolitan Opera's widely available performances enhance, instead of diminish, the local opera fan's interest in the productions staged by her or his local opera company. The second globalization has widened horizons and has facilitated the reception and appreciation of the best of the best on local levels, but it has not displaced local experiences and identities. Instead, it created new ones that have become congruent with the global as in Real Salt Lake's case with Real Madrid and that of the Vienna Vikings with their namesake in Minnesota. In the course of the second globalization, layers of culture, consciousness, and identities emerged in the topography of sports in Europe and America that were unimaginable before the late 1980s.

But let us invoke James Flege's speech-learning model as an apt analogy to what we would like to convey here. In this model, Flege demonstrates that a person's "phonetic space" becomes committed very early in her or his life and that any acquisition of a new language becomes increasingly difficult because these newcomers will have to fight for room in a construct that has already been occupied.[15] In a sense, not only is the space limited, but even in the areas in which the newcomers might be accommodated, the terrain will have been predisposed by the original language. The later one learns another language, the less possible it becomes to sound native in it. In a study of Italian-English bilinguals who differed in their age of arrival in Canada, Flege found that the earlier in life one arrived in Canada, the less of an Italian accent one had in English. Indeed, it is very rare for anybody to speak a new language, acquired after the age of twelve or thirteen, like a native. One's hearing as well as sound reproduction has been hopelessly compromised by one's native language that continues to shape one's phonetic space for life. This finding is corroborated by onomatopoeia, which curiously is immensely language-specific in its reception and reproduction. Every language renders identical sounds in its own way that is different from other languages, meaning that both our hearing of sounds and their reproduction are particular and local. Thus, even though presumably pigs make identical sounds in German-speaking

---

[15] Amanda C. Walley, "Speech Learning, Lexical Reorganization and the Development of Word Recognition by Native and Non-native English-speakers," in Ocke-Schwen Bohn and Murray J. Munro, eds., *Language Experience in Second Language Speech Learning: In Honor of James Emil Flege* (Amsterdam: John Benjamins Publishing Company, 2007), pp. 315–30. We are grateful to John Lucy of the University of Chicago for sharing his insights into language and sports.

and English-speaking regions of the world, German-speakers reproduce the pigs' sound as "gruntz, gruntz" whereas English speakers say "oink, oink." Thousands of other examples abound.

This in no way means that one cannot learn to speak, read, and write a new language perfectly and master it even better than its native speakers. It merely means that one's ability to emulate its sounds like a native is severely compromised, actually well-nigh impossible. And a similarly rigid path dependence pertains to our world of sports. Every day, baseball speakers become fluent soccer speakers as well as vice versa; and both can, and do, master the languages of basketball or cricket or hockey or rugby or football. But they will pronounce these newly acquired sports languages with accents that will be unlike a native speaker's—neither better nor worse, just different. In our cacophonous and interconnected world, purity of accents might become as obsolete in the world of sports as it has in many other forms of communication, language included. This is the essence of what we in our book have called cosmopolitanism.

ACRONYMS ◇◇◇◇◇◇◇◇◇◇◇◇◇◇◇◇◇◇◇◇◇◇◇◇◇◇◇◇◇◇◇◇◇◇◇◇

Alleanza Nazionale (AN/National Alliance)

American Football Conference (AFC)

Anschutz Entertainment Group (AEG)

Atlantic Coast Conference (ACC)

American Youth Soccer Organization (AYSO)

Association for Intercollegiate Athletics for Women (AIAW)

Basketball Association of America (BAA)

Canadian Interuniversity Sport (CIS)

Center for Advanced Study in the Behavioral Sciences (CASBS)

Commando Ultra Curva Sud (CUCS/Ultra Command Southern Stands)

Confederation of North, Central American, and Caribbean Association Football
(CONCACAF)

Dansk Boldspil-Union (DBU/Danish Football Federation)

Deutscher Akademischer Austausch Dienst (DAAD/German Academic Exchange
Service)

Deutscher Fußball-Bund (DFB/German Football Federation)

English Women's Football Association (WFA)

European Broadcasting Union (EBU)

Federation of Independent European Female Football (FIEFF)

Fédération Internationale de Basketball (FIBA/International Basketball Federation)

Fédération Internationale de Football Association (FIFA/International Federation of
Association Football)

Fédération Internationale des Associations de Footballeurs Professionnels (FIFPro/
World Soccer Players' Union)

Federazione Italiana Gioco Calcio (FIGC/Italian Football Federation)

Football Against Racism in Europe (FARE)

Football Association (FA)

Football Bowl Subdivision (FBS)

Football Championship Subdivision (FCS)

Freiheitliche Partei Österreichs (FPÖ/Freedom Party of Austria)

Freedom Party of Austria (FPÖ)

Gaelic Athletic Association   (GAA)
German Academic Exchange Service   (DAAD)
Harlem Globetrotters   (the "Trotters")
International Olympic Committee   (IOC)
Irish Rugby Football Union   (IRFU)
Italian Communist Party   (PCI)
Kontinental Hockey League   (KHL)
Major League Baseball   (MLB)
Major League Soccer   (MLS)
Movimento Sociale Italiano   (MSI/Italian Social Movement)
Narodowe Odrodzenie Polski   (NOP/National Rebirth of Poland)
National Association for Girls and Women in Sport   (NAGWS)
The National Association for Stock Car Auto Racing   (NASCAR)
National Basketball League   (NBL)
National Collegiate Athletic Association   (NCAA)
Nationaldemokratische Partei Deutschlands   (NPD/National Democratic Party of
    Germany)
National Football League   (NFL)
National Hockey League   (NHL)
National Invitational Tournament   (NIT)
National Professional Soccer League   (NPSL)
New York Renaissance Five   (the Rens)
Norges Fotballforbund   (NFF/Norwegian Football Federation)
North American Soccer League   (NASL)
Norwegian Football Association   (NFA)
Partito Comunista Italiano   (PCI/Italian Communist Party)
Real Federación Española de Fútbol   (RFEF/Royal Spanish Football Federation)
Rugby Football   (RFA)
Russian Super League   (RSL)
Soccer Association for Youth   (SAY)
Soccer Industry Council of America   (SICA)
South Eastern Conference   (SEC)
Sozialdemokratische Partei Deutschlands   (SPD/Social Democratic Party of
    Germany)
Sozialdemokratische Partei Österreichs   (SPÖ/Social Democratic Party of Austria)
Svenska Fotbollförbundet   (SvFF/Swedish Football Association)
Union of European Football Associations   (UEFA)
United Nations Children's Fund   (UNICEF)
United Soccer Association   (USA)
United States Soccer Federation   (USSF)

United States Soccer Football Association   (USSFA)
United States Youth Soccer Association   (USYSA)
University of Texas at El Paso   (UTEP)
Women's Professional Soccer   (WPS)
Women's United Soccer Association   (WUSA)
World League of American Football   (WLAF)
World Wrestling Entertainment   (WWE)
Young Men's Christian Association   (YMCA)

INDEX ◇◇◇◇◇◇◇◇◇◇◇◇◇◇◇◇◇◇◇◇◇◇◇◇◇◇◇◇◇◇◇◇